FRIENDS AND OTHER STRANGERS: BOB DYLAN EXAMINED

By Harold Lepidus

Oakamoor
Publishing

Published in 2017 by Oakamoor Publishing, an imprint of Bennion Kearny Limited.
Copyright © Oakamoor Publishing

ISBN: 978-1-910773-40-6

Published by Oakamoor Publishing, Bennion Kearny Limited
6 Woodside
Churnet View Road
Oakamoor
Staffordshire
ST10 3AE
United Kingdom
www.BennionKearny.com

For Debby …

"If not for you, Babe …"

About the Author

Harold Lepidus has been studying Bob Dylan's work since he was a teenager on Long Island, when a concert by Dylan and The Band in 1974 tore down all of his preconceived notions of what art could accomplish, and changed the trajectory of his musical taste. This simple event led to an endless supply of Dylan-related books, records, magazines, bootlegs, videos, CDs, cassettes, posters, t-shirts, movies, and uncounted miles traveled across New England and up and down the east coast, from California to the New York Island, attempting to uncover the secrets of Dylan's magic.

From 2009 to 2016, Lepidus' *Bob Dylan Examiner* column was viewed over 3 million times. His articles have been linked as authoritative by *Rolling Stone*, *npr.org*, *Paste*, *Ultimate Classic Rock*, *Wolfgang's Vault*, *Uncut*, *Glide*, *American Songwriter*, and other sites.

Lepidus has a B.A. in Journalism from Northeastern University, and an M.A. in Video Production from Emerson College. He lives in Massachusetts, has two adult sons, and is surrounded by way-too-many used LPs.

Acknowledgements

There are so many people to thank, those with whom I've traveled lo these many years, that acknowledging them all presents a challenge. Whom to include, whom have I forgotten?

I must begin with Karl Erik Andersen, webmaster at *Expecting Rain*. Originally a Dylan-based news site, it has expanded over time to cover like-minded artists, and a visit to expectingrain.com is the way most Dylan fans begin their day. After about a decade of submitting articles by others for Karl Erik to post, my goal was for my *Examiner* column – whatever it was to become – to appeal to like-minded folks. Not only has Karl Erik supported me by posting links to most of my articles on his site, but he has also defended me against my detractors. *Expecting Rain* has led more people to my writings than any other source. If not for him, there's a very good chance this book would never have materialized.

Thanks also to *Billboard's* Steve Marinucci. Back at the turn of the century, his *Abbeyrd* website became my favorite source for Beatles news. We communicated often, and he even encouraged me to start my own Beatles-related blog. When he began writing about the Fabs for *examiner.com*, I soon applied to do the same as the *Bob Dylan Examiner*. Kudos also to Jim Cherry, *The Doors Examiner*, with whom we often exchanged whatever news we found about our respective subjects. Cherry's writings were anthologized in book form by Bennion Kearny, and he helped me get in contact with publisher James Lumsden-Cook with the idea of compiling my own articles after *Examiner* went belly-up this summer. From across the pond, James was enthusiastic from the start, and worked tirelessly with me over the past few months in order to make sure this became a reality. Thank you, James.

Thanks to my childhood friend, Daniel Horwitz, who tirelessly tried to get me into Dylan back in the day. He convinced his parents to shell out for a copy of Bob Dylan's *Greatest Hits, Vol. II* (a double album!!), for my birthday in 1971, and helped secure an extra ticket for me to see Dylan and The Band at the Nassau Coliseum on January 29, 1974, an event which forever changed the trajectory of my life.

To Seth Rogovoy, Dylan and Klezmer scholar, and "the brother I never had," whose writing I've admired since he was the music critic for the *Islip High School Buccaneer*. In 2009, Seth honored me by asking if I would be the line-editor for his authoritative book on Dylan's religious roots, *Bob Dylan: Prophet, Mystic, Poet* (Scribner). We've shared our passion for Dylan, The Band, Patti Smith, Bruce Springsteen, The Beatles, and the like, throughout the decades via visits, phone calls, emails, and CDRs. Who would have thought our talks about Dylan in the late 1970s would lead us to where we are today?

Thanks also to the following people who agreed to be interviewed for the articles found within: Robyn Hitchcock, Betsy Siggins, Carolyn Hester, John Byrne Cooke, John B. Sebastian, Dom Flemons, Jeff Gold, Al Kooper, Harvey Brooks, Harvey Mandel, D.A. Pennebaker, Michael Gray,

Sean Wilentz, Thomas May, Anneke Derksen, Bucks Burnett, Danielle Labadie, Michael Perlin, Sandi Bachom, and Carol Stief.

In addition, there are so many people who have generously contributed in one way or another, both big and small, without whom this book would not have been as in depth, as accurate, or as rewarding: Liz Thomson, Masato Kato, Alan Fraser (*Searching For A Gem*), Manfred Helfert (*Bob Dylan Roots*), Paul Zollo (*Songwriters on Songwriting*), "Thrasher" (*Thrasher's Wheat*), John A. Baldwin (*Desolation Row Information Society*), Adam Selzer, Sally Kirkland, the folks at *Examiner*, *Blasting News*, and *No Depression*, Larry Jenkins, Dan Levy, and at Sony – Tom Cording, Greg Linn, and David V. Smith.

Fellow travelers who have supported me in other ways: Michael Simmons, David Kinney, Greg Reibman, Scott Warmuth, Andrew Muir, Jeff Slate, Richard Senicola, Mark Krieger, Scott Collins, Beth MacGrory Dube, Brandon Jesse, Trev Gibb, Peter Stone Brown, Rob Stegman, Todd Kwait, James DeSimone, Reb Stephan Pickering, Chris Francescani, April Melody, Jon Friedman, John Fugelsang, and Sean Curnyn, and *Turn It Up's* Patrick Pezzati.

To all of my other friends, virtual and otherwise, who have read, liked, followed, favored, shared, retweeted, commented upon, or otherwise promoted my articles: not only did you help spread the word, but each act never failed to brighten up my day. The same goes to everybody who sent me a scoop of some kind. I owe you all a deep debt of gratitude. Thanks also to those who criticized my work for one reason or another. You all helped by keeping my feet to the fire, and strengthening my resolve. This book is partially your fault.

Special thanks to Linda Friedner Cowen.

Thanks to all of my family, especially my mother Luba, my sister Barbara, and my sons Joe and Sam ... who have put up with my musical diatribes for decades, and probably received cassettes, CDRs, and DVDs I made for them over the years, which have been gathering dust in their closets ever since. The spirit of your love, support, patience and indulgences can be felt in every page of this book.

My father, Marshall, instilled in me the love of art, music, accuracy, and humor. He was conscientious and compassionate, and a stickler for details with an amazing memory. Thankfully, I seem to have inherited most of those traits. He came to my mind quite often while writing, and I think he would have been proud of me for writing this book. May his memory be a blessing.

Finally, I can never repay the help, support, kindness, and love provided by Debby Hax Walker, who encouraged me from the start, tirelessly and unselfishly editing almost everything I wrote, helping me clarify my thoughts, and sharing with me all of my successes. Although she detests clichés (unless used ironically), I really could never have done this without you. This is your book as well.

Table of Contents

Let's Begin

This did not start out as a book.

In August, 2009, I began writing for *examiner.com*. Following the lead of my friend and colleague, Beatles scholar Steve Marinucci, I too applied for a writing position at the online newspaper. Within a matter of days, I officially became *The Bob Dylan Examiner*, and off I went on this new adventure.

As my column (*not* a blog, they were quick to point out) was being set up, there was an incredulous (non-)news story emanating from the U.K. about to go viral. BBC 6 was finally broadcasting *Theme Time Radio Hour With Your Host Bob Dylan*, months after it had originally aired exclusively on XM (and later SiriusXM) satellite radio here in the U.S. The 100th and final scheduled episode aired in April, 2009, but in August, the BBC was only up to *Street Maps* (episode 83), which had debuted here the previous December. With his typically bone-dry delivery, Dylan mentioned, while introducing Ray Charles's version of *Lonely Avenue*, that he was in negotiations to be a voice for GPS devices, back when they were a relatively new phenomenon and celebrity voices were all the rage.

No one initially took Dylan's words seriously, but abroad it was now being reported as legitimate news in the British newspaper, *The Telegraph*. The story was quickly picked up by Britain's premiere music weekly, *NME*, and again on the BBC's website. It then came back *here* as a "news" story, printed as "fact" without journalistic due diligence, in *The New York Times*, and then *The Washington Post*. (A sign of things to come?) Soon, people all over the web thought they were being clever by mocking the future Nobel Prize-winning songwriter and musician's new vocation. However, the joke was on them – The Jokerman was only joking. (Unless, of course, any of these media outlets decide to critique this book, in which case it clearly wasn't their fault.) Every day the story got better, and I couldn't wait to jump through the hoops necessary in order to submit this hot little item.

On August 29, 2009, my first *Bob Dylan Examiner* article became a reality. Titled *Bob Dylan's joke taken seriously by The New York Times, Washington Post*, it was an immediate hit, mostly thanks to *Expecting Rain*, a Dylan-based online website, where it was posted the following morning. After a decade of informative – and occasionally snarky – posts on various Internet fan sites, I now had to "behave." I suddenly had instant cred, and was soon cited on *npr.org* and other sites as the authoritative debunker of this myth, the newest in a very long line of Dylan-centric fabrications. I would later take *The Daily News* to task for referring to Dylan as a "devout Christian," and Maureen Dowd of *The New York Times* for accusing Dylan of "selling out" when he toured China in 2011, among other items. I also had a handful of colorful, devoted followers back in the day – Maddy, Lawfanda, DarkEyez. I wonder where they all are now?

While Dylan was, and still is, an active artist, I wondered what I could write about on days when there was no real news to report. Here, I began using my memory, my archives, and the Internet, to construct articles which made a connection to some anniversary or another. I would continue to report on Bob-based news when I found something worthy to say, but on an "off" day – of which there were many – I would either revisit a relevant event in Dylan history, or tie it to a person associated with him in some way, often to either celebrate the anniversary of their birth, or pay tribute after their death.

It was interesting doing the research back when I had the time and inclination to indulge in such an activity. I wanted my *Examiner* column not only to be entertaining and informative, but something that could be used as a research tool. For instance, if you wanted to know the connection between Dylan and, say, Otis Redding, Sheryl Crow, Tiny Tim, Elizabeth Taylor, or President John F. Kennedy, my article would hopefully show up in that person's Google search.

I also had the privilege of interviewing a myriad of people who have been associated with Dylan in one way or another, including documentarian D.A. Pennebaker, sidemen John B. Sebastian, Harvey Brooks, and Harvey Mandel, DJ Billy Faier, Club 47's Betsy Siggins, Dylan scholars Michael Gray and Sean Wilentz, and Dylan disciple Robyn Hitchcock. The column also allowed me to dispel some myths, including those concerning Dick Clark, Billy Preston, Robert Johnson, and Dylan himself.

It also gave me a soapbox from which to preach. Much like the GPS story above, people found it easy to criticize or mock Dylan for his singing, his setlists, or his 2009 album, *Christmas in the Heart.* Insulted by their shortsightedness and condescension, I offered alternative ways to interpret these subjects. One of the lessons I had learned from studying Dylan's work over the years was there could easily be more than one way to interpret *anything,* if you opened your mind and put in the effort. The greatest irony I found from interacting with Dylan fans was that a large percentage were quite closed-minded in their thinking, and I got a kick out of bursting their bubbles. One of the great debates was over the effects of Dylan's short association with The Grateful Dead in 1987. It was pretty clear to me that it was a catalyst for Dylan to rethink, re-energize, and revitalize his career, which Dylan touched upon in his somewhat fictionalized memoir, *Chronicles: Volume One.* Even though it is probably the most cited story in the book, I never believed his version of events about this time period. He wrote about being frustrated by his rehearsals with the Dead for their joint six-stadium date tour, and left to wander into a nearby bar, where some anonymous singer gave Dylan the inspiration to reconnect with his own music. In reality, it was more likely Jerry Garcia and company were the only musicians weird enough, and sympathetic enough, to tackle that job (although Dylan's tale made for a good yarn). The following year, Dylan started his so-called "Never-Ending Tour," which was based on the Dead's unconventional model, and would often cover their material. However, much like those who have never taken the time to really understand what Dylan was about, a large segment of *his* fans have taken the same close-minded view of The Dead and their tribal followers. Dylan could be music's ultimate Rorschach test: what you think about him reveals more about you than it does about him. Whenever possible, my articles would try to point that out.

As *The Bob Dylan Examiner,* I was given the freedom and the space to use my column as a forum for expressions of my own design, and for that, I will be forever grateful. It changed my life in ways that were previously unimaginable. It gave me the opportunity to connect with people I'd admired from afar, and I made many new friends who suffered from the same affliction. I've even had the opportunity to help people by answering their questions, or solving some of their problems. A personal highlight was when a link to my concert review of a 2014 concert in Providence was posted on Dylan's official website.

It was a fun ride, but that chapter has now closed. *Examiner* decided to shut down this past July, the home of my work for almost six years. A thousand-plus articles, with more than 3 million views, would soon be scrubbed from the Internet. During the last days of *Examiner,* I realized that some of the articles I had written, but not saved, had disappeared without my knowledge. Additionally, once the site was taken down, no one would have access to any of them, except those that were copied and posted online elsewhere without authorization. This book is one way to preserve my work for those who may be interested in adding them to their Dylan library. I chose about 10% of what I had written, with the theme of "Friends and Other Strangers," for this anthology. Almost every column has been recently edited and updated in some way, but the gist of the originals remain.

The main thing I wanted to get across in these articles was that, although I took my job, and my responsibility as a journalist, seriously, I had fun – *yes, fun* – writing about Dylan. (Humor, of course, has always been one of Dylan's secret weapons, and a central reason why his work resonates and endures.) Sure, all of this *Examiner* business was time-consuming, but my passion to discover even more about this endlessly fascinating character led to my fact-finding missions of digging for hidden truths, and uncovering previously unknown, at least to me, connections in his art. This often led me down a rabbit hole of deeper and more complex meanings and references, which was rewarding in-and-of itself. Once my work was completed, I then wanted to share my archaeological findings with like-minded folks. However, I hoped not to come across as pretentious or snobbish, but as an enthusiastic fan and admirer of Dylan and his work, and to treat him not only as an exceptional artist, but also a mortal one. The choice of subjects was often random, and the content was as complete as could be expected at the time. These were daily missives, accumulated and disseminated, my findings formatted as telegrams from the trenches, hopefully presented with a unique slant, and then sent out into the ether.

The Bob Dylan Examiner may be no more, but I continue to write a column for *Blasting News*, and a blog for *No Depression*. Who knows where the future will lead? Hopefully, I'll see you there.

Thanks for your support. I hope you like the book, especially if you paid for it.

Harold Lepidus

Former Bob Dylan Examiner

Somewhere in Massachusetts

December, 2016

Hank Williams

For a young Bobby Zimmerman, before there was Woodrow Wilson Guthrie there was . . . Hiram King Williams.

At a 1966 press conference, Bob Dylan said, *"Hank Williams was the first influence, I would think, I guess, for a longer period of time than anybody else."* [1] In 1978, Dylan told Robert Shelton, *"If it wasn't for Elvis and Hank Williams, I couldn't be doing what I do today."* [2] In his 2004 memoir, *Chronicles: Volume One*, Bob Dylan again praised Williams, saying that before Woody Guthrie, Williams had been his *"favorite songwriter,"* although he initially *"thought of him (more) as a singer."*

Hank Williams was born on September 17, 1923. He was an early influence on Bob Dylan, who listened to Williams on the radio, performing at The Grand Ole Opry. Dylan has repeatedly referenced the country music legend in interviews, in books, and with music, covering a handful of songs associated with Williams.

Williams was mentioned in the liner notes of Dylan's first two albums. In turn, a 1962 out-take of *(I Heard That) Lonesome Whistle* finally received a limited European release in 2014.

Les Crane: When did you start writing original tunes?

Dylan: Well, I started writing a long time ago. You know, you write different things down, when you really don't know what else to do. That's when I started writing. I started writing songs ... that's a different story, you know ... I started writing songs after I heard Hank Williams.

Crane: Hank Williams? Did he really inspire you?

Dylan: Yeah.

Crane: Cold Cold Heart? Jambalaya? Things like that?

Dylan: Yeah. Cole Porter. (Possible some wordplay relating to "Cold Cold Heart.")

Crane: Cole Porter?!?

Dylan: Yeah.

Crane: Now you're putting me on!

Dylan: No. (laughter) . [3]

And at a 1965 press conference, [4] **Dylan was asked whether Hank Williams was an influence.** *"Hey look, I consider Hank Williams, Captain Marvel, Marlon Brando, The Tennessee Stud, Clark Kent, Walter Cronkite, and J. Carrol Naish all influences. Now what is it – please – what is it exactly you people want to know?"*

In 1967, MGM Records was interested in signing Dylan to their label, enticing him with unfinished writings by Williams, according to Bob Spitz in his book, *Dylan - A Biography*. Dylan ended up staying with Columbia Records, so the project was abandoned. The idea of completing Williams' writings eventually led to the *Lost Notebooks* release, a mere 44 years later.

On his *Right Wing Bob* site, Sean Curnyn posted an interesting story about Robert W. Wilson, Jr. giving a copy of Williams' wartime employment records and files to Bob Dylan in 1976. [5]

---

[1] *Circulating Montreal interview tape*, Martin Bronstein, Canadian Broadcasting Corp., 2/20/66

[2] *How Does It Feel To Be On Your Own -Bob Dylan talks to Robert Shelton*, Robert Shelton, Melody Maker, 7/29/78

[3] *The Les Crane Show* (ABC-TV), 2/17/65

[4] *Dylan Meets the Press*, J.R. Goddard, The Village Voice, 3/25/1965

[5] http://www.rightwingbob.com/weblog/bob-dylan-hank-williams-and-an-application-for-a-job/3690/, *Bob Dylan, Hank Williams, and an application for a job*, Retrieved 11/20/16

Spin magazine, December 1985

Who would you want to interview?

A lot of people who aren't alive: Hank Williams, Apollinaire, Joseph from the Bible, Marilyn Monroe, John F. Kennedy, Mohammed, Paul the Apostle, maybe John Wilkes Booth, maybe Gogol.

In 1991, Dylan gave a fascinating, in-depth interview with Paul Zollo for *Song Talk* magazine: [6]

Dylan: To me, Hank Williams is still the best songwriter.

ST: Hank? Better than Woody Guthrie?

Dylan: That's a good question. Hank Williams never wrote This Land Is Your Land. *But it's not that shocking for me to think of Hank Williams singing* Pastures of Plenty *or Woody Guthrie singing* Cheatin' Heart. *So in a lot of ways those two writers are similar. As writers. But you mustn't forget that both of these people were performers, too. And that's another thing which separates a person who just writes a song...*

People who don't perform but who are so locked into other people who do that, they can sort of feel what that other person would like to say, in a song and be able to write those lyrics. Which is a different thing from a performer who needs a song to play on stage year after year.

In 1997, while promoting *Time Out Of Mind*, Dylan told Jon Pareles of the New York Times:

"Those old songs are my lexicon and prayer book. All my beliefs come out of those old songs, literally, anything from "Let Me Rest on that Peaceful Mountain" to "Keep on the Sunny Side." You can find all my philosophy in those old songs. I believe in a God of time and space, but if people ask me about that, my impulse is to point them back toward those songs. I believe in Hank Williams singing "I Saw the Light." I've seen the light, too." [7]

Time Out Of Mind's lead-off track was *Love Sick*, which may have been inspired by Williams' *Lovesick Blues*.

Bob Dylan's memoir, *Chronicles: Volume One* [8] mentioned Williams several times. When Dylan heard Hank on the radio, playing the Grand Ole Opry, he wrote that he loved the mix of humorous and spiritual material. He got hold of a few of Hank's 78s and played them endlessly: *"The sound of his voice went through me like an electric rod,"* and that he felt he was too young to have experienced what Williams had gone through. Dylan also wrote that when Robert Shelton's early review of Dylan stated that he was *"breaking all the rules in songwriting,"* Dylan wrote that they *"were Hank's rules, but it wasn't like I ever meant to break them. It's just that what I was trying to express was beyond the circle."* He also recalled hearing the rumors that Hank had died in the back of his Cadillac on New Year's Day, 1953, hoping it wasn't true: *"It was like a great tree had fallen."*

Bob Dylan has actually played Hank Williams' guitar. At Neil Young's concert at the Ryman Auditorium in Nashville on August 18, 2005, he introduced the song *This Old Guitar* by saying:

"This is Hank Williams' guitar [he points to the guitar]. *I try to do the right thing with the guitar. You don't want to stink with Hank's guitar. I lent it to Bob Dylan for a while. He didn't have a tour bus so I lent him mine and I left the guitar on the bed with a note saying Hank's guitar is back there. He used it for a couple of months."* [9]

Dylan played a number of Williams' recordings on his *Theme Time Radio Hour*, including *My Son Calls Another Man Daddy, Too Many Parties and Too Many Pals* (as Luke the Drifter), *No, No Joe,* and *Lost Highway.* Here is Dylan from the *Friends and Neighbors* episode:

---

[6] *Songwriters On Songwriting - Expanded Edition,* Paul Zollo, Da Capo Press, New York, 1997

[7] *A Wiser Voice Blowin' in the Autumn Wind,* Jon Pareles, New York Times, 9/28/97

[8] *Chronicles: Volume One,* Bob Dylan, Simon & Schuster, New York, 2004

[9] http://thrasherswheat.org/jammin/dylan.htm, *Bob Dylan and Neil Young: Master & Disciple - Jammin' with Neil,* Retrieved 11/20/16

"One of the greatest songwriters who ever lived was Hank Williams, of course. Hank could be headstrong and willful, a backslider and a reprobate, no stranger to bad deeds. However, underneath all of that, he was compassionate and moralistic." [10]

Dylan's long-awaited project, *The Lost Notebooks of Hank Williams*, was released in 2011. Dylan, Jack White, Lucinda Williams, Alan Jackson, Norah Jones, Dylan's son Jakob, and others, took unfinished writings found after Hank's death on January 1, 1953, and turned them into new songs. According to an article in the September 1 issue of *Rolling Stone*, Dylan originally hoped to record an entire album by himself, but realized it was too big a task.

Here's a list of songs associated with Hank Williams that Dylan has performed over the years, originally expanded from *Bob Dylan Roots* [11] with additional help from Olof Bjorner [12] and *It Ain't Me, Babe.* [13]

(I Heard That) Lonesome Whistle, Freight Train Blues (Although probably not Dylan's source), *Lost Highway, I'm So Lonesome I Could Cry, Weary Blues From Waitin', Be Careful Of Stones That You Throw, You Win Again, Kaw-Liga, Cold Cold Heart, Half As Much, Your Cheatin' Heart, Lost On The River, Thank God, A House of Gold, Hey, Good Lookin', Honky Tonk Blues, I Can't Get You Off Of My Mind,* and *The Love That Faded* (Started by Hank Williams, fleshed out by Bob Dylan, *The Lost Notebooks of Hank Williams*).

[10] *Theme Time Radio Hour With Your Host, Bob Dylan,* "*Friends & Neighbors,*" Season One, Episode 17

[11] http://www.bobdylanroots.com/williams.html, *Hank Williams*, Retrieved 11/20/16

[12] http://www.bjorner.com/still.htm, *Still On The Road*, Retrieved 11/20/16

[13] http://rateyourmusic.com/list/Dylanlennon/it_aint_me_babe___all_the_songs_covered_ by_bob_dylan/, *It Ain't Me Babe - All the songs covered by Bob Dylan.* Retrieved 11/20/16

Frank Sinatra

November 18, 2010

Francis Albert "Frank" Sinatra was born on December 12, 1915.

Bob Dylan performed a moving version of *Restless Farewell* for a television special celebrating the 80th birthday of Ol' Blue Eyes. The program was taped on November 19, 1995, at the Heinz Pavilion of the Shrine Auditorium in Los Angeles, by ABC-TV for future broadcast. [14]

Among the other performers who participated in *Sinatra: 80 Years My Way* were Bruce Springsteen (*Angel Eyes*), Natalie Cole (*They Can't Take That Away From Me*), Ray Charles (*Ol' Man River*), Little Richard (*That Old Black Magic*), and Tony Bennett (*I've Got The World On A String*), along with various comedians, actors, and sports figures.

There were reports Dylan had originally planned to cover *That's Life* for the program. Although Sinatra was allegedly unhappy with the idea of a tribute, he reportedly requested Dylan sing his rarely performed composition, the defiant *Restless Farewell*, the closing track from 1964's *The Times, They Are A-Changin'* LP. In the United States, an edited version was aired, while the complete performance was shown in most other countries.

Sinatra died on May 14, 1998, and Dylan reportedly attended his funeral on the 20th. The following night, he reprised *Restless Farewell* at a Los Angeles concert, as a final encore:

"I played at the Frank Sinatra Tribute show a few years back, and I played this next song. We had it all worked out and everything, but then they said they wanted to hear this one instead so ... I hadn't played it up till that time and I haven't played it since, I'll try my best to do it." [15]

However, according to *His Bobness*, [16] Dylan had performed the song at least three times in concert: Chicago (December 27, 1963), Berkeley (February 22, 1964), and London (May 17, 1964). He also sang it for the 1964 Canadian TV show, *Quest*.

Dylan previously recorded an unreleased version of a song associated with Sinatra, *That Was My Love*, during the *Infidels* sessions.

In *Chronicles: Volume One*, Dylan wrote about frequently listening to Sinatra's version of *Ebb Tide*, writing it filled him "awe." In it, he said it evoked thoughts of mortality, spirituality, and more. [17]

Update: Recently, of course, Dylan recorded and released two albums of Sinatra-centric songs, *Shadows in the Night*, and *Fallen Angels*, with a new triple album of standards, *Triplicate*, scheduled to be released at the end of March 2017.

"Happy birthday, Mr. Frank."

---

[14] http://www.bjorner.com/DSN16550%20-%201995%20Fall%20Classics.htm#DSN16870, *Still On The Road*, Retrieved 11/20/16

[15] http://www.bjorner.com/DSN19160%20-%201998%20US%20Spring%20Tour.htm#DSN19210 *Still On The Road*, Retrieved 11/20/16

[16] http://hisbobness.info, *His Bobness*, Retrieved 11/20/16

[17] *Chronicles: Volume One*, Bob Dylan, Simon & Schuster, New York, 2004

Buddy Holly

Charles Hardin Holley was born on September 7, 1936. After a brief time in the spotlight, Buddy Holly left an undeniable legacy. From The Crickets' two-guitar-bass-drums set-up, to Holly writing his own songs, to his geeky-cool fashion sense, his influence has lasted more than half a century since "the music died" in Clear Lake, Iowa, in the early hours of February 3, 1959. Holly, Ritchie Valens, and J. P. "The Big Bopper" Richardson, and pilot Roger Peterson, all died in a plane crash that morning.

On January 31, 1959, a 17-year-old Bobby Zimmerman saw Buddy Holly's Winter Dance Party stop at the Duluth Armory from the front row. A few days later, Holly was dead.

The line-up was Buddy Holly and the Crickets (including new members Waylon Jennings and drummer Carl Bunch), Ritchie Valens, the "Big Bopper" (J.P. Richardson), Dion & the Belmonts, Frankie Sardo, and MC Lew Latto. The entire crew traveled 368 miles from Fort Dodge, Iowa, by bus, to get to Duluth. [18]

Soon after Dylan arrived in New York in early 1961, he played on a Carolyn Hester session. Writing in *Chronicles: Volume One*, he wrote about her beauty, and felt Hester, who had played with Holly, was Dylan's connection to Holly's *"royalty."* [19]

Hester told John Bauldie for *The Telegraph* in 1992:

"Bob was really startlingly different than most everyone. He hadn't started writing an awful lot, but just as a performer he was so outstanding and magnetic. And afterwards we started talking… We talked about Buddy Holly and I told him that Buddy had actually helped me get recorded originally and he enjoyed that. But of course, I had no idea that Bob would be a rock'n'roll musician eventually." [20]

On *Theme Time Radio Hour*, Dylan said, after playing The Spaniels' version of *Stormy Weather*, that he "probably" saw them, and Link Wray, at the Duluth Armory, with Holly, that evening in 1959. Dylan visited Wray in 1975, and told him, *"Link, I was sitting in the front row when you and Buddy Holly were at Duluth, and you're as great now as you were then."* [21] However, it appears that neither the Spaniels nor Link Wray performed on that tour. [22]

In 1984, Dylan again commented on Holly, telling *Rolling Stone,* [23] *"He was great. He was incredible. I mean, I'll never forget the image of seeing Buddy Holly up on the bandstand."*

The most famous and direct acknowledgment of seeing Holly on stage occurred on February 25, 1998, when Dylan accepted his Grammy award for "Album Of The Year," *Time Out Of Mind*:

"And I just want to say that when I was sixteen or seventeen years old, I went to see Buddy Holly play at Duluth National Guard Armory and I was three feet away from him...and he looked at me. And I just have some sort of feeling that he was – I don't know how or why – but I know he was with us all the time we were making this record in some kind of way." [24]

---

[18] http://www.startribune.com/buddy-holly-the-tour-from-hell/38282249/, *Buddy Holly: The tour from hell*, Pamela Huey, The StarTribune, Retrieved 11/20/16

[19] *Chronicles: Volume One*, Bob Dylan, Simon & Schuster, New York, 2004

[20] *Carolyn Hester Interview (John Bauldie)*, 5/24/1992, The Telegraph, No. 43, Autumn, 1992, pp. 50-52. via http://www.bobdylanroots.com/hester.html, Retrieved 11/20/16

[21] *No Direction Home: The Life and Music of Bob Dylan*, Robert Shelton, Revised and Updated Edition Edited by Elizabeth Thomson and Patrick Humphries, Backbeat Books/Hal Leonard Corp., Milwaukee, WI, 2011

[22] https://www.surfballroom.com/winterdanceparty/1959-wdp-tour/, *1959 Winter Dance Party Tour*, Retrieved 11/20/16

[23] *Bob Dylan: The Rolling Stone Interview*, Kurt Loder, Rolling Stone Magazine, 6/21/1984

[24] Acceptance Speech, Radio City Music Hall, New York, 2/25/98

In an interview published in *Guitar World*, Dylan mentioned how he'd randomly hear Holly's music during the time he was making *Time Out of Mind*. [25] *"It was spooky. [laughs] But after we recorded and left, you know, it stayed in our minds. Well, Buddy Holly's spirit must have been someplace, hastening this record."*

Dylan has covered some of Holly's material throughout the years: [26] [27]

- Bobby Zimmerman and his teenage friends would often crash local parties, and reportedly sing Holly's songs.

- Holly opened the Duluth concert with a solo electric version of *Gotta Travel On* on the tour. Dylan later recorded it for 1970's *Self Portrait*, and revived it on the 1976 leg of the Rolling Thunder Revue.

- On February 6, 1986, at the Park Royal Hotel in Wellington, New Zealand, Dylan rehearsed *Everyday*, *Not Fade Away*, and possibly *Maybe Baby*, with Tom Petty & The Heartbreakers, Stevie Nicks, and the Queens of Rhythm.

- *Listen To Me*, *Down In The Groove* sessions, May 1, 1987.

- Dylan rehearsed *Oh Boy* with the Grateful Dead in 1987, and performed it with "The Dead" on August 5, 2003.

- *Not Fade Away* and *Everyday*, rehearsal, May, 1989.

- *Not Fade Away* has been covered other times as well: with the Grateful Dead in 1989, at a soundcheck in 1997, and live in Hartford (1997) and Vancouver (1998), plus numerous times in 1999, 2000, 2001, 2002, and 2009.

- In 1999, Dylan dueted with Paul Simon on their joint tour, often playing a medley of Holly's *That'll Be The Day* and Dion's *The Wanderer*.

- In November 2014, Bob Dylan and his band played a special concert for one person, Fredrik Wikingsson, in Philadelphia. Dylan played four covers, beginning with a version of Buddy Holly's *Heartbeat*.

Adam Selzer noted that 40 years after the Winter Dance Party, in February 1999, Dylan *"played mostly smaller markets, covering* Not Fade Away *regularly, with Brian Setzer Orchestra opening. He never SAID that he was commemorating the 40th anniversary of the* Winter Dance Party *by doing one himself, but I'd say he was."* [28] Support act Brian Setzer played Eddie Cochran in *La Bamba*, the 1987 movie biography of Ritchie Valens. Collectors have footage of Dylan live in Duluth on July 3, 1999, at Bayside Festival Park, where he can be seen beaming as he finally gets to pay tribute to Holly by covering *Not Fade Away* in the same city where he once saw the man in concert.

Will Brennan had an interesting interpretation of the *"When the last rays of daylight go down Buddy, you'll roll no more"* [29] lyric from *Standing In the Doorway*, saying it related to Holly and the plane crash. [30]

I was thinking of Dylan seeing Holly in concert while I was reading Andrew Muir's January 2011 post on Michael Gray's *Bob Dylan Encyclopedia* blog. [31] Muir reported Dylan was no longer the most

[25] *Maximum Bob*, Murray Engleheart, Guitar World, 3/99

[26] http://www.bjorner.com/still.htm, *Still on the Road*, Retrieved, 11/20/2016

[27] http://rateyourmusic.com/list/Dylanlennon/it_aint_me_babe___all_the_songs_covered_by_bob_dylan/5/, *It Ain't Me Babe - All the songs covered by Bob Dylan*, Retrieved 11/20/2016

[28] Personal correspondence, 11/14/2016

[29] *Standing in the Doorway*, *Time Out of Mind*, Bob Dylan, 1997.

[30] http://www.muddywatermagazine.com/Bob-Dylan-Buddy-Holly-Time-Out-of-Mind.html, *Bob, Buddy and Time Out of Mind*, Muddy Water, Retrieved 11/20/16

popular artist in the "rare" records market. Neil Young and The Rolling Stones were still selling, with Bruce Springsteen becoming the new number one artist (The "New Dylan," as it were).

The readers' comments veered toward Dylan's current tours, and while many felt Dylan is still worth seeing live, a recording of the show no longer held the appeal of his older, pre-2003 (keyboard) shows. While no one could quite explain why Dylan is down while Springsteen and Young remain popular, it is interesting that Dylan appears to have finally succeeded at killing his own bootleg market. Dylan not only to wants control over his own "rare" releases (note *The Bootleg Series*), but he tries to connect directly through his music - no video screens, no cameras, no recordings, etc. The music he plays on stage now - as others have noted - works in the moment.

When Dylan recalled seeing Buddy Holly on stage, he said he felt that the two made eye contact. The young Bobby Zimmerman wasn't waving an iPhone or checking his recording levels or watching a mega-screen . . . He was letting the music transport him, directly (see Nobel Prize Chapter). It appears that Dylan wants to make that same connection to his audience.

Holly's ghost still appears to follow Dylan. At the end of his 2009 tour, he added a special support act – Dion DiMucci – who Bobby Zimmerman saw on stage at the Duluth Armory, on January 31, 1959.

---

[31] http://bobdylanencyclopedia.blogspot.com/2011/01/guest-post-from-andrew-muir.html, *A Guest Post by Andrew Muir*, Retrieved 11/20/16

Carl Perkins

Rockabilly legend Carl Lee Perkins, one of the early stars at Sun Records and author of such classics as *Blue Suede Shoes* and *Everybody's Trying To Be My Baby*, was born on April 9, 1932.

While often associated with The Beatles and Sun-mates Elvis Presley, Jerry Lee Lewis, and Johnny Cash, Perkins also had a number of significant connections to Bob Dylan.

The earliest Dylan recordings listed on Bjorner's *Still On The Road* site [32] took place on Christmas Eve, 1956, at Terlinde Music in St. Paul, Minnesota. Of the eight song fragments by Bob Zimmerman, Howard Rutman, and Larry Kegan, captured on tape, the second one listed was *Boppin' The Blues*, written by Perkins and Howard "Curley" Griffin. The song was released on Sun Records by Perkins in May of that year.

On February 18, 1969, [33] Dylan and Cash spent the day in Nashville's Columbia Studio A, recording with Perkins and Bob Wotton on guitars, Marshall Grant on bass, and drummer W.S. Holland. Among the songs covered was Perkins' *Matchbox*, and Cash even namechecked Perkins during his guitar solo.

Around that time, Dylan gave Perkins an unfinished song, *Champaign, Illinois*. According to his autobiography – *Go, Cat, Go!* [34] – Perkins worked out a rhythm and improvised some lyrics. Dylan said, *"Your song. Take it. Finish it."* It was released on Perkins' 1969 album, *On Top*. Incidentally, the initial Dylan-inspired Farm Aid, in 1985, took place in Champaign, Illinois.

On May 1, 1970, at New York's Columbia Studio B, Dylan, Charlie Daniels, Russ Kunkel, and Perkins' greatest disciple, George Harrison, jammed on a diverse set of oldies, including Perkins' *Matchbox* and *Your True Love*.

Dylan, Harrison, and John Fogerty surprised the crowd at Hollywood's Palomino Club in February, 1987, by joining Taj Mahal and Jesse Ed Davis on stage for a 45-minute improvised set. Although Dylan mostly kept in the background, four Perkins compositions were performed - *Matchbox*, *Gone, Gone, Gone*, *Honey Don't*, and *Blue Suede Shoes*. [35]

Perkins joined Dylan on stage in Carl's hometown of Jackson, Tennessee, on November 10, 1994, at the Oman Auditorium. [36] Their performance of *Matchbox* was captured on video by a fan. Dylan also rehearsed *Matchbox* with his band in early 1996, [37] and at a soundcheck on October 1, 1997. [38] His most recent performance of the song was on August 24, 1998, in Adelaide, Australia. [39]

---

[32] http://www.bjorner.com/DSN00003%201960.htm, *Still on the Road*, Retrieved 11/20/16

[33] http://www.bjorner.com/DSN01679%201969.htm#DSN01690, *Still on the Road*, Retrieved 11/20/16

[34] *Go, Cat, Go!: The Life and Times of Carl Perkins, the King of Rockabilly*, Carl Perkins, David McGee, Hyperion Books, 1996

[35] http://www.bjorner.com/DSN08560%20-%201987%20Early%20Sessions.htm#DSN08560, *Still on the Road*, Retrieved 11/20/16

[36] http://www.bjorner.com/DSN15420%20-%201994%20US%20Fall%20Tour.htm#DSN15730, *Still on the Road*, Retrieved 11/20/16

[37] http://www.bjorner.com/DSN18450%20-%201997%20UK%20Fall%20Tour.htm, *Still on the Road*, Retrieved 11/20/16

[38] http://www.bjorner.com/DSN18450%20-%201997%20UK%20Fall%20Tour.htm, *Still on the Road*, Retrieved 11/20/16

[39] http://www.bjorner.com/DSN19570%20-%201998%20Australian%20Tour.htm#DSN19600, *Still on the Road*, Retrieved 11/20/16

Carl Perkins died on January 19, 1998, in Jackson, Tennessee. Dylan was on tour with Van Morrison at the time. On the 21st in New York, [40] and the 24th in Boston, [41] Dylan joined Morrison to pay tribute by covering *Blue Suede Shoes*.

At Perkins' funeral, which featured Harrison performing *Your True Love*, Wynonna Judd read a note from Dylan:

"He really stood for freedom. That whole sound stood for all the degrees of freedom. It would just jump right off the turntable. We wanted to go where that was happening." [42]

(Thanks to the *It Ain't Me, Babe* site for the list of cover versions.) [43]

---

[40] http://www.bjorner.com/DSN18860%20-%201998%20US%20Winter%20Tour.htm#DSN18915, *Still on the Road*, Retrieved 11/20/16

[41] http://www.bjorner.com/DSN18860%20-%201998%20US%20Winter%20Tour.htm#DSN18930, *Still on the Road*, Retrieved 11/20/16

[42] http://www.southcoasttoday.com/article/19980125/News/301259899, *Rock stars pay tribute to Perkins*, The Associated Press, Retrieved 11/20/16

[43] http://rateyourmusic.com/list/Dylanlennon/it_aint_me_babe___all_the_songs_covered_by_bob_dylan/8/, *It Ain't Me Babe - All the songs covered by Bob Dylan*, Retrieved 11/20/2016

Bob Dylan pays tribute to Bobby Vee at St. Paul gig

July 11, 2013

Bob Dylan surprised the AmericanramA crowd at Midway Stadium in St. Paul, Minnesota, last night by paying tribute to early 1960's heartthrob Bobby Vee. In 1959, Dylan played piano on a couple of dates for Vee under the name Elston Gunn (sic). Vee, who last year announced [44] he had Alzheimer's disease, was in attendance.

Vee stood in Buddy Holly's place after Holly's plane went down in February, 1959:

"The promoters asked for local talent to help fill in that sad night and as the curtain came up that evening, a new voice was introduced to the world. A "fifteen-year-old" voice that knew all the words to all the songs." Bobby Vee. [45]

According to audio evidence and an article in Citypages, [46] Dylan said: *"I used to live here, and then I left ... I've shared the stage with everyone from Mick Jagger to Madonna, but the most beautiful person I've ever been on stage with is Bobby Vee. He used to sing a song called* Suzie Baby *... Please show your appreciation ... with a round of applause. We're gonna try and do this song, like I've done it with him before once or twice."*

In a 1992 interview with John Bauldie in *Wanted Man*, Vee recalled his time with a young Bobby Zimmerman, in the North Dakota area. [47] Vee was quoted as saying he wanted to add a piano player to the combo. This was not long after he replaced Holly in the 1959 Winter Dance Party Tour. *"So we sort of asked around the Fargo area and a friend of ours suggested a guy that had been staying at his house, and was working at a café as a busboy ... and so my brother met him and they went over to the radio station to use the piano and they sort of plunked around a bit and played* Whole Lotta Shakin' *in the key of C, and he told my brother that he had played with Conway Twitty, which was a lie, but for openers he thought, "Phew!" He didn't even want to audition the guy - he got the job."*

Vee went on to say Bob Zimmerman wanted to use the name Elston Gunn, and they went out and bought a matching shirt. Vee described him as *"scruffy,"* but *"really into it."* He also liked to do the handclaps, like Gene Vincent and the Bluecaps. But there was no piano, so the band decided to continue without a piano player. *"We paid him $15 a night,"* Vee said, *"so we paid him $30 and he was on his way."*

According to another interview, in *Goldmine* from 1999, [48] Vee said the surname "Gunnn" was spelled with three "N's." However, in Dylan's *Chronicles: Volume One*, the name is spelled "Gunn." Dylan went on to write that he *"had a lot in common"* with his friend, Vee, citing a common musical background, and complimenting his voice. Dylan also wrote about meeting up with Vee in New York soon after (*"as down-to-earth as ever"*). Although they didn't meet up again for another 30 years, Dylan wrote, *"I'd always thought of him as a brother."* [49]

[44] *Bobby Vee's Alzheimer's*, Bob Collins, Minnesota Public Radio News, 4/30/2012

[45] http://www.bobbyvee.com/bio.html, *Bobby Vee Biography*, Retrieved 11/20/2016

[46] *Bob Dylan at Midway Stadium, 7/10/13*, Reed Fischer, CityPages, (Minnesota) 7/11/2013

[47] *Bobby Vee Interview*, John Bauldie, *Wanted Man - In Search of Bob Dylan*, London, 1992. Archived: http://www.bobdylanroots.com/inter04.html Retrieved 11/20/2016

[48] *Bobby Vee & Sons - The Buddy Holly Connection Continues*. Goldmine, 8/27/1999, via http://expectingrain.com/dok/who/g/gunnnelston.html, Retrieved 11/20/2016

[49] *Chronicles: Volume One*, Bob Dylan, Simon & Schuster, New York, 2004

Frankie Valli's 'joke' tribute to Dylan

May 3, 2011

Francis Stephen Castelluccio was born on May 3, 1934, [50] in First Ward, Newark, New Jersey.

From 1962 to 1965, as Frankie Valli, he had massive success as the lead singer of The Four Seasons with such hits as *Sherry*, *Big Girls Don't Cry*, *Walk Like a Man*, *Rag Doll* (all number 1's), *Candy Girl*, *Stay*, and *Ronnie*. It has been estimated that The Four Seasons sold 50 million records between 1962 and 1966, and 100 million in total.

In 1965, The Four Season's label, Vee-Jay, was having financial problems, and was unable to pay royalties to the band. The band and the label went to court whilst the group went on to sign with Philips Records. Valli and The Four Seasons then entered the studio with the idea of recording an album comprised entirely of Bob Dylan compositions. However, the concept changed to also include material written by Burt Bacharach and Hal David.

According to Wayne Jancik in *The Billboard Book of One-Hit Wonders*, [51] Valli was frustrated with his interpretation of *Don't Think Twice, It's All Right*, and decided to record a "joke" falsetto vocal to reduce the tension in the studio. An executive at Philips heard the recording and decided to release it. Possibly due to the lawsuit with Vee-Jay, a single was issued under the name "The Wonder Who?"

The record, *Don't Think Twice/Sassy*, was released as Philips 40324 in October, 1965. It peaked at #12 on the Hot 100 singles chart. The album, *The 4 Seasons Sing Big Hits by Burt Bacharach...Hal David...Bob Dylan*, was released the following month.

Track listing:

Side One: Burt Bacharach, Hal David

1 *What the World Needs Now Is Love*

2 *Anyone Who Had a Heart*

3 *Always Something There to Remind Me*

4 *Make It Easy on Yourself*

5 *Walk on By*

6 *What's New Pussycat?*

Side Two: Bob Dylan

1 *Queen Jane Approximately*

2 *Mr. Tambourine Man*

3 *Like a Rolling Stone*

4 *Don't Think Twice*

5 *All I Really Want to Do*

6 *Blowin' in the Wind*

Credits: Frankie Valli (Vocals), Frankie Valli (Performer), Bob Crewe (Producer), Bob Crewe (Liner Notes), Charles Calello (Conductor), Charles Calello (Orchestral Arrangements), Gordon Clark (Engineer), Ron Harris (Cover Photo).

---

[50] http://www.thesmokinggun.com/mugshots/celebrity/music/frankie-valli, *Mugshots: Frankie Valli*, Retrieved 11/20/2016

[51] *The Billboard Book of One-Hit Wonders* (Paperback), Wayne Jancik, Billboard Books, Penguin, Random House, New York, 1998

Here's one interpretation of the single, from *All Music Guide:* [52]

"Of course, in the middle of the Dylan side comes the "love it or hate it" send-up of Don't Think Twice, It's All Right, *sung by Frankie Valli in his falsetto impersonation of Rose Murphy and, as credited to The Wonder Who?, a Top 20 hit. Those who hate it tend to be humorless Dylan acolytes who consider it sacrilegious; but the reason it was a hit in the fall of 1965 was precisely because the Dylan phenomenon had become so overwrought by then; it was a balloon that needed to have a little air taken out of it, and The Wonder Who? came along at just the right moment to do so."*

[52] http://www.allmusic.com/album/the-4-seasons-sing-big-hits-by-burt-bacharachhal-davidbob-dylan-new-gold-hits-mw0001226771, *The Four Seasons: The 4 Seasons Sing Big Hits by Burt Bacharach... Hal David... Bob Dylan/New Gold Hits,* AllMusic Review by William Ruhlmann, Retrieved 11/20/2016

Johnny Otis

December 27, 2010

Johnny Otis was born John Alexander Veliotes on December 28, 1921.

"Johnny's career just dazzles the mind. From discovering Esther Phillips and Jackie Wilson, to being a drummer, singer, piano player, bandleader, hit maker, right down to sculpting and painting. He even lost a seat for the California State Assembly. You can't top that. Willie and the Hand Jive indeed." - Bob Dylan, quoted in *Midnight at the Barrelhouse: The Johnny Otis Story* by George Lipsitz. [53]

Another revelation in the book was that Dylan purchased some artwork created by Johnny Otis.

Three songs associated with Johnny Otis were played on *Theme Time Radio Hour With Your Host Bob Dylan*:

1. Dylan played *Castin' My Spell* by Otis, Marie Adams, and The Three Tons of Joy, during the *Halloween* episode, saying the versatile Otis recorded this song at about the same time as his hit, *Willie and the Hand Jive*.

2. On the November, 2006, *Leftovers* program, Dylan played *The Turkey Hop*, and only introduced it as a song by The Robins (who evolved into The Coasters). However, it was recorded with the Johnny Otis Orchestra.

3. On the Christmas & New Year's episode of *Theme Time Radio Hour*, Dylan played *Far Away Christmas Blues* by Little Esther with the Johnny Otis Orchestra, complete with an introduction from Otis. After playing the track, Dylan mentioned that he was told by Frank Zappa that his mustache was inspired by Otis' facial hair.

After playing a track by Etta James on the *Theme Time Telephone* episode, Dylan noted that James had been discovered by Johnny Otis.

In his book *Chronicles: Volume One*, Dylan discussed the difficulties of recording *Most Of The Time* with producer Daniel Lanois. At one point, Dylan wrote that he was considering a big-band treatment for the song, imagining himself singing with Otis' orchestra.

On February 16, 1983, [54] Dylan joined former Band mates Rick Danko and Levon Helm at The Lone Star Cafe gig in New York City. They played five songs together, including *Willie and the Hand Jive*.

Bob Dylan surprised the crowd at the Providence (Rhode Island) Marriott Hotel in the early hours of July 10, 1986, [55] by joining Etta James and Shuggie Otis (Johnny's son) on stage. Dylan was on tour with Tom Petty & The Heartbreakers at the time. Shuggie wrote *Strawberry Letter 23*, and played with Al Kooper and Frank Zappa, among others.

---

[53] https://www.upress.umn.edu/book-division/books/midnight-at-the-barrelhouse, *Midnight at the Barrelhouse: The Johnny Otis Story (Reviews)*, Retrieved 11/20/2016

[54] http://www.bjorner.com/DSN06920%20-%201983%20Sessions.htm#DSN06920, *Still on the Road*, Retrieved 11/20/2016

[55] http://www.bjorner.com/DSN07990%20-%201986%20US%20Summer%20Tour.htm#DSN08230, *Still on the Road*, Retrieved 11/20/2016

Bob Dylan and Tiny Tim

December 1, 2009 (Updated 2016)

Last week, Bob Dylan, in an interview with *The Big Issue* [56] credited Brave Combo for the arrangement of *Must Be Santa*, found on his newest album, *Christmas In The Heart*. When asked where he first heard it, Dylan replied initially from Mitch Miller, but his take was based on a version by Brave Combo. Tiny Tim's manager, Bucks Burnett, told me he sent a copy to Dylan's management, and it was later played on Dylan's *Theme Time Radio Hour Christmas* episode. Dylan introduced the song on air by saying, like his own program, Brave Combo wanted to *"expand the musical taste of their listeners."* In the *Big Issue* interview, Dylan added, *"You oughta hear their version of Hey Jude."*

What Dylan left out was that Brave Combo was the backing band on that cover version of The Beatles' classic. The lead singer was Dylan's old chum, Tiny Tim. The recording comes from a 1996 Rounder Records release, titled *Girl*, named after another Beatles' song which opens the collection. The album was completed eight years after the project started. According to the liner notes by Carl Finch and the rest of the band, they *"didn't want it to be written off as 'just another novelty record.'"* [57] The collection includes versions of everything from *Bye Bye Blackbird* to Led Zeppelin's *Stairway To Heaven*. It also features Tiny Tim singing in a lower register than usual. The cha-cha version of *Hey Jude* is certainly one of the standout tracks.

Bob Dylan's and Tiny Tim's paths had crossed before. Dylan recalls, in *Chronicles: Volume One*, his early days in Greenwich Village. In the first chapter, *Markin' Up The Score*, [58] Dylan writes that Tim *"played the ukulele and sang like a girl - old standards from the '20s."* According to Dylan, they hung out a bit, and shared French Fries.

While Dylan was recuperating in Woodstock from his 1966 motorcycle accident, he and members of The Band began shooting a documentary, which included Tiny. The project led to Dylan and members of The Band recording what are now known as *The Basement Tapes*. (A snippet of Tiny peeking through a window can be seen in an official video promoting the 2014 release of *The Basement Tapes: Complete*.) When more and more unreleased material fell into the hands of collectors over the years, one thing that eventually surfaced was some recordings of The Band with Tiny. Four known songs preserved on tape from this era are *Sonny Boy*, *Be My Baby*, *I Got You, Babe*, and *Memphis, Tennessee*. Dylan probably did not play on these tracks. Around this time, Tiny and The Band also recorded material for the film, *You Are What You Eat*, an obscure movie co-produced by Peter Yarrow (of Peter, Paul and Mary). There are also tales of Dylan and Tim privately performing songs for each other.

Bob Dylan played a Tiny Tim recording on the eleventh episode of *Theme Time Radio Hour*. The subject was *Flowers*, and the song Dylan played, was, of course, Tiny's biggest hit, *Tiptoe Through The Tulips*, from 1968. Here's what Dylan had to say:

"No one knew more about old music than Tiny Tim. He studied it and he loved it. He knew all the old songs that only existed as sheet music." [59]

Tiny Tim died in Minneapolis, Minnesota, on November 30, 1996, when he was 64.

---

[56] *Bob Dylan discusses holiday music, Christmas and feeding the hungry*, The Big Issue: International Network of Street Papers, 11/23/2009

[57] Liner Notes, *Girl*, CD by Tiny Tim, Carl Finch, Rounder Records, 1996

[58] *Chronicles: Volume One*, Bob Dylan, Simon & Schuster, New York, 2004

[59] *Theme Time Radio Hour With Your Host, Bob Dylan*, "*Flowers*," Season One, Episode 11, Grey Water Park Productions

Rick Nelson's *Garden Party*: Who really hid in Dylan's shoes?

May 8, 2010

"OK, Ricky Nelson, he did a lot of my songs, Ricky Nelson. I wanna do one of his called Lonesome Town. *Actually I heard this song when I was about oh, say I dunno, two-years-old (sic). It really had an impression on me . . . Thank you. Thank you, Ricky."* (Bob Dylan, Madison Square Garden, New York City, July 15, 1986) [60]

Eric Hilliard "Ricky" Nelson was born May 8, 1940, in Teaneck, New Jersey. He grew up in the public eye, appearing in various radio programs, movies, and television shows while very young, usually with his parents, Ozzie and Harriet, and his brother, David. Starting in 1957, Ricky began performing as a singer on TV's *The Adventures Of Ozzie and Harriet*, and a string of hit singles followed, including *Poor Little Fool*, *Lonesome Town*, *It's Late*, *Travelin' Man*, and *Hello Mary Lou*.

Nelson recorded top-notch material, but was not taken as seriously as he should have been because of his connections to his famous parents, and appearances on a television sitcom. However, he did have some heavyweight supporters, including Sun Records legends Roy Orbison, Carl Perkins, Elvis Presley, and Jerry Lee Lewis. He also had a big influence on many young listeners, including The Beatles, John Fogerty, Linda Ronstadt, and Bob Dylan.

At first, Ricky was signed to a one-record deal with Verve, thanks to his father. Ozzie then negotiated a deal with Imperial, which gave Ricky more creative control. Soon, Nelson formed his own hand-picked band, featuring future Presley and Shindig! guitarist James Burton.

After his string of hits in the late 1950s and early 1960s ended, Rick Nelson became a pioneer in what is now known as country-rock, although, once again, he was not appreciated in his time. In 1970, Nelson released a live album, *Ricky Nelson In Concert*, which was recorded the previous year at L.A.'s Troubadour club. The record featured three Dylan compositions: *She Belongs to Me* (a top 40 hit for Nelson), *If You Gotta Go, Go Now*, and *I Shall Be Released*. On his 1971 album, *Rudy The Fifth*, Nelson also covered Dylan's *Just Like A Woman* and *Love Minus Zero/No Limit*.

Nelson was still part of the oldies circuit in the early 1970s, even though he had progressed musically over the previous few years. On October 15, 1971, he joined Chuck Berry, Bo Diddley, and others for a Rock and Roll Revival show at Madison Square Garden. Nelson heard the crowd booing at one point, thinking they did not like his new musical direction, and it inspired Nelson to recall the incident in song. The result, *Garden Party*, brought Nelson near the top of the charts one last time.

The song referenced various musicians, including John Lennon (*"Yoko brought her walrus"*) and Chuck Berry (*"Out stepped Johnny B. Goode"*) as well as Dylan - with the song *She Belongs To Me*, and in the line *"Mr. Hughes hid in Dylan's shoes, wearing his disguise."* I had always assumed that this was a reference to Dylan himself, who was thought to have been a rock and roll Howard Hughes at the time - an eccentric recluse. However I came across this interpretation, from *The Straight Dope* website, [61]

"Mr Hughes isn't Howard Hughes, as most people think, but refers to George Harrison, the ex-Beatle. Rick Nelson was good friends and next-door neighbor to Harrison, and was also a good friend of Bob Dylan. "Mr. Hughes" was the alias Harrison used while traveling, and "hid in Dylan's shoes" apparently refers to an album of Bob Dylan covers Harrison was planning that never came to fruition. "Wearing his disguise" is more obscure, but presumably had something to do with Harrison's habit of traveling incognito."

---

[60] http://www.bjorner.com/DSN07990%20-%201986%20US%20Summer%20Tour.htm#DSN08260, *Still on the Road*, Retrieved 11/20/2016

[61] http://www.straightdope.com/columns/read/2173/in-ricky-nelsons-garden-party-who-is-mr-hughes, *In Ricky Nelson's "Garden Party," who is Mr. Hughes?* Staff report, Retrieved 11/20/2016

While hosting his *Theme Time Radio Hour* program, Dylan played some of Nelson's records, including 1957's *Waiting In School* (for the theme *School*), and *Hello Mary Lou* (*Hello*) and *Travelin' Man* (*Around The World Part II*), both from 1961.

On *Theme Time*, Dylan talked about Nelson's *Hello Mary Lou* single, originally the A-side, which went to number 9, then the B-side, *Travelin' Man*, which went to number one.

In *Chronicles: Volume One*, Dylan praised Nelson's music, circa 1961, saying he was a fan, but the music of the 50s teen idol was no longer in style. He went on to write about how Nelson put his own mark on his compositions, and then mentioned how he (Dylan) was mentioned in one of Nelson's songs (*Garden Party*). He also mentioned that Nelson, like Dylan, was *"booed while onstage for changing ... his musical direction."* Ironically, it turns out that the crowd was probably not booing Nelson at the Garden, but some inebriated concert-goers being ejected from the show by security.

Dylan also probably related to Nelson's view of nostalgia in the song – *"If memories are all I sang, I'd rather drive a truck."*

Rick Nelson died in a plane crash, December 31, 1985. In 1986, Dylan performed Nelson's *Lonesome Town* 54 times in concert.

Note: Nelson's guitarist, James Burton, was reportedly offered a place in Bob Dylan's first touring band, but turned it down due to a heavy work schedule. [62]

---

[62] http://www.rockabillyhall.com/JamesBurton.html, *James Burton*, Retrieved 11/20/2016

Bob Dylan and the death of Elvis Presley, August 16, 1977

August 16, 2010

When Elvis Presley died on August 16, 1977, it deeply affected Bob Dylan.

During this time, Dylan was already going through his divorce from his wife Sara. It was also not long after the suicide of Phil Ochs.

Dylan heard the news while he was at his farm in Minnesota, with his children and their art teacher, Faridi McFree. She was playing with the kids and planning a birthday party for Samuel Dylan's 9th birthday. Dylan was writing songs for his next album, which turned out to be *Street-Legal*.

When Dylan told McFree that Presley had died, she replied she was not a fan of Presley's music:

"That's all I have to say - he didn't talk to me for a week…. He really took it bad… He was really grieving. He said that if it wasn't for (Presley) *he never would have gotten started. He opened the door."* [63]

Dylan said, *"I went over my whole life. I went over my whole childhood. I didn't talk to anyone for a week."* [64]

In 1997, after recovering from a life-threatening illness, Dylan said he thought he was going to *"meet Elvis."*

On the last date of his 2009 summer tour, Dylan was playing in Nevada. It was the 32nd anniversary of Presley's death. He performed Presley's first RCA single, *Heartbreak Hotel.* [65]

(Sources: Howard Sounes [66] and Clinton Heylin. [67])

---

[63] *Down the Highway - The Life of Bob Dylan*, Howard Sounes, Grove Press, New York, 2001

[64] *How Does It Feel To Be On Your Own? Bob Dylan Talks to Robert Shelton*, Robert Shelton, Melody Maker, 7/29/1978

[65] http://www.bjorner.com/DSN31230%20-%202009%20US%20Summer%20Tour.htm#DSN31530, *Still on the Road*, Retrieved 11/20/2016

[66] *Down the Highway - The Life of Bob Dylan*, Howard Sounes, Grove Press, New York, 2001

[67] *Bob Dylan: Behind the Shades Revisited*, Clinton Heylin, William Morrow, 2001

Billy Faier, banjo pioneer and DJ who hosted Bob Dylan in '62

January 31, 2016

Billy Faier, the five-string banjo pioneer who traveled with Woody Guthrie and Ramblin' Jack Elliott, and hosted a radio show featuring a very young Bob Dylan, died over the weekend. He was reportedly 85-years-old, although on his website, he humorously wrote he was born in 1978 RPM. I conducted an email interview with Faier more than five years ago, and posted it in installments as part of a celebration of Bob Dylan's 70th birthday in May, 2011.

Billy Faier on neighbor Dylan in the 1960s

Billy Faier is a name that should sound familiar to any serious collector of Bob Dylan's unreleased recordings. Sometime in October, 1962, Bob Dylan was one of the many guests that performed on Faier's WBAI radio program, *The Midnight Special*. For this appearance, Dylan played four songs, including a name-check of his host during the soon-to-be controversial number, *Talkin' John Birch Paranoid Blues*, a song requested by Faier.

Intrigued by Faier's covers of Beatles' songs, someone from the Robyn Hitchcock fan-site *Fegmaniax* posted a link to Faier's website. I went to investigate, and was fascinated by all the tales Faier told. They appeared to only touch the surface of an amazing adventure. I contacted Faier, he agreed to be interviewed, and we began emailing each other. The more Faier replied, the more questions I had. There was an even deeper connection to Bob Dylan than I had anticipated, and Faier does not mince words on what he thinks of him.

It turns out that, besides being a disc jockey, Faier is also a banjo player who released a handful of albums, including one with liner notes by Pete Seeger, and who had traveled with Woody Guthrie and Ramblin' Jack Elliott. He was even interviewed for the documentary *Bob Dylan In Woodstock*. Faier had so many fascinating tales - some directly involving Dylan, others that would be of interest to anyone interested in Dylan's influences and acquaintances - that I decided to share all of them here.

Billy Faier lived in Woodstock at the same time as Dylan, and knew him well enough to photograph Dylan playing chess and building his shed. He also owns a postcard sent to Dylan by John Lennon, and kept a letter from Big Bill Broonzy, who was (unsuccessfully) trying to convince Faier's wife to leave Faier and travel to Europe with the blues legend.

Describe the atmosphere in Woodstock in the mid-1960s, before the big Woodstock festival.

My family moved from Brooklyn to Woodstock, New York, when I was 14-years-old. Woodstock had been an artists' colony since 1903. There were artists of all kinds, classical musicians, writers, painters, sculptors, etc. But no jazz, folk or pop musicians that I knew of. It remained my main home until I sold my place in 2003, though I did lots of traveling in those years.

In the early sixties, I booked folk singers for weekend gigs at the Cafe Espresso which was owned by my good friends Bernard and Mary Lou Paturel. I can't remember all of them but for a year I booked one a week which included many of the now-known names of the folk world. Dave Van Ronk, Tom Paxton, John Winn, come immediately to mind. There were many more but I can't remember now. I forget names these days. They got a place to stay, excellent food and fifty dollars for the gig. I performed there many times over the years. I didn't book Dylan but he undoubtedly heard of the place from his friends, many of whom I did book. When he finally got to Woodstock, he became good friends with the Paturels and spent a summer living upstairs at the Cafe. He was already a well-known star. That summer Joan Baez was in Woodstock along with the Farinas and many other well-known figures and many an evening and afternoon was spent at the cafe playing music, though Dylan rarely appeared from upstairs. Grossman bought a house in Woodstock and the Band arrived to work with Dylan. I think one of the Band was an early fan of mine because Al Grossman called me and asked to bring them over to meet me.

By the end of that summer, the town had changed, and changed forever. There were now hordes of people, mostly youngsters coming to get a look at Dylan and Baez. Business was booming; a couple of head shops opened, tie-dye clothes stores, a few more coffee shops, the usual tourist stuff that happens in art colonies when they become known past the artist community. Not only ordinary tourists but many, many musicians from all walks of pop music could be found on the street looking for action, drugs, etc.

I remember running into The Incredible String Band on the corner in the middle of town, looking for something to do. I took one of the guys (can't recall his name) back to my place and we played music for a couple of hours. But the town was still fun for me and most others.

There was a weekly outdoor concert called the Sound Out about six miles out of town where the early rock and folk singers performed, attracting a few hundred people. I think they charged a dollar to get in. Many of the old time Woodstock characters (of which I am one) will tell you that is where they got the idea for the Woodstock Festival which was held 60 miles away from Woodstock in Bethel (or was it White Lake), New York.

Then, in '69, the Aquarian Festival of Music and Art happened. I had a gallery, The Light Box, where I sold my psychedelic light creations, near the center of town, right across the street from the Cafe Espresso, which had changed hands. It was now mainly a rock and roll joint. On weekends, when the town was loaded with tourists, I would sit out on the porch in front of my gallery playing my banjo until ten o'clock in the evening when the music started across the street, drowning me out. Mike Lang, one of the promoters of the festival, now called the "Woodstock Festival" asked me to bring my light boxes to the festival, promising me a good tree and all the electricity I could use, but I refused, fearing rain.

After the Woodstock Festival, the town exploded again, no longer loaded, but now bursting with tourists. Hundreds, maybe thousands of people came to the town of Woodstock for the festival, only to be told by locals that it was 60 miles away. Dozens of us were on the streets all weekend, directing concertgoers to the right location. The tourists have never stopped coming to find the place where the legendary festival happened.

By this time, Dylan had bought a place in upper Byrdcliff, outside the town of Woodstock. Bernard Paturel was now working for him as general factotum, chauffeur, etc. He was being constantly bombarded by tourists looking to see his house, going through his garbage cans, etc. I had constructed my own house by then and had a little carpentry skill. Dylan was justifiably paranoid about strangers near his house so, as a favor, to Bernard, I took on the job of building a little lockable shed for Dylan's garbage cans. Bob saw me working from his window and was greatly amused (this reported to me by Bernard) to see me with really long hair. Up to then, he had only seen me with a crew cut.

Before I write about Dylan I must say that I consider him a great songwriter-poet. One of the very greatest of our day. He had the great fortune, or misfortune, depending on how you look at it, of having his genius displayed to the world long before he knew how to cope with it. I have not followed his career at all since those early days. I can only hope, for his sake, that he has matured and learned how to deal with his life. I also feel that one of his lines completely transcends the folk world, the music world, and the literary world - "If God's on our side, he'll stop the next war."

I first became acquainted with Bob Dylan in the early sixties, mainly through seeing him with mutual friends at the Limelight in Greenwich Village, New York, where many of the folk singing crowd hung out. He and I were not close friends. He seemed to have a lot of difficulty relating to people. So did I. He once complimented me on a song I had written which he had seen in Broadside. Other than that, I cannot remember any positive conversation between us from those Greenwich Village days.

You took a picture of Dylan, taken at the Cafe Espresso, which can be seen on your website. Please describe the Cafe. What can you remember about that day? What were Dylan and Victor Maymudes like?

In Woodstock, Bob had two 'sidekicks' that he hung out with and seemed to be his constant companions. The first was a good friend of mine, Victor Maymudes, whom I had known since 1953 in Los Angeles. I took the two pictures of him and Bob playing chess at the Cafe Espresso mainly because of the light contrast between them; Bob's face lit up, Victor's in silhouette. After Victor had been replaced by Bob Neuwirth, he had a great deal of difficulty accepting the fact that, since he was no longer part of Dylan's inner circle, he no longer enjoyed the standing among the other members of that circle, including Al Grossman and Grossman's associates. Victor asked me to accompany him on a visit to Grossman's house one day, assuring me that we would be welcome. I went with him because he was a good friend of mine, but with great foreboding because I was aware of Victor's compulsive need for recognition from the elite. I was never part of anyone's inner circle so I had nothing at stake. When we arrived, Grossman was at a long table with many others, enjoying an al fresco lunch being served up by Sally, his wife. He completely ignored us, as did all of his guests; not even a greeting. Victor was devastated. He sat down on a large rock. I joined him there for a minute or two. He looked like he was about to cry. I told him, "Victor, these people are not your friends. Let's go." We left.

In the picture Dylan documentary Dont Look Back, *there is a scene in which Dylan is being interviewed by a teenage reporter from a school paper. Dylan, with Neuwirth's constant encouragement and backup, treats the lad disgustingly, using his logic and his quick brain to make the lad feel awful. I was really amazed this 'truth attack' - as it and similar events have been called - was left in the film.*

One evening I was visiting my good friends Bernard and Mary Lou upstairs at the Cafe Espresso where Dylan was staying at the time. I was telling them of my desire to run for office in the local Woodstock elections. Dylan and Neuwirth walked in and joined the conversation. They immediately attacked my idea as being useless with such questions as, "Even if you won, do you really think you could do any good?" This, from two people who had never favored me with a hello, though we saw each other frequently around town. I had seen the movie with the similar event and so I tried not to take their insulting and rude behavior personally, realizing that it was a neurotic need on Dylan's part to make people feel small so that his own tiny self-image grew larger by comparison.

Billy Faier on interviewing Bob Dylan, WBAI, '62

Sometime in October, 1962, Bob Dylan brought his acoustic guitar and harmonica to WBAI for the *Midnight Special* radio program, with host Billy Faier. A partial tape has survived. I received this particular recording in a trade, about a decade ago, on a Maxell cassette. Dylan performed four songs - *Baby Let Me Follow You Down, Talkin' John Birch Paranoid Blues, The Death Of Emmett Till,* and a rare take of *Make Me A Pallet On Your Floor,* a traditional song most often associated with Mississippi John Hurt.

When I asked Faier about what he remembered about the October 1962 appearance of a young Bob Dylan on his *Midnight Special* radio program, this is what he had to say:

Bob Dylan was on my radio show, The Midnight Special, *along with many other folksingers on station WBAI, a Pacifica Station in New York City in the very early sixties. (It was) a live show every Saturday night. His appearance was quite unmemorable. The only reason I'm sure of it is that I have a photo of him at the occasion. It will take a lot of time to find it because my only copy of it is in a file of all my photos on disc, but not in my computer. And it is a too dark shot, hardly recognizable.*

In my memory there was no interview. There may have been a couple of introductory questions because I'm sure I introduced him before he sang. At the time he was one of many unknown kids who came to sing a song or two. He was certainly not a superstar yet, and I don't think he had recorded his first album. However, I must admit my own memory is very shaky. I have about three or four tapes of those couple of hundred shows I did, and I don't remember him being on any of them. I could be wrong about that.

I find it fascinating that Dylan did not leave much of an impression on Faier. After I received Billy's reply, I did some research. Dylan's debut had indeed been released in March of that year. He had already written *Blowin' In The Wind,* and begun recording his second album, *The Freewheelin' Bob Dylan.* He had also been making the rounds, giving interviews, playing various gigs and hootenannies, and showing up at radio programs hosted by Oscar Brand, Cynthia Gooding, and others. When I asked Faier if he had a copy of the appearance, he replied that he did not. I told him I had it on an old cassette in the closet, and I would try to dig it out, transfer it to CD, and send him a copy. Faier replied:

If you find a copy of his performance on my show I would love to hear it. It would have to be from someone's aircheck. It is great to be reminded of stuff I completely forgot.

Luckily, it was not that difficult to find. I hooked up my cassette deck, and made the CD. I probably had not heard the recording, myself, in seven years. It was fascinating to listen to, especially after corresponding with the host of this legendary program. The tape began with a slightly problematic version of *Baby Let Me Follow You Down.* It's unclear if the guitar is out of tune, a capo is causing problems, or Dylan is just having trouble playing the song, but it appeared to improve by the second verse. When the song ends, after a smattering of in-studio applause, someone - presumably Billy - asks Dylan if he was taking requests, and then asks for *Talking John Birch Paranoid Blues.* After adjusting the microphone, while Dylan was tuning his guitar, Faier can be heard saying that they like to give all points of view on the station. Dylan then does a spirited take of the unreleased song, even adapting the lyrics to sing, *"The rest are fellow Birchers like me… and Billy Faier."* (Note that this was about seven months before Dylan was censored from performing this song on *The Ed Sullivan Show*.) Dylan then performed another request, *The Death Of Emmett Till*. Dylan is asked if he wrote that song (he replied in the affirmative), and then is told that he can rest if he prefers, but decides to perform a rare, impromptu version of *Make Me A Pallet On Your Floor*. The tape fades out as an interview seems to be beginning. It ran about 18 minutes.

I made the CD, and sent it off to Texas. The following week, I received the following reply:

Harold, CD arrived today and I got a kick out of listening to it. It made Dylan a little more real to me since I haven't followed him at all for many years. But from my few words with him on the CD I know that I must have liked him then, even though he was sometimes hard to take socially. (Otherwise I wouldn't have adjusted the mike for him.)

Dylan's Woodstock friends:

Billy Faier spent time with many of Dylan's friends and associates, as well as legends in the world of folk music. I asked him to comment on a few of them:

Pete Seeger:

From my seventeenth year - when I started playing the banjo - Pete Seeger has, for a good part of my life, been the closest to an idol that I ever had. Like most others, folk musicians especially, I was swept away by his charisma, his extraordinary ability to get people singing, and his incredible banjo playing. The very first time I ever heard his banjo was on an Asch recording of Cindy *at Wolfe O'Meara's house in Woodstock. When I hear it today, I am still in awe of it because its absolute simplicity still bears the full ring of truth for me as it did sixty-four years ago. I was raised in a radical household; my earliest memories included watching my mother harangue a street crowd from a soap box or playing under the table while she conducted a communist party meeting. While I never subscribed to the Communist line, Communism was never the bug-a-boo to me that it was (and is) to most Americans. Some of the finest people I ever knew were either communists or sympathizers and Pete Seeger was a fine example of this group. But it was not his politics, whatever they may have been at the time, that interested me. Playing and singing folk music was the very first thing that ever seized and moved me to my very core and Pete was the voice that helped me have the confidence in my own feelings about it. He never preached any political ism from the stage. He concentrated on the issues of the time. In the early days (late forties for me) it was peace, union organizing, peace, civil rights for all colors and creeds of people, peace, always peace, throughout the Korean War, the War in Viet Nam, always peace. I believed in all the issues that moved him. But I brought those beliefs to his concerts and what I, and many, many others I knew, wanted was for him to SHUT UP AND SING. None of us ever dared to shout that from the audience. We all loved Pete Seeger.*

Naturally I collect all of his recordings I could find and figured out everything he ever did on record, but always with the acute awareness that, while I could play the notes, I didn't have the drive or the indescribable quality that made his banjo playing so unique. I was at what may have been the first public performance of the Weavers. It was in a photographer's studio on East Tenth St. in New York City, I believe. My wife, Lori, and I visited Pete and Toshi at their cabin they were building in Beacon, New York. Many young folksingers had spoken of visiting them to help build their cabin and I wanted to do the same but never had the nerve to call and ask if I could come up.

But my wife had gotten to know them when the Weavers sang at the Village Vanguard so we called and were invited to stop by. I played the tapes Lori and I had made of Pop Green and Will Calvin in Modesto, California for Pete. In 1948, Pete and Toshi spent the summer at her parents' house in Woodstock, New York where I lived. The campaign to elect Henry Wallace for President on the Progressive Party ticket was in full swing and I got to see and speak to the Seegers a few times that summer. One amusing incident bears telling.

Jackson MacLow, a young, bearded, recorder playing, anarchist poet lived on the Maverick in Woodstock. He could often be seen walking up and down the roads playing his recorder. Being an anarchist he detested communists whom the anarchists always referred to as Stalinists. Jackson and I, along with Bill and Betty Keck, were going to hitchhike to Boston to visit some of the anarchists there. I had to go to Kingston for something and the plan was to meet them at the old viaduct in Kingston. There I was waiting and along comes Pete driving his Jeep station wagon. He stopped across the road from me and leaned out and shouted, "Hey Billy, I hear you're going to Boston." As he spoke, Jackson and the Kecks got out of the station wagon. Pete drove off. He had picked them up hitchhiking and, being a great recorder player he borrowed it from Jackson and played it while he steered with his knees.

"'Do you know that guy?" Jackson asked me, still in awe at Pete's recorder playing. "Sure," I replied. "That's Pete Seeger." "That's PETE SEEGER," shouted Jackson. "My God, I had no idea a Stalinist could be so nice." Pete roared in pleasure when I related this story to him months later.

In that summer of '48 there was a hootenanny at Dr. Kingsbury place in Shady. Pete, Betty Sanders, Fred Hellerman, and others sang. Along with the usual left-wing songs, I remember Freddy singing Eatin' Goober Peas.

In 1957 I recorded my first album, The Art Of The Five String Banjo, *for Riverside Records. Pete did the liner notes for this album. This was - and still is - a great honor to me.*

There were many meetings with Pete over the years. I will describe three more.

Folk music was getting to be big time in the entertainment industry. The Hootenanny *program on prime time TV was all the rage. (That was the program that taught the American public to mindlessly clap in rhythm to every song from start to finish. Thank God they are forgetting it in the past decade or so.) Pete was barred from appearing on the show because of his political leanings. I was the chairman of the folksinger's committee formed to protest that policy. Pete and Toshi came to my apartment to a meeting of the group. At this meeting, Pete made it clear that he was against making an issue of it because the program was airing songs of the people that would never be heard by such a large audience, and giving high paid work to progressive singers that would not be heard otherwise. We dropped the protest. But the thing that is memorable to me from that meeting is that it was the first time I ever became truly aware of the depths of Pete and Toshi's commitment to the all the causes of which Pete spoke and sung. Before the meeting got started, Toshi read to us a letter she had gotten from Woody Guthrie. I do not remember the content of the letter. What I remember is Toshi crying, tears coming down her face. Somehow this affected me deeply. It was a glimpse into the souls of these people to whom I had always wanted to be close. It brought me closer.*

Pete called me at my house in Woodstock to ask if I would appear at a concert in Kingston to raise money for the Clearwater, the Hudson River Sloop that was about to be launched. I was flattered and delighted to be asked. But the thing that stuck in my mind about the call was the way in which he spoke. It was as if he were addressing a crowd of thousands of people, not just me. It felt strange and I determined, if I ever got the chance, to engage him in a one to one conversation to see if he was able to do so. The chance came many years later. I was sitting on a pile of wood on Rondout Creek at the Kingston waterfront admiring the Woody Guthrie, a small version of the Clearwater. Suddenly, and unexpectedly, Pete Seeger came up from the cabin, saw me and greeted me. He came and sat with me and we spoke together like two friends, one to one. I consciously avoided any talk of folk music, politics, or any great issues. I asked him how the sixties had affected his life. Did he still eat meat? Were any of his three kids on drugs? I don't recall any of his answers, but he satisfied my curiosity. Pete was as average as they come in many ways. I loved him for it.

But my fondest memory of Pete has to do with the first thing that attracted me to him - Banjo playing! The Beacon Branch of the Sloop Club meets every Sunday at the Beacon waterfront. I have been there about five or six times over the years. Pete, of course, is the main attraction when he is there, and visitors are constantly vying for his attention. A completely informal situation. I was on stage, playing my banjo and singing You Won't See Me, *my favorite Beatle song. Pete was sitting on the edge of the stage turned toward me and listening to me. Some guy came up to him and tried to engage him in conversation. Pete put his hand up in the guy's face to silence him, without even turning his head from me. It was the greatest compliment I ever had.*

The Band:

(Manager Albert) Grossman brought all The Band over one night. I sat on a box and entertained them with my banjo for a while. I recall the bass player (Rick Danko) being intrigued by one song, Funniest Thing, *which is in 11/8 time, trying to count the beats as I played. I don't remember how they looked or dressed, but they certainly were not clean cut. I would remember that. There was one with a beard, Levon, I think. They were quite nice and friendly. I eventually became friends with all of them, except Robbie Robertson.*

25

On Tiny Tim:

I don't remember seeing Tiny Tim in Woodstock. But I did meet him when I was on the staff of WBAI in New York City. I had a Saturday midnight live show, The Midnight Special. *(WBAI DJ) Bob Fass brought Tim up to the show one night. No one had ever seen anything like him before. It was great.*

On Van Morrison:

Van Morrison was a good friend. He loved to play Woody Guthrie songs with me when he got drunk.

Betsy Siggins on running Club 47, and hanging out with Bob Dylan and Joan Baez

June 9, 2012

Betsy Siggins' Boston University freshman roommate was Joan Baez. Her first husband was a member of the Charles River Valley Boys. She hung out with Bob Dylan in Cambridge and New York, had the Rev. Gary Davis sleep on her couch, and ran Cambridge's legendary Club 47.

Betsy Minot Siggins has lived a full life, a testament to the ideals of the 1960s folk movement. During her two decades away from the Boston area, she worked for nonprofit organizations where she fed the hungry, then founded programs for homeless people with AIDS. Now she's back in Massachusetts where she has founded the *New England Folk Archives*, and recently appeared in the documentary, *For The Love Of The Music - the Club 47 Folk Revival*.

"I was into folk music a little early," Siggins told me recently over the phone. *"I went to a small artistic school (Cherry Lawn) in Connecticut, with a class of about 12 people. Most were theater-bound, writing bound, music bound. I was a high school sophomore, and the Weavers were getting heard on the radio. There were the Everly Brothers, with a hint of R&B. I also overdosed on Gilbert and Sullivan as a teenager."*

Siggins was also influenced by her stepmother, a classical pianist, and the far away, flickering signals from the West Virginia country music station WWVA.

"They were my musical bookends," she said. When she arrived at B.U., Siggins' roommate was a young, aspiring folk singer with long, black hair, and the voice of an angel. Her name was Joan Baez.

"We spent a lot of time not paying attention to academics. She had a great wit. We spent time talking about silly things, and we laughed a lot. I was captivated by this inner strength she didn't know she had, but others saw."

Siggins started waitressing at the Cafe Yana, then moved over to the Golden Vanity. *"Both clubs featured folk music. Cafe Yana was in a tiny basement outside of B.U., while the Golden Vanity was an opened warehouse near the Mass. Pike. Inside was a nautical theme, and there were lofts above that were rented to painters. It was a multicultural hangout."*

One day while working at the Golden Vanity, she met her future husband Bob Siggins of the Charles River Valley Boys. *"He probably told me about Club 47. He had funny friends that knew so much about old-timey music. It certainly was an education!"*

The couple married in 1960 and spent a year in Europe, along with the other members of the Valley Boys. *"I spent my honeymoon with four other guys!"* she laughed. *"The band played, which paid for booze and food. The boys recorded an album at Dobell's Record Shop, and all the British folkies came to hang out."*

When the newlyweds returned to the U.S.A., Siggins worked at Club 47, doing whatever needed to be done. *"I really liked the community, the camaraderie ... That's when I got my real education, at the cusp of world changes. I do remember it being a turning point in my life. At the beginning, everybody thought (the Vietnam conflict) was a just war. People were brainwashed. Friends went to Canada. There were hard choices, and not a lot of support."*

These were also the early days of the Civil Rights Movement, and Cambridge was not excluded from racist incidents. In fact, Siggins said that someone had to buy a piece of clothing for blues singer Elizabeth Cotten (*Freight Train Blues, Shake Sugaree, Oh Babe, It Ain't No Lie*), because she was unable to do it herself. *"Elizabeth Cotten wanted to buy a blouse in a department store in Harvard Square, and they refused to sell it to her,"* Siggins told me. *"It was like being hit by lightning. Nancy Sweezy, one of the Club's first board members, had to go in and buy it for her."*

Many of the blues musicians stayed with Siggins because they were not allowed to stay elsewhere. *"I had the Rev. Gary Davis sleep on my couch. He never took off his coat. It was like he was always waiting for a train."*

Siggins later divorced, then married Benno Schmidt, the future president of Yale University. She left Boston in 1974 and the couple moved to New York City. *"I spent five years being a mom, then ran soup kitchens for hungry and homeless people with AIDS. I worked in East Harlem. There was so much need, never a dull moment. I embraced it completely, worked hard for 12 or 13 years."* Her second marriage ended, and she's been with her partner Hugh McGraw since 1979, but said, *"Two marriages is enough."* The couple moved back to Massachusetts in 1996.

Siggins soon fell in with Club 47 again, just as it was on the brink of folding completely. *"They turned it into a non-profit, and I just had 10 to 12 years experience with soup kitchens in New York. I called on a lot of old friends, and tried to turn the ship. There were lots of good feelings from my contemporaries. We had concerts at the Sanders Theater to celebrate Club 47, I was writing grant proposals.*

"But after 11 years, after the 2009 crash, four or five of us got laid off. I thought, 'What am I going to do now?' Then a light bulb went off three or four years ago."

The epiphany came just by looking around her place. *"I stared at all these boxes with photographs, and bags with tapes, and realized that what I have is an archive, even though I never thought of that word. I had been working with the Smithsonian, and thought, 'This could all go in the trash after I die!' So I started the* New England Folk Music Archives.

"We didn't have any money, but we soon received two grants from the GRAMMY *foundation, enough to transfer some reel-to-reel tapes, which were extremely fragile. They've been moved to the Harvard (University) Audio Preservation department.*

"The Harvard Historical Society partnership was an endorsement that the collection is worthy of living there. I knew enough that the artists would never have an archive of their own, except for the few at the top. It's for people to see, to document a turning point of this country."

Siggins now works for a small gallery in Harvard Square, and another in Somerville's Armory, where there are workshops, salons, and classes that teach the history of music culture in schools. *"It's an easy access to their history. We've got over 200 pieces in archival frames, and that's a pretty big show."*

Back in the day, while the performances were going on at Club 47, the music was often being captured for posterity. *"I ended up with all the tapes. Most of the artists were not aware they were being recorded. I have 25 songs of Doc Watson before he ever recorded, some Joan, a few Dylan pieces* (from April, 1963) *which can be heard in the* For The Love Of The Music *documentary, with Eric* (von Schmidt).

"That movie was a great gift. I sent Todd (Kwait, who, along with Rob Stegman, co-produced and directed the film) *an email after seeing his* (jug band documentary) Chasin' Gus's Ghost. *I asked if he would be interested in doing a Club 47 documentary, and he loved the idea. I asked how we would do this, and he said, 'Let's get started.' I thought it would be tough! The film meant a lot to Todd and Rob, and a great deal to me. I think it's very intimate, and it gave me a clearer vision of my own life.*

"We were all 17, 18, 19, at the time ... We were all green kids, now we're the seniors in the group, and have stayed connected through the years. It's comforting that I'm back in Cotuit, the town I grew up in, and I can call Tom Rush and get an answer."

Speaking of old friends, Siggigs met up with Dylan after a gig when he played three nights at Boston's Wang Theatre in 2009. *"Maria Muldaur was playing in Cambridge the night before* (November 13 at the First Parish Church). *I had been at her show, and we were talking about my first exhibit,* Forever Young. *Then the next day, Maria called and said, 'You'll never guess who called?' Dylan was bored to death* (in his hotel room) *and called her for some coffee and a chat. He gave her five passes, and we all went. There were two backstage passes, and Maria and I were escorted and told where to stand.*

"Dylan saw me, and I said, 'You know I'm 70!' He said, 'No, you're not!' We went back and forth, it was as silly as can be. I gave him an 'Archives Soup Kitchen' poster. It was as he was leaving, and nothing stops the flow of his moving forward."

Siggins recalled the time she found something Dylan had left in her apartment back in the 1960s. *"He left a draft one night of free flowing poetry that he typed on my typewriter. A copy can be seen at the Cambridge Historical Society.*

"Dylan was a funny enigma. He talked about people and life. He was well into who he was going to be, but in such a way we could hang out with him. There was no wall up around him. He and Joan were very funny together! I found him so unique. We went to Washington Square in New York, and he smoked, his leg would be shaking, and he'd talk about Rimbaud. I not sure what he was talking about, but it was cool to listen to.

"He is one of the great wordsmiths," Siggins said in closing. *"People say he's a recluse, but you don't need to do everything in public. He's given so much, and he's still doing a lot."*

Bob Dylan's praise for Charlie Louvin

January 26, 2011

"Do you have a favorite Christmas album?"

"Maybe the Louvin Brothers. I like all the religious Christmas albums. The ones in Latin. The songs I sang as a kid." - Bob Dylan, 2009. [68]

Charlie Elzer Loudermilk, better known as Charlie Louvin, has died at the age of 83.

In the 1940s, Charlie and Ira Loudermilk, the Depression-era country music duo, changed their last names to something easier for others to spell and remember, and became the legendary Louvin Brothers. Usually, Charlie played guitar and sang lead vocals while his older brother played mandolin and sang high tenor harmonies. Their recordings were a huge influence on future country and rock musicians.

Dylan has performed many songs recorded by the Louvin Brothers, including *In The Pines*, *Blues Stay Away From Me*, *Mary Of The Wild Moor*, and *Searching For A Soldier's Grave*, although, obviously, they were also previously interpreted by other artists.

On *Theme Time Radio Hour*, Bob Dylan played the Louvin Brothers' *Knoxville Girl* on the *Musical Maps* episode, *Satan Is Real* from *The Devil* program, and *When I Stop Dreaming* on *Dreams* week. The Louvin Brothers were also referenced on the *Drinking* and *Eyes* programs.

During *The Devil* episode, Dylan praised the brothers for their harmonies, the mix of mandolin with the guitar of Chet Atkins, then instructed listeners to look at the cover of the LP, *Satan is Real*. From *Musical Maps*, in response to an (alleged) email, he spoke about the *"lust, murder, and mayhem"* in hillbilly music, while taking a dig at the technique of sampling in modern music.

---

[68] *Bob Dylan discusses holiday music, Christmas and feeding the hungry*, The Big Issue: International Network of Street Papers, 11/23/2009

The ballad of Bob Dylan and Earl Scruggs

March 29, 2012

"He wasn't writing too much then (1987), still isn't. I think he was looking for a new direction in which to take his songs... We talked about people like Elizabeth Cotten, Mississippi Sheiks, Earl Scruggs, Bill Monroe, Gus Cannon, Hank Williams ... Trouble was, Bob seemed to prefer to do these rather than rehearse his own songs." - Jerry Garcia on Bob Dylan [69]

Bluegrass legend Earl Scruggs died yesterday at the age of 88. From *The New York Times:*

"(H)e also helped shape the "high, lonesome sound" of Bill Monroe, often called the father of bluegrass, and pioneered the modern banjo sound. His innovative use of three fingers rather than the claw-hammer style elevated the five-string banjo from a part of the rhythm section — or a comedian's prop — to a lead or solo instrument.

What became known as the syncopated Scruggs picking style helped popularize the banjo in almost every genre of music." [70]

After leaving Monroe's Blue Grass Boys with Lester Flatt, the Flatt & Scruggs duo reached their biggest audiences with their recordings of *Foggy Mountain Breakdown*, used to great effect in the 1967 film *Bonnie and Clyde*; and *The Ballad of Jed Clampett*, the theme song of *The Beverly Hillbillies* television sitcom.

According to *Dylan Cover*, Flatt & Scruggs covered the following Dylan songs between 1966 and 1969:

Mama, You Been On My Mind (1)

Don't Think Twice, It's All Right (2)

Blowin' In The Wind (2)

It Ain't Me Babe (2)

Down In The Flood (2)

Mr. Tambourine Man (2)

Like A Rolling Stone (3)

I'll Be Your Baby Tonight (3)

The Times They Are A-Changin' (3)

Rainy Day Women No. 12 And 35 (3)

Nashville Skyline Rag (4)

Maggie's Farm (4)

Wanted Man (4)

One More Night (4)

One Too Many Mornings (4)

Girl From The North Country (4)

Honey, Just Allow Me One More Chance (4)

(1) released on single b/w *Last Thing On My Mind*, Columbia 4-43803, 1966

---

[69] http://deadessays.blogspot.com/2010/08/byrds-and-dead.html, *Grateful Dead Guide - The Byrds and the Dead*, Retrieved 11/20/2016

[70] *Earl Scruggs, Bluegrass Banjo Player, Dies at 88;* Christopher Lehmann-Haupt, The New York Times, 5/29/2012

(2) released on *Changin' Times*, Columbia 9596, 1968

(3) released on *Nashville Airplane*, Columbia CS 9741, 1968

(4) released on *Final Fling - One Last Time (Just For Kicks)*, Columbia CS 9945, 1970

All tracks were released on *1964-1969*, Bear Family Records 6-CD set (BCD 15879).

In addition, *Frieda Florentine*, from *Nashville Airplane*, has been described as a "rewrite" of Dylan's *Nashville Skyline Rag*.

The last Flatt & Scruggs recordings took place in August 1969. According to Roots of Bob Dylan, [71] the sessions were conducted to fulfill a contractual obligation. They were produced by Dylan's producer Bob Johnson, and featured the Dylan covers that appeared on *Final Fling*.

Scruggs felt stifled in recycling the same bluegrass material, and after Flatt & Scruggs split, continued to support contemporary songwriters.

He covered an instrumental version of *Love Is Just A Four-Letter Word* for the Johnston- produced Nashville's Rock. Scruggs also interpreted Dylan songs with his Earl Scruggs Revue (featuring his sons):

It Takes A Lot To Laugh, It Takes A Train To Cry

Down In The Flood

Tomorrow Is A Long Time

Watching The River Flow

Song To Woody

In late 1970, Dylan appeared in a documentary on Scruggs. Here is the information, courtesy of Olof Bjorner: [72]

The Home Of Thomas B. Allen Carmel, New York December 1970; Earl Scruggs Documentary;

1. *East Virginia Blues (trad.)*

2. *Nashville Skyline Rag*

Bob Dylan (guitar & vocal), Earl Scruggs (banjo), Randy Scruggs (acoustic guitar), Gary Scruggs (electric bass).

Broadcast by National Education TV, New York City, New York, 10-17 January 1971.

2 (only) released on *Earl Scruggs Performing With His Family And Friends*, Columbia KC-30584, Summer 1971. Released on commercial video *Earl Scruggs' Festival Of Music*, 1985

The *Earl Scruggs Performing With His Family And Friends* album also featured covers of *Love Is Just A Four-Letter Word* (with Joan Baez) and *You Ain't Goin' Nowhere* (with The Byrds).

Charlie Daniels, who appeared in the show and played on Dylan sessions circa 1970, tweeted: *"He meant a lot to me. Nobody will ever play a five string banjo like Earl."*

---

[71] http://www.bobdylanroots.com/scruggs.html, *Earl Scruggs (and Lester Flatt)*, Retrieved 11/20/2016

[72] http://www.bjorner.com/DSN01790%201970.htm#DSN01880, *Still on the Road*, Retrieved 11/20/2016

Pete Seeger, 92 years young today

May 3, 2011

Paul Zollo: I interviewed Pete Seeger recently --

Bob Dylan: He's a great man, Pete Seeger.

Paul Zollo: I agree. He said, "All songwriters are links in a chain." Without your link in that chain, all of songwriting would have evolved much differently. You said how you brought folk music to rock music. Do you think that would have happened without you?

Bob Dylan: Somebody else would have done it in some other kind of way. But, hey, so what? So what? You can lead people astray awfully easily. Would people have been better off? Sure. They would have found somebody else. Maybe different people would have found different people, and would have been influenced by different people." - From Song Talk Magazine, interview April 4, 1991. [73]

Peter Seeger was born on May 3, 1919. It has been well-documented that Seeger was an early supporter of Bob Dylan.

In May, 1962, Dylan appeared with Pete Seeger, Gil Turner, and Sis Cunningham on the *Broadside* program at WBAI Studios in New York City. It was not broadcast until the fall of that year.

Dylan performed three of the eight songs during the one-hour broadcast: *Ballad Of Donald White, The Death Of Emmett Till,* and *Blowin' In The Wind.* Seeger, Turner, and Cunningham sang backup on the last song. Part of *Emmett Till* was included on the Interactive Music CD-ROM *Highway 61 Interactive,* while the others were released on the Folkways 1972 release, *Broadside Reunion.*

Seeger and Dylan shared the stage twice at the 1963 Newport Folk Festival. On July 26, 1963, at the evening finale, Dylan led Pete Seeger, Joan Baez, the Freedom Singers, and Peter, Paul & Mary, through *Blowin' In The Wind,* and joined in singing the traditional *We Shall Overcome.* The following day, at the Topical Song workshop, Seeger joined Dylan on *Playboys and Playgirls.*

You can see and hear some of these performances on the DVD/Blu-Ray, *The Other Side Of The Mirror, the Vanguard LPs Evening Concerts At Newport, Vol. 1* and *Newport Broadside, and* the Vanguard CDs *Evening Concerts: Newport Folk Festival 1963 and Newport Folk Festival.*

There has been some controversy surrounding Seeger's reaction to Dylan's "going Electric" two years later. In 2001, Seeger has this to say to David Kupfer, in an interview for *Whole Earth* magazine, Spring 2001:

"It was at Newport, 1965. I couldn't understand the words. I wanted to hear the words. It was a great song, Maggie's Farm, and the sound was distorted. I ran over to the guy at the controls and shouted, "Fix the sound so you can hear the words." He hollered back, "This is the way they want it." I said, "Damn it, if I had an axe, I'd cut the cable right now."

Seeger went on the say he could have pointed out that Howlin' Wolf performed with electric instruments the previous day, and that was apparently already considered acceptable. [74]

Dylan next shared the stage with Seeger at a tribute to Seeger's friend and colleague, Woody Guthrie, in 1968. There were two shows at Carnegie Hall on January 20, 1968. For each show, Dylan did a three-song set with members of The Band. For the afternoon show, Dylan joined Seeger, Judy Collins, Arlo Guthrie, Odetta, and others for the finale of *This Land Is Your Land,* while the evening show had the same artists performing *This Train Is Bound For Glory* instead.

---

[73] *Songwriters On Songwriting - Expanded Edition,* Paul Zollo, Da Capo Press, New York, 1997

[74] http://www.wholeearth.com/issue/2104/article/116/pete.seeger.interviewed.by.david.kupfer, *Pete Seeger interviewed by David Kupfer,* Spring 2001

Dylan, Seeger, Arlo Guthrie, Melanie, Phil Ochs, Dave van Ronk, and Larry Estridge performed at Friends of Chile Benefit Concert at New York's Felt Forum on May 9, 1974. Guthrie did his father's song, *Deportee*, while Dylan sang versions of *North Country Blues*, *Spanish Is The Loving Tongue*, and *Blowin' In The Wind*.

According to *Dylan Cover*, Seeger has covered Dylan's *Blowin' In The Wind*, *Hard Rain's A- Gonna Fall*, *Masters Of War* [with spoken Japanese translation], *Paths Of Victory*, and *Who Killed Davey Moore?*

Carolyn Hester recalls appearance at BobFest, the 1992 Bob Dylan tribute concert

November, 2010

Carolyn Hester, "The Texas Songbird," should be familiar to any fan of Bob Dylan. She got her start in the late 1950s as a singer of traditional folk songs, including *The House Of The Rising Sun*, *The Water Is Wide*, and *Dink's Song*. Hester's first album, *Scarlet Ribbons* (Coral Records, 1957), was produced by Norman Petty, and she later recorded with fellow Texan Buddy Holly. (See the chapter on Buddy Holly for Dylan's thoughts on Hester.) Carolyn's second LP was recorded on the Clancy Brothers' Tradition label. She was briefly married to folk singer Richard Fariña in the early 1960s.

On September 30, 1961, Hester hired Dylan to play harmonica on a session for her Columbia Records debut, after playing a shared bill at Club 47 up in Cambridge, Massachusetts. According to Hester, *"I was surprised to find that Bob was opening for Richard Fariña and me at Club 47 (now Club Passim). I didn't even have his phone number until the day after we played Club 47... When he asked about gigs and I offered to have him play harp on the Columbia session."* The album's producer, John Hammond, was impressed with Dylan and quickly signed him to Columbia.

Martin Scorsese's documentary *No Direction Home* featured Dylan's 1963 performances of *Blowin' In The Wind* and *Man Of Constant Sorrow* from the Westinghouse TV special, *Folk Songs and More Folk Songs*. Among the other artists on the program were the Brothers Four, Barbara Dane, The Staples Singers, and Carolyn Hester. The finale featured all the artists performing Woody Guthrie's *This Land Is Your Land*.

Two years later, Hester covered Dylan's *Playboys and Playgirls* on her *At Town Hall* live album.

In 1969, Hester married jazz musician David Blume. She continues to record and perform with their daughters, Amy and Karla Blume. They recently released a new album entitled *We Dream Forever*, which features a cover of Bob Dylan's *Boots Of Spanish Leather*.

Carolyn appeared at the 1992 Bob Dylan 30th Anniversary Celebration Concert at New York's Madison Square Garden. She graciously agreed to answer some questions about that historic night via email.

What are your favorite memories of the *Bob Dylan 30th Anniversary Concert Celebration*?

Any musical artist would be totally delighted to be invited to this tribute to Bob Dylan. As he is a musical icon, with so many friends he could have invited, it was an honor for those of us who gathered at Madison Square Garden to share this fabulous evening with Bob and with each other. We can never forget how stirring it was, for ourselves and the 20,000 or so in the audience, who were treated all night long to enjoying Dylan songs interpreted so lovingly. It seemed as though New York City itself was even more "switched on" than usual. Everyone knew it was "Bob Dylan Night" ... the cabbies, the police force, the media, and the people in the streets.

How did you get involved with "BobFest"?

When the news of this special tribute was announced, my long time friend and sometimes booking agent and producer, Steve Goldston, got in touch with one of Dylan's managers, Jeff Rosen, in N.Y.C. They stayed in touch, and six weeks or so before the event I was told that there was a question and a request. "Since Carolyn participated with Nanci Griffith on her album Other Voices, Other Rooms, *(as did Bob, who played harmonica on* Boots of Spanish Leather*), would Carolyn care to join Nanci in singing* Boots? *Nanci's then Manager, Ken Levitan, confirmed this idea in the affirmative, so that is how "our" Dylan song was determined.*

How did you prepare for the concert?

The day before the big concert, I arrived at JFK from my home in L.A. It was a little unusual for a folksinger to be greeted by a limo driver and then to get swallowed up in the huge back seat, with a bar at my disposal all the way from JFK to the Rihga Royal Hotel. I was too happy to be back in the city to do anything but enjoy the scenery and chat with the driver. He seemed to know all about the upcoming event. He told me that he had heard that "The Donald" (Trump) would be there. And that was what the weekend was like... The entire city seemed to be involved.

What were rehearsals like? Where were they held?

I understand that rehearsals were held over several days... rumors of "certain" rehearsal studios. Nanci and I rehearsed at the hotel... Nanci and Frank Christian on guitars. The next day I had an interview with ABC-TV News and it was broadcast that same day, late in the afternoon. Nanci and I and Frank had soundcheck in the early afternoon and went back to the hotel to dress. About that time, Willie Nelson's harmonica player, Mickey Raphael, came up to me and said, "I love Nanci and I know that Bob is on harp on her CD about to come out... I wondered if you might ask her if she would like me to join you on harp for "Boots?" So I asked, Nanci said "yes" and that's how Mickey joined our little band. Another run through with Mickey and we were good to go. (Mickey played that evening with both Willie and Nanci).

What are your thoughts of the pay-per-view broadcast? The home video version?

"Nanci and I and the other folkies were not being considered as being part of the Pay Per View portion... However, the audience gave Nanci, myself, Frank and Mickey a standing ovation for Boots of Spanish Leather. *A message came down from Jeff Rosen that they didn't have room for all these many artists on the CD and ALL the videos... and he wanted us to enjoy ourselves and realize that we were much appreciated. Of course, they paid us well, provided travel and hotel, plus we participated with each other in an historic evening! The hospitality and the company was outstanding... the audience enraptured! But, after all that, we DID end up on the VHS release, as well as the VH1 broadcast."*

What were your favorite performances?

"My favorite performances of the evening is a long list, but I would say that in my memory some that seem most vivid would be Bob's own performance, Neil Young, Johnny Cash & June Carter (who have both passed away), and Stevie Wonder (who wasn't booked but who called one of Dylan's managers and volunteered to come on over and sing Blowin' In The Wind.) *I could go on... what about* Masters of War *sung by Pearl Jam's Eddie Vedder? WOW! Don't get me started... it was ALL powerful. And for the ending, we all sang with gusto on* Knockin' On Heaven's Door.

What is your take on the whole Sinead O'Connor incident?

Sinead O'Connor's situation ... to get booed on being introduced ... due to an appearance on TV when she tore up a photo of the Pope. Kris Kristofferson seemed to help her the most. All the women performers in the dressing room, including Nanci and myself, tried to comfort her. Seems to me that this moment did affect her career. But she seems to have come through it all now. She has recorded some folk albums of Irish songs, which I like so much. Paddy Clancy remarked later that her "butting heads" with authority was no surprise ... "She's a purist," he said.

It was reported Bob Dylan stayed alone somewhere waiting to go on. Did you get a chance to speak with him that week?

I did get to visit briefly with Bob backstage and then again at the party later, which was held at Tommy Makem's Irish Pavilion on E. 57th St. Dylan himself seemed truly happy with the tribute! That was the best "walk away present" of it all!

Enjoyed our visit and at the same time renewed my acquaintance with George Harrison. I had met him in U.K. in the sixties through Ravi Shankar (who celebrated his 90th birthday this year). Also, I so much enjoyed my visit with the Clancy Brothers and Tommy Makem. Paddy and Liam Clancy, as well as Tommy Makem, have passed away now.

How did you decide to cover *Boots Of Spanish Leather* on your new album, *We Dream Forever?*

My daughters Karla & Amy Blume do the concerts with me now, as my husband, David Blume, passed away in 2006. The girls asked me to record my version of Boots of Spanish Leather. *So it is included on this CD... just me and my guitar. It is available online, but of course! And you get to hear the next generation of singer-songwriters on the CD, too.*

John Byrne Cooke recalls 1964 New England road trip with Bob Dylan

February 11/12, 2011

In the early 1960s, musician John Byrne Cooke got to hang out with Bob Dylan, even accompanying and photographing the legendary singer-songwriter on numerous occasions, including a Massachusetts road trip from Cambridge to Amherst.

Cooke was born [75] in New York City, studied photography at Vermont's Putney School, and went on to attend Harvard University in the early 1960s. While there, Cooke became immersed in the emerging folk music movement, hung out at Club 47, and joined the Harvard-based bluegrass band, the Charles River Valley Boys. Their first record was produced by Paul Rothchild, who went on to have the same responsibility with such artists as The Doors, The Lovin' Spoonful, The Paul Butterfield Blues Band, and Janis Joplin, among others. Besides a musician, Cooke is an author, actor, and photographer. [76] From 1967 until her death in 1970, he was Joplin's road manager. He is also the son of British journalist and television broadcaster Alistair Cooke, and the great-grandnephew of Ralph Waldo Emerson.

In April, 1964, Cooke spent some time hanging out and traveling with Dylan during a New England tour, which included stops at Providence, Brandeis University, Boston's Symphony Hall (the 24th), Cambridge's Club 47 (the 25th), and "The Cage" at the University of Massachusetts ("UMass") at Amherst (the 26th). Dylan had also recently played Tufts University in early March.

Cooke recently spoke with me about that trip, over the phone from his studio in Jackson Hole, Wyoming, his home since 1982.

"There were very few folk clubs. The folk community was very small at the time," Cooke told me. *"This was the peak of the folk music community. There was a connection between Greenwich Village and Cambridge. There are more folk clubs now, but they are not getting on the cover of* Time *magazine. Boston had the Golden Vanity in 1963, '64, but Club 47* (now Club Passim) *was the most important coffee house in the greater Boston - or even eastern Massachusetts.*

"I was done with Harvard one year before, April 1964," Cooke recalled. *"I had known Dylan for a few years by then. Dylan was the first guy that had a road manager. We'd heard that jazz musicians had them, but not folk singers. Victor (Maymudes) would drive, he would take care of everything. We thought, 'This is really neat,' and it was a new thing - 'Look how Bob's doing!'"*

Dylan was touring New England after his following grew, due in large part to Joan Baez.

"In 1963, Dylan played Newport. People knew him, but few had seen him. Peter, Paul & Mary's version of Blowin' in The Wind *went high up the charts just before. Baez was the reigning 'Queen of Folk.' After Newport 1963, Baez introduced Dylan to her audience in a fall concert tour, which gave a substantial boost to his career. In October 31, 1964, Dylan played Philharmonic Hall - now Avery Fisher - and by that time sold it out. Thanks to Joan's help, from July 1963, to October 1964 - just over a year - Dylan became more famous than Joan."*

While conversing with Cooke, it's obvious he remembers a lot about his time with Dylan, but the years have blended the events together, and he would often refer to his own photographs to confirm various people and moments. Luckily for Dylan fans, he is a stickler for accuracy.

Dylan made a guest appearance at Club 47 on April 25th. The next day, Dylan, Maymudes, Cooke, and others drove their cars out west to Amherst.

"We had a least two cars, possibly three, although I don't see a third one in the photographs. I was in the same car as Bob. You can see my picture of Bob sitting in the front seat (on his website). [77] *You can also see that's their*

---

[75] http://www.cookephoto.com/bio.html, *John Byrne Cooke Biography*, Retrieved 11/20/2016

[76] http://www.johnbyrnecooke.com, *John Byrne Cooke*, Retrieved 11/20/2016

[77] http://www.johnbyrnecooke.com, *John Byrne Cooke*, Retrieved 11/20/2016

(Maymudes' and Dylan's) *Ford station wagon. I want to point out that it's navy blue. It's been described as a red car, I think, in some book.*

"We were kind of like his extended road crew - except we were not paid or anything!" Cooke laughed.

There were also some other people along for the trip that would later make their mark in the music scene, including two that Dylan first worked with in 1964. [78]

"Paul Rothchild, way before he produced The Doors, was in another car. John Sebastian, just before he formed The Lovin' Spoonful, was there. At the time, we just knew him as this guy who played a mean blues harp." Sebastian would later be part of the *Bringing It All Back Home* sessions. [79]

Also along for the ride was one of Cooke's oldest friends, fellow photographer Charlie Frizzell ("with two Z's," Cooke points out). Cooke also has portraits of Dylan and Frizzell backstage at the 1964 Brandeis Folk Festival on his website. [80]

After the gang arrived at Amherst, Cooke met blues musician Taj Mahal for the first time. *"I know he was a student there,"* Cooked remembered, *"although he may have graduated by that time."*

Back in the mid-1960s, Dylan and other traveling musicians often had to play in makeshift auditoriums, and UMass Amherst was no exception.

"There was this place (The Curry Hicks Cage) . . . *It was a big room, a gymnasium. The stage was specifically constructed for the concert, and they brought in rows of folding chairs, I believe."*

While "The Cage" still stands, Dylan now usually plays the newer Mullins Center when he plays Umass, Amherst.

"It was in four sections, a pipe-constructed stage. There wasn't even a curtain," Cooke said, then looked at his photographs from April 26, 1964. *"Well, there wasn't a curtain in my photograph, but that may have just been from the soundcheck."*

"During this period, from 1963 until 1965, it was just one man and a guitar. The power of performing under one spotlight … It would mesmerize the audience."

Dylan did not seem to be under much pressure during the road trip, according to Cooke.

"There was usually some Beaujolais around. It was just hanging out with a friend, and his road manager. (Dylan) could laugh, but he could also be cryptic and opaque - but he was not striking a pose."

"At the time, to people like Pete Seeger and Alan Lomax, (Dylan) was the apotheosis, he was the new folk poet. They put their expectations on him. This was not a daily topic (on the Amherst trip). *It was not really brought up."*

"What's interesting is that while people really know his protest songs, The Times, They Are A- Changin', Hattie Carroll, *the ones that lasted were the love songs …* Don't Think Twice, Baby Blue, *and* It Ain't Me, Babe *and* Like A Rolling Stone, *which are, I guess, the anti-love songs.*

"When it comes to Dylan, you have to be careful not to over-intellectualize. Dylan was writing the gospel truth. You can't listen to his songs and not think that he cared about what he was writing about. For people saying otherwise, it was just bullshit. I reject that. He put it all in the music - Hattie Carroll, Emmett Till. *He did not want to come out and say we needed civil rights. It was in the music."*

---

[78] http://www.bjorner.com/DSN00630%20%2864%29.htm#_Toc490790205, *Still on the Road*, Retrieved 11/20/2016

[79] http://www.bjorner.com/DSN00785%20%2865%29.htm#DSN00790, *Still on the Road*, Retrieved 11/20/2016

[80] http://www.cookephoto.com/cfrizzell.html, *John Byrne Cooke Photography: Image No. 64-7-25*, Retrieved 11/20/2016

Dylan's complex friendship with Donovan

May 10, 2011

"Do I like Donovan's "Colours"? No. He's a nice guy, though." - Bob Dylan, 1965 San Francisco press conference.

Scottish singer-songwriter and guitarist Donovan Philips Leitch was born on May 10, 1946.

The relationship between Donovan and Bob Dylan is almost as confusing as the reports of Dylan "going electric" - an event Donovan witnessed. The problem started with an encounter on May 8, 1965, when the rising star Donovan hung out with Dylan at The Savoy Hotel in London. The moment was captured by D.A. Pennebaker in the 1967 documentary, *Dont Look Back*.

In the spring of 1965, Donovan's Dylan-esque *Catch The Wind* was number five on the U.K. singles charts, while Dylan had climbed to number 13 with 1964's *The Times They Are A- Changin'*. Meanwhile, *Subterranean Homesick Blues* was rising up the U.S. charts at the same time. In the film, Dylan appeared to have been amused/annoyed by this new upstart, one of the first "new Dylans," before the summit occurred, commenting (to Alan Price of The Animals): *"Who's this Donovan?"* Price assured Dylan that Donovan is a good guy and a superior guitarist. Dylan replied that he wants to meet him.

When Albert Grossman (Dylan's Manager) asked Dylan, possibly aware he was being filmed, about mailing an award he has been recently given, Dylan tells him: *"I don't even want to see them. Tell them to give it to Donovan."* After opening a newspaper, Dylan said *"Donovan, Donovan, our next target. He's our target for tomorrow."*

In the car, Dylan asked Donovan's tour manager, Fred, (who was also Dylan's), about Donovan's tour: *"Uh, not so good,"* Fred replied, and Bobby Neuwirth (Dylan's friend) laughed. Dylan lit up a cigarette and turned to the window, saying nothing.

Before the last concert, Dylan talked to Neuwirth in the backstage and asked, *"Donovan out there?"* Neuwirth replies, *"Hey, I can't see him... people like Donovan... they look just like ordinary... everybody... out there."* Dylan, again, said nothing. [81]

In *Dont Look Back*, we can see a party in progress, and a timid-looking Donovan starts to play a gentle original song, *To Sing For You*. Realizing that he was no threat, the film shows Dylan eviscerating Donovan with his recent composition, *It's All Over Now, Baby Blue*.

Or did he?

Donovan hinted [82] that he performed *To Sing For You* to diffuse a situation with a belligerent drunk who was harassing Dylan, with Bob praising the song midway through. Also, if you listen closely, it sounds like Donovan requested *Baby Blue*, so it was would not have been Dylan's idea of a put-down.

Pennebaker added that Dylan requested he not film anything when Donovan first arrived. *Then Donovan debuted a new song, based on the melody of* Mr. Tambourine Man, *titled* My Darling Tangerine Eyes. *Dylan remained pokerfaced, while his friends were in hysterics. Donovan then told Dylan,* "Well, I heard you sing this somewhere and I thought it was a folk song so I thought the tune was up for grabs." *Dylan said,* "There have been a lot of songs that people said I swiped, but that wasn't one of them." *And he let it go.* [83]

Reportedly, Dylan handed Neuwirth and Pennebaker Halloween masks, which they were all wearing when Donovan arrived. Donovan, to his credit, said nothing.

---

[81] http://donovan-unofficial.com/video/documentaries.html, *Documentaries - Dont Look Back*

[82] *Donovan: Bob Dylan, the Beatles, Buddha and me*, John Walsh, The Independent (U.K.), 5/21/2011

[83] *Q&A with D.A.Pennebaker*, Carolina A. Miranda, Time Magazine, 2/25/2007

According to Olof Bjorner, Dylan also sang two other new songs, *Love Minus Zero/No Limit* and *She Belongs To Me*, plus *Let Me Die In My Footsteps.* [84]

While on tour, Dylan added a line while performing *Talkin' World War III Blues*, singing *"I looked in the closet, and there was Donovan!"* While the crowd laughed, Dylan told reporters after the show that *"I didn't mean to put the guy down in my songs. I just did it for a joke."* [85]

The headline in *Melody Maker* on the fifth day of May, 1965, proclaimed *"Dylan Digs Donovan"* and the issue appeared to have been settled.

It turns out that Dylan and Donovan actually met earlier in the day of The Savoy summit, during the filming of the promotional *Subterranean Homesick Blues* short. According to Donovan, [86] it was the beat poet Allen Ginsberg who suggested he, Donovan, and Dylan write some of the lyrics from *Subterranean Homesick Blues* on the backs of large, white cards for what turned out to be the opening scene of *Dont Look Back*. Dylan encouraged Donovan because he admired his penmanship. According to other sources, D.A. Pennebaker, Alan Price, and Joan Baez also helped. Donovan said he and Bob swapped songs, and Dylan said he particularly liked *To Sing For You*. Dylan, Donovan, and Price then attempted to go to a club in Soho, but were mobbed by teenyboppers and returned to safety and the Savoy.

Before Dylan went back to the U.S., Donovan was invited to see Bob one more time. All four members of a certain British pop combo from Liverpool were in the room, hidden in the darkness. Bob asked, *"Have you met these guys yet?"* It was, of course, The Beatles.

In the May 15 issue of *Record Mirror*, Donovan reviewed Dylan's new album, *Bringing It All Back Home*, track-by-track. Here are a few examples:

She Belongs To Me: *"Yea, it's beautiful. His Buddy Holly influence comes out. Very pretty harmonica on it, it's nice.*

Maggie's Farm: *"This is the ...* (Turns volume up and laughs). *It's a good send-up. It's just amusing. You know, all these things he does they're just personal, you can't understand them. It's just to make one person laugh, probably Maggie. Don't like this much."* (Takes it off).

It's Alright Ma (I'm Only Bleeding): *"He's written a lot of poems and he's just picked these few to put to song. You've got to be a genius to understand them. To me he's just a guy that writes poems and puts a lot of feeling in them. It's hard for me to say what I think of him. I couldn't write a story of what I think of him for any paper. I like him because he shoots down a lot of people who shoot a load of crap."* [87]

By 1966, the heavy Dylan influences were gone. Donovan would soon be hanging around with the Beatles (helping to write *Yellow Submarine*, and teaching them his finger-picking technique) and the Maharishi Mahesh Yogi.

Ten years ago, Donovan was asked to comment on Dylan for his 60th birthday. He said when he first heard *Blowin' in the Wind*, *"It was the clarion call to the new generation - and we artists were encouraged to be as brave in writing our thoughts in music."* He admitted that he was heavily influenced by Dylan, but only for a short while. He was also supportive of Dylan going electric at Newport in 1965. *"I was there when it happened! The audience at Newport Folk in the USA were still naive - the girls in Bobby Sox and ponytails and the boys in plaid shorts and crewcuts - what did they or the press know about folk and R&B?"* [88]

---

[84] http://www.bjorner.com/DSN00785%20%2865%29.htm#DSN00970, *Still on the Road*, Retrieved 11/20/2016

[85] *Hurdy Gurdy Man - The Autobiography of Donovan*, Donovan,St. Martin's Press, New York, 2005

[86] *Bob Dylan: A meeting of minds*, David Hepworth, Independent (U.K.), 9/22/2005

[87] *Donovan Review New Dylan Album*, Richard Green, The Record Mirror, 5/15/1965

[88] http://news.bbc.co.uk/2/hi/entertainment/1347199.stm, *Donovan Remembers Dylan*, Retrieved 11/20/2016

Bob Dylan and Maria Muldaur - From the Village to Newport '65, and beyond

September 12, 2011

Singer Maria Grazia Rosa Domenica D'Amato, better known as Maria Muldaur, was born on September 12, 1943, in Greenwich Village, New York.

Muldaur was part of the same early 1960s Village folk scene that nurtured Bob Dylan. At the time, she hung out with Son House, Rev. Gary Davis, Victoria Spivey, and other blues legends. According to her website, [89] Muldaur *"became involved with The Friends of Old Timey Music, a group ... that traveled to the rural South to find legendary artists like Doc Watson, Bukka White, Skip James and Mississippi John Hurt, then bring them north to present them in concert to urban audiences."*

Maria D'Amato got her start as a member of the Even Dozen Jug Band, with John Sebastian, David Grisman, and Stefan Grossman, followed in 1963 by Jim Kweskin & His Jug Band. Kweskin's combo included her future husband, Geoff Muldaur.

The couple later married, and after Kweskin's band broke up, performed as a duo until their divorce in 1972. As a solo artist, Maria had major hits with *Midnight At The Oasis* and a cover of Leiber and Stoller's *I'm A Woman*. In the mid-1970s, Muldaur toured with the Grateful Dead, and eventually sang backing vocals as a member of the Jerry Garcia Band.

When Muldaur met Dylan at Gerde's in 1963, he was telling her about all the wine he'd learned about in Europe. Later that year, at the Third Side coffeehouse, he played Maria his brand new composition, *Only A Pawn In Their Game*.

For Elektra Records' *Blues Project* sessions, Dylan, as "Bob Landy," played piano on the 1964 recording of *Downtown Blues*, along with John Sebastian, Fritz Richmond, Eric von Schmidt, and Geoff Muldaur. [90]

After he plugged in at the 1965 Newport Folk Festival, Dylan appeared to be shell-shocked from the experience. In an attempt to lift his spirits, Muldaur asked Dylan if he wanted to dance. Dylan enigmatically replied, *"I would, but my hands are on fire."*

The Kweskin Band split up in 1968. The couple then moved up to Woodstock, where Muldaur and her daughter would visit Dylan's home, and their kids would play on the front porch.

In 1972, three years before The Rolling Thunder Revue, Dylan reportedly asked Muldaur, *"Wouldn't it be great if we got a train, and put a revue together that would travel across the country?"* [91]

When Dylan performed at the Warfield Theater in 1979, he alienated much of his audience by playing only his new "gospel" material, mainly songs from *Slow Train Coming* and the as-yet-unrecorded follow-up, *Saved*. Around this time, Muldaur had also been "saved" after struggling with substance abuse and her daughter's near-fatal car accident.

Maria wrote Bob a letter of support. Dylan got in touch with Muldaur, and she attended one of his shows. Backstage, she noticed that Dylan was completely calm and relaxed, without his usual leg-twitching. Soon after, Dylan met with Muldaur at her place, and they discussed religion.

Muldaur later joined Dylan on stage at San Francisco's Fox Warfield Theatre, on November 19, 1980, performing Blind Willie Johnson's blues classic, *Nobody's Fault But Mine*. This time, Muldaur

---

[89] http://www.mariamuldaur.com/bio.html, *Maria Muldaur Bio 2014*, Retrieved 11/20/2016

[90] http://www.bjorner.com/DSN00630%20(64).htm#_Toc490790205, *Still on the Road*, Retrieved 11/20/2016

[91] *Dylan: A Biography*, Bob Spitz, W.W. Norton Company, New York-London, 1989

noticed that backstage, Dylan was again acting restless. By the *Shot Of Love* sessions, Muldaur felt Dylan was acting distant and aloof.

After all these years, Dylan and Muldaur still appear to be friendly. He is said to have donated the song *Well Well Well*, co-written with Danny O'Keefe, for her 1996 album, *Fanning The Flames*. She also participated in the Martin Scorsese documentary, *Bob Dylan - No Direction Home*. (Also, see the chapter with Betsy Siggins for a reunion in 2009, after Dylan played the Wang Center in Boston.)

According to *Dylan Cover*, Muldaur has covered many other Dylan songs over the years, including *I'll Be Your Baby Tonight* (1967 with the Kweskin Jug Band, 1970 with her husband), *Ain't No Man Righteous*, *John Brown*, *License to Kill*, *Lord, Protect My Child*, and *Masters of War*.

2006 saw the release of *Heart of Mine: Maria Muldaur Sings Love Songs of Bob Dylan*. Here's the track listing:

1. *Buckets Of Rain* 4:12

2. *Lay Baby Lay (Lay Lady Lay)* 3:38

3. *To Be Alone With You* 4:15

4. *Heart Of Mine* 3:13

5. *Make You Feel My Love* 3:29

6. *Moonlight* 4:16

7. *You're Gonna Make Me Lonesome When You Go* 4:53

8. *Golden Loom* 5:21

9. *On A Night Like This* 3:30

10. *I'll Be Your Baby Tonight* 4:08 (Third version)

11. *Wedding Song* 4:36

12. *You Ain't Goin' Nowhere* 3:42

Thanks to Howard Sounes, *Down The Highway*, Grove Press, for some of the above information. [92]

---

[92] *Down the Highway - The Life of Bob Dylan*, Howard Sounes, Grove Press, New York, 2001

Interview: John Sebastian on touring, jug bands, Kotter, and Dylan

November 28, 2013

What better way to celebrate Thanksgivikkah eve than by getting a phone call from legendary singer-songwriter-musician John Sebastian.

I could have spoken to Sebastian for hours. He was in The Lovin' Spoonful, and played an impromptu solo set at Woodstock. He's in the Rock and Roll Hall Of Fame, and the Songwriters Hall Of Fame as well. You know his songs: *Do You Believe In Magic?*, *Daydream*, *She's A Lady*, *I Had A Dream*, *Nashville Cats*, *Summer In The City*, *You're A Big Boy Now*, and others too numerous to list here. He's played with everyone from Donovan and NRBQ to The Doors and The Who. David Crosby, Stephen Stills, and Graham Nash all played on his debut solo album before they were even an official band, and he played harmonica on the title track on the 1970 CSNY album, *Déjà Vu*.

However, I decided to focus on just a few specific topics, as much of the above information has been covered elsewhere.

First of all, his biggest solo hit, *Welcome Back*, the title song from the 1970s sitcom, *Welcome Back, Kotter* (featuring a young John Travolta), can now be heard in a new TV ad for Monk Fruit In The Raw. I asked Sebastian how something like this would come about. When answering, his voice, like his songs, is full of wonder and intonation, and frequently punctuated with laughter.

"Usually it comes through in a very straightforward way. A company or an advertising agent calls and says, 'We're interested in this,' and they mainly talk with my publisher, not to me. And as it gets OK'd, at that point, usually, I get a call to ask, 'Is this, or that, OK?' It is actually a very nice gesture the publisher makes that he technically doesn't have to make. I've turned down ... a lot of money when it wasn't the right client. This (product) *is terrific."*

I remembered that the program was originally titled *Kotter* but was changed when Sebastian was hired to write the theme song.

"You have it right! I asked them to please not make me write a song of that title, because the only thing rhyming I could think of was 'otter'! It doesn't make a great pop song. The main thing I had to impress on the group was that I thought of the song, oddly, as a thing that might transcend the television show. This was not a normal thought in those days. It was one of my biggest hits, but just to keep me humble, I got beat out by (Rick Dees' novelty hit) *Disco Duck."*

Sebastian is currently on tour, playing the Bull Run in Shirley, Massachusetts, this Friday, with more dates scheduled on the east coast later this year.

"I'm touring, but I'm not tearing up the turf or anything," he told me. When I mentioned I'd try to rush out the article in order to promote the Bull Run show, he said, *"Maybe we should make mention of what the hell these people are going to see when they come to see me. Not a bad idea! So, here's what's going on.*

"I, in all of this time, have now begun to really center on playing as a soloist. It is a very unusual thing to have this opportunity to play with Paul Rishell and Annie Raines on the bill, whose vocal and instrumental expertise will astonish you. My job here is to try to get around to tunes that folks are expecting to hear, and also to include what we really had been doing for about 15 years now. It was also to pay homage to the music that brought up into this funny obsession.

"And where we all did end up was chasin' Gus Cannon's ghost, and just trying to capture that jug band moment. God knows why we decided to do it?" he asked himself, letting out a big laugh. *"I guess it was like an antidote to what was happening as pop music was being absorbed by ... um ... whatever ..."*

"The bottom line?" I ventured.

"Yeah ... yeah ..." he replied, with his voice trailing off.

"Paul and Annie have been involved over the years in my jug band that they participated in. Occasionally, we get these chances to get together and do kind of a jug band finale to our various shows we do together. The way it usually plays out is, I spend a little time getting the Spoonful catalogue out for the folks that came to see that, then Paul and Annie

come out and show what a cool little blues duo they are, and then we get together and play pretty much from a set list that started in 1993."

I asked if he spent time speaking with his fans after the show. *"I do. I hang around, and sign old vinyl, and sell CDs, and yeah, have a jolly good time. My audience is mostly procrastinators! They will mostly wait and go, 'Look, Daisy, we could go see John tonight!'"*

While I had Sebastian on the line, I couldn't help but ask a couple of question about playing with Bob Dylan in the early-to-mid 1960s. However, he told me, *"I don't know all that much about Dylan, had very limited access over the years, and don't want to be portrayed as someone who is going to tell you about Dylan."* As it happens, he doesn't really remember the specifics of the January, 1965, *Bringing It All Back Home* session, anyway. When I told him I'd emphasize that, he laughed and said, *"That's a better lead story: 'Sebastian doesn't remember!'"*

This, however, is what he did share with me:

"You know, to this day, (Lovin' Spoonful bassist) Steve Boone and I puzzle over who might have been on that album. Because Dylanology is a real thing, people actually do ponder this (stuff)! The fact is, at that point, before that extreme high visibility, Bob and I were friends, back in the Gerde's Folk City days, and I think he kind of invited me to those sessions, to explore how I might do. And, in fact, he did later ask me if I wanted to come along on some adventure or another and play bass. It was before the excitement of The Band, and all of that. But it was a thing that became a kind of a subject of discussion and dispute among Dylanologists, and Steve Boone and I, who were both at that session, find ourselves totally puzzled as to whether which, or the other, or any of us were on the particular sides that are disputed or described.

"The way that it went down on that session was ... Bob said, 'Oh, here's this, why don't you play bass?' Fine, I play bass. Then we do a cut, then Boone walks in, and I immediately tell Bob, 'Wait! Now we have a real bass player! So why don't you let Steve play it?' So, I believe Steve played one time through. And then we're all standing around, then Harvey Brooks, a prominent session guy, shows up, and both Steve and I go, 'Jeez, now you've got like a triple session guy! We're not going to stand in your way!' I believe Harvey, who I frequently played with in later days, did a few takes.

"So I really don't know, and that's from the bottom of my heart. It has been questioned a lot of different times."

I also mentioned that I interviewed photographer-musician John Byrne Cooke, and he spoke about a New England road trip they all took in the spring of 1964. (See earlier chapter.)

"We did have a week or so where I had the opportunity to see him play in his really exciting, first burst onto the scene, mostly colleges, and he brought me to tears every night that I saw it. I saw it every night, and the same thing happened. So that was a perfect moment. I thank him for that."

Gordon Lightfoot

October 10, 2012

Once again, Bob Dylan did not perform anything from his new album at his concert in Edmonton, Alberta, last night. However, fans witnessed something even more special.

Dylan played an unexpected 'request' at the show, according to a *Drawing Book* post. [93] It was the live premiere of *Shadows*, a song by Canadian singer-songwriter Gordon Lightfoot. Dylan has been a long-time supporter of Lightfoot's, even covering *Early Morning Rain* on 1970's *Self Portrait*, and performing *I'm Not Supposed to Care* on stage. Lightfoot, like Dylan, was managed by Albert Grossman.

In 1986, Dylan inducted Lightfoot into the Canadian Music Hall Of Fame, where he called the singer *"someone of rare talent."* Lightfoot also made an appearance at a Rolling Thunder Revue's Maple Leaf Garden show in 1975, and his cover of *Ballad In Plain D* appeared in the film *Renaldo & Clara*. He also performed *Just Like Tom Thumb's Blues* on *The Tonight Show* with Johnny Carson, and more recently covered *Ring Them Blues* on the album *Waiting For You*, according to *Dylan Cover*.

Dylan praised Lightfoot many times, once saying, *"He became a mentor for a long time. I think he probably still is to this day."* [94] He also had this to say about Lightfoot, and *Shadows*, in 2009:

Bill Flannigan: Who are some of your favorite songwriters?

Bob Dylan: Buffett I guess. Lightfoot. Warren Zevon. Randy (Newman). John Prine. Guy Clark. Those kinds of writers...

Bill Flannigan: You and Lightfoot go way back.

Bob Dylan: Oh yeah. Gordo's been around as long as me.

Bill Flannigan: What are your favorite songs of his?

Bob Dylan: Shadows, Sundown, If You Could Read My Mind. I can't think of any I don't like. [95]

---

[93] http://www.thedrawingbook.com/comics-1_dylan-yeg12.html, *Bob Dylan in Edmonton*, Retrieved 2/2/2017

[94] http://www.corfid.com/vbb/showthread.php?t=12880, *Lightfoot-Dylan-jam session in Rosedale*, Retrieved 2/2/2017

[95] http://www.huffingtonpost.com/2009/04/15/bob-dylan-exclusive-inter_n_187216.html. (Originally posted on bobdylan.com), *Bob Dylan Exclusive Interview: Reveals His Favorite Songwriters, Thoughts On His Own Cult Figure Status*, Retrieved 2/2/2017

Carolina Chocolate Drops' Dom Flemons on opening for Bob Dylan in Kettering, OH

August 8, 2011

When Leon Russell agreed to be this summer's support act for Bob Dylan's North American tour, his management must have forgotten to tell someone he already had plans on August 5.

It turns out that Russell was previously booked at Detroit's free admission concert, "Rockin' on the Riverfront," on that date. To fill in the August 5 slot in Kettering, Ohio, the Carolina Chocolate Drops were fortunate enough to get the gig.

"We've been reaching out to Dylan's people for a while. I think the main thing is that one of our managers (Dolphus Ramseur) *also manages the Avett Brothers, who played with Dylan at the Grammys,"* band member Dom Flemons told me over the phone.

"People know I've been into Dylan for years, and now it's come full circle. It was a wonderful experience. People told us that he's been a fan for a while, and he never has anyone on the bill that he doesn't like."

The Carolina Chocolate Drops are an old-time string band from Durham, North Carolina. Their 2010 album, *Genuine Negro Jig*, won the Grammy Award for Best Traditional Folk Album at the 53rd Annual Grammy Awards (where Dylan sang *Maggie's Farm* with the Avett Brothers and Mumford & Sons).

The current line-up is Dom Flemons, Rhiannon Giddens, Adam Matta, and Hubby Jenkins. Matta and Jenkins joined earlier this year when founding member Justin Robinson left the band.

"The music our group plays is based in the old-time fiddle and banjo music while we incorporate elements of country blues, old-time jazz, country music and R&B. Rhiannon and I first met at an event called the Black Banjo Gathering in 2005. It was one of the first events exploring the black and African roots of the banjo. A lot of people don't know that the banjo is an African-derived instrument evolving through the slave trade transitioning from parts of West Africa to the Caribbean and finally into the United States. We also got to study with Joe Thompson, a 92-year-old black fiddler from North Carolina which is the basis around the group's core sound.

"I first really got into Dylan through a PBS special about the history of rock and roll," Flemons said. *"There was an episode about the* (1960s) *folk revival. I got into* (Jimi) *Hendrix and Dylan, but also at the same time Phil Ochs, Lightnin' Hopkins, Pete Seeger ... into the* (Alan) *Lomax stuff.*

"A lot of the Alan Lomax collection has not been performed live and made to be a living music in quite a long time. When I first heard a lot of the stuff on Rounder Records' Deep River of Song series I knew we had to do some of those songs and contextualize it for a new generation of people not familiar with it.

"For me personally, since Dylan was into old rock and roll, Chuck Berry, Fats Domino, Muddy Waters, Charley Patton, Hank Williams, Jimmie Rodgers, it was also getting me into different types of music.

"Since we got this gig, people have been really enthusiastic, saying, Good job!" Flemons told me.

When I spoke to Flemons before the show, he expressed doubt about getting to meet Dylan. *"Hopefully we'll get to meet Bob,"* he said, *"but I'm not expecting to. His privacy is legendary."*

However, much to the surprise and delight of the Carolina Chocolate Drops, Dylan did greet the band before sound check.

"We got to shake Bob's hand, get a little of the crystal touch. It was really short, just a few seconds. He just said that he was happy to have us on the show. He was being really cordial toward us. Everyone was bowled over by it! We were actually able to meet Bob Dylan!"

It turns out that the Drops know someone in common with Dylan's long-time bassist, Tony Garnier.

"We saw Tony backstage as well. We were talking about music, and he mentioned that he had a brother who played Zydeco music and it turned out to be a good friend of mine, D'Jalma Garnier. He plays Zydeco fiddle and bass with

The Creole Cowboys and Cedric Watson. Tony said, 'Wow! You know D'Jaima!' That was neat too. Tony was really nice to us the whole time."

Needless to say, Flemons enjoyed Dylan's set.

"I've seen Dylan about six times, going back to his 1999 tour with Paul Simon. The set was really good, very good stripping down the band's sound. Mississippi was really the best one all night. His keyboard playing was really good, it was nice to hear that too."

Flemons also said that he liked playing at Kettering's Fraze Pavilion.

"We had a great time. The people seemed to enjoy it! It was fun, and it was cool to shake 'The Man's' hand. Opening for Dylan was a wonderful thing."

[update: January 26, 2012]

Last summer, the Carolina Chocolate Drops played a one-off opening slot at a Bob Dylan concert in Kettering, Ohio. The band just contributed a cover of *Political World* to the benefit album, *Chimes of Freedom: The Songs of Bob Dylan Honoring 50 Years of Amnesty International.*

I interviewed Flemons after his return from Europe, on one of his off days before returning to the road.

When people are associated with Bob Dylan in any way, it often leads to good fortune. How has the band's career changed since you shared the bill with Dylan last year?

I think the prestige of having opened for Dylan has had a great effect on a "street cred" level, but I can't say it has changed anything in our career so far. If Bob has put a good word behind for us is hard to tell, but that is the best way I could answer that question. I don't know. I will say on a personal level, and for fans of ours knowing we opened for Bob, it is a great thrill and another great feather in the cap. A big one at that.

You recorded a Dylan song for the new benefit album, *Chimes of Freedom: The Songs of Bob Dylan Honoring 50 Years of Amnesty International*. How did that come about?

Well, we got asked to do the album. Our manager Dolphus Ramseur, I believe, got the call. He manages the Avetts (who played with Dylan at the 2011 Grammy Awards ceremony), *who contributed a track as well, so I think we were at the right place at the right time with that.*

How did you decide to cover *Political World* for the album?

There are two tracks that we recorded for the project. One is Political World, *and the other one is* George Jackson, *which will be a digital bonus track for our coming album* Leaving Eden. *I'll break the story down in a few ways 'cause it was very interesting how this all came together.*

I'm a pretty big Dylan fan, so I wanted to pick some obscure cuts just so that we wouldn't have to do any of the well-known tunes. As a Dylan fan myself, it's a real drag to hear a Dylan cover of, say, Like A Rolling Stone, *and not like it, just because I would rather hear Dylan's definitive version. There are times when artists are able to transcend, but that's not usually how I like to do things.*

Also (band member) *Rhiannon* (Giddens) *is not much of a Dylan fan. I needed to pick something that was not too Dylanesque for her to be interested, so I picked out some different pieces I thought the group could tackle. I picked stuff from* Dark Eyes *to* Golden Loom *to* One More Night, *and figured maybe she'd go for one of these. As it turned out, she picked out* George Jackson *because of the words. I had never looked up who George Jackson, the person, was. When I did, I knew this would be a great fit. We strip the song down to just the skeleton of the melody and worked from there, creating an arrangement with just banjo, patting juba, and vocal bass, along with Rhiannon and I passing off vocals.*

This is the original list of songs I thought would be neat to rearrange with our group:

1. Black Crow Blues

2. I'll Keep It With Mine (from Biograph)

3. Abandoned Love (from Biograph)

4. Tangled Up In Blue (from Blood On The Tracks and Real Live for the alternative lyrics)

5. Eternal Circle

6. Santa Fe

7. Golden Loom

8. Black Diamond Bay

9. Dark Eyes

10. Nobody 'Cept You (Live version from Genuine Bootleg Series Vol. 3)

11. One More Night

12. Went To See The Gypsy

13. Where Teardrops Fall

14. Man In The Long Black Coat

15. Turkey Chase

16. On A Night Like This

17. George Jackson (Big Band Version, from Masterpieces)

After having worked up the piece, we were in need of a producer, and to our great fortune we were able to book a studio date with the legendary producer Jac Holzman. Nonesuch Records is, of course, an offshoot of Elektra, and was started by Jac, so Nonesuch president David Bither reached out to him. Last February, we met up with Holzman at the Folk Alliance conference where he laid a great compliment on us, and even told an interviewer that we were a current band that he enjoyed listening to, and that he'd like to work with us someday.

Holzman gave the okay to record, but he was not impressed with the thought of us doing George Jackson. *He had heard Dylan do the song at the Bitter End when it had first been written, and proclaimed that it was not one of Dylan's best songs and suggested several others. These songs were* Political World, High Water *and* Spirit on the Water. *We were most drawn to* High Water *and* Political World *and finally chose* Political World *because we all felt the words were a bit more poignant in the world now than ever before.*

I love the arrangement. It retains the integrity of the original, yet it still sounds like the Drops. Did it come together quickly?

Rhiannon wrote the melody "break" as we were working the tune out to section out the verses, but besides that, it was again trying to strike that balance between interpretation and doing the original justice. It was pretty quick working the piece up.

Are there any plans on playing *Political World* in concert?

There are plans to play it live. We just haven't gotten the words all down. That was the hardest part. There are a lot of words and they come on very fast. Also that song comes from a period when Dylan's writing was very much set to a certain phrasing, so trying to break that when performing it was hard too. But the short answer is, 'Yes, we will do it live at some point.'

Have you had a chance to hear the *Amnesty* album yet?

I haven't yet. I can't wait though. I've heard several different reviews, and the names on the albums are of interest. I can't wait.

The Drops have a new album coming out soon. What can you tell us about it?

Our new album, Leaving Eden, *is a new phase in the group's career. We will have a new line-up and the music is taking another step forward because of it. There is a wide variety of tunes, from old-time to blues to jazz. There's a South African tune, a few recent compositions* (one by Rhiannon), *and several surprises along the way.*

Any other plans?

Just to keep on touring. With the new album we'll put in another big year of touring, and see how far we can with the new ensemble. We're also hoping to cut another album in the next year if it all works out.

I've got a few different projects coming along myself that are of note. I have an album called The Uptown Strut *coming out, which I did with Sule Greg Wilson, who worked with Rhiannon and I, early on, as Sankofa Strings. The group on this album is called just Sankofa. That will be coming out on Kingswood Records in late March.*

There is another album I have that features me backing an older blues songster by the name of Boo Hanks. That will be coming on Music Maker Relief Foundation in late March as well.

The Chocolate Drops will be making an appearance on Voice of Ages, *which is the 50th anniversary CD for the Chieftains.*

Also, the Chocolate Drops are featured in a recent PBS documentary on the history of the banjo called Give Me The Banjo. *The show premiered on PBS in November, but the expanded DVD will be coming out in April.*

I think that's it. I'm excited to see what the next year brings.

Note: Flemons left the band soon after this interview. Rhiannon Giddens participated in *Lost on the River: The New Basement Tapes* album, featuring music set to unused lyrics Dylan wrote during the original *Basement Tapes* sessions of 1967. It was produced by T-Bone Burnett, and featured Elvis Costello, Taylor Goldsmith (Dawes), Jim James (My Morning Jacket), Marcus Mumford (Mumford & Sons), and Giddens, all finishing the compositions in different combinations, and then performing them for the project.

Bob Dylan and T-Bone Burnett, from Rolling Thunder through *Dharma and Greg*

January 14, 2011

Joseph Henry "T-Bone" Burnett was born on January 14, 1948.

Burnett has been awarded ten Grammy Awards and one "Oscar." As a record producer, Burnett has worked with Elvis Costello, the Wallflowers, Gillian Welch, Roy Orbison, Robert Plant & Alison Krauss, Willie Nelson, John Mellencamp, B.B. King, Los Lobos, Elton John & Leon Russell, and Kris Kristofferson, among others. He was also the man behind many soundtracks, including *Crazy Heart*, *O Brother, Where Art Thou?*, *Walk The Line*, and *Cold Mountain*. His first session was as the drummer (and producer) of The Legendary Stardust Cowboy's *Paralyzed*. He has also released a handful of critically-acclaimed solo albums.

Bob Dylan and Burnett have collaborated on and off since the mid-1970s, when T-Bone was a member of The Rolling Thunder Revue. He got the gig through a chance meeting with Bob Neuwirth, and would sing lead on one song each evening, usually *Hula Hoop*, *Silver Mantis*, or Warren Zevon's *Werewolves of London*.

Burnett has been credited as one of the influences that led to Bob Dylan's late 1970's interest in Christianity. T-Bone has been reluctant to address this issue, but has said, *"People like myself, Bruce Cockburn, Bono and Bob Dylan have tried to bring love and perspective and Christ to people who can't hear Jerry Falwell . . . I've made it a policy not to talk about Bob Dylan. But I will say this, his career has been about Bob Dylan's search for God."* [96]

After the tour with Dylan ended, Burnett hooked up with Revue members David Mansfield and Steven Soles to form The Alpha Band.

Burnett later participated in Dylan's May, 1986, sessions for the album *Knocked Out Loaded*: Skyline Recording Studios, Topanga Park, California: 1 May 1986

1. *Without Love* (Clyde McPhatter)

2. *New Danville Girl* (Bob Dylan & Sam Shepard)

3. *Unchain My Heart* (James Freddy/Agnes Jones)

Bob Dylan (vocal & guitar), T-bone J. Henry Burnett (guitar), James Jamerson Jr. (guitar), Ira Ingber (guitar), Steve Douglas (tenor saxophone), Al Kooper (keyboards), Vito San Filippo (bass), Steve Madaio (trumpet), Raymond Lee Pounds (drums), Carolyn Dennis, Sharon "Muffy" Hendrix, Madelyn Quebec (background vocals).

Notes

2 is an overdub on the basic take recorded at Cherokee Studios, Hollywood, Los Angeles, California, 6, 10 or 11 December 1984. This take was not used on *Knocked Out Loaded*.

1 may be a Bob Dylan composition.

1 and 3 are not circulating.

---

[96] http://www.jesusjournal.com/index2.php?option=com_content&do_pdf=1&id=120, *Being T-Bone Burnett*, Retrieved 11/20/2016

Skyline Recording Studios, Topanga Park, California: 2 May 1986

1. *New Danville Girl* (Bob Dylan & Sam Shepard)

2. *Unchain My Heart* (James Freddy/Agnes Jones)

Bob Dylan (vocal & guitar), T-bone J. Henry Burnett (guitar), Cesar Rosas (guitar), James Jamerson Jr. (guitar), Ira Ingber (guitar), Al Perkins (steel guitar), Larry Myers (mandolin), Steve Douglas (tenor saxophone), Al Kooper (keyboards), Vito San Filippo (bass), Steve Madaio (trumpet), Raymond Lee Pounds (drums).

Notes

1 is an overdub on the basic take recorded at Cherokee Studios, Hollywood, Los Angeles, California, 6, 10 or 11 December 1984. This take was not used on *Knocked Out Loaded*.

2 is not circulating.

According to the album's credits, Burnett also plays guitar on the opening track, *You Wanna Ramble*. [97]

When Dylan gave a performance at the San José Event State Center on May 9, 1992, Burnett played guitar on three songs. [98]

In 1999, Bob Dylan made a surprise appearance on the *Play Lady Play* episode of the TV sitcom, *Dharma & Greg*, probably at the invitation of Eddie Gorodetsky. [99] The band consisted of Bob Dylan, T-Bone Burnett, John Field, Tony Gilkyson and Joe Henry, with actress Jenna Elfman on drums.

Burnett included Dylan's recording of *The Man In Me* on the soundtrack to *The Big Lebowski*, while in 2002, Dylan contributed a new song, *Waitin' For You*, to the soundtrack of *Divine Secrets of the Ya-Ya Sisterhood*, released on Burnett's DMZ label.

Last year's Speaking Clock Revue was inspired by Burnett's Rolling Thunder Revue experience.

[97] http://bobdylan.com/albums/knocked-out-loaded/, *Knocked Out Loaded*, 1986, Retrieved 11/20/2016

[98] http://www.bjorner.com/DSN13060%20-%201992%20US%20West%20Coast%20Spring%20Tour.htm#DSN13170, *Still on the Road*, Retrieved 11/20/2016

[99] http://expectingrain.com/dok/who/g/gorodetskyeddie.html, *The Bob Dylan's Who's Who: Eddie Gorodetsky*, Retrieved 11/20/2016

When Bob Dylan praised Barry Manilow at Burt Bacharach's Passover Seder

June 16, 2011

Barry Manilow was born on June 17, 1943. He has more in common with Bob Dylan than you might think:

- Like Robert Allen Zimmerman, Manilow changed his name. He was born Barry Alan Pincus.

- Both were born Jewish (Manilow's mother and paternal grandfather were Jewish), and have released Christmas albums.

- Dylan and Manilow each collaborated with Bette Midler. Manilow worked with the Divine Miss M from 1971 to 1975, while Dylan sang with her on at least three occasions: A duet on *Buckets Of Rain* in 1975, plus the group projects *We Are The World* and the 1986 tribute to Rev. Martin Luther King, Jr.

- Both worked with Clive Davis; Dylan at Columbia, Manilow at Arista.

- Each walked out on a television program. Dylan would not allow himself to be censored by *The Ed Sullivan Show*, while Manilow backed out of an interview on *The View* because of Elisabeth Hasselbeck's conservative political views.

- Both appeared in television commercials. Dylan and his songs have appeared in numerous ads, most notably Victoria's Secret and Cadillac, while Manilow wrote and occasionally sang jingles, including State Farm Insurance (*"Like a good neighbor, State Farm is there..."*) and Band-Aid (*"I am stuck on Band-Aid, 'cause Band-Aids stick on me!"*).

- Bob Dylan has been known to take drugs while, in an April 1979 *Ladies Home Journal* interview, Manilow admitted to experimenting with marijuana, saying he lost the taste for it quickly.

- Elizabeth Taylor was friends with both performers. Dylan was close to Taylor (and reportedly wrote a song for her), while Manilow was the Master of Ceremonies for Taylor's 60th birthday bash at Disneyland in Anaheim, California.

- Both artists have won Grammy awards and have been inducted into the Songwriter's Hall of Fame.

- Dylan and Manilow have appeared in public wearing disguises. In 2002, Dylan wore a wig and fake beard when he returned to the Newport Folk Festival, while the following year Manilow wore dark glasses and a blonde wig in the streets of Beverly Hills, California, after reportedly receiving a facelift.

In 1988, Manilow met Dylan. According to an article in the *Star Tribune*: [100]

"It was an odd meeting," he recalled. It took place at a Seder, a ceremonial Passover dinner, at the home of songwriting legend Burt Bacharach. "He [Dylan] came over to me and said, 'Keep doing what you're doing, man. You're inspiring all of us.' Isn't that nice?"

A couple of months later, Dylan began what is often called his "Never Ending Tour," which resumes tonight.

---

[100] *Music: Barry's bonds: Manilow talks about his connections with Clive Davis, rock 'n' roll, Bob Dylan and the Twin Cities*, Jon Bream, StarTribune (Minnesota), 1/4/2008

Mutual admiration society - Bob Dylan, Leonard Cohen, and that *Hallelujah* song

September 20, 2011

"Dylan blew everybody's mind, except Leonard's." Allen Ginsberg. [101]

Happy birthday to Leonard Norman Cohen, CC, GOQ, born September 21, 1934.

Cohen and Bob Dylan are two of the most respected songwriters of the last half-century. Both men have received many of the highest and most prestigious awards and honors bestowed in the world of arts and entertainment. They have also expressed admiration for each other.

There are many similarities between the two. Here is a sampling:

- Born Jewish, each explored other religions, even though Cohen's world was *"rocked"* when Dylan went Christian. [102]

- Cohen and Dylan are poets, recording artists, actors, authors, singers, songwriters, and performers, although not necessarily in that order.

- Both spent time with Andy Warhol's Factory crowd, especially Nico.

- Dylan and Cohen were each signed to Columbia Records by John Hammond. Recording in the studio soon after signing, Cohen started singing and Hammond said on the intercom: *"Watch out, Dylan!"* [103] Like Dylan, Cohen briefly left the label, but soon returned.

- Judy Collins recorded cover versions of songs by both artists early in their careers. Each stayed at New York's Chelsea Hotel, and the building is referenced in the songs *Sara* (Dylan) and *Chelsea Hotel #2* (Cohen). Cohen went to Nashville in 1968, not long after Dylan recorded there.

- Cohen was originally produced by John Simon (The Band), then Bob Johnston (taking Dylan's sidemen – Ron Cornelius and Charlie Daniels – with him).

- Cohen played the 1970 Isle of Wight Festival, one year after Dylan.

- Dylan and Phil Spector visited Cohen backstage in 1975. [104] In 1971, Spector co-produced Dylan's songs for *The Concert For Bangla Desh*. Spector produced Cohen's 1977 album, *Death Of A Ladies' Man* (originally released on Warner Brothers,) with Dylan and Allen Ginsberg singing background vocals on one track. Soon after, Dylan was reportedly involved with a friend of Cohen's named Malka Marom.

- Both artists have been counted out many times, only to return with great songs and albums, and continue to tour into their 70s.

On December 4, 1975, at Canada's Forum de Montréal, Cohen went to see The Rolling Thunder Revue. That night, Dylan introduced a new composition by saying, *"Here's a song about marriage, this is called 'Isis' ... This is for Leonard, if he's still here."* It has been written [105] that Cohen had left the venue by this time, but Larry Sloman, in his book *On the Road with Bob Dylan*, wrote that after the show:

---

[101] *Songwriters On Songwriting - Expanded Edition*, Paul Zollo, Da Capo Press, New York, 1997

[102] *Down the Highway - The Life of Bob Dylan*, Howard Sounes, Grove Press, New York, 2001

[103] *Who held a gun to Leonard Cohen's head?*, Tim de Lisle, The Guardian (U.K.), 9/27/2001

[104] *Cohen's New Skin*, Harvey Kubernik & Justin Pierce, Melody Maker, 3/1/1975

[105] http://hobomagazine.com/essays/the-energy-of-love/, *The Energy of Love - Words by Stephen Scobie*, Retrieved 11/20/2016

"Ratso (Sloman) rushes back to Leonard's party and escorts them backstage, worming their way through the crowds, stepping over the huge rolls of toilet paper that were thrown from the rafters by the enthusiastic audience ... Backstage, Leonard greets the troops, and everyone repairs to the hotel for a party in one of the downstairs banquet rooms." [106]

In 1988, Bob Dylan twice sang Cohen's *Hallelujah* in concert: July 8, at Montréal's Forum de Montréal (see introduction to *Isis* above,) and at the tour ending August 4 show at Hollywood's Greek Theatre.

"It's a rather joyous song. I like very much the last verse. I remember singin' it to Bob Dylan after his last concert in Paris. The morning after, I was having coffee with him and we traded lyrics. Dylan especially liked this last verse 'And even though it all went wrong, I stand before the Lord of song With nothing on my lips but Hallelujah.'" - Leonard Cohen interview, *Paroles et Musiques*, 1985. [107]

There is an oft-repeated story of Dylan and Cohen exchanging anecdotes about songwriting. This is from a 1992 interview with Cohen by Paul Zollo: [108]

"That was a song that took me a long time to write. Dylan and I were having coffee the day after his concert in Paris a few years ago and he was doing that song in concert. And he asked me how long it took to write it. And I told him a couple of years. I lied actually. It was more than a couple of years ... Then I praised a song of his, I and I, *and asked him how long it had taken and he said, "Fifteen minutes." [Laughter]*

A similar quote was printed in *The Telegraph*, issue 41, page 30.

The story has been embellished to varying degrees ever since, although the point is the same. Here are some examples:

"There is a story about Dylan and Cohen meeting each other in a Parisian café in the early 1980s. Bob says how much he likes Leonard's song Hallelujah *(which he was later to perform), and asks Leonard how long he took to compose it. Leonard hesitates, and mutters something like "four or five years," not liking to admit that versions of this song had been in the works for a whole lot longer, and that manuscript pages of revisions ran into the hundreds. As always, the process of composition had been long and difficult. Then, feeling the need for reciprocation, he asks Bob how long it had taken him to write* I and I. *"Oh," says Bob, "about fifteen minutes.""* Hobo Magazine [109]

Bob Dylan and Leonard Cohen are both on tour in Europe when they find out they're playing near to each other one night and arrange to meet up for lunch. Over the extended meal Bob turns to Leonard and says "Hey man, I love Hallelujah. *How long did it take you to write that one?" Leonard considers for a moment and says "About three or four months. Molding it and getting it perfected." "By the way, Bob" continues Leonard, "I think* Make You Feel My Love *is fantastic. How long did that one take?" Bob pulls on his cigar, stares into the distance and says "20 minutes." Postscript: Leonard was later asked did it really take 3-4 months to write* Hallelujah. *He replied: "Actually it took much longer, but I didn't want Dylan to think I was slacking." - Jack Stow* [110]

One day, Leonard Cohen met Bob Dylan. They started talking about their writing style and how long it took them to write songs. "How long did it take you to write Hallelujah?*" Dylan asked. "The best part of two years," replied Cohen.*

---

[106] *On the Road With Bob Dylan - Rolling With the Thunder*, Larry Sloman, Bantam Books, New York, 1978.

[107] http://www.leonardcohen-prologues.com/hallelujah.htm, Interview (Magazine "Paroles et Musiques" 1985). Retrieved 11/20/2016

[108] *Songwriters On Songwriting - Expanded Edition*, Paul Zollo, Da Capo Press, New York, 1997

[109] http://hobomagazine.com/essays/the-energy-of-love/, The Energy of Love - Words by Stephen Scobie. Retrieved 11/20/2016

[110] http://www.jackstow.com/blog/post/2010/09/27/Bob-Dylan-And-Leonard-Cohen-Have-Lunch.aspx, Dead Link

"Two years? Really?" Dylan said, surprised, trying to hold back a grin. "How long did it take you to write Highway 61?" Cohen retorted. Dylan shrugged his shoulders. "Oh, all of fifteen minutes." - Comment on Drowned In Sound. [111]

Talking in 2008 about a Dylan concert, Cohen said he wore earplugs at a gig at St.John's, since it was louder than his own concerts, then went on to say:

"As Sharon Robinson said, Bob Dylan has a secret code with his audience ... Some were hard to recognize. But nobody cared. That's not what they were there for and not what I was there for. Something else was going on, which was a celebration of some kind of genius that is so apparent and so clear and has touched people so deeply that all they need is some kind of symbolic unfolding of the event ... It's a very strange event." [112]

However, in a 2009 *Rolling Stone* interview, Dylan claimed he doesn't see Cohen, or any other singer-songwriters, perform these days, saying he was familiar with *"what Leonard does,"* but is not compelled to see him, or "anybody," preferring plays and symphonies. [113]

Here are a few more Cohen quotes about Dylan from Zollo's interview:

Is Anthem *in any way an answer to Dylan's song* Everything is Broken?

I had a line in Democracy *that referred specifically to that Dylan song* Everything is Broken, *which was "The singer says it's broken and the painter says it's gray..." But, no,* Anthem *was written a long time before that Dylan song. I'd say '82 but it was actually earlier than that that that song began to form.*

... I think Dylan has lines, hundreds of great lines that have the feel of unhewn stone. But they really fit in there. But they're not smoothed out. It's inspired but not polished. That is not to say that he doesn't have lyrics of great polish. That kind of genius can manifest all the forms and all the styles.

Dylan said, around the time that Hallelujah *came out, that your songs were almost like prayers. I didn't hear that but I know he does take some interest in my songs. We have a mutual interest. Everybody's interested in Dylan but it's pleasant to have Dylan interested in me."* [114]

[111] http://drownedinsound.com/community/boards/music/4150395, A nice Jeff Buckley vs XFactor related rant, Retrieved 11/20/2016

[112] http://www.macleans.ca/authors/brian-d-johnson/cohen-wore-earplugs-to-a-dylan-show/, *Leonard Cohen wore earplugs to a Dylan show?* Retrieved 11/20/2016

[113] *Bob Dylan's Late-Era, Old-Style American Individualism*, Douglas Brinkley, Rolling Stone, 5/14/2009

[114] *Songwriters On Songwriting - Expanded Edition*, Paul Zollo, Da Capo Press, New York, 1997

Chuck Berry, Leonard Cohen, honored at JFK Library - Bob Dylan sends his regards

February 26, 2012

Chuck Berry and Leonard Cohen were honored at Boston's John F. Kennedy Library this afternoon, receiving the first annual PEN New England Awards for Song Lyrics of Literary Excellence. [115]

Bob Dylan could not attend, but sent his regards yesterday:

"To Chuck, the Shakespeare of rock and roll, congratulations on your PEN award, that's what too much monkey business will get ya . . . Say hello to Mr. Leonard, Kafka of the blues, and Lord Byron Keith (Richards) *if he shows up. In all seriousness, Chuck, congratulations on this prestigious honor.*

"You have indeed written the book with a capital B, and congratulations to Leonard, who's still writing it - Bob Dylan" [116]

The *"monkey business"* Dylan mentioned was no doubt a nod to Berry's *Too Much Monkey Business*, an influence on Dylan's 1965 single, *Subterranean Homesick Blues*.

At today's ceremony, Cohen was first honored in a speech by Salmon Rushdie, then by Shawn Colvin's cover of *Come Healing*. (Rosanne Cash also sent a note.)

To honor Berry, Paul Simon read some of Chuck's lyrics. Elvis Costello sang a solo cover of *No Particular Place to Go*, then Richards joined him for a version of *Promised Land*. Berry performed a bit of *Johnny B. Goode* during his speech.

Others in attendance included Caroline Kennedy, Al Kooper, Peter Wolf, and writers Bill Flanagan, Tom Perrotta, and Peter Guralnick. [117]

The event was live-streamed at the JFK Library, and the official video is archived online.

---

[115] https://www.jfklibrary.org/Asset-Viewer/_HlVdJ4Y3UqgCA7mEb4yAg.aspx, *Song Lyrics of Literary Excellence*, Accessed 11/21/2016

[116] https://www.jfklibrary.org/Asset-Viewer/_HlVdJ4Y3UqgCA7mEb4yAg.aspx, *Song Lyrics of Literary Excellence*, Accessed 11/21/2016

[117] https://www.bostonglobe.com/arts/2012/02/27/leonard-cohen-and-chuck-berry-celebrated-jfk-library/9mPNrgSYjClyq1StBni90M/story.html, *Leonard Cohen and Chuck Berry celebrated at JFK library*, Retrieved 11/21/2016

Nana Mouskouri and email pal Dylan

May 4, 2011

"Playboy Magazine (1978): What musicians do you listen to today? . . . Any popular stuff?

Bob Dylan: Well, Nana Mouskouri." [118]

"People like Bob Dylan and Neil Young and Leonard Cohen, I was as much in love with their writing as I was with my Greek poets and composers." - Nana Mouskouri, 2005. [119]

Ioánna Moúschouri, more commonly known as Nana Mouskouri, is a Greek singer who has sold 300 million records over five decades (according to her label, Universal).

"I know Dylan very well," Mouskouri told Liz Thomson in late 1983, *"I mean if you can say very well. I met him in 1975 or '76 in Los Angeles because we had some common friends. He came to one of my concerts... He came to say hello and said he wasn't going to stay long. He ended up staying all through the concert in the wings. I thought at the beginning that he was an intimidating person but when he starts it's impossible to stop him. I was amazed about how he was afterwards. We got together a few times. He wanted to know everything about me. He didn't know that I did a lot of his songs in French and German. At the end we became... you can't say 'friends', but if he's somewhere I go to see him and we talk on the phone every now and then."* [120]

According to another source, the date was actually September 10, 1979. when Leonard Cohen brought Dylan backstage before her performance at the Greek Theater in Los Angeles. Cohen introduced Mouskouri to Dylan, who claimed to be unfamiliar with her work. [121]

Mouskouri told Thomson Dylan sent her a demo of *Every Grain of Sand*. [122] The song arrived in the mail at her Geneva home sometime after that LA meeting, completely unexpected, and she was the first to record it. [123] Mouskouri said the song was written after Dylan attended one of her concerts. However, Dylan's version was released in 1981, the year before it appeared on Mouskouri's album, *Song For Liberty*. According to a 1981 interview in London with WNEW-FM DJ Dave Herman, Dylan said he wrote the song the previous summer.

Dylan and Mouskouri shared some late-night dinners, but she revealed it never went any further. [124]

Mouskouri and Dylan have apparently stayed in touch over the years. She told *Bunte* magazine, *"I love emails . . . but it is pretty tough with Bob Dylan, he writes so rarely."* [125]

In addition to *Every Grain of Sand*, Mouskouri has recorded numerous Dylan compositions over the years, including *Farewell Angelina* (1967), *Love Minus Zero/No Limit* (1969), *Farewell* (1970), *A Hard Rain's A-Gonna Fall* (1974), *Tomorrow Is A Long Time* (1979), *I'll Remember You* (1987), *Dignity* (1997), and, with Stig Rossen, *Make You Feel My Love* (2000). Mouskouri also performed a medley of three

---

[118] *Playboy interview: Bob Dylan: a candid conversations with the visionary whose songs changed the times*, Ron Rosenbaum, Playboy, 3/1978

[119] http://www.theage.com.au/news/music/shy-and-retiring/2005/08/25/1124562976353.html, *Shy and retiring*, Retrieved 11/24/2016

[120] *Elizabeth Thomson interview*, Savoy Hotel, London. Personal correspondence, 11/24/2016

[121] http://www.nana-mouskouri.net/index.php?article9/nana-and-bob-dylan, *Nana & Bob Dylan*, Retrieved 11/24/2016

[122] http://www.independent.co.uk/arts-entertainment/books/reviews/still-on-the-road-the-songs-of-bob-dylan-vol-2-1974-2008-by-clinton-heylin-1996796.html, *Still on the Road: The Songs of Bob Dylan Vol 2: 1974-2008*, by Clinton Heylin, reviewed by Liz Thomson. Retrieved 11/24/2016

[123] *Elizabeth Thomson interview*, Savoy Hotel, London. Personal correspondence, 11/24/2016

[124] *Nana Mouskouri: Diva with specs appeal*, Andy Miller, The Telegraph U.K., 11/10/2007

[125] http://www.rightwingbob.com/weblog/bob-dylan-is-a-lazy-emailer/2627/, *Bob Dylan "is a lazy emailer,"* Retrieved 11/24/2016. Originally *Bunte* magazine DEAD LINK

Dylan songs with Hugues Aufray on French television in 1976: *Adieu Angelina (Farewell Angelina)* and *Le ciel est noir (A Hard Rain's A-Gonna Fall)* in French, and *Blowin' In The Wind* in English. Aufray has also covered many Dylan compositions, including two tribute albums.

Bob Dylan content in HBO's Mavis Staples documentary: 'We may have smooched!'

March 1, 2016

Bob Dylan agreed to allow 15-year-old interview segments to be included in Jessica Edwards' new documentary about gospel legend Mavis Staples, which made its television debut on HBO Sunday night. The film, titled *Mavis! - The Documentary*, traces her career from the early days with her family gospel group The Staple Singers, through her ups, downs, and triumphant return to glory as a solo artist. While the film covers her collaborations with Jeff Tweedy, Prince, The Band, and others, as well as testimonials from Bonnie Raitt, Chuck D., and the late civil rights leader and politician Julian Bond, here we will focus on the Dylan content.

There are two segments featuring Dylan. The first, about 14 minutes in, features Dylan talking over The Staple Singers' performance of *Sit Down Servant*. In an interview from November, 2001, [126] Dylan recalled listening to the radio, in bed under the covers, when he was young. *"At midnight, the gospel stuff would start. The Staple Singers came on once, and they were just so different ... Pops (Mavis' father) has an easy kind of flow voice and kind of a gentle voice, but then this other voice came on, which I found out was Mavis. One of the first songs I heard that made my hair stand up on end was called* Sit Down Servant, *that just made me stay up for a week after I heard that song."* [127]

About 20 minutes later, there's a longer segment featuring Dylan. It begins with the credits for the 1963 TV special, *Folk Songs and More Folk Songs!*, with Dylan, the Staple Singers, and others walking in front of the singing Brothers Four, followed by a snippet of Dylan performing *Blowin' in the Wind*, while Mavis talks about their first encounter. Mavis said she wasn't familiar with Dylan at the time, but he certainly was familiar with her. Mavis said Pops immediately related to Dylan's lyrics, especially the lines about *"How many roads,"* because in Mississippi, he had to cross the street when a white man walked by. The Staple Singers learned it, and then recorded it.

"(Dylan) was a cute guy, curly hair ... but I didn't have flirtin' on my mind back then," Mavis said, *"but he did!"* After telling her father he wanted to marry Mavis, Pops told Dylan to ask Mavis directly, but when he did, she *"didn't take it to heart ... I was a young girl."* At the 1964 Newport Folk Festival, Dylan told her he was serious. *"We wrote letters, we kept in touch ... We may have smooched!"*

Talking about the 1964 Newport performance, Dylan said, *"The atmosphere was high charged with plenty of different kinds of musicians around ... I think we kind of got friendly at the time and I knew the Staple Singers at the time, so I probably was in hotels, and hanging around with them."* [128]

Dylan and Mavis have collaborated musically twice since then, although neither performance is covered in the documentary. In 1992, Mavis appeared on stage with Bob Dylan at the taping of the David Letterman 10th anniversary special, singing backup in an all-star band on *Like a Rolling Stone*. In 2002, Dylan and Mavis duetted on a rewritten version of his composition, *Gonna Change My Way of Thinking*.

In a 1969 interview with Jann Wenner in *Rolling Stone*, Dylan said he'd always liked Mavis Staples ever since she was a little girl. *"She's always been my favorite... she's always had my favorite voice."* [129]

Addendum: In 2016, Dylan and Staples toured together, and she told *Rolling Stone* magazine Dylan had written a new song for her.

---

[126] http://www.davehoekstra.com/wp-content/uploads/2014/03/mavis_staples.pdf, *Mavis Staples*, Feb. 22, 2002 By Dave Hoekstra. Retrieved 11/24/2016

[127] http://www.mavisfilm.com Mavis! Official Website

[128] http://www.mavisfilm.com Mavis! Official Website

[129] http://www.jannswenner.com/Archives/Bob_Dylan.aspx, *The Rolling Stone Interview: Bob Dylan*, by Jann S. Wenner, RS47: November 29, 1969. Retrieved 11/24/2016

Loudon Wainwright III, a former 'New Bob Dylan'

September 4, 2011

Loudon Snowden Wainwright III was born on September 5, 1946. He is a singer, songwriter, and actor. Like many singer-songwriters of the early 1970s, including Bruce Springsteen, Wainwright was (incorrectly) labeled "The New Dylan." Dylan reportedly praised Wainwright's novelty hit, *Dead Skunk*, saying, *"Man, that skunk song is pretty good."* [130]

Loudon is the son of Martha Taylor, a yoga teacher, and Loudon Wainwright, Jr., a columnist and editor for *Life* magazine. One of his siblings, Sloan Wainwright, is also a singer. He was married to the late Kate McGarrigle. Both their son, Rufus, and daughter, Martha, are successful musicians in their own right. Loudon also had a daughter, Lucy Wainwright Roche (with singer Suzzy Roche), and another daughter, columnist Alexandra "Lexie" McKim Kelly Wainwright.

Wainwright has said that he was inspired after seeing Bob Dylan at the Newport Folk Festival (probably in 1963).

His recording career began in 1970, and had his biggest hit a couple of years later with *Dead Skunk (In The Middle Of The Road)*. In 2010, he won the Best Traditional Folk Album, *High Wide and Handsome - The Charlie Poole Project*, at the 52nd Annual Grammy Awards.

In 1993, Wainwright spoke about Dylan's *Visions Of Johanna* on the program *Hits of the Sixties* at the BBC. He said was not a fan of his early albums when he first heard them, finding them derivative, but then saw him in concert.

"Then I went to the Newport Folk Festival at some point in the early 60s ... and I SAW him play. And that was kind of a shattering experience 'cause he was so charismatic and ... just this kind of scruffy, skinny guy ...

But, Blonde on Blonde *is a magical record, the songs are great, the lyrics are amazing. It's still kind of painful to listen to it -- it's just SO GOOD. Even though it's a young man, probably on drugs, and the imagery is sometimes a little silly, but it's the power of the performance, the harmonica playing, the singing, and the production ...*

He was a middle-class white guy like me. And yet he was so poetic and mysterious ... and charismatic and exciting to watch that it seemed like a pretty interesting idea to be a songwriter..." [131]

In 1992, Wainwright released the album *History*, which featured the song *Talking New Bob Dylan*, about Dylan turning 50. It began:

Hey, Bob Dylan, I wrote you a song.

Today is your birthday if I'm not wrong. [132]

---

[130] http://theseconddisc.com/review-loudon-wainwright-iii-40-odd-years/, *Review: Loudon Wainwright III, "40 Odd Years"* by Joe Marchese. Retrieved 11/24/2016

[131] http://www.bobdylanroots.com/wainwr.html, *Transcript of Loudon Wainwright III interview*, BBC Radio broadcast, May 24, 1993. Retrieved 11/24/2016

[132] *Talking New Bob Dylan, History*, Loudon Wainwright III, 1991.

Paul Simon

October 12/14, 2010

Paul Frederic Simon was born on October 13, 1941.

Bob Dylan and Paul Simon go back a long way, to Greenwich Village in the early 1960s. They have covered each other's songs, and even toured together in 1999, performing duets during each show.

Simon's first hit with Art Garfunkel was *Hey, Schoolgirl* in 1957, released under the name Tom and Jerry. Like Dylan, Simon worked under different aliases, releasing singles as Jerry Landis, Paul Kane, and True Taylor. Simon also had some success as a member of Tico and The Triumphs.

Simon joined a fraternity while in college, much like the young Bobby Zimmerman.

According to Victoria Kingston's biography of Simon & Garfunkel (Fromm International), when Simon first visited Dylan at his home in the early 1960s, the place was a mess, and while Dylan paced, Simon put little scraps of paper into his pocket to learn more about songwriting: *"I wanted to find out if he was doing it like I was doing it. But I couldn't find out what he did."*

In 1964, Clive Davis signed Simon & Garfunkel to Columbia Records. It was decided that, unlike Dylan, the duo would use their real, ethnic-sounding names. Their debut album, *Wednesday Morning, 3 A.M.*, was released later that year. It was an acoustic album (with some additional backing), with Dylan's producer, Tom Wilson, at the helm. Like labelmate Dylan's debut, the record mixed Paul Simon originals with covers, including versions of *The Times They Are A-Changin'* and *Peggy-O*. It was not a success when it was first released, so Simon & Garfunkel decided to go their separate ways.

After the folk-rock boom in the wake The Byrds' cover of Dylan's *Mr. Tambourine Man*, Wilson overdubbed electric instrumentation over the original acoustic version of *The Sound(s) Of Silence* on *Wednesday Morning, 3 A.M.*, to give it a more contemporary feel. This was done on June 15, 1965, just after Wilson had recorded Dylan's *Like A Rolling Stone*, retaining Al Gorgoni and Bobby Gregg from the earlier session. It became a huge hit, leading to Simon's return to the U.S. from England, and a reunion with Garfunkel. The next two albums were produced by Bob Johnston, who had also replaced Wilson as Dylan's producer.

While in England in 1965, Paul Simon recorded an early, solo version of a Dylan pastiche/parody originally titled *A Simple Desultory Philippic (or How I was Lyndon Johnson'd into Submission)*, included on his album *The Paul Simon Songbook*. The lyrics referred to Dylan's songs *It's Alright, Ma (I'm Only Bleeding)* and *I Shall Be Free No.10*, producer Tom Wilson, and Dylan Thomas. For the third Simon & Garfunkel album, *Parsley Sage Rosemary and Thyme*, an updated folk-rock version was recorded, and now subtitled *(or How I was Robert McNamara'd into Submission)*. In the fade-out of the newer version, Simon says, *"Folk-rock . . . I've lost my harmonica, Albert,"* a reference to Dylan's manager Albert Grossman. It also quoted Dylan's *Rainy Day Women #12 & 35*.

In 1970, Bob Dylan released his cover of Simon's *The Boxer*. It has often been cited as one of the more unusual tracks from *Self Portrait*, a controversial choice from a controversial album. It featured Dylan singing harmonies as both Simon AND Garfunkel, and it puzzled just about everybody, including Simon. Dylan must have put some thought into recording, however, since he changed the word *"glove"* to *"blow"* in his version. There was speculation that the song was about Dylan, but Simon denied this:

"Like anything Dylan does, it has its own thing. . . Dylan's version makes me smile . . . One thing is certain, I've never written anything about Dylan, and I don't know his personal life." [133]

In a 1970 issue of *Rolling Stone*, Simon said that he was flattered that Dylan would record one of his songs, but (obviously) preferred Simon & Garfunkel's original. [134]

---

[133] *Simon & Garfunkel: The Biography*, Victoria Kingston, Fromm International, New York, 1999

According to Garfunkel, Dylan surprised the duo by showing up while they were yelling in the studio during their recording of *Baby Driver*, the b-side of *The Boxer*.

The traditional English ballad *Scarborough Fair* was the basis for both Bob Dylan's *Girl From The North Country*, and Simon & Garfunkel's *Scarborough Fair/Canticle*.

In October, 1975, Bob Dylan recorded a rewritten version of *Buckets Of Rain* with Bette Midler, with the title phrase changed to *"Nuggets of Rain."* During the fade, Midler can be heard cooing, *"Ooh, you don't even know. You have no idea."* Dylan replied, *"I don't want to know … You and Paul Simon should have done this one."*

Dylan and Simon officially recorded together in 1985 as part of USA For Africa's *We Are The World* benefit single. Simon was originally scheduled to appear at Live Aid but allegedly withdrew because the organizers were pressuring a reunion with Art Garfunkel. [135]

When Bob Dylan was rehearsing with the Grateful Dead in June, 1987, at Club Front in San Rafael, California, he sang backup vocals on a version of *Boy In The Bubble*, a song from Simon's recent album, *Graceland.* [136]

Bob Dylan covered Simon's *Homeward Bound* three times while on tour in 1991: June 6 in Rome, June 14 in Innsbruck, Austria, and July 6 in Nashua, New Hampshire. [137]

When interviewed by Larry King for his CNN television show, Simon revealed the right to use the Columbia master tapes of Simon & Garfunkel material on his solo *1964-1993* box set was granted as part of a trade with Warner Brothers to use material by Neil Young, George Harrison, Chrissie Hynde, Lou Reed, and Eric Clapton on the Columbia release, *Bob Dylan - The 30th Anniversary Celebration Concert.* [138]

In 1999, Simon and Dylan went on two tours together, with each artist alternating as the headliner. When the first act finished his portion, the other performer would join the opener for a mini-set. It would include one of Simon's songs (*The Sound Of Silence* or *The Boxer*), an oldies medley (*I Walk The Line/Blue Moon Of Kentucky* or *That'll Be The Day/The Wanderer*), and one of Dylan's songs (*Forever Young* or *Knockin' On Heaven's Door*). Toward the end of the summer tour, when Simon would hold out his arms during the line *"10,000 people, maybe more"* (from *The Sound Of Silence*) to much applause, Dylan would often be seen with his back to the audience, apparently pretending to look for his harmonica.

Simon mentioned earlier this year [139] that he was reissuing his solo catalog with Columbia Records after a few decades with Warner Brothers (a much longer defection than Dylan's time with Asylum). According to Roger Friedman, *"He's thinking of asking Bob Dylan, with whom he's toured, 'to sing something on (his next album).'"* It is unclear what label will release Simon's next album, or if Dylan will actually participate. (Update: He did not)

---

[134] *Paul Simon: The Rolling Stone Interview*, Jon Landau, Rolling Stone, July 20, 1972

[135] http://rateyourmusic.com/list/yellowbrick/the_alternate_live_aid/, *The Alternate Live Aid*, Retrieved 11/24/2016

[136] http://www.bjorner.com/DSN08630%20-%201987%20Dylan-Dead%20Tour.htm#DSN08628, *Still on the Road*, Retrieved 11/24/2016

[137] http://www.bjorner.com/still.htm#y91, *Still on the Road*, Retrieved 11/24/2016

[138] https://groups.google.com/forum/m/#!topic/alt.music.paul-simon/M8cKcjIkCxs, *S&G FAQ - Greg Nesteroff*, Retrieved 11/27/2106

[139] http://www.showbiz411.com/2010/06/01/paul-simon-may-record-with-bob-dylan-taking-catalog-back-to-sony, *Paul Simon May Record with Bob Dylan, Taking Catalog Back to Sony*, Roger Friedman, Showbiz 411. Retrieved 11/24/2016

In 1991, Dylan gave a major interview with Paul Zollo for *Song Talk* magazine. [140] According to a friend of Zollo's, one of the reasons he got the Dylan interview was because of a previous in-depth talk with Simon. In the Simon interview, he said the following about his change in songwriting from *Hey Schoolgirl* to *The Sound Of Silence*:

"Well . . . I'm trying to find out if there's anyone besides Bob Dylan who could have influenced me. But I can't really imagine . . . that there was . . ."

[140] *Songwriters On Songwriting - Expanded Edition*, Paul Zollo, Da Capo Press, New York, 1997

Bob Dylan and Van Morrison

August 31, 2010

George Ivan Morrison, OBE, was born on August 31, 1945. Van the Man and Bob Dylan have been friends and mutual admirers for decades. Dylan referred to Morrison as the *"great Irish poet, the Bard of Belfast,"* on *Theme Time Radio Hour*.

Morrison grew up in Belfast, Ireland. His father, George, traveled to Detroit in the early 1950s, and brought back a massive and diverse collection of vinyl, which educated and influenced the younger Morrison.

Dick Rowe, the man who turned down The Beatles, signed Morrison's band, Them, to Decca Records. They had a string of hit singles, including *Baby Please Don't Go/Gloria, Here Comes The Night, Mystic Eyes*, and a cover of Bob Dylan's *It's All Over Now, Baby Blue*. This recording was sampled by Beck on his 1996 track, *Jack-Ass*.

After Morrison left Them, the band's producer Bert Berns convinced him to come to New York and record in 1967. The sessions produced one of Morrison's most popular songs, *Brown-Eyed Girl*. Burns died suddenly on December 30, 1967, and Morrison was soon involved in some contractual disputes. He moved to Cambridge, Massachusetts, where he hung out with DJ and future J. Geils singer Peter Wolf, who promoted Morrison on his radio program. (Wolf also hung out with Dylan in Greenwich Village in the early 1960s.)

Morrison was a big fan of The Band. After recording his landmark album *Astral Weeks*, Morrison and his wife Janet Planet moved to Woodstock in February, 1969, partially because The Band created *Music From Big Pink* there. Morrison started hanging out with The Band, although he didn't get to know Dylan during this period.

The Band's influence is all over Morrison's hit album *Moondance*. *Brand New Day* was Morrison's response to first hearing The Band's version of Dylan's *I Shall Be Released*:

[Brand New Day] *"expressed a lot of hope. I was in Boston and having a hard job getting myself up spiritually...Then one day this song came on the FM station and it had this particular feeling and this particular groove and it was totally fresh. It seemed to me like things were making sense... I didn't know who the hell the artist was. It turned out to be The Band. I looked up at the sky and the sun started to shine and all of a sudden the song just came through my head. I started to write it down, right from "When all the dark clouds roll away.""* [141]

Appropriately enough, Van first shared the stage with Dylan at The Band's Last Waltz in 1976, singing back-up on that song.

Dylan toured with Morrison numerous times in the 1980s and 1990s. Morrison sang *Baby Blue* three times with Dylan on the 1984 European Tour (and, once, *Tupelo Honey*).

In 1989, Dylan spent some time with Morrison in Athens, Greece. The two songwriters were filmed at Philopappos (The Hill Of The Muses) on June 27, performing *Crazy Love, And It Stoned Me, Foreign Window*, and *One Irish Rover*. Some of the footage was used for the 1991 BBC documentary, *Arena: One Irish Rover – Van Morrison in Performance*. The next evening, Morrison joined Dylan on stage in Athens, singing *Crazy Love* and *Stoned Me*.

On February 6, 1991, when Dylan played in Dublin, Morrison again guested, with Dylan singing *Tupelo Honey* while Morrison sang *Why Must I Always Explain*. On June 8, Dylan joined Morrison during his opening set, playing harmonica on *Whenever God Shines His Light* and *Enlightenment*.

The night after Dylan played The Point in Dublin on February 5, 1993, Morrison played the same venue. Dylan played harmonica on *Baby Blue*, while Chrissie Hynde, Kris Kristofferson, and Steve Winwood joined on backing vocals. Later that year, on June 12, Dylan played a short set at London's

---

[141] *Van Morrison: Into the Music*, Ritchie Yorke, Futura Books, Leander, Texas, 1975

Fleadh Festival. Morrison joined Dylan for a version of *One Irish Rover*. When Dylan returned to The Point as the last stop of his spring 1995 tour, his was joined during the encores by Carole King, Elvis Costello, and Morrison.

The next on-stage collaboration was at Norway's Molde Jazz Festival on July 19, 1996, when Morrison sang *I Shall Be Released* and *Real Real Gone*, which, like *One Irish Rover*, was covered by Dylan on his own.

In early 1998, Dylan and Morrison toured North America. While sharing a bill at The Theater in Madison Square Garden, Dylan joined Morrison's band for a duet of the Webb Pierce/Merle Kilgore song, *More and More* on January 18th, and Carl Perkins' *Blue Suede Shoes* three nights later (Perkins had died on the 19th). While playing in Boston on the 24th, Dylan again joined Morrison for *Blue Suede Shoes* while Van joined Dylan during his set for *Knockin' On Heaven's Door*.

In May of 1998, Dylan and Morrison toured again, this time with Joni Mitchell. On the 16th, in Gorge, Washington, Van and Joni reprised their roles in The Last Waltz by joining Bob for *I Shall Be Released*. In June, during Dylan's summer European tour, Dylan and Morrison shared the bill for a handful of shows, with Morrison singing *Heaven's Door* with Dylan in Birmingham, England. In September, Dylan and Morrison hit the road again, but did not perform together. Dylan and Morrison were scheduled to tour Europe together in 1997, but Dylan had to cancel while he was recovering from histoplasmosis.

Dylan played numerous Morrison songs on his *Theme Time Radio Hour* program, including *Brown Eyed Girl* (1967), *One Irish Rover* (1986), *Youth of 1000 Summers* (1990), and *The Last Laugh* with Mark Knopfler (2000).

Both Dylan and Morrison have each reportedly used *The Web Sheriff* to protect their material from being exploited on the web.

I was fortunate enough to meet Van Morrison in January, 1998. I was invited to a lunchtime meeting with employees of Sony Records in Harvard Square, in Cambridge, Massachusetts. Dylan and Morrison were scheduled to play the Fleet Center (the old Boston Garden) that evening. I looked to my right and saw Morrison arriving alone, then walking over to sit by a window at the opposite side of the dining hall. I do not know what he ordered, but I did see a couple of large glasses filled with what looked like orange juice. The Sony meeting coincidentally ended at the same time as Morrison ended his meal. As we all headed for the exit, a rep I knew from a different label was arriving. It turned out that she was there to meet Van for lunch, but was late. She knew I was a fan, and introduced me to the Belfast Cowboy. I said something like, *"It's an honor to meet you, Mr. Morrison."*

Van the Man grumbled something, then disappeared behind a partition.

Bob Dylan and Marianne Faithfull

December 29, 2010

Marianne Faithfull was born on December 29, 1946. For more than four decades, Marianne Faithfull, despite personal ups and downs, has been a successful singer, songwriter, actress, and author. While she is most closely associated with The Rolling Stones, Faithfull has also been friends with Bob Dylan since the mid-1960s, and hung out with him in his hotel room during his U.K. tours of 1965 and 1966.

In her autobiography, *Faithfull,* she described Dylan as *"nothing less than the hippest person on earth. The zeitgeist streamed through him like electricity . . . (he) stared at me for so long I thought I was going to melt."* [142]

Marianne appeared in the 1965 U.K. tour documentary, *Dont Look Back.* She can be seen about 31 minutes in, sitting in a chair while Joan Baez sang and Bob Dylan typed.

From the DVD commentary by Bob Neuwirth, to director D.A. Pennebaker:

"There's Marianne Faithfull, wondering about her husband John (Dunbar) who was pacing outside, nervously. Do you remember . . . we went to an Indian restaurant, and Bob sat at one end, and (Marianne) sat on the other. Bob was, kinda, obviously, the master, the head of the table . . . and she was telling about her first big hit, she then said, 'Well I had this hit, then I got pregnant'. Then Joan said, 'get pregnant, and you fall right off the charts.'" [143]

Faithfull also recalled an early encounter, when Dylan spent many hours writing a poem for her, with the expectation of them sleeping together. Although Faithfull was interested, she refused because she was about to marry her first husband, with whom she was expecting a child. *"I told him all this and he was furious and ripped the poem up in front of me. We are still very fond of each other and still talk about that night. I'll always say to him, 'But Bob, I was only 17' and he always says, 'Yeah, but I was only 22 myself!' ... The saddest thing for me was not that we didn't go to bed together,"* Faithfull wrote in her autobiography, *"but that I never got to see that poem."* [144]

Faithfull also witnessed other pivotal events, including Dylan cutting up a newspaper in front of a reporter to explain how he wrote his book, *Tarantula,* and walking out of a room when Paul McCartney played an experimental track from the upcoming Beatles album, *Revolver.*

Marianne got hold of *The Basement Tapes* demos in 1967 or '68, and, according to an article in *Mojo* magazine, played them for her boyfriend, Mick Jagger. These recordings helped influence the direction of the Stones from the dead-end of psychedelia to the "golden age" of the Stones, beginning with *Jumping Jack Flash* and *Beggar's Banquet* in 1968, on through to 1972's *Exile On Main Street.*

In 1970, Faithfull recorded an LP titled *Rich Kid Blues,* [145] but it remained in the vaults until the mid-1980s. The released version included three Dylan covers - *It's All Over Now, Baby Blue, It Takes A Lot To Laugh, It Takes A Train To Cry,* and *Visions Of Johanna.* It was recorded just before Faithfull hit rock bottom (and later, resurrected herself). Faithfull reportedly hates the album, but many disagree with her assessment.

According to *Dylan Cover,* Faithfull also covered *Blowin' In The Wind, I'll Be Your Baby Tonight, I'll Keep It With Mine,* and *Gotta Serve Somebody.*

---

[142] *Faithfull: An Autobiography,* Marianne Faithfull and David Dalton, Little Brown and Company, New York, 1994

[143] *Dont Look Back,* D.A. Pennebaker, Criterion Collection, 2015

[144] http://www.twentyfourbit.com/2009/03/marianne-faithful-reveals-bob-dylans-poetry-sex-ploy/, *Marianne Faithful Reveals Bob Dylan's Poetry Sex Ploy,* Retrieved 11/24/2016

[145] http://www.mariannefaithfull.org.uk/music/rich-kid-blues/, Discography: *Rich Kid Blues,* Marianne Faithfull, Retrieved 11/24/2016

On February 17, 2003, Dylan met Faithfull backstage at the Sydney Entertainment Centre after his Sydney concert.

Twenty years ago, when asked what she wished for Dylan on his 50th birthday, Faithfull replied, *"A brand-new leopard-skin pill-box hat."* Interestingly, in 1989, Rolling Stones guitarist Keith Richards commissioned a *"Brand new leopard-skin pill-box hat"* silver skull box with 18ct gold lid, as a gift for Dylan's 50th birthday. [146]

---

[146] http://www.courtsandhackett.com/ch_pillbox.html, *Brand New Leopard-Skin Pill-box Hat 1989*, Retrieved 11/24/2016

Tina Turner goes country with Dylan covers

May 6, 2011

Anna Mae Bullock is one of the most successful rock singers of all time, selling over 180 million albums and singles since the late 1950s. You probably know her better as Tina Turner.

In August, 1974, while still a member of the Ike and Tina Turner Revue, Tina released her first solo album, titled *Tina Turns The Country On!* The United Artists LP, as the title suggested, was rooted in country music, and featured compositions by Hank Snow, Kris Kristofferson, Dolly Parton, and James Taylor, as well as two by Bob Dylan - *Tonight I'll Be Staying Here With You*, and *(S)he Belongs To Me*. Turner received a Grammy Nomination for Best R&B Vocal Performance, Female, in 1974, but the release was only a moderate success, and has never been issued on CD.

In 1971, the Ike & Tina Turner Revue had a major hit with a cover of the Creedence Clearwater Revival song *Proud Mary*. In 1987, at an impromptu jam with Taj Mahal and Jesse Ed Davis at Hollywood's Palomino Club, the song's author, John Fogerty, found himself on stage with Dylan and George Harrison. Fogerty has stopped performing Creedence material since the early 1970s because he did not want to add any revenue to the pockets of Fantasy Records owner, Saul Zaentz. At Dylan's urging, Fogerty played it for the first time in years at the Palamino that night, saying, *"We're gonna do this, ah, because Bob Dylan asked me to do this."* Dylan reportedly told Fogerty he should start playing his Creedence material because *"if you don't, the whole world's gonna think* Proud Mary *is Tina Turner's song."*

In 1985, Dylan and Turner participated in the USA For Africa and Live-Aid projects. They sang on *We Are The World*, both in the studio and as the finale at Live Aid, although Dylan walked out halfway through the Philadelphia performance.

Dylan had the unfortunate honor of closing Live Aid in Philadelphia. I say "unfortunate" because his set was disrupted by the backstage set-up for the *We Are The World* finale, and he had to follow a sexy, energetic duet by Turner and Mick Jagger, which included Jagger ripping off Tina's skirt. (What that had to do with starving children, I don't know).

Listen to her unique, soulful interpretation of *She Belongs to Me*. The lyrics could now be addressed to Dylan himself: *"Salute him when his birthday comes."*

Stephen Stills

January 3, 2011

"Those first passionate (songs) are really special. And later in life you might get deeper and more resonant and more crafted, but they're not as free as those first ones. You end up out-crafting yourself. You get too cute. Losing the point. Getting contrived. Which is why I admire Bob Dylan so much. He's managed not to do that." - Stephen Stills to Paul Zollo [147]

Stephen Arthur Stills was born on January 3, 1945, in Dallas, Texas. The first two-time Rock and Roll Hall of Fame inductee has been a member of numerous iconic bands, including Buffalo Springfield, Manassas, and Crosby, Stills, Nash & Young.

Like Bob Dylan, Stills went to Greenwich Village in the early 1960's, but arrived just as Dylan was moving on to bigger things. Stills told *Rolling Stone* that when he arrived, he had heard a story which he admitted may not have really happened. After his initial success, Dylan reportedly raced through Greenwich Village, wearing a black top hat and big black cape, carrying with him about a hundred one dollar bills. He found a *"wino … in a doorway,"* and apparently *"made it rain"* (to use a modern phrase), with the money flying everywhere. [148]

Late in the decade, Dylan and Stills were both approached to contribute new material for the film *Easy Rider*. Uncredited, Dylan wrote a few lines for Roger McGuinn's *Ballad Of Easy Rider*, while Stills' song, *Find The Cost Of Freedom*, was not used. [149]

In 1970, while playing the Fillmore East with CSNY, Stills reportedly decided to hog the spotlight one night in order to impress Bob Dylan, who was sitting in the audience.

On July 22, 1974, Dylan previewed at least a half-dozen *Blood On The Tracks* songs for Stills and Tim Drummond at the St. Paul Hilton Hotel, after a CSNY gig. [150]

In 1976, Stills and Dylan appeared at both Night Of The Hurricane 2 and The Last Waltz, although they never appeared on stage at the same time.

Dylan and Stills finally collaborated at The Absolutely Unofficial Blue Jeans Bash (For Arkansas), as part of the Bill Clinton Presidential Inaugural. The performance took place at the National Building Museum in Washington, D.C., on January 17, 1993. Here's the breakdown, according to Olof Bjorner: [151]

1. *To Be Alone With You* (Bob Dylan-lead vocal)

2. *Key To The Highway* (Stephen Stills-lead vocal)

3. *I Shall Be Released* (The Cate Brothers - lead vocals)

4. *(I Don't Wanna To) Hang Up My Rock And Roll Shoes*

Bob Dylan (guitar), Stephen Stills (guitar), Rick Danko (bass), Garth Hudson (keyboards), Levon Helm (drums), Jimmy Weider (guitar), Richard Bell (piano), Randy Ciarlante (drums), Ronnie Hawkins (guitar), Don Johnson (guitar) and The Cate Brothers.

---

[147] *Songwriters On Songwriting - Expanded Edition*, Paul Zollo, Da Capo Press, New York, 1997

[148] http://www.bobdylanroots.com/stills.html, *The Rolling Stone Interviews, Vol. 2*, New York, NY, Editors of Rolling Stone, Warner Library, 1973

[149] https://30daysout.wordpress.com/2009/10/07/40-years-out-easy-rider/, *40 Years Out: "Easy Rider"*, Retrieved 11/25/2016

[150] *Bob Dylan: Behind the Shades Revisited*, Clinton Heylin, William Morrow, 2001

[151] http://www.bjorner.com/DSN13790%20-%201993%20Early%20Sessions.htm#DSN13810, *Still on the Road*, Retrieved 11/25/2016

Stills covered *Ballad Of Hollis Brown* on his 1991 solo album *Stills Alone*, and *Girl From The North Country* on the CD/DVD set, *Live at Shepherd's Bush*. The latter song is slated for inclusion on the next CSN album. (Note: The project was abandoned.) Stills also cut *It Takes A Lot To Laugh, It Takes A Train To Cry* with Al Kooper for the *Super Session* album.

When CSNY reunited in 1999 to record the album *Looking Forward*, it included a song called *Seen Enough*, which was "inspired by" Bob Dylan's *Subterranean Homesick Blues*. (Originally, Dylan received a co-writing credit.) [152]

On *Theme Time Radio Hour*, for the *Birds* episode, Dylan couldn't decide whether to play The Beatles' *Blackbird* or Buffalo Springfield's *Bluebird*, so he flipped a coin. *Bluebird*, written by Stills, won.

Note: For his first studio session ever, [153] Harvey Brooks played bass on Dylan's *Highway 61 Revisited* album. Later, he played on 1968's *Super Session* album with Michael Bloomfield, Al Kooper and Stephen Stills. Stills has also played at the three most famous rock festivals of the late 1960s: Monterey Pop, Woodstock, and Altamont.

[152] http://www.human-highway.org/pages/album/LF.html, *Looking Forward* (October 26 1999, Reprise 9 47436-2) Crosby, Stills, Nash, & Young. Retrieved 11/25/2016

[153] http://www.goldminemag.com/article/harvey-brooks-electric-flag-and-beyond, *Harvey Brooks: Electric Flag and beyond*, Retrieved 11/25/2016

The Bob Dylan - Neil Young saga

March 26, 2011

Bob Dylan and Neil Young are friends and mutual admirers. They have appeared on stage together numerous times, and have even referred to each other in their songs.

Thrasher's Wheat is the premier Neil Young fan site. It's not just my opinion - Neil Young himself has acknowledged the site, and expressed his appreciation and support for all their dedication and hard work:

"This is the most respected site on the net for this type of activity. Let me take this opportunity to thank you for your interest in what I am doing." [154]

Webmaster "Thrasher" had been dealing with the Bob Dylan vs. Neil Young comparisons for years. He discusses the "battle" here:

Bob Dylan and Neil Young: A Fascinating Saga by Thrasher [155]

The relationship between Bob Dylan and Neil Young is a fascinating saga.

While Dylan is universally acknowledged as the most influential and important 20th-century singer-songwriter performing today, Young is among a very small contingent of contenders for second place. Young's integrity and credibility place him among a distinguished group of artists to be compared to Dylan.

As a long time Neil Young fan, we've never really perceived any rivalry whatsoever between the Bob and Neil fan bases, and find the whole Bob vs. Neil discussions to be a bit tiresome. It seems no matter your preference, both men are living legends and musical geniuses.

Nevertheless, the whole Bob and Neil business can be quite humorous.

Back in 2006, we linked over to a blog post on Top 10 Reasons Why Neil Young is Better Than Bob Dylan. The tongue-in-cheek posting created quite a bit of an uproar generating nearly 100 comments from outraged Dylan fans. So what exactly would any Dylan fan find objectionable??

Top 10 Reasons Why Neil Young is Better Than Bob Dylan: [156]

1. Better Voice

2. Better Guitar Player

3. Better Good-to-Bad Song Ratio

4. Neil Never Sold His Music To a Commercial

5. Neil Embraces the Younger Generation of Musicians

6. No One Plays Neil Songs Better Than Neil

7. Farm Aid & The Bridge School Benefit Concerts

8. Neil Is More Diverse

9. Neil Never Played With The Dead (Note - Yes he has! - HL)

10. Because I Like to Piss People Off

---

[154] http://neilyoungnews.thrasherswheat.org/2010/08/vista-and-muse.html, *The Vista and The Muse*, Retrieved 11/25/2016

[155] http://neilyoungnews.thrasherswheat.org, Courtesy "Thrasher"

[156] http://neilyoungnews.thrasherswheat.org/2006/01/top-10-reasons-why-neil-young-is.html, *Top 10 Reasons Why Neil Young is Better Than Bob Dylan*, Retrieved 11/25/2016

The Eight Track Mind *blog goes on to deconstruct each argument point by point. To say some of the reasoning is provocative would be an understatement.*

In "retaliation," the Dylan community returned fire with both humor and wit to which we waved the flag on Top 10 Reasons Not to Goof Around With Bob Dylan Fans. [157] *For example, Dylan fan Mikey spoofs:*

More Top Ten Reasons Dylan is Better:

1. Neil's tendency to make one-off right wing political statements (e.g. "Let's Roll").

2. Neil's Everybody's Rockin'.

3. Neil does not regularly tour with Crazy Horse, his best band and he obviously knows this fact.

4. Neil stopped selling "Greendale High" t-shirts on-line.

5. Bob's influence allowed The Beatles to write and record Rubber Soul.

6. Bob is an American and Neil is Canadian.

7. If there is another CSNY reunion and I have to see Graham Nash on stage, I may off myself.

8. More Star Wars Jawas on stage would have made Live Rust *a better video.*

9. Neil has never been called Judas.

10. Neil hasn't invited me to the Broken Arrow ranch yet.

In the end, this comment from Karen sums up where many serious music lovers stand on the Bob vs. Neil debate:

"I love Neil Young. I am a fanatic. First and foremost, a Rustie (Neil Young fan). But I also love Bob Dylan.

"Neil has been very clear over the years on his own admiration and appreciation for Bob Dylan, he (Neil) has called Dylan the master on several occasions. Neil has said many times over that Dylan was an inspiration to him. One of the funniest, more recent comments was during a recent radio interview about Prairie Wind, *Neil's latest album, the interviewer had apparently heard that Neil does a great impression of Bob Dylan (presumably Dylan's speaking voice, given the context of the interview.) Neil pauses, and as his manager literally breaks into the studio to make sure Neil is NOT going to impersonate Bob Dylan on air, Neil says, Impersonate Bob Dylan, huh? Hey, I've been doing that for forty years. Haven't you been listening?"*

Great comment. Makes it clear how Neil feels about Dylan. Neil Young is my Mecca, no one loves the man and his music more than I do, but we all should bow down to Mr. Bob Dylan. Noooo question. So. Whether you like Bob, Neil, both or neither, it's all one song..."

"I'm listening to Neil Young, I gotta turn up the sound

Someone's always yellin', 'Turn him down'."

Bob Dylan's *Highlands* (Copyright © 1997 by Special Rider Music)

"You're invisible

You got too many secrets Bob Dylan said that Somethin' like that"

Neil Young's *Bandit* (Copyright © 2003 Silver Fiddle Music ASCAP)

---

[157] http://neilyoungnews.thrasherswheat.org/2006/01/top-10-reasons-not-to-goof-with-bob.html, *Top 10 Reasons Not to Goof With Bob Dylan Fans*, Retrieved 11/25/2016

Neil Young debuts new song about Dylan's 'Like A Rolling Stone' in Albuquerque

August 4, 2012

Neil Young and Crazy Horse began their first joint tour in eight years at the Hard Rock Pavilion in Albuquerque, New Mexico, last night. On stage, they mixed old material and new, with concert staples like *Powderfinger* and *Cinnamon Girl* alternating with seven live debuts, six apparently from their next, still unreleased album. Of special interest to Bob Dylan fans is a new song reportedly referencing the 1965 hit single, *Like A Rolling Stone.*

Rolling Stone magazine reported the lyrics read, in part, *"Poetry rolling off his tongue like Hanks (sic) Williams Jr. bubblegum…"* [158] Maybe it was *"Hank Williams chewin' bubblegum?"* Only time will tell.

According to posts at Young fan site *Thrasher's Wheat*, the song is apparently called *Twisted Road*, the same title given to his 2010-11 solo Le Noise tour. Young referenced Dylan in the song *Bandit* from 2003's *Greendale* album.

Young has interpreted Dylan songs throughout his career. Since 1976, Young has covered *All Along The Watchtower*, *Everything Is Broken*, *Just Like Tom Thumb's Blues*, *My Back Pages*, *Blowin' In The Wind*, *I Shall Be Released*, *Forever Young*, *This Wheel's On Fire*, and with the band Spirit in 1976, *Like A Rolling Stone*, according to *Dylan Cover*.

In the fall of 2002, Dylan frequently covered Young's *Old Man* in concert. Young and Dylan shared the stage numerous times between 1975 and 1994.

So, I attempted to contact Crazy Horse drummer Ralph Molina to hopefully get some additional information, or at least clarification, on *Twisted Road*:

Mr. Molina ... Are you able to shed any light on the song "Twisted Road" ... ?

Here was the typed reply, from 3:47 a.m. this morning:

"It has nothing to do with… bob. Just the, rolling stone line… Roy (Orbison) is in there too. It's just a song. Songs and people, that inspire… we don't ask each other, what a song is about, nor why, etc… and please… call me Ralph…"

---

[158] http://www.rollingstone.com/music/news/neil-young-and-crazy-horse-launch-tour-with-new-tunes-in-albuquerque-20120804, Neil Young and Crazy Horse Launch Tour With New Tunes in Albuquerque. Retrieved 11/25/2016

Neil Young upgrading sound of classic Bob Dylan albums for new 'Pono' device

September 30, 2012

Neil Young has been upgrading the sound of classic Bob Dylan albums for a new device he's helped develop called a "Pono."

While appearing on *The Late Show With David Letterman* last Thursday, Young discussed a variety of subjects, including his stake in Lionel Trains, his LincVolt car, a new memoir (*Waging Heavy Peace*), and last weekend's concert in Central Park with Crazy Horse.

He also brought a new hand-held, pyramid-shaped, iPod-like device, which, according to Young, has superior sound. It's called a "Pono," which Young explained is Hawaiian for "righteous." (Pono rhymes with Ono, as in Yoko.) Young pulled out a "working prototype" from his jacket pocket.

Young has been criticizing mp3 and other inferior audio formats for years, because he believes "sound matters," and music suffers when heard through below-par audio systems. He told Letterman the Pono *"plays back master files ... the best sound anybody can get ... This is what they get in the studio, the highest resolution ... "*

Then Neil dropped this bombshell:

"Tomorrow we're in the studio. We're transferring Highway 61 Revisited *from the original tapes, and* Freewheelin' *from the original tapes... of Bob Dylan classics. And we're negotiating with Sony (which owns Columbia Records, Dylan's label) so that we can put all these things out."* [159]

---

[159] *The Last Show with David Letterman,* 9/27/2012, Worldwide Pants/CBS-TV

Jewel: On tour, Bob Dylan, Neil Young were 'mentors' early in her career

February 5, 2013

During an interview today, [160] the singer Jewel referred to Neil Young and Bob Dylan as her "mentors" when she was a support act during their respective tours early in her career.

At the end of a nearly one-hour interview on Howard Stern's SiriusXM satellite radio show this morning, Jewel said that after her first album *Pieces Of You*, produced by Young's pedal steel guitarist Ben Keith, stalled after selling 3,000 copies during the grunge/gothic era, she was booked as Dylan's support act, because *"he believed in me."*

Jewel said they were her mentors. She went on to say Dylan *"went over my lyrics with me every night,"* and gave her advice on books and music to explore. His belief in her, she said, gave her confidence.

After touring with Dylan, Jewel said she went into the studio to record a follow-up album, and began changing her sound to get airplay. She abandoned her album when Young asked her to be his support act. He told her to *"stick to what you do … just like, screw it all."* Soon afterwards, she said her song *You Were Meant For Me* began to get airplay, and began selling half a million records a month.

The interview came to a sudden halt at this point, as Jewel had another commitment.

---

[160] *The Howard Stern Show, 2/5/2013*, SiriusXM

Neil Innes (Rutles, Monty Python) 'salutes' Bob Dylan

May 15, 2011

Last night, I attended a delightful concert by Neil Innes at the Narrows Center for the Arts in Fall River, Massachusetts.

Neil Innes infiltrated my life surreptitiously in the mid-1970s. He got his start with the Bonzo Dog (Doo Dah) Band in the late 1960s, and I heard their legendary *The Intro and the Outro* numerous times on WNEW-FM in New York. Next, I saw The Beatles' TV movie, *Magical Mystery Tour*, in a movie theater as a double feature with Mel Brooks' *Blazing Saddles*. The Fab's film included the Bonzos performing a song called *Death Cab For Cutie* (Yes, that's where they got their name).

In the spring of 1976, I bought tickets to see a live Monty Python's Flying Circus matinee performance at New York's City Center. While I knew the Pythons would put on an hysterically funny show, there was an unexpected treat waiting for me.

Neil Innes was a name I barely knew. I was aware he was in *Monty Python and the Holy Grail* (which I had seen about eight times in the theater) but was not prepared for him to almost steal the show. He was featured in at least four bits - *How Sweet to Be An Idiot* (with a giant plastic duck on his head), Stoop Solo's *Short Blues* (performed on stilts), *I'm The Urban Spaceman* (the only hit single from the Bonzo days - originally produced by Paul McCartney - and accompanied by a tap-dancing Carol Cleveland), and, as Raymond Scum, *Protest Song*.

I was sitting in the audience with five of my high school friends, none of whom understood my Bob Dylan fixation. When Innes began *Protest Song*, complete with acoustic guitar and screeching harmonica, I could feel them looking at me to see my reaction. I doubt anyone laughed harder than I did. Most Dylan imitations are not very funny - in fact, they are usually obvious, superficial, and predictable. However, Innes nailed it by getting to the heart of Dylan's art, and turning it inside-out, with accuracy, affection, and humor.

After the show, while the Pythons were signing autographs by the backstage door, Innes slipped away when Eric Idle arrived, although my friend, future comedian Paul Bond did ask Terry Jones what he thought of New York. He answered, in his high-pitched lady Python voice, *"Better than a dead crab!"*

Innes went on to other projects, most notably The Rutles, a George Harrison-approved, Python-associated Beatles parody featuring Innes as "Ron Nasty." Besides Innes' portrayal of the Lennon-esque character, the highlights included 20 songs he wrote in about a week, all modeled after the Fab's catalog and every bit as brilliant as *Protest Song*. The secret of Innes' musical genius is his ability to mock "heavy" pop music philosophy with songs that are every bit as insightful, without the pretentiousness.

Last night's solo concert in Fall River was an entertaining mix of story and song, loosely based around the theme "A People's Guide to World Domination." Innes' shows continues to evolve as he weaves music and anecdotes from his days with the Bonzos and Python (*Brave Sir Robin*, Bruce's *Philosopher Song*, and an out-take from The Holy Grail, *Run Away*) to the Rutles (including Ron Nasty's last song), up to "modem times" (pun intended, from the song *Face Mail In The Meat Zone*).

After the show, Innes met with audience members. When I told him about this column, he said, *"Please wish the great man 'Many Happy Returns' for me!"*

Unfortunately, in order to fit in some of Innes' newer material, we did not get to hear some classics like *Urban Spaceman* and *Protest Song*.

Trivia: The band Oasis borrowed part of the melody included in their hit *Whatever* from *How Sweet To Be An Idiot*. Innes' publisher sued, and Innes is now credited as the co-author, according to an article in *Q Magazine*. Innes included the melodic line in question on The Rutles' 1996 reunion track, *Shangri-La*.

The night Bob Dylan offered *Just Like A Woman* to Otis Redding

September 9, 2011

Soul legend Otis Ray Redding, Jr., was born on September 9, 1941, and grew up in Macon, Georgia. Like Dylan, he was heavily influenced by Little Richard, who also lived in Macon. Also like Dylan, Redding wrote much of his own material.

In early April, 1966, Redding played four nights at the Whiskey A Go Go, with the Rising Sons opening. According to a contemporary article in the *Los Angeles Times*, [161] "Drawn by his growing popularity, a fervid audience shoe-horned into the club . . . Redding was assured of an In Group [sic] following Thursday night (April 7) when from among his spectators emerged Bob Dylan, trailed by an entourage of camp followers." Dylan evidently was scheduled to fly to Hawaii that day, but delayed the trip, presumably to oversee the mixing for *Blonde On Blonde*.

Among those followers attending the show with Dylan was filmmaker D.A. Pennebaker. On the commentary track included on the Criterion edition of the Monterey Pop DVD, Pennebaker said that he first saw Redding when Dylan took him to see him at the Whiskey.

In a 1969 *Rolling Stone* interview with publisher Jann Wenner, [162] Dylan said that, after Redding's Whiskey A Go Go gig, he was asked if he had any material he could cover. Dylan played him a dub of the as-yet-unreleased track, *Just Like a Woman*. Dylan said Redding planned on recording it, but never did. He also said their paths never crossed again.

Here's Robbie Robertson's take: [163]

"We were in Los Angeles, and we found out that Otis Redding was playing somewhere. So, the manager at the time — Albert Grossman — hooks it up for Bob and I to meet Otis, and [Redding manager, later Capricorn Records impresario] *Phil Walden. So, we get together and I'm kind of pitching this song, and Otis says: 'That sounds great to me.'"*

(According to Dylan's drummer Mickey Jones, Redding was very impressed and told Dylan that he would record the song as soon as he could. [164])

When the song was not included on Redding's next album, Robertson asked Walden to explain. Apparently, Redding *"went in and recorded it, and he couldn't sing the bridge. He said, 'I don't know how to sing the bridge.'"* Walden told Robertson, *"In the bridge, the words are about amphetamines and pearls, and he couldn't get those words to come out of his mouth in a truthful way. So, we had to put it aside."*

Redding told *Melody Maker*, *"Yes, I like Dylan — he's my favorite singer now. I love the Rolling Stones as well … Bobby is the greatest, though. He gave me* Just Like a Woman *to make as a record, y'know. But I didn't do it because I just didn't feel it. Mind you, I dig his work like mad."* [165]

Bob Dylan played some of Redding's recordings on his *Theme Time Radio Hour* show, including *Cigarettes and Coffee, I've Got Dreams to Remember*, and a "Stay in school" promotional ad.

On March 3, 1970, during the *Self Portrait* sessions, Dylan ran through *(Sittin' On) The Dock Of The Bay*, and eventually covered it live at the Champs de Brionne Music Theater, George, Washington,

161 http://www.otisredding.com/2010/05/buy-now-otis-redding-live-on-the-sunset-strip/ Dead Link

162 http://www.jannswenner.com/Archives/Bob_Dylan.aspx, *The Rolling Stone Interview: Bob Dylan*, by Jann S. Wenner, RS47: November 29, 1969. Retrieved 11/25/2016

163 http://somethingelsereviews.com/2014/01/15/he-would-just-tear-it-up-robbie-robertson-wanted-otis-redding-to-cover-a-key-bob-dylan-song/, *'He would just tear it up': Robbie Robertson wanted Otis Redding to cover a key Bob Dylan song*, Retrieved 11/25/2016

164 http://www.newworldencyclopedia.org/entry/Otis_Redding, *Otis Redding*, Retrieved 11/25/2016

165 https://www.theguardian.com/music/2015/oct/21/otis-redding-interview-rocks-back-pages-mr-cool-and-the-clique-from-memphis, *Otis Redding: Mr Cool and the clique from Memphis*, Retrieved 11/25/2016

on August 18, 1990. Dylan also participated in an all-star version of Redding's *I Can't Turn You Loose*, at the Guitar Legends Expo '92, (Leyendas de la Guitarra), Auditorio de la Cartuja, Seville, Spain, on October 17, 1991, featuring Keith Richards, Dave Edmunds, Richard Thompson, Phil Manzanera, Robert Cray and Steve Cropper on guitars, Jack Bruce and Charley Drayton on bass, Chuck Leavell and Ivan Neville on keyboards, Simon Phillips and Steve Jordan on drums, Ray Cooper on percussion, and the Miami Horns.

Steve Goodman, Monty Hall, and Robert Milkwood Thomas

May 18, 2011

Steve Goodman was a singer, songwriter, guitarist, and legendary Chicago Cubs fan. He is probably best known as the author of *City Of New Orleans*, a song recorded by Arlo Guthrie, Willie Nelson, Johnny Cash, and Judy Collins, among others. ABC News' morning show, *Good Morning America*, which started in the mid-1970s, took its name and original theme music from the chorus of this song.

He also wrote David Allan Coe's *You Never Even Called Me By My Name*, and a few songs dedicated to his beloved Cubs - *A Dying Cub Fan's Last Request*, *When the Cubs Go Marching In* and *Go, Cubs, Go*.

He was discovered by Kris Kristofferson, after opening for one of his shows in Chicago:

As it happened, Kristofferson was singing a song written by Paul Anka. Anka was also playing a different club in town and on one of his nights off, he decided to drop by and listen to Kris's set. While waiting to listen to Kristofferson's set, Anka listened to Goodman's show. Anka was so impressed that he paid Goodman's way to New York and set up for some demo's to be cut. This led to his first record contract with Buddah. [166]

His eponymous debut included *City Of New Orleans*, but was not a big seller. For his next album, 1973's *Somebody Else's Troubles*, Goodman received help from some heavyweight friends - John Prine, Marvin Gardens, and Robert Milkwood Thomas. Gardens was actually Jimmy Buffett, and Thomas was none other than Bob Dylan. (One of Dylan Thomas' best-known works was his verse play *Under Milk Wood*). Dylan apparently was unable to show up on time for the *Somebody Else's Troubles*, which disappointed Goodman. [167]

According to *Searching For A Gem*: [168]

Bob took part in the Steve Goodman Somebody Else's Troubles sessions at Atlantic Recording Studio, New York, in mid-Sep 1972. ...It was presumably released as an A-side to coincide with the 1972 US Presidential election, but then dropped from the 1973 album because it was no longer topical! ... It first appeared on album on The Essential Steve Goodman. *Buddah Records US 2LP compilation, 1976.*

For *Election Year Rag* and *Somebody's Else's Troubles*, Dylan played piano and provided harmony vocals.

One of my favorite examples of a Dylan passage incorporated into another song is Goodman's *Door Number Three*, written with Buffett. The song was included on the 1975 album, *Jessie's Jig and Other Favorites*, and includes one of Dylan's most famous verses in a song based on the game show, *Let's Make A Deal*.

Goodman died in 1984 at the age of 36, after a 16-year battle with leukemia. On August 3, 2010, President Barack Obama signed into law a bill to rename a Chicago post office after Goodman.

(2016 update: The Chicago Cubs finally won the World Series for the first time in 108 years.)

---

[166] http://steve-goodman.hegewisch.net/newbio.html, *The Professional Life*, Retrieved 11/25/2016

[167] http://steve-goodman.hegewisch.net/newbio.html, *The Professional Life*, Retrieved 11/25/2016

[168] http://www.searchingforagem.com/1970s/1972.htm, *Searching For A Gem - Bob Dylan's Officially Released Rarities and Obscurities*, Audio: 1972. Retrieved 11/25/2016

Bryan Ferry

April 6, 2011

"No, it's not atomic rain, it's just a hard rain. It isn't the fallout rain. I mean some sort of end that's just gotta happen... In the last verse, when I say, 'the pellets of poison are flooding the waters', that means all the lies that people get told on their radios and in their newspapers." – Bob Dylan, Studs Terkel's Wax Museum, 1963. [169]

Bryan Ferry, solo artist, former lead singer of Roxy Music, and debonair Bob Dylan interpreter, spoke to NY Rock about Dylan in 2002. He said he covered so many of Dylan's songs because of *"The quality of the writing, really. Simple as that. Beautiful words. It's very nice as a singer to do great songs, which have wonderful lyrics and strong feelings underneath the song."* Even then, Ferry had been talking about recording an album's worth of Dylan's songs. However, at the time he said he didn't have any plans to do so, but added, *"I mean, there are so many of his songs that I like that I could easily do that one day."*

Ferry added that he *"never have (and) probably never shall"* meet Dylan, but liked the idea of singing a duet with him. *"Wouldn't that be nice? That would be a very good idea. He's a friend of Dave Stewart's, who I know."* [170]

Ferry has sprinkled Dylan songs throughout his solo career: *A Hard Rain's A-Gonna Fall* (1973), *It Ain't Me, Babe* (1974), and *Don't Think Twice, It's All Right* and *It's All Over Now, Baby Blue* (2002). Of course, in 2007, Ferry did release *Dylanesque*, a collection of 10 Dylan covers, plus *Baby, Let Me Follow You Down*.

I've always been intrigued by Ferry's suave persona tackling Dylan's more rootsy material. Ferry's take on *Hard Rain*, in particular, has always been one of my favorites. I remember someone describing this unique take as the song being sung from the point of view of . . . Satan! Talk about taking someone's song and making it his own.

Bryan, this one's for you.

---

[169] http://www.slate.com/blogs/browbeat/2013/12/16/bob_dylan_interview_by_studs_terkel_in_1963_on_wfmt_listen_audio.html, *When Studs Terkel Talked With Bob Dylan*, Retrieved 11/27/2016

[170] http://www.nyrock.com/interviews/2002/ferry_int.asp, *An Interview with Bryan Ferry*, Talia Soghomonian, NY Rock, Retrieved 11/25/2016

Robyn Hitchcock on Bob Dylan, *The Basement Tapes*, and Greek Curses

February, 2015

Who better to discuss Bob Dylan and the Band's legendary 1967 *Basement Tapes* sessions with than Robyn Hitchcock? Who better to analyze why a bunch of half-baked songs by a room full of fully-baked musicians would have such an influence on music, which still resonates to this day?

Like Dylan, Hitchcock's career has lasted decades, covering a multitude of styles, collaborations, and media. His desire to become a songwriter was triggered by such poetic Dylan compositions as *Visions of Johanna* back in the 1960s. Besides the 20-plus albums of original material he has released since the 1970s, Hitchcock has sporadically covered Dylan's songs, including two all-Dylan shows last May to celebrate the bard of Hibbing's 73rd birthday, with one focusing exclusively on *The Basement Tapes*. Like Dylan, Hitchcock writes, paints, and draws, has appeared in films (including three directed by Jonathan Demme), and continues to release some of the best music of his career, including 2014's folk-influenced *The Man Upstairs,* modeled after Judy Collins' 1967 album, *Wildflowers. The Man Upstairs* is a collection of half covers, half originals produced by Joe Boyd, who, among his many accomplishments, mixed the sound for the 1965 Newport Folk Festival.

I spoke with Hitchcock last December through Skype on a Tuesday night, while he was sitting at a cafe in Sydney, talking on his cell, on a Wednesday afternoon. He answered my questions easily and articulately, with great enthusiasm. His thoughts were occasionally interrupted by quiet bursts of laughter, as if he realized the effect Dylan still had on him was as ridiculous as it was influential. Hitchcock had clearly thought a lot about Dylan over the years, and was eager to share his memories and observations. Along with other early influences like The Beatles, Syd Barrett, The Byrds, and Captain Beefheart, Dylan continues to influence Hitchcock's art, as well as his wardrobe. However, he is not one of those people who worships, or even follows, all of Dylan's exploits. Everything he said to me about Dylan was couched in love and respect, but with a keen critical, but non-judgmental, eye. Much like his songs, Hitchcock's answers were intelligent and full of insight, with a reverential attention to detail, and an added pinch of surreal, metaphorical asides to place his answers in a colorful, psychedelic context.

In your personal musical chronology, I've heard you give interviews where you said the first album you ever bought was 1965's *Highway 61 Revisited,* about a year or two after it came out. Now, The Beatles exploded on the scene in England a few years earlier, in 1963, when you were about 10-years-old. How did The Beatles enter your life before you discovered Bob Dylan?

Well, The Beatles appeared through the pretty tiny musical portholes that were available in Britain. We had one Top 20 (BBC radio) program on Sunday afternoons, and we had Saturday Club *on the* Light Programme, *and then there was Radio Luxembourg, which actually played pop music every night, which is where you were more likely to hear pop singles. It was quite hard to hear stuff. Nonetheless, it got around, so I would say by the middle of 1963, pretty much every single person in Britain between the ages of six and 14 knew who The Beatles were, and loved them. And a lot of adults did too, but it was music that appealed to children, and I was a kid. I think what was interesting to my generation particularly, was that as I grew ... I was 10 when I heard* Please Please Me, *and I was 16 when* Abbey Road *came out.*

So I was moving from childhood into adolescence into being essentially a very, very, young adult. The Beatles music moved with me. It's almost as if they were moving along in the train beside me. I even lived in Weybridge, in Surrey, for a while where three of The Beatles bought houses, so it was an odd thing. People of my age tracked The Beatles, who were all a decade older. They were just there. I couldn't afford records at all when I was a kid, but by the time I was able to afford to buy an LP, I was in a school where a lot of other people already had albums. I didn't have to worry, I would just hear them anyway.

I bought Sgt. Pepper *when it came out, too. I think I bought* Highway 61 *about a year after it came out. I mean, it was extremely ahead of its time. It was ahead of Bob Dylan's fans' time. There had never been anything like it. It was kind of the marriage between Bo Diddley and T.S. Eliot. He name checks both of them. Me, hearing this as a*

13-year-old, that was my Bar Mitzvah, and I'm not even Jewish. It was, "Aw, fuck, that was it, mate." I was decided (laughs). I wasn't going to go anywhere else. Here I am, 50 years later, still suffering from the polka dot shirts and sunglasses. It sent me in a good direction. As I've said before, it gave me something to aim at and miss, and it completely changed everybody.

The Beatles lost their innocence. He stole their psychic virginity. He gave them marijuana. They no longer produced fun songs, they produced thoughtful songs, and eventually they fell apart. But it also meant that it allowed their songs to grow up. Dylan injected wisdom into popular music in a way that hadn't really been there before. By nature, pop was trivial, it wasn't for serious minded folk. Noel Coward talked about the tremendous power of cheap music. ("Strange how potent cheap music is." — Noël Coward, Private Lives.) Pop music's gone back to being trivial. It's not like you listen to Justin Bieber or One Direction or whatever and you're plugged into W.H. Auden (laughs) or Milton or Shakespeare or something like that, but it just gave it a capacity, to get people to write songs ... Someone like me would never have gotten involved with pop or rock if it hadn't been for Dylan. ... So, yeah, that was Dylan arriving on Planet Hitchcock.

When I first starting listening to Dylan lyrics, I'd sometimes get them wrong. *Like in Tears of Rage*, **I thought the phrase** *"Life is brief"* **was** *"Like this bridge,"* **like it was some sort of symbolic, existential ...**

Yeah, "And like this bridge" (laughs) ... That's good, yeah.

And in *Memphis Blues Again*, **is he saying "headlines" or "headlights?" It sounds like he's trying to say two words at once.**

I still don't know which it is. Which one do you think it is?

"Headlines" makes (slightly) more sense, but some people still think it's "headlights." It could be "head lice" for all I know!

Head lice! (laughs) Maybe! Maybe that is what he was really trying to say!

So I was wondering what you thought about his vocal delivery, because it was so unusual ...

It was immaculate! You could hear every word he sang, and for that period, he was completely on. He may have done some gigs better than others, but he got to a point where he Simply! Emphasized! Every! Word! And! It! Mattered! It was brilliant! You know, he used up a lot of talent credits ... I've heard tapes of him live from before he went electric. He'd be singing one or two notes just hypnotically over this slightly out-of-tune guitar, in an echoey hall. It was magic.

I could see why people complained about the band (The Band) coming, because you couldn't quite make out the words so much, but at least on the records, you could totally make out the words. I think the big difference between Bob Dylan now and then, one of the many differences, is that in the old days, Dylan came out and he grabbed you! You may not like him, but you'd have to repel him, throw him away, push him away. But Dylan grabbed you, and now, in the last 20 years, you've had to lean into him. "What's that old guy saying? What's that? Oh, that's a good line. Oh, sorry, I've lost the next one." Dylan no longer needs to attract attention, so I think he's quite happy to bury his vocal in the music. And I do miss that terrific clarity. You know, I remember listening to people like Mick Jagger, and I couldn't make out what he was singing. I remember him doing "Hahf-ahsed" (British accent) or "Haylf-ayssed (American accent) games" in It's All Over Now, and I thought it was "half-past games," like instead of "half-past one," it was "half-past games." Jagger you could always misinterpret, he was singing in a more soul-y way. Bob Dylan was extremely clear and lucid with his words. I loved it.

So getting to *The Basement Tapes*, **you must have been aware of it all coming to light as it was happening, to a certain extent, once people started covering songs, and so on.**

Well, it was very murky. Information traveled slower then, and there wasn't much of it. As I sort of swam into adolescent consciousness and became a Dylan fan, almost the first thing I heard was that he was very badly hurt in a car crash, and that transmogrified into a motorcycle crash, and there were rumors that he'd signed with MGM, and there were rumors that he was making a TV special, and then there were rumors that he was really ill. I started buying the music press, the Record Mirror and the Melody Maker, just to see if I could find out anything about it, but there wasn't anything at all. There were no photographs. Meanwhile it's 1967, the flowers were growing on the carpet (laughs), Are You Experienced? (the debut album by the Jimi Hendrix Experience) was coming out, and the kind of change that had been brewing, brooding, for the previous three or four years, erupted. That was the year everything tipped, if you like, into modern life, and Dylan was completely absent. And then towards the end of the year, there were a couple of bits in the Melody Maker *and the* Record Mirror. *I remember the exclusive (in* Melody Maker, *November 4, 1967) – 'Nick Jones listens to seven secret tapes! Titles include* Ride Me High! Waters of Oblivion! This Wheel's on Fire!' *and I pretty much memorized those articles. But I didn't know anything about... The first thing I heard about* The Basement Tapes. ... *I think Manfred Mann covered* The Mighty Quinn ...

Actually, John Wesley Harding *came out before this, and we knew nothing about* John Wesley Harding *at all. It just appeared. It came out in the second freezing week of January (1968) with no publicity, and immediately sold out because we were so desperate for Dylan. I do think that* John Wesley Harding *would have made more sense (laughs) if we'd heard* The Basement Tapes *first, because they are a key, transitional phase. The Basement Tapes have (almost) no harmonica, which was interesting. I wondered if Dylan had hurt his neck and so couldn't play harp, and he just changed his way of writing songs. He was writing with choruses without the harp break and all that, and harmonizing with The Band. We didn't know anything about that. All we knew is that there'd been these songs, and then suddenly this album came out completely unannounced, a very allegorical, short, sober record, almost, you know, personally, justifiably calculated to kind of puncture and snub* Sgt. Pepper, *and the effect it had was amazing. The Beatles and the Stones immediately got back, lost the colored clothes ... Psychedelia was like vanished by* John Wesley Harding. *It was the first great step backwards, and* The Basement Tapes, *I just didn't know anything about. I finally heard a bootleg in 1969 ... No, in 1970. By that time* Self Portrait *had come out, and it was the* Great White Wonder *with* Tears of Rage, *and I loved them. Not great quality, which enhanced their enigma, and then more and more of them have been coming to light ever since.*

The thing that gets me as I'm re-experiencing *The Basement Tapes: Complete* these days is that, unlike anything that's recorded now, where there's a chance of it coming out on something ... In those days, the technology to do that easily didn't exist. There were no rock music bootlegs. It really was secret. There's a voyeuristic, almost pornographic aspect to it, like it's the forbidden fruit you were not supposed to hear ...

That's brilliant! It couldn't have been better for the whole mystique. Can you imagine Blonde on Blonde *that badly recorded, or primitively recorded? It would have been a loss. Can you imagine* The Basement Tapes *properly (laughs) recorded? The fact that it's sort of clear, but misty, was absolutely right. There's no photographs of the sessions. Was Dylan bald and wearing an afro? Had he grown a beard? Was he in a wheelchair? Were they all drunk? Probably. Were they all off hard drugs? Hopefully, at the time. I don't know.*

Funny coincidence was that Brian Wilson, his sort of alleged masterpiece SMiLE, *and* The Basement Tapes, *were both done at the same time, and were never finished. And they both became grails ... (Parenthetically)* Greil Marcus *... It was the Holy Grail. I'm sure it wasn't intentional, Harold, but just think about it. It does so much for the legend and the mystique ...*

After you spoke to a roomful of songwriting students at the Berklee College of Music clinic in November, you told me you were working on fleshing out a version of *I'm Not There*.

Well I did, I wrote it. I painstakingly transcribed the five verses, and I filled in the gaps with what I thought Dylan might have said if he'd finished it (laughs) ... I wasn't sort of pretending to be him, but obviously I have a Dylan app in me, a "Dylan 66-67 app," so I kind of used it. I also just made it so it sounded good, but I've left it in storage. I should have brought it with me. I had it all written out on the dining room table in Sydney, but I took it back to Britain, and it's in storage. I'll see if I could dig it up again. I'd have to re-transcribe it. But you know, it's pretty atmospheric, it's almost kind of like a sort-of Leonard Cohen song.

It's so brilliant to do something ... I love the way he'd come up with something as great as that, and then decides to discard it (laughs), and decides not to finish it. Anyone else, you would think might go, "Hey, I've got something here. I'll land this fish properly." Dylan's just sort of, "Wow, that was it," and moves on. I like the sort of disdain and ... the sort of confidence, in a way, that he could go, "Oh, fuck it, I'll leave that. I've probably done the best version." You can imagine the guys in the Band going afterwards (imitating the voices), "Oh, what was that, Bob?" "I don't know man, that's not happening. Let's do something else." It's just terrific.

But anyway, I somewhere have finished it, did my version. I sang it at McCabe's in Santa Monica. I don't know if somebody was taping it, in June. If they would have, there's a recording. I memorized all my verses. Yeah, great song.

I think I love Dylan's voice on The Basement Tapes *(because) I think he's a bit affected by the Band. He started singing along in a more high, plaintive way, less kind of knowing and cynical. In some way, I think that was when his voice peaked. There's a sort of wisdom and regret and feeling in his voice there. It's almost the most mature* (phone connection dropped out for ten seconds) *it's a brilliant record, and long way off from where he started. Almost like he and The Beatles had swapped places at the end of the 60s. They were writing all these meaningful songs, and he was writing these beautiful little pop things. I think after that he rather lost his momentum, as all those people did. Then he split from his* (first) *wife and he started sounding petulant and everybody loved him, because he was angry and writing long songs again. I thought his soul had just gone to Hell, actually. I think he's been profoundly unhappy from then on.*

But The Basement Tapes *... that, and* John Wesley Harding, *may be the summary of Bob Dylan as a wise man, a young man who was way wiser than he should have been. His curse seemed to be an older man who had to forsake the wisdom that he had as a youth, because there hasn't been enough to sustain him. Now he sounds ... I know there's soul there, and he is still capable of great lines and great performances, and when he's on, there's nobody who tells a story like he does. But I just feel as an entity, he was sort of damaged after that.* The Basement Tapes *was the last of the kind of ... I wouldn't say "innocence"* (laughs) *... you know, the young wise man. Dylan travels backwards in time even as he travels forwards in time* (laughs). *He's a strange chromel unit ... We'll be talking about him forever, and we'll miss him when he's gone.*

When Bob Dylan puts out a new album, is that something you go out and buy?

No ... no... I just listened to (2009's) Together Through Life *on a plane, and I rather enjoyed it more than I thought I would. It's hard work. You really have to sit down and listen to it. Sometimes, with the Christmas record* (2009's Christmas In The Heart), *it just seems like an elaborate joke, but it may sound brilliant in 30 years time, who's to say? But no, I haven't bought a Dylan record when it came out since* Street-Legal, *I think.* (That would be 1978, when Hitchcock's own career with his band, The Soft Boys, began to take off.)

You recently tweeted that you'd seen Dylan live in Australia, and said it was one of the best Dylan shows you'd ever seen, or in a long time, anyway.

Yeah. It was odd. I always think Dylan is usually either kind of brilliant or terrible in a way, and this was more like he was very good. He was pronouncing the words, being very sober, the band played as well as (laughs) *frightened employees can play, and Dylan was playing a lot of piano and he seemed to be into it. I think, in the end, all you can say for the last 30 years, either he's into it or he's not. When he's into it, it's still got something, and when he's not, you may as well listen to almost anybody else. You know, he has so much unconditional love from his followers, he knows he can give them any shit and they'll sound off and justify it. He's totally walled in by his legend, and the love people have for it, like a Greek curse, "The Man Who Saw Too Much." Everybody then says, "See it again! See it again, O Wise One! What does it mean?" "I've already seen it once." "O, look! Look again, O Wise One!" It's a bit like* (Monty Python's) Life of Brian, *"How should we fuck off, O Lord?"*

I'm very happy being a cult figure (laughs). *It must drive him nuts about that stuff, but he brought it upon himself, like everybody in Greek curses does* (laughs). *I really wish him well, but I thought the show was good. Maybe the second half was a bit less exciting than the first, that was more* (to do with) *the set list.*

The other thing I liked was that he mostly did songs from the last 20 years, and I think he actually loses interest in his songs after a while. He doesn't sing them like they were, the paint doesn't dry. I know he sang a perfect version of The Times, They Are A-Changin' *for the Obamas when they got into the White House, but unless there's some sort of gun to his head, he doesn't ... Someone like Paul McCartney, he finishes a song, and then he sticks with it, and plays it just the same 50 years later. As long as he could hit the notes, Paul will sing* Hello Goodbye, *or* Got To Get You Into My Life, *just as he did when he was a guy in his 20s. Dylan, the paint doesn't dry on his work. Just because it sounded like that once, doesn't mean it has to now. In a way, I admire that, that he has a complete contempt for nostalgia. He'll serve up* Like A Rolling Stone, *but not like you'd expect it* (laughs). *I do admire that, but I can't always follow what he's up to, and I don't always enjoy it. I thought he was good in Sydney, and he'll always have his phrasing and his timing and his depth, and I just do prefer it when he's actually making the words clear.* (laughs) (Asking himself:) *"What would you like for Christmas?" "Clarification, Bob. Sing those words so you can hear them, like I do." (laughs) Give him a copy of* Fegmania! *(Hitchcock's 1985 album with the Egyptians.) Like I said, I just know we're gonna miss him when he's gone. So I wish him well, and I will probably go and see him again. I've seen some awful Dylan gigs over the years, but I think he's sort of stabilized a bit.*

Did you hear about Dylan's next album (*Shadows in the Night*)?

That's the one that's all Frank Sinatra songs ...

Yeah ...

Yes, I heard one. He's singing very clearly and carefully. I expect he's going to do his version of Fegmania! *next, anyway ... He loves to confound expectations, doesn't he? (laughs) I love the cover, it looks like he's in jail! Have you heard the whole thing?*

Only a couple of songs, including one live in concert. It sounded like he's trying to sing clearly. His voice sounded a little cracked, which is not necessarily a bad thing, but as I wrote when I reviewed the show I saw in Providence, that you can't really drink the drinks and smoke the smokes that he did and then sing with smooth tones at the age of 73. This is what is going to happen to you if you're going to be a Bob Dylan.

I think it's more than alcohol and tobacco. You know, I still drink and smoke, and I can hit a lot of those notes (laughs). I don't know what he's done. I don't know how he did it. I think perhaps by singing way too high, it sounds to me like what happens when you damage your larynx by singing without warming up. I mean, after eating and drinking and doing God-knows-what-else ... I'm sure there's extra stuff in there ... He's definitely singled his own voice out for special treatment (laughs).

Well, OK, I'll definitely hear it, one day when I have time to sit down and do some painting and really take some time off - which never seems to happen - I'll listen to the last few records, contemplatively, by myself.

This brought the conversation to a close. When the interview ended, he asked, *"So, you've got everything you need? You know, I'll rattle on about Dylan indefinitely!"*

Yeah, I know the feeling.

Chrissie Hynde of The Pretenders

September, 2010

Christine Ellen "Chrissie" Hynde was born September 7, 1951, in Akron, Ohio.

Hynde attended Kent State University, and was on campus during the 1970 Kent State shootings. In 1973, Hynde moved to England, where she eventually started to write for the *New Music Express*, followed by a job working at a little-known clothing store, SEX, run by Vivienne Westwood and future Sex Pistols' manager Malcolm McLaren. Chrissie went home for a while, then returned to England. After failed attempts to join or form bands with future members of The Damned, The Clash, Visage, and The Psychedelic Furs, she formed her own band, the massively successful Pretenders.

Hynde is also known for her animal right activism. Her current musical project is JP, Chrissie & The Fairground Boys.

Chrissie has appeared on stage with Bob Dylan five times. The first was in 1984, when Dylan played at Wembley Stadium in London, on July 7. [171] She was on stage for half of the ten song encore. After playing harmonica and singing backup on *Leopard-Skin Pill-Box Hat*, Dylan said, *"I'm sure you all know Chrissie Hynde. She's gonna make an announcement to you now!"* Hynde then said, *"The announcement is, Van Morrison!"* who then performed *It's All Over Now, Baby Blue*. She then left the stage temporarily, but returned to sing backup on the last three songs. Other encore guests included Carlos Santana and Eric Clapton.

Bob Dylan's 30th Anniversary Celebration Concert took place at Madison Square Garden in 1992. She performed *I Shall Be Released*, introduced George Harrison, and sang during the *Knockin' On Heaven's Door* finale. Earlier in the year, she sang and played rhythm guitar on *Like A Rolling Stone* when Dylan performed on David Letterman's Late Night 10th Anniversary show. [172]

In 1993, when Van Morrison played in Dublin, Bob Dylan guested and played harmonica while the Belfast Cowboy sang *It's All Over Now, Baby Blue*. Singing backup were Kris Kristofferson, Steve Winwood and Hynde. [173]

When Dylan played London's Brixton Academy on March 31, 1995, Elvis Costello, Carole King, and Hynde joined in on the last two songs. Costello talked about it later that year: [174]

"Chrissie's always been really cool. Recently I did this gig with Bob Dylan and we were doing I Shall Be Released. *Bob had Chrissie and Carole King up on stage doing backgrounds, while Bob and I were doing a duet. I turned round and Carole King was really excited, dancing and shaking her head around. But Chrissie was just standing at the mic like one of the Vandellas, doing the chick singer thing with finger snaps and everything. It looked great."* [175]

On February 9, 1986, there was a benefit concert at London's Royal Albert Hall. According to *Wolfgang's Vault*:

. . . (the) all-star benefit (was) in response to the November 1985 Nevado del Ruiz volcano explosion, which caused an immense natural disaster in Colombia and killed over 25,000 people. Colombian musician Chucho Merchan, with

---

[171] http://www.bjorner.com/DSN07010%20-%201984%20Europe%20Tour.htm#DSN07310, *Still on the Road*, Retrieved 11/25/2016

[172] http://www.bjorner.com/DSN12845%20-%201992%20Early%20Sessions.htm#DSN12850, *Still on the Road*, Retrieved 11/25/2016

[173] http://www.bjorner.com/DSN13820%20-%201993%20Europe%20Winter%20Tour.htm#DSN13830, *Still on the Road*, Retrieved 11/25/2016

[174] http://www.bjorner.com/DSN15790.htm#_Toc471532734, *Still on the Road*, Retrieved 11/25/2016

[175] http://www.pretenders.org/arelvis.htm, *How We Met Chrissie Hynde and Elvis Costello*, Nicholas Barber, The Independent (London), 10/8/1995, Retrieved 11/25/2016

the help of *Who* guitarist, Pete Townshend, began organizing a charity event, which ultimately included Hynde (who was taking a break from the Pretenders at the time), as well as Townshend, Pink Floyd's David Gilmour, Annie Lennox, and others. [176]

Hynde ended her set with a cover of Dylan's *Property Of Jesus*.

Arthur magazine published an interview with Chrissie in 2008, and asked about her song - *Boots of Chinese Plastic*:

A: Does "Boots of Chinese Plastic" have anything to do with Dylan's "Boots of Spanish Leather"?

CH: Yeah, it's kind of a nod to that. And the way things have changed, and I'm personally trying not to promote leather. [177]

The Pretenders also covered Dylan's *Forever Young* on their 1994 album, *Last Of The Independents*.

---

[176] http://www.concertvault.com/chrissie-hynde/royal-albert-hall-february-09-1986.html, *Chrissie Hynde, Royal Albert Hall* (London, England), 2/9/1986, Retrieved 11/25/2016

[177] https://arthurmag.com/2008/12/17/pretenders-qa/, *"Way to Go, Ohio": Arthur's exclusive Q&A with THE PRETENDERS' Chrissie Hynde and James Walbourne*, Retrieved 11/25/2016

Sheryl Crow - 'Bob Dylan took voice lessons' for 1994 Japan concert

December 22, 2010

In May, 1994, Bob Dylan appeared at the Todaiji Temple, in Nara, Japan, for three nights. [178] For these special "Great Music Experience" concerts, Dylan performed impassioned versions of *A Hard Rain's A-Gonna Fall*, *I Shall Be Released*, and *Ring Them Bells*, backed by Phil Palmer (guitar), Paul "Wix" Wickens (keyboards, now with Paul McCartney), Pino Palladino (bass, The Who, John Mayer, Simon & Garfunkel), Jim Keltner (drums) and The Tokyo New Philharmonic Orchestra, conducted by Michael Kamen. For the finale, Dylan once again performed *I Shall Be Released* with all participating artists, including Joni Mitchell, the Chieftains, Jon Bon Jovi, Richie Sambora, Ry Cooder, Roger Taylor, and the members of INXS and X Japan.

From IMDb (by Neil McCartney): [179] *"The Great Music Experience", produced by Tony Hollingsworth of Tribute and backed by UNESCO and the United Nations, was staged at Todai Ji, an eighth-century Buddhist temple, the world's largest wooden building containing the world's largest statue of Buddha. It challenged top international artists to immerse themselves in Japanese culture, explore their differences and perform a show that was rich in its influence.*

Along with his appearance at Woodstock '94 later that year, these performances helped restore Dylan's somewhat tattered reputation, and according to a new interview with Sheryl Crow in *Popeater*, [180] he even took voice lessons in preparation for the event. Crow praised Dylan for not being "Static," and mentioned he took voice lessons for the "Great Music Experience" concerts. After being Dylan's support act at a New York gig, she said, *"He invited me to work with him. Meeting heroes can be terrifying, but Bob was just so cool. We drank coffee, hung out and became friends."*

Crow later covered his *Time Out Of Mind* outtake *Mississippi* on her 1998 album, *The Globe Sessions*, a few years before Dylan released it on 2001's *"Love & Theft."* They also appeared together at Eric Clapton's 1999 Crossroads Benefit. When Crow was diagnosed with breast cancer, Dylan sent flowers. [181] Crow also credits Dylan with advice to overcome writer's block while working on her album, *C'mon, C'mon*. *"I knew he'd suffered from it and I rang him. He asked me questions, talked me through it and I worked it out. There are times like that when you can't believe your own reality. Not even my nine Grammys mean as much to me as having the friendship of a man like him.* [182]

Some of the performances from Nara, Japan, were broadcast on television [183] in over 50 countries all over the world, as well as on radio. *Hard Rain* was released in some territories as part of the *Dignity* single. In the August, 1994, issue, *Q* magazine said of the performance, *"(It was) no ordinary version...*[he] *really opens his lungs and heart and sings, like he's not done for many a year...The only word for it majestic."* [184]

---

[178] http://www.bjorner.com/DSN14790%20-%201994%20Spring%20Sessions.htm#DSN15060, *Still on the Road*, Retrieved 11/25/2016

[179] http://www.imdb.com/title/tt1055285/, *The Great Music Experience* (1994), Retrieved 11/25/2016

[180] http://www.musicstop.org/sheryl-crow-works-out-her-passion-for-classic-soul-music/, *Sheryl Crow Works Out Her Passion for Classic Soul Music*, Retrieved 11/25/2106

[181] http://www.gossiprocks.com/forum/gossip-archive/22314-sheryl-crows-vanity-fair-interview.html, *Sheryl Crow Talks About Beating Cancer and Losing Lance Armstrong; Armstrong Talks About Crow*, Vanity Fair, Retrieved 11/25/2016

[182] http://www.dailymail.co.uk/home/moslive/article-1027121/How-Sheryl-Crow-took-Klan-White-House-depression-cancer.html, *Sheryl Crow Talks About Beating Cancer and Losing Lance Armstrong; Armstrong Talks About Crow*, Retrieved 11/25/2016

[183] http://www.imdb.com/title/tt1055285/, *The Great Music Experience* (1994), Retrieved 11/25/2016

[184] http://theendlessfurther.com/dylan-at-todai-ji/, *The Endless Further*, Via Q Magazine, Retrieved 11/25/2016

The day Whitney Houston sang with Bob Dylan in 1986 (Sort of)

February 11, 2012

Pop icon Whitney Houston has died at the age of 48.

According to Olof Bjorner, [185] Houston once sang with Bob Dylan for a television special on January 20, 1986. However, they did not perform from the same location.

The occasion was the celebration of the first Martin Luther King, Jr., day. For the event, some artists, including Bob Dylan, performed from the John F. Kennedy Performing Arts Center Opera House in Washington, D.C., while others sang from New York's Radio City Music Hall. The show ended with a group finale of Stevie Wonder's 1981 tribute to King, *Happy Birthday*. Dylan and others sang from D.C., while a large group of background singers, including Houston, simultaneously joined in from New York City.

The two-hour television special, *An All-star Celebration Honoring Martin Luther King Jr.*, was first broadcast by NBC-TV that evening after a two-hour delay. [186] Among the other performers were Joan Baez, Harry Belafonte, the Boys Choir Of Harlem, Andraé Crouch, Neil Diamond, Amy Grant, Dick Gregory, Charlton Heston, Gregory Hines, Quincy Jones (Conductor), Coretta Scott King, Patti LaBelle, Cyndi Lauper, Bette Midler, Yoko Ono, Peter, Paul & Mary, The Queens Of Rhythm (Possibly, from Dylan's band), Lionel Richie, Diana Ross, Elizabeth Taylor, Cicely Tyson (Houston's aunt), Dionne Warwick (Houston's cousin), and host and performer Stevie Wonder, with his band, Wonderlove.

Bob Dylan's grandson, Pablo, tweeted **@PabloDylan**, "RIP Whitney Houston."

Two more selected tweets:

@aliciakeys Alicia Keys: I feel sick.... Life is precious, we are fragile souls. Let's love each other! I miss you beautiful Whitney, the whole world misses you!!

@iamwill will.i.am: I'm so sad...whitney houston was so kind, sweet, wonderful, amazing, talented, and a true gift to the world...#iwillalwaysloveyou

---

[185] http://www.bjorner.com/DSN07630%20-%201986%20Early%20Sessions.htm#DSN07630, *Still on the Road*, Retrieved 11/25/2016

[186] http://www.imdb.com/title/tt0321152/, *An All-Star Celebration Honoring Martin Luther King Jr*, (1986). Retrieved 11/25/2016

Al Kooper chimes in on the Bob Dylan Newport electric guitar controversy

July 12, 2012

On Tuesday night, PBS will air the season premiere episode of *History Detectives*. The centerpiece of the show is whether the electric Fender guitar that Bob Dylan played at the 1965 Newport Folk Festival is in the possession of the New Jersey daughter of a pilot who flew Dylan to concerts in the mid-1960s. The guitar even came with sheets of paper containing some of Dylan's unpublished poetry, with lines that ended up on his 1966 album, *Blonde On Blonde*.

While there is reportedly compelling evidence that it is indeed the guitar Dylan strummed on that fateful day, Dylan's camp has denied the claim, saying he drove, not flew, to the concert, and still retains possession of the original, legendary, Fender Stratocaster.

I asked Al Kooper, who played keyboards with Dylan at Newport, on the albums *Highway 61 Revisited* and *Blonde and Blonde*, and other projects on and off through 1996, if he had any recollection of how Dylan traveled to the gig that changed the world.

Here was his response via email:

In all truthfulness, I have no idea how he arrived in Newport, but I would guess he took to the roads as airplanes were only used for more distance than the comparative hop from New York to Newport. And having once owned one of Jimi Hendrix's guitars, I can only conjecture that the guitar you speak of was probably also just made out of wood and metal like all the other Stratocasters in the world. Have they tried DNA ? Good luck / @l k%oper

The defense rests.

Jeff Gold on skeptics and Bob Dylan's electric Newport guitar

July 16, 2012

Initially, Jeff Gold was skeptical. There were so many people trying to pass off fake Bob Dylan memorabilia as the real thing. This, however, felt different.

A woman in New Jersey thought she might have the electric guitar Dylan played at the Newport Folk Festival in 1965. It was originally in the possession of her late father, pilot Victor Quinto, who flew Dylan to concerts in the 60's. Dylan had left it on her father's plane, and she had reached out to the television show *History Detectives* to see if it was, indeed, the Newport guitar.

Gold was asked to determine if lyric sheets found in the guitar case were written and typed by Dylan, but was initially noncommittal. Then he saw scans of the manuscripts. He was in.

Gold began collecting records and rock music memorabilia in 1971. He is a former Executive Vice President/General Manager of Warner Bros Records, a Grammy Award winning art director, and a longtime Dylan collector who was a curatorial consultant and major lender to the traveling exhibition "Bob Dylan's American Journey" (organized by Seattle's Experience Music Project.) He now buys and sells music memorabilia and blogs about music - and Dylan - on his website, *Recordmecca*.

Gold has studied Dylan's handwriting and manuscripts extensively, and was recommended by Howard Kramer, curatorial director of the Rock and Roll Hall of Fame, to evaluate the lyrics for *History Detectives*. His initial reaction to the scans was that they were indeed by Dylan, but he needed more evidence than just a gut response. After carefully examining the lyric sheets, Gold noticed one stanza had the line *"the six white horses,"* which also appears in Dylan's *Absolutely Sweet Marie* - a song Gold owns a manuscript for. He compared the line on the *History Detectives* page to his own - written not too long after Newport - and they were a perfect match.

According to Gold, the History Detectives hosts also interviewed Jonathan Taplin, Dylan's road manager at Newport, who pointed out that the guitar case was stenciled "Property of Ashes & Sand," the little-known of name of Dylan and manager Albert Grossman's touring company. Taplin noted the equipment was flown home after the concert in Peter Paul & Mary's plane - a band also flown by Victor Quinto.

Gold also told me, *"Quinto's daughter, Dawn Peterson, had her father's address book, which includes Dylan's former Woodstock phone number.* History Detectives *called every number in the book and managed to locate a friend of Quinto's, a pilot, who confirmed that he had indeed flown Dylan, Peter Paul & Mary, and The Band."*

The next step was to analyze the guitar itself. Vintage guitar expert and Rock and Roll Hall Of Fame staff consultant Andy Babiuk was called in. He took the instrument apart, and was able to confirm that the Fender Stratocaster was made in May 1964, over a year before Dylan's first electric Newport Folk Festival appearance. Babiuk told Gold that the serial number on a Stratocaster isn't that important, it's on a metal plate attached by 4 screws that can easily be changed. So he had to open the guitar up to make sure it was from the right time and all original, and then try to match the wood grain.

Babiuk then compared the wood grain on the guitar to large, very detailed color photographs taken from the edge of the stage at Newport by John Rudoff. Babiuk told Gold that *"wood grain is like a fingerprint. No two pieces of wood have exactly the same grain."*

Babiuk was able to identify sections of the grain on the guitar body, near the input jack, and on the fingerboard that exactly matched the grain on the guitar in the photographs. His wood grain comparison allowed him to determine that this was indeed the Newport guitar.

While there are skeptics, Gold says the show makes a very compelling argument. In fact, *"The program sets up the evidence like a court case,"* Gold said. *"Some people may have doubts, but when they see all the evidence, including the wood grain, I think they'll be convinced."*

The show also reveals that in 2005, Peterson had a lawyer write to Dylan's management, requesting that he relinquish all rights to the guitar. At the time, Dylan's lawyers responded that the guitar was Dylan's property, and asked for its return. This week, Dylan's lawyer issued a press release claiming that Dylan still possesses the Newport original guitar, but similar ones were stolen, along with some unpublished lyrics.

The episode premieres Tuesday night on PBS, 9 Eastern, 8 Central. In addition to the Dylan piece, there are also investigations into an artwork possibly made by Frank Zappa, and previously unknown - and possibly genuine - Beatles' autographs.

When George Martin mixed the sound for Bob Dylan

March 10, 2016

In May, 1994, Bob Dylan participated in The Great Music Experience, a three-day concert event that took place at the eighth-century Buddhist temple of Todai-Ji, in Nara, Japan. The May 20, 21, and 22 shows were organized in cooperation with UNESCO, [187] and also featured Joni Mitchell, The Chieftains, Ry Cooder, INXS, Jon Bon Jovi and Richie Sambora, Roger Taylor, Wayne Shorter, and various Japanese acts.

For the first time in his career, Dylan sang in front of an orchestra, in this case the Tokyo New Philharmonic conducted by Michael Kamen. There was also a house band consisting of Phil Palmer on guitar, Paul "Wix" Wickens on keyboards, Pino Palladino on bass, and Jim Keltner on drums. Each night Dylan featured the same set list: *A Hard Rain's A-Gonna Fall, I Shall Be Released,* and *Ring Them Bells,* with a reprised group finale of *I Shall Be Released* with all acts participating. According to British impresario and Great Music Experience producer Tony Hollingsworth, [188] Dylan was forced to be a follower instead of a leader, and *"it was a huge relief for him, and he told Hollingsworth as he came off stage that he hadn't sung as well for 15 years."* According to a 2010 interview with singer Sheryl Crow in *Popeater,* [189] Dylan even took voice lessons in preparation for the event. (See Sheryl Crow chapter.)

A television and radio program documenting the event *The Great Music Experience Countdown* was broadcast in over 50 countries on May 22, 1994, and on the BBC in the U.K. on the 29th. Taking on the role of an "elder statesman" [190] was George Martin, who acted as an emollient in the organization of the collaborations, and headed the team of technicians in charge of the audio. Martin's son, Giles, was appointed co-music director for the television and radio music countdown show. According to *Endless Further,* "The music [for the program] *was later mixed by Beatles producer George Martin."* [191]

Dylan's breathtaking version of *Hard Rain* from the final night was added to the CD5 single of *Dignity,* released in various configurations in different countries in 1994 and 1995. However, Martin is not credited on the CDs, so he may not have been involved in that particular mix. If you'd like to experience Dylan's performance at The Great Music Experience as mixed by George Martin, your best bet is to search out the original footage.

---

[187] http://theendlessfurther.com/dylan-at-todai-ji/, *The Great Music Experience* (1994), Retrieved 11/25/2016

[188] http://tonyhollingsworth.com/?q=content/great-music-experience, *The Great Music Experience,* Peter Elman, Tribute Inspirations Limited, Retrieved 11/25/2016

[189] http://www.musicstop.org/sheryl-crow-works-out-her-passion-for-classic-soul-music/, *Sheryl Crow Works Out Her Passion for Classic Soul Music,* Retrieved 11/25/2106

[190] http://tonyhollingsworth.com/?q=content/great-music-experience, *The Great Music Experience,* Peter Elman, Tribute Inspirations Limited, Retrieved 11/25/2016

[191] http://theendlessfurther.com/dylan-at-todai-ji/, *The Great Music Experience* (1994), Retrieved 11/25/2016

Bob Dylan and John Lennon

October, 2010

John Winston Ono Lennon was born on October 9, 1940.

I was fortunate enough to have seen John Lennon perform at the 1972 One-To-One Benefit, the only time he played a rehearsed, full-length, post-Beatles concert. The only other concert that had as much of an impact on me was seeing Bob Dylan and The Band a year-and-a-half later.

Dylan and Lennon have been called the two most influential artists of the 1960s. They were similar on many levels, ranging from their primitive musical styles to their interest in art, filmmaking, and literature. They also focused on the same instruments - guitar, keyboard, and, for a while, harmonica.

Bob Dylan became intrigued with Lennon and The Beatles when he first heard them on the radio while driving to San Francisco in mid-February, 1964. The Beatles were already Dylan fans, playing his second album, *Freewheelin'*, non-stop since their January, 1964, trip to France.

Dylan inspired The Beatles to write more mature lyrics, while Lennon and The Beatles were a catalyst in Dylan's decision to "go electric."

In honor of Lennon's birthday, I'm going to give an overview of the various times his career crossed paths with Dylan's. The focus will be on Lennon as an individual, but the rest of the Fab Four will obviously be included.

In 1964, John Lennon started wearing a cap similar to the one Dylan wore on the cover of his debut album.

According to Marianne Faithfull, *"Dylan didn't pay much attention to The Beatles at all actually, except for John. John he adored, so hanging out with John was always good."*

Dylan is said to have turned The Beatles on to "jazz cigarettes," although at least one person has reported that Lennon had tried marijuana the previous month.

Starting in 1964, many of John's songs, most notably *I'm A Loser*, *You've Got To Hide Your Love Away*, and *Norwegian Wood* were heavily influenced by Dylan. (Replace the flute at the end of *Hide Your Love Away* with a harmonica, and you'll see what I mean). Later songs like *I Am The Walrus*, *Working Class Hero*, and *Steel and Glass* can also be traced back to Dylan.

Bob also recorded his own Lennon-esque songs, including *4th Time Around* (his response to *Norwegian Wood*) and *I Wanna Be Your Lover*.

In 1965, Lennon bought a jukebox. One of the 45's he allegedly included was Dylan's *Positively 4th Street*.

Lennon specifically refers to Dylan or his songs in a number of his own recordings, including *Yer Blues*, *Dig It*, *Give Peace A Chance*, *God* (originally "Dylan," but later changed to "Zimmerman"), and an alternate version of *How Do You Sleep?*, where Lennon sings *"How Does It Feel?"* at the very end. Lennon quotes *Like A Rolling Stone* in his 1974 song, *Scared*, and imitated Dylan on an out-take version of *Bring On The Lucie (Freda Peeple)*.

A short clip from *Eat The Document* featured Dylan and Lennon in the back of a cab in May, 1966. A much longer outtake has been widely bootlegged. [192]

Lennon, along with George Harrison and Ringo Starr, hung out with Dylan around the time of Dylan's 1969 Isle of Wight concert. It was rumored Dylan played piano on an unreleased version of *Cold Turkey* around this time.

---

[192] http://www.recmusicbeatles.com/public/files/bbs/etd.html, *"Permission to land, Tom"* - *Transcript of two film reels from the Eat The Document archives*, Retrieved 11/25/2016

When John and Yoko arrived in New York City in 1971, they started hanging out with A.J. Weberman. For a while, Lennon even wore a "Free Bob Dylan" badge. They later denounced Weberman.

In 1972, Lennon and Ono were trying to launch a tour to get young people to vote against the reelection of President Richard Nixon. According to Jerry Rubin in Jon Wiener's book, *Come Together, John Lennon In His Time*, John and Yoko were trying to convince Dylan to join after he had recorded the protest song, *Come To San Diego*, [193] with Allen Ginsberg. It was almost released as a single on The Beatles' Apple Records label.

Around this time, Dylan released a song about the murdered Black Panther prisoner George Jackson, while Lennon and Yoko Ono recorded an album track about Angela Davis, who tried to free Jackson while he was imprisoned, and was later charged with kidnapping, conspiracy, and murder.

In 1974, Lennon produced the Harry Nilsson album, *Pussycats*. In a contemporary radio interview, Lennon said that both he and Nilsson chose the cover versions recorded for the album. While Lennon said the Nilsson picked most of them, it's probable that *Subterranean Homesick Blues* was Lennon's idea.

Shortly before his death, Lennon made some home recordings featuring imitations of Dylan, and as well as a parody of Dylan's *Gotta Serve Somebody*, entitled *Serve Yourself*.

In early January, 1981, Dylan was sighted in Greenwich Village, which has led to speculation that he had visited Lennon's widow, Yoko Ono, at The Dakota.

Some have interpreted Dylan's 1981 song, *Lenny Bruce* as really being about Lennon (notice the similar names), especially the reference to sharing a cab. The "babies" mentioned in the lyrics could be a nod to The Beatles' notorious "Butcher Cover" of 1966.

Media consultant and publicist Elliot Mintz was employed by both the Lennons and Dylan.

Dylan visited Lennon's childhood home, Mendips, in 2009. Guide and custodian Colin Hall told *The Daily Mail*. He recalled that in the future Beatle's bedroom, Dylan noticed a copy of "Just William, *which was one of John's favorite books. Dylan was fascinated by the book, and I remember thinking, 'I'm standing in John Lennon's bedroom with Bob Dylan.' It was a totally surreal moment."* [194]

Lennon on Dylan

Lennon commented on Dylan many times over the years. Here are a few examples.

On September 13, 1964, when journalist Larry Kane asked Lennon what he liked best about New York when he was there earlier in the year, Lennon replied, *"I just like cities, you see, and preferably big ones. That's why I liked it. And we met some good people like Bob Dylan and Joan Baez, you know, and I enjoy meeting people I admire."* [195]

[193] http://www.bobdylanroots.com/allen.html#dylgins, *In Memoriam Allen Ginsberg* (Jun 3, 1926 - Apr 5, 1997), Retrieved 11/25/2016

[194] http://www.dailymail.co.uk/femail/article-1316904/I-Beatle-bath-John-Lennons-childhood-home-museum-visited-thousands--whats-like-live-there.html, *I had a Beatle in my bath: John Lennon's childhood home is now a museum visited by thousands - including Bob Dylan...but what's it like to live there?* Retrieved 11/26/2006

[195] http://www.beatlesinterviews.org/db1964.0913.beatles.html, *Beatles Interviews Database: John Lennon Interview*, Larry Kane, Baltimore 9/13/1964. Retrieved 11/26/2016

In 1970, Lennon told *Rolling Stone*'s Jann Wenner [196] that he referred to Dylan as "Zimmerman" on the song *God*, *"Because Dylan is bullshit. Zimmerman is his name. You see, I don't believe in Dylan and I don't believe in Tom Jones, either in that way."*

Dylan was also referenced in 1968's *Yer Blues*. Lennon felt "self-conscious" singing the blues, as opposed to rock and R&B. He complimented Dylan's ability to it. Lennon thought when Dylan was insecure, he'd use *"double entendre. So therefore he is secure in his Hipness."*

In 1980, Lennon told *Playboy* he didn't care what most other musicians were up to, from the other Beatles to Elton John and Bob Dylan, saying his own life was busy enough. Later he quoted Dylan's *Subterranean Homesick Blues*, saying *"Don't follow leaders, watch the parking meters,"* after saying that it was OK to follow examples. When asked about Dylan's current Gospel phase, he declined to comment, but acknowledged it was a personal choice. He also said not to depend on presidents, messiahs, John & Yoko, or Dylan to get things done. [197]

Dylan on Lennon

"John and The Beatles were doing things nobody was doing. Their chords were outrageous, and their harmonies made it all valid. Everybody else thought they were for the teeny boppers, that they were gonna pass right away. But it was obvious to me that they had staying power: I knew they were pointing in the direction where music had to go." [198]

In a 1978 interview with *Playboy*, [199] Dylan said publishers were "encouraged" by Lennon's book, *In His Own Write*, which is what lead to his own *Tarantula*. He complimented Lennon's innovative poetic style, and credited him with coming up with *"key expressions … are symbolic of some inner reality and probably will never be said again."*

Dylan wrote a letter to the INS, in his own handwriting, supporting Lennon's right to stay in the U.S., sometime around 1972, during the John Lennon deportation proceedings. It reads:

JUSTICE for John & Yoko!

John and Yoko add a great voice and drive to this country's so called ART INSTITUTION / They inspire and transcend and stimulate and by doing so, only can help others to see pure light and in doing that, put an end to this will dull taste of petty commercialism which is being passed off as Artist Art by the overpowering mass-media. Hurray for John & Yoko. Let them stay and live here and breathe. This country's got plenty of room and space. Let John and Yoko stay! - Bob Dylan [200]

"I was thinking about (Jimi Hendrix) the other night -- I really miss him a lot, him and Lennon." (Dylan quoted in the *Biograph* booklet, 1985.)

Update 2016: Dylan included a song about Lennon on his 2012 album, *Tempest*, titled *Roll On John*.

[196] http://imaginepeace.com/archives/4385, Rolling Stone issues # 74 & 75 (21 Jan & 4 Feb, 1971), *John Lennon: The Rolling Stone Interview* by founding editor Jann S. Wenner. Retrieved 11/26/2016

[197] *The Playboy Interviews With John Lennon and Yoko Ono: The complete texts plus unpublished conversations and Lennon's song-by-song analysis of his music*, conducted by David Sheff, Playboy Press, New York, 1981.

[198] *Bob Dylan: An Intimate Biography*, Anthony Scaduto, W.H. Allen, London/New York, 1972.

[199] *Playboy interview: Bob Dylan: a candid conversations with the visionary whose songs changed the times*, Ron Rosenbaum, Playboy, 3/1978

[200] http://lennonfbifiles.com/natl_comm_john_yoko/bob_dylan.html, *The John Lennon - Deportation Proceedings, Letters to the INS - Bob Dylan*, Retrieved 11/26/2016

Bob Dylan and George Harrison through the years

February 24, 2011

"And I'd felt very strongly about Bob when I'd been in India years before - the only record I took with me along with all my Indian records was Blonde On Blonde. *I felt somehow very close to him or something, you know, because he was so great, so heavy and so observant about everything." -* George Harrison, *Crawdaddy*, February 1977. [201]

George Harrison was born on February 25, 1943.

Bob Dylan and Harrison were friends for decades. They co-wrote songs and covered each other's material. Dylan collaborated with Harrison on many occasions: in the studio, on stage, and in Dylan's home. Here's a list, courtesy of Olof Bjorner: [202]

- Late November 1968: The Home Of Bob Dylan, Woodstock, New York

- 1 May 1970: Columbia Studio B, New York City, New York

- 1 August 1971: Concert For Bangla Desh, Madison Square Garden, New York City, New York

- 19 February 1987: Palomino, Hollywood, Los Angeles, California (Guest Appearance at a Taj Mahal concert).

- 17 October 1987: Wembley Arena, London, England

- 20 January 1988: The Grand Ballroom, Hotel Waldorf-Astoria, New York City, New York (Rock and Roll Hall Of Fame)

- May 1988: Bob Dylan's garage, and Dave Stewart Studios, Los Angeles, California (*Traveling Wilburys Vol. 1*)

- March to May 1990: Oceanway Studios, Los Angeles, California (*Under the Red Sky*).

- April 1990: Wilbury Mountain Studio, Bel Air, Los Angeles, California (*Traveling Wilburys Vol. 3*)

- Mid-October 1992: Bob Dylan 30th Anniversary Concert Celebration, including rehearsals, New York City.

Harrison would often quote Dylan's lyrics like it was scripture. Here are a few examples:

"I'm really quite simple. I don't want to be in the business full-time, because I'm a gardener. I plant flowers and watch them grow. I don't go out to clubs and partying. I stay at home and watch the river flow." [203]

"One body is called the causal body, the next body is called the astral body and the third is called the gross physical body. So death is only relative to birth - If you don't wanna die, you don't get born. But as long as you're born, you've got to die, because just as sure as night time is gonna follow daytime, death is gonna follow birth. Like Bob Dylan said, "Look out kid, it's something you did. God knows when, but you're doing it again."" [204]

"I said, "You don't have to have a Number 1. You want to be number one. The record is second." I say, if you set yourself up looking for success, when you have a failure, you fall much deeper. I say, bring the two together. As Bob Dylan said, "When you find out you are at the top, you are at the bottom."" [205]

---

[201] *The George Harrison Interview*, Mitchell Glazer, Crawdaddy, 2/1977

[202] http://www.bjorner.com/still.htm, *Still on the Road*, Retrieved 11/26/2016

[203] *I Me Mine*, George Harrison, Genesis Publications, 1980.

[204] *The George Harrison Interview*, J. Kordosh, Creem magazine

[205] http://www.superseventies.com/ssgeorgeharrison.html, *George Harrison - In His Own Words*, Retrieved 11/26/2016

George had this to say about writing *I'd Have You Anytime* with Dylan:

"I was saying to him, 'You write incredible lyrics,' and he was saying, 'How do you write those tunes?' …And I was saying, 'Come on, write me some words,' and he was scribbling words down. And it just killed me because he'd been doing all these sensational lyrics … The idea of Dylan writing something, like, so very simple." [206]

Harrison also recycled a riff from Dylan's *I Want You* for his 1973 hit single, *Give Me Love (Peace On Earth)*, and the Dylan song title, *It's All Over Now, Baby Blue*, was used in Harrison's song, *When We Was Fab*.

Here's Dylan on Harrison, late 2001:

"He was a giant, a great, great soul, with all of the humanity, all of the wit and humor, all of the wisdom, the spirituality, the common sense of a man and compassion for people. He inspired love and had the strength of a hundred men. He was like the sun, the flowers and the moon, and we will miss him enormously. The world is a profoundly emptier place without him." [207]

The following year, Dylan performed Harrison's *Something* at Madison Square Garden:

"Thank you. There's a tribute coming, I guess it's the next week or the week after, it's over in England, for George Harrison and <inaudible> lots of people <inaudible> I'm not sure who. But we can't make it. I just want to do this song <inaudible> for George because we were such good buddies." [208]

For what it's worth, I always associate the "Quiet Beatle" with the song, *Ain't Talkin'*, where Dylan is in a *"mystic garden"* and *"someone hit me from behind,"* and now *"the gardener is gone."* Harrison died on November 29, 2001.

---

[206] *The George Harrison Interview*, Mitchell Glazer, Crawdaddy, 2/1977

[207] http://www.ew.com/article/2012/02/25/george-harrison-birthday-video, *Happy Birthday, George Harrison! Celebrate with Evan Rachel Wood's cover of his classic Bob Dylan collab 'I'd Have You Anytime' – EXCLUSIVE*, Retrieved 11/26/2016

[208] http://www.bjorner.com/DSN24270%20-%202002%20US%20Fall%20Tour.htm#DSN24570, *Still on the Road*, Retrieved 11/26/2016

Bob Dylan content in Scorsese's George Harrison documentary, or the lack thereof

October 7, 2011

Martin Scorsese's documentary, *George Harrison: Living In The Material World*, premiered in the U.S. over the last two nights on HBO.

Bob Dylan, like Harrison, enjoys his privacy and rarely participates in projects such as this. However, Dylan and Harrison were such good friends that it would be impossible to leave Dylan out of the picture entirely. Scorsese and Olivia Harrison, George's widow, must have made some difficult decisions of what to include in *Living In The Material World*. Harrison did not need to be overshadowed by Dylan as he had been in The Beatles.

In part one, Dylan is only acknowledged in two passing images - The chart placing of *Like A Rolling Stone* just below a Beatles' single, and Harrison seen reading the paperback version of *Dont Look Back*.

The start of the second half features a couple of photographs of Dylan and Harrison, presumably taken at Dylan's Woodstock home in late 1968, although his name is not mentioned. Dylan's name is finally uttered during the segment about the unexpected success of the Harrison-produced *Hare Krishna Mantra* by the Radha Krishna Temple. The record was played between acts at Dylan's 1969 Isle of Wight concert.

It was up to producer Phil Spector to discuss Dylan's appearance at 1971's Concert For Bangla Desh, explaining how he went to Dylan's apartment to retrieve the reluctant musician. Later, while it is not an obvious reference, Harrison's recycled riff from Dylan's *I Want You* can be heard in *Give Me Love (Peace On Earth)*.

The Dylan-Harrison composition, *I'd Have You Anytime*, was used as a juxtaposition for a series of family home movies after a sequence about financing the controversial film, *Monty Python's Life Of Brian*.

It was interesting that an unreleased recording of Harrison covering *Let It Be Me* was used in the film after the report of the 1980 murder of John Lennon. In 1981, Dylan unexpectedly issued his second version of the song as the b-side to *Heart Of Mine* in Europe.

Dylan's presence is most felt in the Traveling Wilburys' segment. He is first seen in a photograph behind a microphone, wearing headphones and holding up a sheet of paper, while Tom Petty recalled the origins of the band. The video *Handle With Care* was shown next, with Petty describing how the song was written.

The previously unseen footage of Dylan snapping his fingers, then swaying back and forth while listening for instructions as he was recording his vocals for *Margarita*, was probably the highlight for Dylan fans. There's also a clip from the end of the *Dirty World* recording session, when each Wilbury took a turn at the mic. Some of this footage was used with a voiceover in the documentary *The True History of the Traveling Wilburys*, but this is "clean" with a slightly different edit.

Toward the end of the movie, there's a revealing scene when Olivia Harrison interprets George's lyrics of *I'd Have You Anytime* as a way for him to communicate with Dylan about letting Harrison into his life, while a photo of both musicians from 1968 was shown on the screen.

The three-and-a-half hour documentary barely scratched the surface of Harrison's life. The pacing reminded me of *A Hard Day's Night*, which started off claustrophobic, then featured a liberating escape sequence halfway through. In the case of *Living In The Material World*, Harrison was able to free himself from The Beatles and forge his own path, although the pressures of fame still waited in the shadows.

Unfortunately, many aspects of Harrison's life were not covered, including most of his solo recording career, the success of Cloud Nine, and his 1991 tour of Japan with Eric Clapton. There could also have been more about George and Bob, including the joy of hanging out with Dylan and the Band in 1968 and how it contrasted with the tension within The Beatles, stories of Harrison secretly taping Dylan's performances, and other anecdotes.

However, this is Harrison's story. In the first half, Harrison could barely get a word in. In the second, the "Quiet Beatle" finally had his say.

All things must pass - The Bob Dylan-George Harrison connection

November 28, 2011

George Harrison left his earthly body ten years ago, on November 29, 2001.

The Martin Scorsese documentary *Living In The Material World* premiered in theaters and on television in October. While the fate of a U.S release is still a mystery, some territories have the opportunity to buy a box set that includes a DVD/Blu-Ray, book, and CD featuring 10 previously unreleased tracks. (Update: It was eventually released in the U.S. separately.)

While I've already written about Harrison's friendship and collaborations with Bob Dylan, the movie and CD made me think of connections I had not covered before.

In early 1974, Bob Dylan and The Band returned to the road touring North America. Dylan's set featured radical reworkings of his classic catalog to mostly positive reviews. Over the summer, a recovering Eric Clapton and a reunited Crosby, Stills, Nash and Young followed suit.

The year was to end with the first U.S tour by a former Beatle. Three years after The Concert For Bangla Desh, George Harrison was hitting the road.

I saw Harrison's evening performance at Long Island's Nassau Coliseum on December 15, with John Lennon watching from the wings. I loved it, but understood why others did not.

In some ways, the show was similar to Dylan's Before The Flood tour. Like Dylan with The Band, Harrison shared the bill with other named artists, including Billy Preston, Tom Scott, and a lengthy Indian music section which was to feature Ravi Shankar. Unfortunately, Shankar did not appear at this stop due to health concerns, but his compositions were still performed.

Harrison, unused to touring, lost his voice early in the tour. He also had some personal problems, including his wife recently having left him for his friend Clapton (which bothered him less than you would think). In addition, Harrison, like Dylan, radically rearranged his back catalog. This is where the problems really started.

I don't know why anyone going to a Harrison concert in 1974 would be expecting a Beatles show, but that's what they wanted. Instead of seeing Harrison express himself, they wanted to preserve their image of Beatle or Bangladesh George. The crowd reacted more to Preston's R&B hit singles than Harrison's musical meditations.

Personally, I loved what Harrison was doing. It was real. It was a statement. He wasn't even going to perform any Beatles material, but was talked into it by Shankar. Sure, it might have been passive aggressive, even immature. However, it was something you rarely see. A rock legend not trying to please an arena crowd. Like Dylan, he was challenging his audience, sharing what he had experienced.

"The dream is over," Lennon sang in 1970, but people wouldn't accept it. So Harrison hit them over the head, with big band parodies of Fab classics like *Something* (*"Go and find yourself another lover"*), *While My Guitar Gently 'Smiles'*, a boogie jam version of *For You Blue*, and a cover of Lennon's *In My Life* (*"I love God more"*). You could hear the crowd moan after some of these lyric changes. It was not what they wanted, but Harrison knew what he was doing. He was saying, *"Wake up, The Beatles are over. It is time to move forward. There are more important things in life."*

The songs from his recent albums *Living In The Material World* and *Dark Horse* were faithful to the originals, but even his hits from *All Things Must Pass* - the closing *What Is Life* and encore *My Sweet Lord* (based on Preston's soulful Apple Records arrangement) - met the same fate as his Beatles classics. Harrison turned *My Sweet Lord* into a religious sing along, calling out the names Jesus Christ (*"I don't want to hear any swearing!"* he joked), Buddha, and, of course, Krishna. The crowd was hopping up and down at this point, clapping along, but they did not like being lectured. Only seven years before, The Beatles released *Sgt. Pepper*, taking everyone on a magical ride to open their minds. Now the crowd that dropped acid and danced naked to Jimi Hendrix at Woodstock wanted nostalgia, and was ready for disco. Or punk. Of course, some of Dylan's fans in the mid-1960s didn't like his new sound or arrangements either, but by 1974, they finally got it.

I had another thought about Dylan and Harrison. While listening to the audio tracks from the *Living In The Material World* set, it occurred to me that in some ways Harrison was mining territory in 1970 that Dylan would also visit from another angle at the end of the decade. Rock and Roll music has been linked to religion from the start. The most obvious example would be Elvis Presley, who released his first Christmas album in 1957, and first gospel LP three years later. While Harrison's religious beliefs were occasionally expressed in some of his later Beatles-era compositions, *All Things Must Pass* can be seen as much of a manifesto as Dylan's *Slow Train Coming*. Harrison's 1970 triple album was pretty much accepted for what it was, with many fans hearing Eastern philosophies for the first time. Aside from songs like the smash hit *My Sweet Lord*, the "lessons" were subtle, and easier for the listener to swallow.

On the other hand, *Slow Train Coming* baffled and alienated old fans while attracting new ones. It took years for many to get past the shock of Dylan exploring the New Testament and finally realize the richness of this music.

However, the public soon tired of Harrison's religious dogma, as he tired of his own fame and audience. For the rest of his career, Harrison would continue to do what he pleased, often taking many years off between albums, occasionally returning to the stage as he did on October 16, 1992, when I saw him perform for the second and final time at "Bob-Fest" in New York's Madison Square Garden.

Paul McCartney, marriage, and Mother's Day

May 7, 2011

"The judge, he holds a grudge" - Bob Dylan, 1966.

"And the county judge, who held a grudge" - Paul & Linda McCartney, 1973.

Congratulations to Paul McCartney on his engagement to Nancy Shevell. Third time's a charm. First one too. The second, not so much.

It is generally acknowledged that Bob Dylan and The Beatles were two of the biggest forces in 1960s popular music. In 1985, McCartney was chosen to close the U.K. Live Aid concert, while Dylan had the honor in the U.S.

While Dylan's friendships and collaborations with John Lennon, George Harrison, and Ringo Starr have been well documented, he did not appear to have much of a connection with Paul McCartney.

In a 40th anniversary *Rolling Stone* interview, however, Dylan said, he was in *"awe"* of the ex-Beatle, praising his work ethic, and for making it all seem *"so damn effortless."*

In 2008, McCartney commented in a radio interview, [209] *"Bob Dylan would be lovely* [to collaborate with] *because I admire him."* However, after ridiculous rumors spread in 2009 about a secret collaboration - with Starr joining in, no less - McCartney told *Spin* magazine, *"So much has been written about me doing a collaboration with Bob or me doing a collaboration with Ringo and Bob. But that is not happening yet. We're nowhere near. I did say I wanted to work with Bob but that was ages ago and he hasn't been in touch. I can't contact him. That's not cool."* [210]

He was also quoted as saying in *The Independent*, *"No, that's a newspaper thing . . . He just said some very complimentary things about me in some interviews and I love him. I think he's a great poet and writer so I've always admired him. I don't rule it out and I admire him. But we're not the kind of people who would ring each other up."* [211]

While McCartney had obviously been influenced by Dylan in the 1960s, it continued into his solo career as well.

When he formed Wings in 1971, the debut album, *Wings Wild Life*, was recorded quickly, modeling himself after Dylan's recording technique, saying, *"I was inspired by Dylan, the way he just kind of comes in the studio and everyone falls in and makes a track."* [212]

Dylan has paid tribute to McCartney as well over the years. In 1978, when he headlined a massive gig at England's Blackbushe Aerodrome on July 15, 1978, Dylan backed a solo turn by background singer Jo Ann Harris on McCartney's *The Long and Winding Road*. [213]

Also, when George Harrison joined Dylan in the studio on May 1, 1970, they covered McCartney's most famous tune, *Yesterday*. In recent years, McCartney has stated that the song may have unconsciously been written about his mother.

On a personal note:

---

[209] http://www.nme.com/news/music/nme-1317-1336547, *Paul McCartney: 'I want to record with Bob Dylan'*, Retrieved 11/26/2016

[210] http://www.spin.com/2009/06/paul-mccartney-mgmt-and-bob-dylan/, *Paul McCartney on MGMT and Bob Dylan*, Retrieved 11/26/2016

[211] http://www.independent.ie/woman/how-the-maccas-want-to-save-the-planet-26554027.html, *How the Maccas want to save the planet*, Retrieved 11/26/2016

[212] *The Beatles Forever*, Nicholas Schaffner, McGraw-Hill Book Company, New York, 1978

[213] http://www.bjorner.com/DSN04000%201978%20Europe%20Tour.htm#DSN04260, *Still on the Road*, Retrieved 11/26/2016

When the Wings Over America tour was happening in 1976, I wanted to go. I had already seen Lennon in 1972 and Harrison in 1974. One morning, there was a report in *The New York Times* that tickets for the show would go on sale that day, presumably in the morning. I had to go to school, but asked my mother if she - or someone - could try to get tickets.

Not wanting to wait in a long line, my mother decided to give it a try in the mid-morning. She drove 20 minutes to Abraham & Strauss in Babylon, Long Island, and when she arrived, there was no line at all. She asked one of the women at the Ticketron booth if she knew anything about Paul McCartney and Wings tickets. They hadn't, but looked it up in a loose leaf notebook. It said that tickets for the Madison Square Garden and Nassau Coliseum shows would go on sale at 3 p.m.

My mother returned at 2:30. There were only a few people ahead in line. She got floor seats for one of the Madison Square shows.

Thanks, Mom, and Happy Mother's Day!

Note: Dylan contributed a version of *Things We Said Today* to a McCartney tribute album, *The Art of McCartney*, released in 2014.

In November, 2016, after sharing the Desert Trip with Dylan, among other 1960's musical icons, McCartney was asked the following question on the *You Gave Me The Answer* blog on his official website: *"Bob Dylan recently took part in a tribute album featuring your songs. If you were to cover one of Dylan's songs, which would you choose?"* His reply? *"That's a very difficult question to answer, as there are so many great songs. I mean,* Mr. Tambourine Man *just comes to mind because it's something you could cover. Singing Dylan songs can be difficult because something like* Like A Rolling Stone, *it's so Dylan that it would be hard to get the spirit that he puts on it.* A Hard Rain's A-Gonna Fall *is another good one, you know. I'd put that on a list as well."* [214]

The Byrds, 'Chimes Of Freedom'

May 2, 2011

What would be an appropriate song for today? How about The Byrds covering Dylan's *Chimes Of Freedom*?

Bob Dylan wrote most of the song in early 1964 (although he probably started it late in 1963), and began performing it in concert soon after. He recorded the seven-plus minute track in seven takes on June 9, 1964, for the album, *Another Side Of Bob Dylan*.

Recording information: [215]

Studio A

Columbia Recording Studio New York City, New York June 9, 1964, 7-10 pm

Produced by Tom Wilson. Engineers: Hallie and Catero.

However, by 1965 the song was no longer a part of his live repertoire, and Dylan did not perform it on stage again until 1987, while touring with the Grateful Dead and, later, Tom Petty & The Heartbreakers. Dylan dug it up again for the 1993 Bill Clinton presidential inauguration concert; re-recorded it on Halloween, 1998, with Joan Osborne and Al Kooper for the TV movie, *The '60s*; and has performed it sporadically since 2000.

The Byrds, of course, famously covered an outtake from *Another Side*, *Mr. Tambourine Man* in 1965, and ushered in the "folk-rock" era. The success of the single was another catalyst for Dylan to "go electric." For the accompanying album, The Byrds recorded three more Dylan compositions, all from *Another Side*:

Mr. Tambourine Man: Rec. date: January 20, 1965

All I Really Want To Do: Rec. date: March 8, 1965

Spanish Harlem Incident: Rec. date: April 14, 1965

Chimes of Freedom: Rec. date: April 22, 1965

The Byrds' session to cover *Chimes Of Freedom* was apparently not all "peace and love." It was the final track to be recorded for their 1965 debut album, *Mr. Tambourine Man*. The recording session was less than harmonious. According to Jim Dickson, the band's manager, singer-guitarist David Crosby *"announced that he wasn't going to sing on the recording and was instead leaving the studio for the day."* Dickson said he ended up *"sitting on Crosby's chest, telling him 'The only way you're going to get through that door is over my dead body...You're going to stay in this room until you do the vocal.'"* It reportedly brought Crosby to tears. Dickson said, *"It was one of those cathartic moments. He got it all out and sang like an angel.'"* [216]

---

[215] http://www.punkhart.com/dylan/sessions-1.html, *Bob Dylan: The Recording Sessions Part One*, Michael Krogsgaard, Retrieved 11/26/2016

[216] *The Byrds: Mr. Tambourine Man* (1996 Columbia Legacy CD Reissue Notes), Johnny Rogan

Did Dylan influence Eric Burdon and the Animals?

May 11, 2011

"You can't say an icon like Bob Dylan has a great singing voice. He doesn't, but he has impeccable timing and of course it's his writing and what he says, not particularly in the way that he says it, but is important and goes to people's hearts." - Eric Burdon interview for *Classic Bands.* [217]

Eric Victor Burdon was born on May 11, 1941. He is best known as the lead singer of the Animals and, for a while, War (*Spill The Wine*).

When the Animals covered *The House Of The Rising Sun*, it was one of the catalysts that lead Dylan to "go electric."

It was assumed that the Animals heard Dylan's version as *House of the Risin' Sun*, which was released on his 1962 debut album, and decided to cover it with electric instrumentation, as well as change the narrator's gender in the lyrics. It was recorded in one take on May 18, 1964, and produced by Mickie Most. The single came out a month later in the U.K., and August in the U.S., reaching number one in both countries.

Dylan's reaction? Most reports say Dylan was ecstatic. He was excited when he first heard The Animals' version on his car radio and *"jumped out of his car seat."* [218]

In Anthony Scaduto's biography, *Dylan,* after he returned to New York from a U.K. tour in 1964, Dylan raved, *"My God, ya outta hear what's going down over there. Eric Burdon, the Animals, ya know? Well, he's doing* House Of The Rising Sun *in rock! Rock! It's . . .wild. Blew my mind."* [219]

However, lead singer Eric Burdon is also quoted as saying, *"The best aspect of it, I've been told, is that Bob Dylan, who was angry at first, turned into a rocker. Dylan went electric in the shadow of The Animals classic "House of the Rising Sun.""* [220]

Burdon also claimed their version was not learned from Dylan, but from a folk singer named Johnny Handle. However, Animals guitarist Hilton Valentine (born on May 21, 1943), remembers it differently:

"Bob Dylan's version was the one I first heard. But Eric [Burdon] had heard the Josh White version. Bob Dylan got his version from Dave Van Ronk." [221]

Nina Simone's version has also been credited as the inspiration. The Animals would later have a hit with a cover of her record, *Don't Let Me Be Misunderstood.*

On December 8, 1964, producer Tom Wilson overdubbed electric instrumentation to Dylan's version, but it remained unreleased until 1995's Interactive Music CD–ROM, *Highway 61 Interactive.*

Animals' keyboard player Alan Price can be seen in the 1965 U.K. tour documentary *Dont Look Back.* Burdon also reportedly met Dylan in the winter of 1965. Bassist Chas Chandler went on to manage Jimi Hendrix.

Dylan revived the song on stage sporadically since the mid-1980s. When performing in Newcastle, England, on April 12, 2007, he paid tribute to the Animals in their hometown by performing *House*

---

[217] http://www.classicbands.com/EricBurdonInterview.html, *Gary James' Interview With Eric Burdon,* Retrieved 11/26/2016

[218] *Dylan Played His Debt to the Animals,* Graeme Whitfield, The Journal (Newcastle, England), 4/14/2007

[219] *Bob Dylan: An Intimate Biography,* Anthony Scaduto, W.H. Allen, New York/London, 1972

[220] http://www.songfacts.com/blog/interviews/eric_burdon/, *Songfacts Dan MacIntosh: Eric Burdon,* Retrieved 11/26/2016

[221] http://www.tomguerra.com/HiltonValentine.htm, *Hilton Valentine - From Animal to Skiffledog,* Retrieved 11/26/2016

Of The Risin' Sun. House was the second single by the Animals. The first was a song also found on Dylan's debut album, a rewritten version of *Baby Let Me Follow You Down*, retitled *Baby Let Me Take You Home*, credited to Bert Russell (a.k.a. Bert Berns) and Wes Farrell. Did they get that from Dylan? Not according to the band. It turns out that they credit Josh White for this one as well.

Dylan Cover lists Burdon singing *It's All Over Now, Baby Blue* with a reunited Animals in 1977. As a solo artist, Burdon covered Dylan's *Knockin' On Heaven's Door* and *One More Cup Of Coffee (Valley Below)*. The Animals, with Peter Barton on vocals, performed *I Shall Be Released* in 2007.

When asked in 2007 if the "wounds were healed" after Dylan was accused of ripping off the Animals' version of *House of the Rising Sun*, Burdon replied, "*I don't know. I'd have to ask myself who was wounded in the first place? Not me. I think that Bob just had to make some adjustments. I'm not sure there were any wounds that needed to be healed.*" [222]

---

[222] http://www.pennyblackmusic.co.uk/MagSitePages/Article.aspx?id=5654, *Eric Burdon Interview*, Lisa Torem. Retrieved 11/26/2016

Harvey Brooks interview

July, 2013

"Thanks everyone and especially Harvey Brooks! You would know, you the man!" - Duke Robillard (*Facebook*, July 3, 2013)

If you are a music fan, you probably have recordings featuring Harvey Brooks somewhere in your collection. He's played with everyone from Seals & Crofts to Fontella Bass to Jimi Hendrix. If you've heard Bob Dylan's *Highway 61 Revisited*, *Bitches Brew* by Miles Davis, *Mixed Bag* by Richie Havens, or *Super Session* with Al Kooper, Mike Bloomfield, and Stephen Stills, you are familiar with the bass playing expertise of Mr. Brooks.

He was born Harvey Goldstein on the 4th of July, 1944. To help celebrate his birthday, Brooks consented to answer a handful of questions for the *Bob Dylan Examiner* from his home in Jerusalem via email, about a somewhat arbitrary selection of legendary recordings on which he appears.

You were playing with Bob Dylan in 1965 during the *Highway 61 Revisited* sessions, and at a couple of his legendary early electric gigs ...

It was the beginning of my career, incredible times, and the music was great.

When did you go from Harvey Goldstein to Harvey Brooks?

Right after the Highway 61 *album.*

What was it like in the inner circle during the live shows (Forest Hills and the Hollywood Bowl)?

I was aware that the folk traditionalists were having a hard time with the electric-ness of the new folk-rock sound and that certainly added a tension in the air. Bob was committed to his new sound and was not concerned about the attitudes of the non-acceptees of his evolution. He planned the concert perfectly. I was only concerned about playing the music of the songs as good as I could. I would say the same for Levon (Helm), Robbie (Robertson) and Al (Kooper). A good time was had by all.

What was the stage equipment like?

Primitive P.A. and monitor system. We had to depend on hearing each other and watching Dylan. Since the audience was in the stands and not on the field in front of us, until they rushed the stage, we could only hear their rumblings but not see them. Lighting was primitive as well. Bob, Robbie and I were playing Fender Amps. Bob and Robbie I think had Fender Twins and I played through a dual Showman.

Did you have the opportunity to speak with Murray "the K" at Forest Hills? If so, what was he like?

The only strange touch was Murray "the K." Murray was a great New York rock 'n' roll D.J. I worked with him a few times. He was a pro and even though he was the politically correct wrong choice, he delivered his M.C. duties professionally. He really knew his top forty music. Murray also brought Cream and The Who to New York for their first American concerts.

Miles Davis' *Bitches Brew*: The sessions began the day after the Woodstock festival ended. Were you aware of the concert's cultural significance, or were you too busy with your own career?

At the time I was a staff producer at Columbia Records and was tuned into recording and performing.

It was as groundbreaking as *Highway 61* in many ways. Did you sense that at the time? How did the two sessions compare/contrast?

Both sessions were spontaneous and intense. Bob had his tunes written and while he was still messing with the lyrics, he knew how the songs should go musically. Miles offered up tone centers with no written music and the sessions were based on the musician's intuition and Miles's direction. My friend Teo Macero was the producer, and between him and Miles in the editing room, Bitches Brew *was born.*

What was it like playing with another bassist? Did you work things out, or were you free to play as you chose?

I loved playing alongside Dave Holland and Ron Carter. The whole idea for me was to create a groove and lock in and they would play around it.

In 1968, you played on Cass Elliot's first solo album, *Dream a Little Dream*. What was the atmosphere like?

John Simon [The Band, Big Brother and the Holding Company, Leonard Cohen] was the producer on that album, and he called me at the Chateau Marmont Hotel [in West Hollywood] to come down to the studio and record with Cass. The first time I met her was at the studio. She was a pleasure to work with. Very positive and energetic and a great vocalist. The session was filled with excellent L.A. session musicians such as guitarist James Burton and drummers Jimmy Gordon and Hal Blaine, John Sebastian, and Steve Stills, among others.

Speaking of Sebastian, you played on the first solo album he made after leaving The Lovin' Spoonful. It was recorded in late 1968 with an all-star cast, including David Crosby, Stephen Stills, and Graham Nash before they became an official trio. The album *John B. Sebastian* is an underrated gem in my opinion. Unfortunately, the LP's release was delayed until early 1970 due to contractual complications, thus lessening its impact. What can you tell me about how you knew Sebastian, the sessions, and anything else of interest.

When I was working with Cass Elliot on her album, I was staying at her home, rehearsing for her first solo gig in Las Vegas. Steve Stills - we had recorded Super Session *together with Al Kooper - and Graham Nash came over and, while we were floating in the pool, invited me to join their new group which was to be "Crosby, Stills & Nash," and would soon be rehearsing in Sag Harbor, N.Y. ... Paul Harris, Dallas Taylor and I met in Sag Harbor for rehearsals and both Paul and I stayed at John Sebastian's house. I believe that John had influenced the group to rehearse there ... We started rehearsing and when it was time to talk business, both Paul and I could not come to terms. We were then available to record with John who was just beginning pre-production with producer Paul Rothchild [The Doors, Lovin' Spoonful, Janis Joplin] on the album,* John B. Sebastian. *We rehearsed at John's home studio and recorded at Jerry Ragavoy's "Hit Factory."*

You, Harris, and Taylor were asked to be part of CSN? Can you elaborate? As a backing band? Part of a different type of band (i.e. a six- piece band)?

I thought we'd share financially as partners in a six-piece band, understanding that the writers owned their own songs but we could share revenue from sales, merchandising, and live performances. Management did not approve. Things work out for the best.

Paul Kantner's early solo project, *Jefferson Starship: Blows Against The Empire*, sounds very focused, but there were many musicians involved. Were things organized, or kind of crazy? Laid back?

I was at Wally Heider's studio producing a record for Columbia Records called Sweet Apple. *We were on a break and I walked out of the studio and into some of the folks in Jefferson Airplane. They invited me into their studio to play on this jam tune (Starship). I picked up a guitar and joined the festivities.*

You worked with keyboardist Ray Manzarek, who died recently. What was a recording session with The Doors like?

Ray was an innovative musician who created a unique sound with his bass line chord approach. Coming in to play bass with The Doors could have been uncomfortable had Ray not been open to my ideas. The album I played on was Soft Parade, *and their producer, Paul Rothchild, felt the band needed to try some new ideas to keep The Doors fans interested. My good friend and keyboardist/arranger Paul Harris wrote the horn charts.*

You played live on stage with The Doors. Were the shows as wild as legend has it?

Jim Morrison was an exciting performer who laid his soul out on the line for every performance. I played the Forum in L.A. and Madison Square Garden in New York. These shows were on the edge from soundcheck to the last groupie or hanger on.

Richie Havens appeared to be a really nice, genuine guy. You played on his album _Mixed Bag_. How did you meet him?

I met Richie at the Cafe Au Go Go in Greenwich Village. After the Dylan Highway 61 _sessions I started hangin' out in the village. Phil Ochs had an apartment he was leaving on Thompson, right off of Bleecker, so I took over his lease. I was now right around the corner from the Cafe and became the house bass player. I started playing with Richie and we became good friends. When Richie got his deal through GrossCourt productions with Verve Folkways, I was, at that time, living in Mill Valley, California, playing with the Electric Flag. His producer John Court, who also produced the Electric Flag, asked me to arrange the rhythm tracks for the upcoming sessions._

How did you get to jam with Jimi Hendrix?

Cafe Au Go Go and Steve Paul's The Scene were the two hot spots. Jimi and I became good friends. We would start at the Au Go Go and then go uptown to The Scene. At the Go Go, one jam was with Duane Allman, Paul Butterfield, Elvin Bishop & Jimi, and then we went uptown and jammed with Jimi, Buddy Miles, Jim Morrison & Johnny Winter. The Jimi Hendrix Experience and Electric Flag shared many bills and Jimi, Buddy and I once had a killer jam at the Fillmore East.

How did the 1970 sessions for Bob Dylan's _New Morning_ compare to the _Highway 61_ sessions only five years before?

When I walked into Columbia [Studio] A for the Highway 61 _sessions, it was all new for me: People, places and the world of pop music. Five years later, I had (by now) played live concerts with Dylan at Forest Hills and the Hollywood Bowl, moved out to Mill Valley, San Francisco, to play with Mike Bloomfield and the Electric Flag, recorded_ Soft Parade _with The Doors and played live concerts with them at the Forum in L.A. and Madison Square Garden in New York,_ Super Session _with Al Kooper …_

Walking into the studio for New Morning, _there was a pressure that I'd grown to recognize when there was a desire to keep the music real as an artist evolves. Dylan had been working on the album for a while and I think I was part of the second or third group of musicians Bob used. I enjoyed the sessions._

Anything you'd like to add? Say?

LIFE IS GOOD!!!

The Turtles go folk-rock, meet Dylan

March 21, 2011

The Turtles are known for such 1960s classics as *Happy Together, You Baby, She'd Rather Be With Me, She's My Girl, Eleanor,* and *You Showed Me.* In 1970, founding members Howard Kaylan (lead vocal) and Mark Volman (singer/guitarist/saxophonist), along with bassist Jim Pons, went on to join Frank Zappa and the Mothers Of Invention. Soon after, Kaylan and Volman formed their own act, The Phlorescent Leech and Eddie, later shortening it to Flo & Eddie. Kaylan and Volman also sang backup on countless records, including hits for Bruce Springsteen (*Hungry Heart*) and T. Rex (*Bang A Gong (Get it On)*).

In the early 1960s, Kaylan and Volman started a surf-rock combo called The Nightriders, later known as The Crossfires. By 1964, the band morphed into a folk-rock act first called The Turtles. In 1965, The Turtles released their debut LP, titled *It Ain't Me, Babe.* The album included three Dylan covers - *Love Minus Zero, Like A Rolling Stone,* and the title track. The Turtles' version of *It Ain't Me, Babe* became a top five hit. [223]

It Ain't Me, Babe is one of Dylan's most popular songs, even though it was never a hit single for him. The *"No, no, no"* line in the chorus has been interpreted as the antidote to The Beatles' *"Yeah, yeah, yeah"* from their recent hit, *"She Loves You."*

The Turtles actually encountered Dylan while on tour soon after: [224]

When the Turtles played at the Phone Booth in New York, they were pleased to see Bob Dylan sitting a mere eight feet away. He had his shades on and was slumped over. Afterwards, the boys eagerly introduced themselves. Dylan responded, deadpan, to the Turtles live performance of their hit, Dylan's very own "It Ain't Me Babe": "That's a great last song, it should be a record."

Dylan mentioned The Turtles in the Martin Scorsese documentary, *No Direction Home.*

---

[223] http://theturtles.com/downloads/TurtlesLONGHistory_1989.pdf, *The History of The Turtles Featuring Flo & Eddie,* Retrieved 11/26/2016

[224] http://theturtles.com/downloads/TurtlesLONGHistory_1989.pdf, *The History of The Turtles Featuring Flo & Eddie,* Retrieved 11/26/2016

Davy Jones of The Monkees

February 29, 2012

Singer-songwriter-actor David Thomas "Davy" Jones, best known as a member of the television-based rock group The Monkees, died of a heart attack earlier today. He was 66 years-old.

I've been a Monkees fan ever since September 12, 1966, when they first appeared on NBC-TV. For a brief moment, The Monkees eclipsed The Beatles as my favorite band, until my parents sat me down and read an article (probably in *The New York Times*) explaining how The Beatles were a real band that played their own instruments and wrote their own songs. So the pre-fab four were demoted to second place, but I never missed an episode of their show, and still bought their first five albums on the Colgems label, the first four in monaural, as soon as I was able.

When the show was canceled (around the same of another childhood favorite, *Batman*), I moved to much more "cool" interests, but I never really stopped loving The Monkees. I would occasionally see the shows in syndication, watch Dolenz, Jones, Boyce & Hart on *The Mike Douglas Show*, and, even though it felt uncool, bought the *Monkee Business* vinyl picture disc in the early 1980s.

I was fortunate enough to see The Monkees in concert four times between 1986 and 2011. I even took my sons to a free outdoor concert in Boston about ten years ago.

When I saw the band in Lowell last year, they played close to 40 songs, mixing hits with deeper cuts. Jones jokingly announced that he was Davy's father, and "Davy" would be out in a moment. He still looked and sounded great, and it was surprising to hear of his death earlier today.

Looking around my music room earlier today, I saw two issues of *Monkees Monthly*, two Monkees paperbacks, a Mickey Dolenz postcard, a guitar-shaped promo-only Rhino CD compilation, various albums and CDs, and my Monkees t-shirt.

Davey Jones started as a child actor in Britain. He almost became a jockey, but stuck with singing and acting. When The Beatles debuted on *The Ed Sullivan Show* on February 9, 1964, Jones also performed, playing the part of the Artful Dodger with the Broadway cast of *Oliver!*

On July 26, 1965, before he was a Monkee, Davy Jones recorded seven tracks for his first album at United Recorders in Hollywood, California. One of the songs recorded was a cover of Bob Dylan's *It Ain't Me, Babe*. The Turtles had recently charted with their folk-rock version of the song, but Jones' take featured verses not included on that single. Among the heavy hitters on the session were Carol Kaye, Earl Palmer, Emil Richards, and Tommy Tedesco. Jones' version was eventually released as a single in Britain on April 14, 1967, in the wake of The Monkees' success.

There were some other connections between Dylan and The Monkees.

On *Theme Time Radio Hour*, Dylan played Linda Ronstadt's cover of the Michael Nesmith composition *Different Drum* for the *Musical Instruments* edition of the show, while The Monkees' version of *Last Train To Clarksville* was played on the first *Trains* episode. Not only did the latter song, like *It Ain't Me, Babe*, feature a chorus with the antithesis of The Beatles *"Yeah, Yeah, Yeah"* credo of the times, but Dylan mentioned the subversive nature of the The Monkees' hit, written by Tommy Boyce and Bobby Hart, with its hint at an anti-Vietnam war agenda, *"I've always believed that the first rule of being subversive is not to let anybody know you're being subversive."*

In one of the *Theme Time* episodes, Dylan mentioned his musical tastes knew no boundaries, saying that on his shelf, Thelonious Monk could be found right next to The Monkees. There is also an episode of The Monkees TV show where one of Dylan's album covers can be seen, and another where Nesmith makes a joke about *"some kid named Bob Dylan."*

Throughout their hey-hey-day, The Monkees played with some of the same musicians as Dylan, including Kenny Buttrey, Ry Cooder, Charlie McCoy, Dr. John, Leon Russell, Jerry Scheff, and Neil Young.

Dylan has been specifically credited as an influence on one Monkees song. The Nesmith-penned *St. Matthew* was recorded in Nashville and Hollywood, starting in June, 1968, with Nesmith, McCoy, David Briggs, Wayne Moss, Harold Bradley, and others, among those at the sessions. The track, however, was not released until way after the group split up. In the liner notes for the Rhino box set *Music Box*, Nesmith was quoted as saying, *"It's a song about Bob Dylan. The 'steal and kneel' is a reference to* She Belongs To Me.*"* Nesmith, like Dylan, was a pioneer in the field of "Country-Rock," and this is an early example.

Sample tweets and posts:

@carole_king Carole King: *RIP Davy Jones*

@davedavieskinks Dave Davies: *Hey Hey were The Monkees - so sad about Davey - oh man - shocked - will pray for Davey- wow*

@LifeAsWillSmith Will Smith: *R.I.P. Davy Jones. Retweet for respect.*

@kevinbacon Kevin Bacon: *When I was a kid I wanted to BE Davy Jones. Big part of what led me to showbiz. R.I.P. say.ly/TqS1vml*

@smhelloladies Stephen Merchant: *RIP Davy Jones. I adored The Monkees growing up and their songs are still on the iPod. Sad news*

@NeilDiamond Neil Diamond: *I'm sad to hear about Davy Jones. The Monkees were such a sensation that it was a thrill for me to have them record some of my early songs.*

@NekoCase Neko Case: *Mike Nesmith was my "boyfriend" but Davy Jones was my "best friend" in my childhood Monkee-liking politics.*

@WilliamShatner William Shatner: *My condolences go out to the family of Davy Jones. MBB*

@NancySinatra Nancy Sinatra: *Davy Jones leaves a wife, 4 daughters and a great legacy. Gone too soon.*

@peteyorn Pete Yorn: *I'll never forget when Davy Jones was on the Brady Bunch. RIP monkee man.*

@bobdylantheband Bob Dylan & The Band: *It has just been announced that the Monkeys Davy Jones passed away...*

@MonkeesOfficial The Monkees: *Very sad to report the news that Davy Jones has passed away - we will pass along more information as it comes in.*

Now playing (while writing this article): the first two vinyl Monkees albums, in mono.

(Thanks to Andrew Sandoval's book *The Monkees*, Thunder Bay Press [225])

---

[225] *The Monkees: The day-by-day story of the '60s TV pop sensation*, Andrew Sandoval, Thunder Bay Press, San Diego, CA. 2005

Pink Floyd's Roger Waters

September 6, 2011

George Roger Waters was born on September 6, 1943, in Leatherhead, Surrey, England. He's best known as a founding member of Pink Floyd, eventually taking a leadership role after the 1968 departure of Syd Barrett. Waters left the band in 1985 to pursue a solo career, while the other members continued with the name, music, and props, over his objections. Relations between the surviving members have warmed somewhat in recent years, with various permutations of the band performing at isolated events.

The music of Bob Dylan and Pink Floyd is not as diametrically opposed as it might first appear. For starters, they were both steeped in American music, most notably Rhythm and Blues, then went on to compose and perform more lengthy, mind-expanding, ground-breaking music. However, there is not much crossover in the careers of Dylan and the members of Pink Floyd.

Barrett wrote his original song *Bob Dylan Blues* sometime between 1962 and 1964. According to Julian Palacios' 1998 book, *Lost In The Woods*, a young Syd Barrett saw Bob Dylan in London, with his girlfriend, Libby Gausden. It states that Barrett saw Dylan's first major London show in March of 1963, but there is no evidence of such a performance. It must have been either The Royal Festival Hall in 1964, or one of a handful of smaller gigs between mid-December 1962 and early January 1963.

Since the Waters/Floyd split, Pink Floyd is known to have covered *Like A Rolling Stone* at a soundcheck in Tampa, Florida, on the fifth day of May, 1994, according to *Dylan Cover*. Meanwhile, Waters recorded his version of *Knockin' On Heaven's Door* for the score of the late 1990s Israeli film *The Dybbuk of the Holy Apple Field*. It was also included on 1998's *Flickering Flame: The Solo Years Volume 1*.

Here are some comments from Waters about Dylan:

"You can draw a line between what I'm interested in and what I'm not interested in. On one side you can name Dylan and Lennon, who observe the world and have feelings, and write songs directly from those feelings ... I think it is in the nature of all people who do these things - in the Lennon, the Dylan, the Pete Townshend manner, that come from the heart - that the gratification doesn't stay with you and you feel compelled to go start the process all over again." - Musician, November, 1992. [226]

When answering questions from fans on the *Rockline* radio program in 1993, [227] a caller asked if the "Bob" reference in his song, *Too Much Rope*, was about producer, Bob Ezrin. Waters replied, *"The reference when I actually put the word down on tape was to Bob Dylan because at the time, I was going through a kind of Bob Dylan sound-alike period to amuse myself in the studio. Uh, so I would be singing (Dylan style) "Each man has his price Bob", like that. For a joke. But afterwards, it seemed to me a rather appertain lyric for Bob Ezrin so I left it in because of Ezrin as a little gift for Bob Ezrin. Yeah."* Host Bob Cockburn then asked, *"So, Dylan in mind but if it works the other way, no problem with that either, huh?"* Waters replied, again in a Dylan-esque voice, *"That's right. That's right."*

In a special 2004 Pink Floyd edition of *Q* magazine, [228] when asked about punk, Waters replied, *"I've never been very interested in modern music. I might find some of it enjoyable, but it's never really been interesting. I never really heard The Clash, and certainly not The Sex Pistols, so I can't really answer that question. As I still am now, I was listening to Neil Young when all that happened. It passed me by. I'll always listen to a new Dylan album. But it takes an awful lot of something for anyone else to break into what I listen to."* Waters echoed that

---

[226] *Roger and Me - The Other Side of the Pink Floyd Story,* Matt Resnicoff, Musician, November 1992

[227] http://www.rogerwaters.org/atdrockline.html, *Rockline Interview by Bob Cockburn,* February 8, 1993, Retrieved 11/26/2016

[228] http://thrasherswheat.org/jammin/jammin_more.htm#waters, *Pink Floyd Q Special Edition,* October 2004. Retrieved 11/26/2016

sentiment on January 21, 2007, when he was interviewed by Mark Sainsbury of Television New Zealand's *Close Up*, saying he doesn't keep up, nor is he interested in modern music. *"I still listen to music and I listen to a lot of classical music,"* Waters said, *"and I have my few favorite sort of songwriters who, when they produce new work, I'll sort of listen to it. So I always buy the new Dylan album and the new Neil Young album and the new John Prine album and I'll sniff around one or two other things if I catch something on the radio. But by and large I'm not really interested in it."* [229]

Waters appeared on the Howard Stern's satellite radio program on January 18, 2012, back in happier days before Stern critiqued his pro-Palestinian (anti-Israeli) stance. Early on, Stern recalled a private concert he attended at someone's house with Jon Bon Jovi and other musicians, and observed Waters looked extremely unhappy at being invited to join in the festivities. Waters said that type of setup made him uncomfortable, adding he wasn't a *"troubadour … I'm not Neil Young or Bob Dylan."* Later, Waters credited Dylan's 1966 song, the "hypnotic" *Sad Eyed Lady of the Lowlands*, for breaking down the barrier of the short, AM friendly, three-minute pop song, saying *"If Bob can do it, I can do it."* Waters also had no problem with artists like The Who and Dylan having their songs used in commercials, citing the latter's appearance in a Victoria's Secret ad, adding, *"We're all different, and have different furrows to plow."*

Note: The inclusion of Roger Waters in the book is not an endorsement of his political views. Although he professes to be a fan, I doubt he agrees with the sentiments expressed in Dylan's 1983 song, *Neighborhood Bully*.

---

[229] TVNZ via https://www.neptunepinkfloyd.co.uk/forum/viewtopic.php?f=23&t=15754&view=next, *Excellent Interview with TVNZ from Close Up Program*, Retrieved 11/26/2016

Bob Dylan, The Who, and the 1968 TV show that never was

September 13, 2011

In 1968, there was a BBC television project in the works that would star the up-and-coming rock band, The Who. The series, *Sound and Picture City*, never came to fruition, but one of the guests scheduled to appear was Bob Dylan.

Details are scarce, but according to *Anywhere Anyhow Anywhere - The Complete Chronicle of The Who 1958-1978* (dated April 8, 1968):

The group made plans to start rehearsing and recording a (later aborted) BBC pilot for Sound and Picture City, *produced by Tony Palmer, with Radio 1 DJs Chris Denning and Kenny Everett, as well as Caroline Coon, founder of "Release," the drug charge aid organization. The Who were to sing a different song each week, and at the end of the series, an album of tracks would be released.*

Unlike the U.S. television sitcom The Monkees, The Who's *Sound and Picture City* would have been a musical variety show. According to Dave Marsh's book, *Before I Get Old - The Story Of The Who*:

A WMCA fan's newsletter from their spring tour of America spoke of an "upcoming" BBC series - a "one-hour pop music show with other artists filmed by the BBC mostly in America" ... Bob Dylan, The Monkees and Lulu were to be among the early guests. The BBC confirmed plans for the show through a press release from its American office.

Of course, it is unclear how much of a commitment Dylan made, but it would have been quite the coup to get the reclusive singer-songwriter on any television program during his late 1960s post-motorcycle accident phase.

In any case, *Sound and Picture City* was abandoned. Instead, The Who focused on their rock opera, *Tommy*, and went from the brink of bankruptcy to worldwide superstardom.

Sound and Picture City was also a working title for the 1968 BBC television special *Omnibus: All My Loving*, another project produced by Tony Palmer. Among the artists appearing on the show were Pink Floyd, Donovan, Jimi Hendrix, Cream, and The Who. [230] [231]

Dylan would not make any major television appearances until the following year, for the documentary *Johnny Cash: The Man And His Music*, and the premiere of *The Johnny Cash Show*. Dylan's name was also linked to a 1969 Smothers Brothers television special that never saw the light of day.

In 1969, The Who and Dylan both appeared at the Isle of Wight festival, although on different dates. Dylan and The Who would also share the bill at the Prince's Trust concert in London, 1996.

Her are some other Who-Dylan connections:

My Generation was originally based on Dylan's early style as heard in *Talkin' New York*. Townshend has mentioned that he was an early fan of Dylan's first two albums, back in his art school days.

Dylan in mentioned in The Who song, *The Seeker*.

Bob Dylan played The Who track, *La La La Lies* on the *Theme Time Radio Hour* episode, *Truth and Lies*, season three, episode 20.

Pete Townshend covered *Corrina, Corrina* for the charity album, *Chimes of Freedom: The Songs of Bob Dylan - Honoring 50 Years of Amnesty International*.

Cameron Crowe: Did you have any heroes when you were a kid? Townshend: "*Well, there was Bob Dylan. When I was a kid ... well, not a kid, but younger and listening to Dylan, I couldn't wait for the day when somebody would get to him and do that in-depth interview where everybody would find out what really was in the*

---

[230] *Echoes: The Complete History of Pink Floyd*, Glenn Povey, Chicago Review Press; First Edition edition, 2010

[231] http://www.imdb.com/title/tt0814001/fullcredits#cast, *Omnibus* (TV Series) *All My Loving* (1968), Retrieved 11/25/2016

back of his head ... You can't deny ...that Dylan's music marked a new dimension in rock 'n' roll. He opened the door for rock to say bigger and better things." [232]

Many thanks to Mike Segretto at *Psychobabble* for his inspiration and help with the article. [233]

---

[232] http://www.theuncool.com/journalism/pete-townshend-penthouse-magazine/, *Rock Wizard - The Who's Pete Townshend*, Cameron Crowe, Penthouse, 12/1974

[233] http://psychobabble200.blogspot.com. *Psychobabble*, Retrieved 11/26/2016

Stevie Wonder

May 15, 2011

Motown legend Stevie Wonder, born Steveland Hardaway Judkins, was a child prodigy. He began his recording career in 1962, at about the same time as Bob Dylan.

Dylan and Wonder collaborated a few times in the mid-1980:

- Co-presenters at the 1984 Grammy Awards

- The 1985 *We Are The World* session (where Wonder "coached" Dylan)

- 1986 celebration at the John F. Kennedy Performing Arts Center Opera House in Washington, D.C.

Stevie Wonder's cover of *Blowin' In The Wind* is pretty well known. It was included on Wonder's albums *Up-Tight - Everything's Alright* (1966), *Tamla-Motown Festival Tokyo '68* (1968 - Japan only) and *Stevie Wonder Live* (1970). Readers of this column are also probably aware of his performance at 1992's "Bob-Fest" concert.

But how many people are aware of his version of *Mr. Tambourine Man*, also from 1966? It was included on the album *Down To Earth*.

Wonder's cover of *Blowin' In The Wind* was a unique, soulful interpretation, which owed nothing to Bob Dylan, or Peter, Paul and Mary, for that matter. What is interesting about Wonder's take on *Mr. Tambourine Man* is that the version is obviously based on the arrangement by the Byrds, almost note-for-note.

Eric Clapton

March 29, 2011

Eric Patrick Clapton was born on March 30, 1945.

Bob Dylan first crossed paths with Clapton at Levy's Recording Studio, in London, on May 12, 1965. Tom Wilson was there to produce Dylan, with John Mayall's Bluesbreakers, featuring John McVie, Hughie Flint, and Clapton, who had just joined after leaving the Yardbirds. The session was not a success, probably due to the consumption of alcohol. Clapton said it was basically a "jam session" playing blues songs, with Dylan on piano, making it up as he went along.

Ten years later, Clapton showed up at one chaotic session for Dylan's *Desire* album. One track, *Romance In Durango*, made the final cut.

In 1976, Clapton was recording his album, *No Reason To Cry*, at the Band's Shangri-La Studios. Dylan appeared for the sessions, staying in the rose garden, in a tent made out of Ron Wood's clothes. He contributed guitar and vocals to his song *Sign Language*. In November, Clapton joined Dylan for the finale of The Last Waltz.

Dylan and Clapton recorded in London one more time, for the *Hearts Of Fire* soundtrack, in 1986.

Clapton appeared at Dylan's 1978 gig at England's Blackbushe Aerodrome, as well as Dylan's Wembley concert in 1984.

Clapton rehearsed a duet of *It Takes A Lot To Laugh, It Takes A Train To Cry* for the Bob Dylan 30th Anniversary Concert Celebration in 1992, but it was cut due to time constraints. Clapton did perform two songs, and joined Dylan, George Harrison, Roger McGuinn, Neil Young, and Tom Petty for *My Back Pages*, and everybody else for *Knockin' On Heaven's Door*.

In 1999, Dylan and Clapton finally got to perform a set together, including *It Takes A Lot To Laugh*, at the Eric Clapton & Friends To Benefit Crossroads Centre, Antigua.

According to *Dylan Cover*, Clapton has covered the following songs either written or co-written by Dylan: *Born In Time, Don't Think Twice, If I Don't Be There By Morning, Knockin' On Heaven's Door, Love Minus Zero, Not Dark Yet, Sign Language, Walk Out In The Rain*, and *Rainy Day Women #12 & 35*.

Bob Dylan and Jeff Beck

June 23, 2011

Geoffrey Arnold "Jeff" Beck was born on June 24, 1944.

He has played with everyone from Stevie Wonder, Buddy Guy, Mick Jagger, and Joss Stone to Spinal Tap, Donovan, Keith Moon, and David Gilmour. If fact, according to drummer Nick Mason's autobiography, the members of Pink Floyd wanted Beck to replace Syd Barrett in the band, but *"none of us had the nerve to ask him."*

The legendary British guitarist first came to prominence in The Yardbirds during their most commercially successful period. He replaced Eric Clapton in the line-up, and was eventually joined - then replaced - by Jimmy Page. Beck went on to form his own band, the Jeff Beck Group, initially featuring Rod Stewart on vocals and future Faces and Rolling Stones guitarist Ron Wood on bass. His next project was Beck, Bogert & Appice.

Beck reached his commercial peak in the mid-1970s with two instrumental jazz-rock albums, *Blow By Blow* and *Wired*, both produced by George Martin.

After a period of laying low, Beck has become more productive in recent years, recording and performing frequently, including numerous tours with Clapton. Beck has been inducted into the Rock and Roll Hall Of Fame twice - once as a member of the Yardbirds, once as a solo artist.

Beck has shared the stage only once with Bob Dylan, and that was at the 1988 Rock and Roll Hall Of Fame Induction Ceremony, where Beck also shared the stage with his first inspiration, Les Paul:

The Grand Ballroom, Hotel Waldorf-Astoria, New York City, New York: 20 January 1988

1. *Twist And Shout* (Phil Medley/Bert Russell)

2. *All Along The Watchtower* (Bob Dylan)

3. *I Saw Her Standing There* (John Lennon/Paul McCartney)

4. *Stand By Me* (Elmo Glick/Ben E. King)

5. *Stop! In The Name Of Love* (Lamont Dozier/Brian Holland/Eddie Holland)

6. *Whole Lotta Shakin' Goin' On* (Dave Williams/Sunny David) / *Hound Dog* (Jerry Leiber/Mike Stoller) / *Hi Ho Silver* (An early single by Jeff Beck) (Thomas "Fats" Waller/Ed Kirkeby)

7. *Barbara Ann* (Fred Fassert)

8. *Born On The Bayou* (John C. Fogerty)

9. *Like A Rolling Stone* (Bob Dylan)

10. *(I Can't Get No) Satisfaction* (Mick Jagger/Keith Richards)

Musicians: Bob Dylan, Jeff Beck, Les Paul, Sid McGinnis, Paul Shaffer, John Fogerty, Ben E. King, George Harrison, Yoko Ono, Ringo Starr, Little Richard, Mary Wilson, Mike Love, Brian Wilson, Carl Wilson, Mick Jagger, Bruce Springsteen, Johnny Moore, Joe Blunt, Clyde Brown, Elton John, Arlo Guthrie, and Peter Wolf. [234]

Beck is known more for his guitar playing than his singing, and can be found as a backing guitarist on a number of Dylan compositions, including Patti Smith (*All Along The Watchtower* at a 2005 Jimi Hendrix tribute), and Sting with the Secret Police (*I Shall Be Released* from Amnesty International's "The Secret Policeman's Other Ball"). Beck has also been performing the blues classic *Rollin' and Tumblin'* for over a decade, which Dylan rewrote and released in 2006.

---

[234] http://www.bjorner.com/still.htm, *Still on the Road*, Retrieved 11/26/2016

Beck has recorded only one Dylan cover under his own name, *Tonight I'll Be Staying Here With You*. It was included on 1972's *Jeff Beck Group* album, the second with the line-up of Beck, Bobby Tench, Clive Chaman, Max Middleton and Cozy Powell, and their fourth and final LP of all. The band split up soon after the release of the album.

Bob Dylan and Led Zeppelin's Jimmy Page

January 8, 2012

What do Richard Nixon, Joan Baez, and Jimmy Page have in common? Why, they share the same birthday, of course!

Guitarist, songwriter, and producer James Patrick Page, OBE, was born on the 9th of January, 1944. A very short version of his impressive resume would include being an in-demand British session musician in the 1960s (recording with everyone from Nico and Donovan to The Who and The Kinks); following Eric Clapton and Jeff Beck in The Yardbirds' lead guitarist spot; and eventually forming Led Zeppelin.

What does Jimmy Page have in common with Bob Dylan? Well, on the surface, not much. They have never recorded or played together. However, The Yardbirds, with Page, covered Dylan's *Most Likely You Go Your Way (And I'll Go Mine)*, at a BBC session on March 17, 1967.

While Page has not, as far as I can tell, recorded any other Dylan songs (except possibly as a session musician), Zeppelin's former lead singer, Robert Plant, has covered Dylan's *Girl From The North Country* and *One More Cup Of Coffee (Valley Below)*, and bassist John Paul Jones has been hanging around with his neighbor Robyn Hitchcock, so one would assume they probably do the occasional Dylan song. In addition, Jones' side project, Mutual Admiration Society, has been known to perform *Subterranean Homesick Blues* in concert.

Dylan and Page were influenced by many of the same rock, folk, and blues artists, and have both been accused of plagiarism.

Like Dylan, Page was influenced by Joan Baez. On Zeppelin's eponymous debut album, there's a cover of Anne (Johannsen) Bredon's *Babe, I'm Gonna Leave You* based on a version released by Baez. It was originally credited to Page and Plant. Bredon sued in 1980, and since 1990, her name has been added to the credits.

Dylan and The Yardbirds have each recorded the blues classic *Rollin' and Tumblin'* with new lyrics, and claimed authorship. Dylan's version was released on his 2006 album, *Modern Times*. The Yardbirds' recording, retitled *Drinking Muddy Water* was released on the 1967 album, *Little Games*. It was credited to band members Chris Dreja, Jim McCarty, Jimmy Page and Keith Relf. Dylan and Led Zeppelin also each interpreted the old blues song, *In My Time Of Dying*.

Dylan mentioned Page on his *Theme Time Radio Hour* program during the *Heart* and *Presidents* episodes.

Page had this to say about Dylan at the 2011 Ivor Novello Awards:

Question: Bob Dylan turns 70 this month. What does he mean to you?

Jimmy Page: "Bob Dylan...Oh my goodness ... He changed it all, didn't he? Yeah, he's just remarkable, Bob Dylan. His early work ... and still now. He is just head and shoulders above so many people." [235]

---

[235] https://www.youtube.com/watch?v=UjPsKsxqHVc, *Jimmy Page says he's working on new material* (Ivor Novello awards 2011), Retrieved 11/27/2016

Frank Zappa

Bob Dylan and Frank Zappa were both produced by Tom Wilson in the 1960s. Dylan and Zappa each released double album sets in the summer of 1966. Bob Dylan's name was listed on the cover of *Freak Out!* Zappa is quoted as saying, in 1967, that when he heard Dylan's early singles like *Subterranean Homesick Blues* (" *... a monster record"*) and *Like a Rolling Stone*, he *"wanted to quit the music business, because I felt: 'If this wins and it does what it's supposed to do, I don't need to do anything else', but it didn't do anything."* When his envisioned revolution failed to materialize, he felt that *"maybe it needs a little reinforcing."* [236]

When Bob Dylan met with Frank Zappa on December 22, 1982, the session was recorded by an engineer, according to Zappa tape archivist Joe Travers. Dylan had appeared, unannounced, on Zappa's doorsteps. According to Michael Gray, in his book *Mother! Is The Story Of Frank Zappa*, *"I get a lot of weird calls, and someone suddenly called up saying, 'This is Bob Dylan. I want to play you my new songs.'"* [237] Zappa went on to say that he had never met Dylan before, but could see someone (via a video screen) in the cold, with an open shirt, and no coat. Gray quoted Zappa, telling Karl Dallas, that Dylan played 11 new songs on the piano, humming the lyrics. *"I thought they were good songs. He seemed like a nice guy. Didn't look like it would be too hard to work with him … I asked him if it had any Jesus in it … and he said no."*

Unfortunately, it never came to pass. Some of the songs Dylan played may have ended up on his next album, *Infidels*, which was co-produced by Dylan and Mark Knopfler of Dire Straits.

For decades, both Dylan and Zappa fans have wondered what may have transpired during this meeting. It turns out that the session *was* recorded. Masato Kato interviewed Travers over the telephone for *Player* magazine in the spring of 2009. Here's what Travers had to say:

"What happened was, when Bob came to the house, and went and had a meeting with Frank, Frank's engineer at the time, his name was Mark Pinske. And Mark ran off cassettes of the meeting at the time that they were having it. And unfortunately, those cassettes were lent out, and given out to people, and, they are not around any longer. So, unfortunately, those master cassettes of Bob and Frank at the studio talking about a possible working relationship do not live in the vault. They live somewhere else out there in the world." [238]

One moment that has been documented was this quote from Pinske, Zappa's chief recording engineer/live sound engineer from 1980 to 1987:

"My favorite moment with Zappa in the studio was when... I got back at him for saying, "I'm not a robot you know, I can only stay interested in these things for mere moments." That was when Bob Dylan asked him what kind of engineer "this here Pinske was." Frank said, "He gets a better drum sound in 20 minutes than most engineers can get in hours." [239]

I was fortunate enough to meet Zappa at WBCN's Prudential studios in 1977, while he was trying to promote his unreleased album, *Läther*. After the interview, we all got in the elevator, and Zappa was telling a story and quoted Dylan, saying *"more people die in colleges than in old-age homes."*

Thanks to Masato Kato.

---

[236] *No Commercial Potential: The Saga Of Frank Zappa*, David Walley, Da Capo Press, New York, 1996

[237] *Mother! Is the Story of Frank Zappa*, Michael Gray, Proteus Books, London/New York, 1985

[238] Interview courtesy Masato Kato. Personal communication, 11/27/2016

[239] http://archive.ec/w4nlm, *On the Move*, Compiled by Sarah Benzuly, Who: Mark Pinske, COO at Crest Audio, Retrieved 11/26/2016

Don Van Vliet (Captain Beefheart)

December 17, 2010

Don Van Vliet, better known as Captain Beefheart, is dead at the age of 69. It was reported that his death was due to complications from multiple sclerosis.

Van Vliet was a painter, poet, songwriter, singer, and bandleader. He was respected as a revolutionary avant-garde artist. His best-known work was probably the 1969 double-album, *Trout Mask Replica*.

While Van Vliet was most closely associated with Frank Zappa, there have been some instances of similarities between Dylan and Beefheart's over the years.

Both artists changed their names early in their career. Dylan and Beefheart were musicians and visual artists. Dylan has been listed as an influence on Beefheart, and some articles have even listed Beefheart as an influence on Dylan, although that would be harder to prove.

On *Theme Time Radio Hour*, Dylan played two Beefheart tracks. For the *More Trains* episode, *Click Clack* was used. Dylan referred to Beefheart as *"a guy a lot of people think is way out,"* and said his influences - Howlin' Wolf and Louis Armstrong - could be heard in the song. After playing the track, Dylan had *The Simpsons* creator Matt Groening explain the importance of Beefheart.

During the *Birds* episode, after Mel Blanc's *Daffy's Rhapsody*, Dylan played *Ice Cream For Crow*. Dylan's introduction contrasted Blanc's arsenal of voices to Beefheart's unique one. Dylan went on to say that Beefheart retired from music after this record came out, to concentrate on painting, but wished *"he made more records."*

Here's what the Captain had to say about Bob Dylan over the years:

"Bob Dylan? Oh, you mean Robert Zimmerman. He's no genius. Quote me any of his songs and I would pick out the origins of all his imagery. He steals his stuff from real geniuses like Robert Johnson." (1972) [240]

So what kind of rock 'n' roll do you like these days then, Don?

"Oh, I like that Stylistics' record Betcha By Golly Gee Whiz: *that is a great, great song. Also the Stories'* Brother-Louie. *Also, I really like Dylan's new album. I mean, I think that is the most representative Dylan album there is. You know that song* I'll Be Your Baby Tonight? *Incredible. Really advanced music."* (1974) [241]

What sort of music do you listen to these days?

"I don't listen to nothin' - I don't need to. Bob Dylan impresses me about as much as… well, I was gonna say a slug but I like slugs. You gotta serve somebody - shit, trash poetry. Too much LSD. You know, they usually do that - they go right up to Jesus. What about Buddha? He seems like a lot more fun." (Circa 1980) [242]

Dylan and Beefheart songs have appeared on a couple of the same compilations, including the 2003 benefit album, *Where We Live: Stand For What You Stand*, and more famously on the soundtrack for *The Big Lebowski*, which contained the *Clear Spot* version of *Her Eyes Are A Blue Million Miles*.

Side notes:

Two of Dylan's friends, Jack White and Tom Waits, are big Beefheart fans.

One of White's bands, the White Stripes, recorded a limited edition single featuring Beefheart covers, while White, accompanied by Dead Weather co-member Alison Mosshart, visited

---

[240] *The Lives and Times of Captain Beefheart*, John Muir (Ed.), Babylon Books, Manchester, U.K., 1980

[241] *Old Fart at Play*, Nick Kent, NME, 6/1/1974

[242] *Captain Beefheart by Kristine McKenna*, Wet Magazine, 5/1/1980

Beefheart's childhood home last summer. [243] Similarly, Dylan visited the homes of John Lennon and Neil Young in recent years.

Tom Waits' career took a sharp turn when his wife turned him onto Beefheart. In 2005, Waits listed his *"20 most cherished albums of all time."* Number six was Dylan and The Band's *Basement Tapes*, while *Trout Mask Replica* took the third spot. [244]

Ry Cooder played on the first Captain Beefheart album, 1967's *Safe As Milk*. Cooder has played with Dylan on a number of occasions, including the finales during the three-night Great Music Experience Countdown in Nara, Japan, from 1994, and last year's appearance on *The People Speak*.

[243] http://www.csindy.com/coloradosprings/death-becomes-them/Content?oid=1404751, *Death becomes them: Alison Mosshart and Jack White kill some time with the Dead Weather*, Retrieved 11/26/2016
[244] https://www.theguardian.com/music/2005/mar/20/popandrock1, *'It's perfect madness'*, Retrieved 11/26/2016

T. Rex's Marc Bolan

March 28, 2011

T. Rex is best known for such 1970's glam-rock classics as *Jeepster*, *20th Century Boy*, and *Bang A Gong (Get It On)*.

Leader Marc Bolan (born Marc Feld) cited Bob Dylan as one of his main influences. He referred to Dylan in *Telegram Sam* (*"Bobby's alright, Bobby's alright / He's a natural born poet, he's just outta sight"*), and *Ballrooms Of Mars* (*"Bob Dylan knows…"*)

On the album *Live 1977*, Bolan updated *Telegram Sam*, singing *"Bobby's alright, he may be getting dee-vorced."*

Why did Feld choose the name "Bolan"? Possibly from B-O-b d-y-L-A-N, according to comments attributed to Bolan.

Bolan, as Toby Tyler, covered Dylan's *Blowin' In The Wind* in January, 1965, along with *The Road I'm On (Gloria)*, originally by Dion Di Mucci (of Dion and The Belmonts). It was finally released in 1993. Several takes of *Blowin' In The Wind* were included on *Marc Bolan As Toby Tyler: The Maximum Sound Session*.

Elton John's 'unforgettable' first meeting with Bob Dylan

Elton John was recently interviewed for a *Rolling Stone* cover story. [245]

When asked about his most unforgettable moments, John mentioned meeting Groucho Marx, Mae West, Neil Diamond, The Band flying from Connecticut to Philadelphia to see him in concert, receiving a congratulatory telegram from George Harrison, and Neil Young previewing *After the Gold Rush*, on piano, in John's apartment.

He also mentioned meeting Bob Dylan. John said Dylan was at the Fillmore East, standing on the staircase. He told Bernie Taupin, John's songwriting partner, that he really liked the words to *"Ballad of a Well-Known Gun,"* and Bernie feigned a heart attack.

Here's a brief history of Bob Dylan and Elton John:

John went to see Bob Dylan and The Band at the 1969 Isle of Wight festival, according to record producer Stuart Epps [246] who attended the concert with John and some other friends. *"We were going to see Bob Dylan playing in a huge field to about 150,000. Backed by the amazing Band. No-one could have guessed at the time, that almost a year later to this day, Dylan would be going to see Elton in Los Angeles and because of the Headlines that were to follow in the Melody maker, namely ----- DYLAN DIGS ELTON !"* (after seeing John at the Fillmore East, actually, accompanied by members of The Band, on November 20, 1970.)

Dylan shared the stage with Elton John during the January 20, 1988, Rock & Roll Hall Of Fame induction ceremony. (See previous entry)

John also played piano on Dylan's *2 X 2* from the album, *Under The Red Sky*. [247]

Bob Dylan - Acoustic Guitar, Vocals; David Crosby - Background Vocals; Elton John – Piano; David Lindley – Bouzouki; Randy Jackson – Bass; Kenny Aronoff – Drums; Paulinho Da Costa – Percussion.

Dylan was photographed with John and Ryan Adams at the 10th Annual Elton John AIDS Foundation InStyle Party in Los Angeles, March 24, 2002. [248]

John's recent 2010 album, *The Union*, was a collaboration with Leon Russell, and produced by T-Bone Burnett.

[245] http://www.rollingstone.com/music/news/elton-john-on-playing-with-kanye-hanging-with-dylan-and-filling-his-babys-ipod-20110202, *Elton John on Playing With Kanye, Hanging With Dylan and Filling His Baby's iPod*, Retrieved 11/26/2016

[246] http://www.stuartepps.co.uk/eltontheearlyyears.htm, *It was a Little Bit Funny: Elton John*, Stuart Epps, Retrieved 11/26/2016

[247] http://bobdylan.com/albums/under-red-sky/, *Under The Red Sky* (1990), Retrieved 11/26/2016.

[248] http://www.gettyimages.com/event/the-10th-annual-elton-john-aids-foundation-instyle-party-inside-75071502?#ryan-adams-sir-elton-john-and-bob-dylan-picture-id76379222, *The 10th Annual Elton John AIDS Foundation InStyle Party – Inside*, Retrieved 11/26/2016

When Bob Dylan gave Billy Joel *Make You Feel My Love* to record

May 9, 2011

William Martin "Billy" Joel was born on May 9, 1949. According to the RIAA, Billy Joel is the sixth best-selling recording artist and the third best-selling solo artist in the United States. [249] Dylan was a Columbia recording artist, and that was at least a partial reason why Joel chose to sign with that label – over Atlantic Records – in the early 1970s. [250]

The first time I saw Joel on television was in 1974 on Don Kirshner's Rock Concert, where he performed *Piano Man*, *Somewhere Along the Line*, and *Captain Jack*. [251] In addition to vocals and piano, Joel also played a harmonica held in a rack, much like Bob Dylan used to do.

Joel and Dylan met in the early 1980s, and they first worked together on 1985's USA For Africa single, *We Are The World*. Later that year, Joel appeared at the first Farm Aid concert (which was inspired by a quote by Dylan at Live Aid) [252] and attended a party to honor Dylan and his new compilation, *Biograph*. [253]

When Joel toured the Soviet Union in the summer of 1987, he covered The Beatles' *Back In The U.S.S.R.*, and Dylan's *The Times They Are A-Changin'*. Both songs appear on his live album, *Концерт*.

In 1988, Billy Joel joined Dylan, George Harrison, Ringo Starr, Mick Jagger, Bruce Springsteen, Ben E. King, Mary Wilson, Brian Wilson, Elton John, and many others at the Rock & Roll Hall of Fame induction ceremony in New York City. [254]

We Didn't Start the Fire, a #1 hit for Joel in 1989, mentioned Dylan in the lyrics: *"Hemingway, Eichmann, Stranger in a Strange Land / Dylan, Berlin, Bay of Pigs invasion."* [255]

A demo of *Highway 61 Revisited*, recorded on April 28, 1999, was included on Joel's box set, *My Lives*. It was released on November 22, 2005, the anniversary of J.F.K. being "blown away" (1963), and the marriage of Bob and Sara Dylan (1965).

Joel stopped writing and recording pop songs in 1993. According to contemporary interviews with Joel, Dylan's management offered Joel the opportunity to record a new Bob Dylan composition before the composer himself released it on his upcoming album, *Time Out Of Mind*. After Joel agreed, someone from Dylan's office brought a recording of *Make You Feel My Love* to Joel, who had to learn it then and there, as he was not allowed to keep the disc in his possession. The track, slightly retitled as *To Make You Feel My Love*, was one of three newly-recorded cover versions Joel included on his August, 1997, compilation *Greatest Hits, Volume III*. Dylan's version was released the following month.

In the June 7, 1997, issue of *Billboard*, Sony's Peter Asher said that the song had as much hit potential as *Lay Lady Lay*. Joel deadpanned, "I've been writing a different kind of music, which is why I'm recording a Bob Dylan song, actually. He's not a bad writer." [256]

---

[249] http://www.universalmusic.com/legendary-singersongwriter-billy-joel-signs-global-publishing-agreement-with-rondor-music-international-and-universal-music-publishing-group-worldwide/, *Legendary singer/songwriter Billy Joel signs global publishing agreement with Rondor Music International and Universal Music Publishing Group worldwide*, Retrieved 12/7/2016

[250] http://www.onefinalserenade.com/highway-61-revisited.html, *One Final Serenade: Songs of Billy Joel - Highway 61 Revisited*, Retrieved 12/7/2016

[251] https://sites.google.com/site/vintagerocktv/usa/don-kirshner-rock-concert, *Vintage Rock TV Archive. USA > Don Kirshner Rock Concert: Season One*, Retrieved 12/7/2016

[252] http://www.bjorner.com/still.htm, *Still on the Road*, Retrieved 12/7/2016

[253] http://www.gettyimages.com/detail/news-photo/from-left-to-right-judy-collins-bob-dylan-and-billy-joel-news-photo/109707813?#from-left-to-right-judy-collins-bob-dylan-and-billy-joel-attend-a-at-picture-id109707813, *Dylan's Biograph*, Retrieved 12/7/2106

[254] http://www.bjorner.com/still.htm, *Still on the Road*, Retrieved 12/7/2016

[255] *We Didn't Start the Fire, Storm Front*, Billy Joel, 1989

Make You Feel My Love has since been recorded by many artists, most notably the two 1998 versions on the Don Was-produced soundtrack to *Hope Floats* (by Garth Brooks – #1 on the Billboard Hot Country charts and nominated for a Grammy – and Trisha Yearwood), and in 2008, a hit cover by Adele, who finally reached #4 in the U.K. singles charts with the single last September. According to *Dylan Cover*, the song has also been covered by Neil Diamond, Bryan Ferry, Maria Muldaur, Joan Osborne, and Gary Puckett.

Joel was expected to release his memoir, entitled *The Book Of Joel*, this June, but has since decided to cancel the project. "It took working on writing a book to make me realize that I'm not all that interested in talking about the past," Joel said, "and that the best expression of my life and its ups and downs has been and remains my music." [257]

In August, 1997, Joel debuted *To Make You Feel My Love* on *The Late Show with David Letterman*. He also discussed a visit by Dylan at his home at the St. Moritz in New York. Joel was speaking with Dylan's daughter (a Joel fan) with her father hanging out in the kitchen, noting he "was being a good dad." Joel also recalled some advice he was given backstage at a Dylan concert in Milan, Italy. To help him remember the lyrics, Dylan said he kept a published book of his own lyrics while on tour. When asked how he could read them on stage, Dylan replied, "I can't read them. I just feel good knowing they're there." (Letterman on Joel's Dylan imitation: "You sound like Bob Dylan if he had a cartoon show.") [258]

[256] *Billy Joel Updates Sony Music Australia Staff*, Billboard, 6/7/1997
[257] http://www.cbsnews.com/news/billy-joel-cancels-his-memoir/, *Billy Joel cancels his memoir*, CBS News Staff/AP, Retrieved 12/7/2016
[258] *Billy Joel interview: The Late Show with David Letterman*, 8/17/1997, CBS/Worldwide Pants

Did a teen-age Alice Cooper meet Bob Dylan's parents at the mall?

November 3, 2010

Goldmine magazine has posted an interview with Dennis Dunaway, bassist for the Alice Cooper Group. In the article, entitled *10 albums that changed Dennis Dunaway's life,* [259] he had this to say about Bob Dylan's second album (*The Freewheelin' Bob Dylan*):

As old high school buddies, Alice and I thought we were incredibly hip. But when our art teacher made us listen to this album, even though we laughed at the froggy voice, the dead seriousness of most of the lyrics made us realize that our art teacher was way hipper than us. Soon after that, we met Dylan's parents at the local Mall.

Vincent Furnier (Cooper's real name) and Dunaway attended Cortez High School in northern Phoenix. What Abe and Beatty Zimmerman were doing at a shopping mall in Arizona, or how Vincent and Dennis knew they were there, is a bit of a mystery.

Dylan played *School's Out* on *Theme Time Radio Hour.*

---

[259] http://www.goldminemag.com/article/10-albums-that-changed-dennis-dunaway-life, *10 albums that changed Dennis Dunaway's life*, Retrieved 11/26/2016

Duet with Springsteen at opening of Rock and Roll Hall of Fame and Museum

September 1, 2010

In 1995, the Rock and Roll Hall of Fame and Museum opened in Cleveland, after over a decade of debate and construction. As you would expect, there was an all-star, six-hour concert in Cleveland to celebrate the opening of the Hall on September 2, 1995. The event was broadcast live.

Among the musicians present (according to various sources) were Chuck Berry, Jackson Browne, Bruce Hornsby, Natalie Merchant, Sam Moore, Iggy Pop, the Pretenders, Martha Reeves, Little Richard, John Mellencamp, Eric Burdon, Jon Bon Jovi, Aretha Franklin, Lou Reed, Soul Asylum, the Allman Brothers, Sheryl Crow, The Kinks, Ann and Nancy Wilson of Heart, John Fogerty, Booker T. and the MGs, James Brown, Al Green, Johnny Cash, George Clinton, Melissa Etheridge, Carole King, Jerry Lee Lewis, Boz Scaggs, Slash, Robbie Robertson, Jim Keltner, Bruce Springsteen and the E Street Band, and Bob Dylan. The musical director was Dylan's former guitarist, G.E. Smith.

After an introduction by Bruce Springsteen (*"Ladies and gentlemen, one of my favorites"*), Dylan played a strong half-hour set, mixing familiar material with *Empire Burlesque*'s *Seeing The Real You At Last*. According to one attendee, Dylan's appearance was a surprise, as *"he was not on the bill, t-shirts or in the programs."* [260] While segments of the concert have been made available for purchase in different formats, the video of Dylan's portion has never been included. *All Along The Watchtower*, however, *was* included on the Columbia 2 CD set, *The Concert For The Rock and Roll Hall Of Fame*.

The highlight had to be when Dylan introduced a surprise guest:

"A buddy of mine is going to come up and do one of my old songs . . . Mr. Bruce Springsteen . . . Let me hear you say 'Bruce!'" (Smiles all around.)

Then Dylan and Springsteen shared vocals on *Forever Young*.

Courtesy of Olof Bjorner: [261]

Cleveland Stadium, Cleveland, Ohio: 2 September 1995

Opening of the Rock and Roll Hall of Fame Museum.

1. *All Along The Watchtower*

2. *Just Like A Woman*

3. *Seeing The Real You At Last*

4. *Highway 61 Revisited*

5. *Forever Young* - with Bruce Springsteen (guitar & shared vocal).

Bob Dylan (vocal & guitar), Bucky Baxter (pedal steel guitar & electric slide guitar), John Jackson (guitar), Tony Garnier (bass), Winston Watson (drums & percussion).

1 released on *The Concert For The Rock And Roll Hall Of Fame*, Columbia 483 793 2, 17 September 1996.

Broadcast live by various TV stations in the US. Stereo TV broadcast, 28 minutes.

---

[260] http://bobdylan.com/#/tour/1995-09-02-rock-and-roll-hall-fame, Dead Link.

[261] http://www.bjorner.com/still.htm, *Still on the Road*, Retrieved 11/26/2016

Bob Dylan's little tribute to the 'Big Man,' Clarence Clemons

July 7, 2011

Yesterday morning, advanced sale tickets for Bob Dylan's August 14 concert at Asbury Park Convention Hall in New Jersey went on sale.

In order to participate in the pre-sale, one must visit Dylan's official tour page to find out what the "password" is. Sometimes the word is related to the venue or the location, other times the connection is more of a mystery.

Asbury Park is, of course, Bruce Springsteen territory. In case you didn't check it out yet, the password for the Asbury Park show is "clarence," an obvious nod to Clarence Clemons of the E Street Band, who died last month.

Classy.

Dylan was originally rumored to play the PNC Bank Arts Center, Holmdel, New Jersey, on August 14. The Asbury Park show was posted on Dylan's official site June 30.

Bob Dylan's tenuous connections to the late, great, R.E.M.

September 21, 2011

Earlier today, the band R.E.M. officially decided to call it quits.

I know some of you must be asking – what is the connection between R.E.M., one of the most revered bands of the 1980s and 90s, and Bob Dylan, who is still revered, but not calling it quits?

On the surface, not much. Dylan burst onto the Greenwich Village folk scene in the early 1960s, developed his own musical vocabulary, and soon suffered under the weight of being the "Voice Of a Generation." R.E.M. emerged from Athens, Georgia, to become one the most critically acclaimed, and eventually commercially successful acts in what is now known as "Alternative" music, with lead singer Michael Stipe mumbling his way through their early albums.

However, there was something that could be filed under "collaboration" between the prides of Hibbing and Athens. Dylan played harmonica on a track featuring three members of R.E.M. (Peter Buck, guitar; Mike Mills, bass; Bill Berry, drums) during a Warren Zevon session in early 1987. One song, *The Factory*, was released on Zevon's album, *Sentimental Hygiene*. [262]

When Patti Smith toured with Bob Dylan in 1995, Stipe provided emotional support for her.

R.E.M. have covered Dylan songs. Sort of.

- R.E.M. slipped in a few lines from *Like A Rolling Stone* during the song *Country Feedback*, during their 2001 return to MTV's *Unplugged*.

- When playing London under the name Bingo Hand Job in 1991, R.E.M. performed Dylan's *You Ain't Goin' Nowhere*, the *Basement Tapes* classic covered by the Byrds on 1968's *Sweetheart Of The Rodeo*. Of course, the jangly guitar sound of R.E.M. can be traced back to the early Byrds (and The Soft Boys).

- Stipe joined the Indigo Girls for a cover of *All Along The Watchtower* at the Athens (Georgia) Music Festival in 1988.

- As the Venus 3, Peter Buck, and hired R.E.M. members Scott McCaughey and Bill Rieflin, occasionally record and tour with Robyn Hitchcock. In concert, they have performed Dylan covers including *Ballad Of A Thin Man*. They also recorded *Not Dark Yet* for a Dylan birthday celebration issue of *Uncut* magazine earlier this year.

- One of R.E.M.'s most popular songs, *It's the End of the World As We Know It (And I Feel Fine)*, was inspired by Dylan's *Subterranean Homesick Blues*, according to Buck.

Here are some quotes about Dylan from Buck and Stipe:

In October, 2001, Mark Lindquist asked Buck about his five favorite songs. The first one he mentioned was *Like a Rolling Stone*: [263] *"Obviously it's an aggressive song putting someone down, but I don't know who that person is. Assuming that I know a little about Dylan's life, it could be about the people who followed him around. It seems to be a portrait of someone who thinks they're a winner, who's high in society. Who that is, I don't know. I could be completely wrong . . . "The ghost of electricity howls in the bones of her face." That's from* Visions of Johanna, *which is one of my favorite songs, but I have no idea what that means."*

---

[262] http://www.bjorner.com/still.htm, *Still on the Road*, Retrieved 11/26/2016

[263] *Reconstruction Of The Fables: The Dynamic Interplay Of Music And Literature*, Mark Lindquist and Peter Buck, The Hartford Courant, 10/14/2001

"And I don't expect anyone can bring about a revolution in the way that Bob Dylan did - and really didn't - in the 1960s." (Stipe) [264]

"We've sort of flirted with greatness, but we've yet to make a record as good as Revolver *or* Highway 61 Revisited *or* Exile on Main Street *or Big Star's* Third*."* (Buck) [265]

Farewell, R.E.M.

Update, 2016: On Twitter, I asked Mike Mills (@m_millsey) about the Zevon session:

Always assumed Zevon "Sentimental Hygiene" Dylan session was separate overdub?

Mills replied: Overdub, but in the same studio and session #recordone #thevalley

[264] http://borntolisten.com/2016/01/04/jan-4-michael-stipe-was-born-in-1960/, *October 6: R.E.M. released Automatic For The People in 1992*, Retrieved 11/26/2016

[265] http://www.mtv.com/news/1644007/andy-hummel-original-big-star-bassist-dead-at-59/ *Andy Hummel, Original Big Star Bassist, Dead at 59*, Retrieved 11/26/2016

John Mellencamp

Johnny Cougar, a.k.a. John Cougar, a.k.a. John Cougar Mellencamp, a.k.a. John Mellencamp, was born on October 7, 1951, in Seymour, Indiana. In addition to his main occupations as a singer, songwriter, and musician, he is also a painter, director, and actor. He has been inducted into the Rock and Roll Hall Of Fame.

During his set at Live Aid in 1985, Bob Dylan said:

"I'd just like to say I hope that some of the money that's raised for the people in Africa – maybe they could just take a little bit of it – maybe one or two million, maybe - and use it, say, to pay, er, the mortgages on some of the farms . . . that the farmers here owe to the banks."

Dylan's statement inspired Farm Aid. Along with Willie Nelson and Neil Young, Mellencamp was a founding member. While Dylan has not been seen at Farm Aid since the second one in 1986 (and that time only via satellite), Mellencamp continues to be an active participant, and has been involved in various Farm Aid efforts.

Dylan referred to Mellencamp in the July 17, 1986, issue of *Rolling Stone*, questioning the then in vogue *"this Bruce Springsteen-John Cougar-'America first' thing."* He went on to say that he wasn't badmouthing them, and that he shared the same ideals, but focused more on *"eternal"* matters. He then said *"Cougar"* was *"great"* and was *"knocked out"* by his grandmother singing on his latest album.

Fast forward a few years: Mellencamp directs Dylan in a video for his song *Political World*. Asked if there was a "treatment" for it, [266] Mellencamp said, *"No, I called up Bob, and I said, 'Bob, here's what we're going to do . . . ' and he said, 'OK, just don't make me look stupid.' That's all he said."*

In 2008, Mellencamp has this to say to *Time* magazine: [267]

Do you have a list in your back pocket of people you'd like to work with?

Yeah. The one thing I really want to do is to get with Bob Dylan, and he and I would paint. He said, "Let's get together and paint" last time I saw him. That never happened. But it would be fun to learn something from Bob.

Dylan and Mellencamp both appeared at the White House for a salute to the music of the civil rights era. According to Mellencamp: [268]

"Bob was nervous," Mellencamp said during a question-answer-performance session Tuesday at the Grammy Museum, which coordinated the White House event. When a few of the 200 members of the museum audience chuckled at the comment, Mellencamp added, *"No, he was really nervous."*

Dave Lindquist, music journalist for *The Indianapolis Star* and *Metromix*, sent a link to an article in *The Star* which included the following story about Bob Dylan and John Mellencamp:

Mellencamp told Lindquist that Dylan asked him, *"John, are you going to tell that stupid story tonight about you being in a bar band? … Change it. I'm sick of hearing it. Mellencamp was surprised Dylan was listening "You mean like you?" he asked. "Yeah," Dylan said. "I don't talk to the audience. If they don't come to me, then they miss the show." Mellencamp pointed out that he was not in the same position as Dylan. "I'm not like that, Bob. I can't lean on 'Rainy Day Women.' I kind of have to reach out to the audience."* [269]

---

[266] http://www.cmt.com/news/1615363/john-mellencamp-explains-his-influence-or-not-on-country-music/ *CMT NEWS: John Mellencamp Explains His Influence (or Not) on Country Music. He Prepares for Summer Ballpark Tour With Bob Dylan and Willie Nelson*, Retrieved 11/26/2016

[267] http://content.time.com/time/specials/2007/article/0,28804,1638826_1704995_1704987,00.html, *Q & A: Talking with John Mellencamp*, Retrieved 11/26/2016

[268] http://articles.latimes.com/2010/aug/20/entertainment/la-et-john-mellencamp-20100820, *John Mellencamp talks 'No Better Than This' and Bob Dylan at Grammy Museum. The rocker, who's been touring with Dylan and recorded his new album with T Bone Burnett, drops by for a question-answer-performance session*, Retrieved 11/26/2016

[269] *Mellencamp and Dylan: Traveling Companions*, Dave Lindquist, Indianapolis Star, 11/04/2010

On September 25, 2014, Mellencamp was guest on the Howard Stern's satellite radio program, to promote his new album, *Plain Spoken*. Bob Dylan came up a lot in conversation. Mellencamp admitted he was friends with Dylan, and has received plenty of advice from him. He told Stern that they have toured together, talked about how funny Dylan was, and that he stayed at Mellencamp's house when in town, on tour, where they hang around the kitchen and discuss music.

Mellencamp loved Dylan's answer when he asked him about his "Plan." Dylan laughed and said that there wasn't any plan! He could only play a handful of songs when he initially arrived in New York in the early 1960s, Dylan told him. He also said that while still in high school, he went from Duluth to Milwaukee, stayed at his grandmother's sister's house, and played on street corners, as big city practice, in preparation for going to New York.

When Stern asked him if Dylan had an "open door" policy, where he could raid his refrigerator, Mellencamp said that his dressing room was an Airstream, and takes his food and cigarettes.

(The entire interview can be accessed on the SiriusXM app, under Howard Stern interviews.)

Mellencamp was the first musician to perform on the televised portion of 1992's Bob Dylan 30th Anniversary Concert Celebration. One of a handful of acts originally advertised for "Bob- Fest," he performed *Like A Rolling Stone* and *Leopard-Skin Pill-Box Hat*. Mellencamp regularly sang *Like A Rolling Stone* on his 1988 tour. Dylan's version of *People Get Ready* for the *Flashback* soundtrack was recorded at Mellencamp's studio in Indiana. On his 1997 album, *Rough Harvest*, Mellencamp covered Dylan's *Farewell Angelina* as well as *In My Time Of Dying*, which Bob performed on his debut album. Dylan toured with Mellencamp a couple of times. Mellencamp appeared at the 2015 MusiCares Person of the Year tribute concert in honor of Dylan, performing *Highway 61 Revisited*.

Lenny Kravitz on hanging out with Bob Dylan in Paris, in the rain

On September 23, 2014, Howard Stern interviewed singer Lenny Kravitz on his satellite radio program. Stern began asking the musician about the many celebrity friends with whom Kravitz has worked, including Mick Jagger, David Bowie, Paul McCartney, and Michael Jackson. As Stern was listing these artists, Kravitz brought up Bob Dylan's name. Stern and Kravitz discussed Dylan for about seven minutes.

Kravitz told Stern he toured with Dylan when his debut album came out (1990). He went on to say that Dylan was *"cool"* and they stay in contact with each other. When he played in Paris a while ago, Dylan visited Kravitz' house and *"hung out."* Then Dylan wanted them to go walking in the rain, then sit on a bench, for three hours, without umbrellas! Kravitz thought, *"If Bob Dylan wants to take a walk, it could be fucking snowing."* They talked about music, politics, family, and real estate.

When Stern asked Kravitz if it was *"fucking weird,"* Kravitz said he just thought about what he would have thought about this as a youngster. Robin Quivers, Stern's sidekick, asked if Dylan was testing him, to see what he would put up with, but Kravitz said, *"Nah."*

The last time Kravitz saw Dylan was when he was doing a movie in Atlanta, and then went to see him in concert. Afterwards, Dylan gave him his harmonica. Stern asked where he keeps it. He replied it was with his jewelry.

(The entire interview can be accessed on the SiriusXM app, under Howard Stern interviews.)

Guns N' Roses guitarist Slash

British guitarist Slash is best known as the lead guitarist for the bands Guns N' Roses and Velvet Revolver.

He was born Saul Hudson on July 23, 1965, a few days after the release of the single of *Like A Rolling Stone*, and two days before Bob Dylan went "electric" at Newport. Almost 25 years later, in April, 1990, Slash overdubbed a guitar solo on the Dylan track *Wiggle Wiggle*. [270]

The sessions were produced by Don and David Was of the band Was (Not Was), along with "Jack Frost" - Dylan's first use of the pseudonym he would be known by when producing his own records. Don Was was a hot producer at the time, especially after the success of Bonnie Raitt's 1989 "comeback" album, *Nick Of Time*. Was tried to use a similar formula with Dylan on the 1990 album, *Under The Red Sky*. It was also Was' idea to keep the length of the album to under 40 minutes, something he later regretted.

The results were considered disappointing both critically and commercially, especially after the success of 1989's *Oh Mercy* album, although the album does have its supporters. Al Kooper referred to this as "the hood album," since Dylan dressed for the sessions in a sweatshirt, with his head covered by a hood. According to one source, during this period, Dylan would randomly give people he didn't know made-up monikers like "Fred," instead of learning their real names.

Was also brought in many famous "guest stars" for the project, including Stevie Ray Vaughan (who Dylan allegedly did not recognize without his hat) and his brother Jimmie (of The Fabulous Thunderbirds), David Lindley, Bruce Hornsby and Al Kooper. After Dylan's vocals were done, Was brought in more "stars" to overdub their parts, including David Crosby, George Harrison, Elton John, and Slash. According to Was, [271] the Randy Jackson that played on the album was the one who ended up on American Idol, not the Randy Jackson from the Jackson 5.

Dylan looked "beleaguered" [272] at the sessions, according to Was. While it was difficult to know his exact state of mind at the time, Dylan was probably a bit suspicious of the by-the-numbers production and all-star musicians used on the album.

While Dylan had been friends with Crosby, Kooper, and Harrison for years, and must have at least known - or been aware - of some of the other "name" artists in the studio, he did not seem impressed with the appearance of the new kid, Slash.

The Guns N' Roses guitarist was invited by Was to play on *Wiggle Wiggle*, one of the songs on *Under The Red Sky*, after contributing to a Was-produced Iggy Pop session. Fans speculate the song was originally written as a nursery rhyme (albeit with much different lyrics). The album was dedicated to "Gabby Goo Goo," a nickname for Dylan's young daughter, Desiree Gabrielle Dennis-Dylan, although this was not public knowledge at the time.

Slash was famous for being a hard rock guitarist. Dylan asked him to play like the jazz legend, Django Reinhardt. [273] Of course, it is not known what Dylan meant by this remark. The most common interpretations are that Dylan was either putting Slash in his place, or commenting on his excessive equipment. However, it could be that Dylan was trying to get Slash to think outside the box, and play a little differently than usual.

In September, 2014, Slash was interviewed by Howard Stern on his SiriusXM satellite radio program. About 22 minutes in, Stern asked about Slash playing with Dylan.

---

[270] http://www.bjorner.com/still.htm, *Still on the Road*, Retrieved 11/26/2016

[271] http://www.uncut.co.uk/music/bob_dylan/special_features/12271, Dead Link.

[272] *Down the Highway - The Life of Bob Dylan*, Howard Sounes, Grove Press, New York, 2001

[273] http://bobdylanencyclopedia.blogspot.com/2010/01/django-reinhardt-centenary.html, Django Reinhardt Centenary. Retrieved 11/26/2016

Stern began by asking him about playing on an album full of "guest stars," but Dylan ended up not using Slash on the record. Slash said he played a *"really great"* improvised solo, and an acoustic rhythm track, on a *"real basic rhythm and blues track."* When Was sent him a rough mix, Slash heard only the acoustic part. When Slash asked Was what happened to his guitar solo, Was said that Dylan thought it sounded *"too much like Guns 'N' Roses."* Slash wasn't insulted, he said, saying it was *"cool,"* and it was confirmation he had already *"established (a) sound."* Slash also said he was paid *"scale"* for the session, because he was not yet *that* well known.

Wiggle Wiggle (Album credits): [274]

Bob Dylan – Guitar, Vocals; Slash – Guitar; David Lindley – Guitar; Jamie Muhoberac – Organ; Randy Jackson – Bass; Kenny Aronoff – Drums

(The entire interview can be accessed on the SiriusXM app, under Howard Stern interviews.)

---

[274] http://bobdylan.com/albums/under-red-sky/, *Under The Red Sky* (1990). Retrieved 11/26/2016

Bob Dylan's connection to 2011 Rock Hall Of Fame nominees

September 29, 2010

The 2011 nominees for induction into the Rock and Roll Hall Of Fame have been announced:

Alice Cooper, Beastie Boys, Bon Jovi, Chic, Neil Diamond, Donovan, Dr. John, J. Geils Band, LL Cool J, Darlene Love, Laura Nyro, Donna Summer, Joe Tex, Tom Waits, and Chuck Willis.

Bob Dylan has connections with almost all of this year's nominees, obviously some more than others. Here's a quick overview:

Alice Cooper: In an interview published in early 1978, [275] Bob Dylan called Cooper an *"overlooked songwriter."* Cooper later commented, [276] *"That was such a surprise to me. What a compliment that Bob Dylan even knows I'm alive. He must have listened to* Only Women Bleed *or one of those songs that felt like a touching ballad. I had four ballads in a row that were hits and maybe that was what that had to do with."* Dylan played *School's Out* on *Theme Time Radio Hour.*

Beastie Boys: Dylan has been sampled by the Beasties, and he also played *No Sleep Til Brooklyn* on *Theme Time.*

Bon Jovi: Dylan was the inspiration for their song *Last Man Standing.* Guitarist Richie Sambora presented an acoustic guitar signed by Dylan to Jon Bon Jovi with the inscription, *"To Jon, 'Keep Livin' On A Prayer', Happy Birthday, Bob Dylan."* [277] Bon Jovi has covered Dylan's *Knockin' On Heaven's Door* and *Seven Days.*

Chic: Nile Rodgers produced, and played guitar on, Dylan's 1996 version of *Ring Of Fire* for the *Feeling Minnesota* soundtrack. Chic's Bernard Edwards played bass.

Neil Diamond: Dylan and Diamond both appeared at The Band's Last Waltz in 1976. The following year, Dylan enlisted Diamond's management team.

Donovan: Dylan met Donovan during his 1965 U.K. tour. It was documented in the film, *Dont Look Back.* (See previous.)

Dr. John (Mac Rebennack) wrote in his autobiography, [278] *"A lot of different artists pitched in to give me lines on the song* Right Place, Wrong Time. *Bob Dylan started it off by laying a line on me - 'I'm on the right trip, but in the wrong car.'"* Both Rebennack and Dylan participated in the 1972 Doug Sahm sessions, and The Band's Last Waltz. Dylan played *Such A Night* and *Right Place, Wrong time* on his *Theme Time Radio Hour.*

J. Geils Band: In the early 1960s, future J. Geils Band lead singer Peter Wolf used to hang out with Dylan in Greenwich Village, trying to sell Bob his paintings, and witnessed Dylan's premier performance of *A Hard Rain's A-Gonna Fall.* Wolf contributed to *Theme Time*, and Dylan played both J. Geils and Wolf solo tracks on the show. Dylan guitarists Stu Kimball and Larry Campbell participated on Wolf's recent albums. When Dylan played Boston's Avalon club in 2004, I spotted Wolf in the audience.

LL Cool J: Dylan "rapped" part of *Mama Said Knock You Out* on the second episode of *Theme Time.*

---

[275] *Bob Dylan: The Rolling Stone Interview*, Jonathan Cott, Rolling Stone, 1/26/1978

[276] http://www.intelligencer.ca/2010/07/16/cooper-ready-to-rock-the-friendly-city, *Cooper ready to rock The Friendly City*, Retrieved 11/26/2016

[277] https://www.pinterest.com/pin/341358846726255374/, *LOST HIGHWAY ERA: Jon & Richie backstage holding Bob Dylan-signed guitar Richie presented to JBJ as a birthday gift † Bon Jovi It reads "To Jon, keep livin' on a prayer. Happy birthday '08 Bob Dylan "*, Retrieved 11/26/2016

[278] *Under a Hoodoo Moon: The Life of Dr. John the Night Tripper*, Dr. John (Mac Rebennack) with Jack Rummel, St. Martin's Press, New York, 1994

Darlene Love: Dylan played the Phil Spector-produced track *(Today I Met) The Boy I'm Going to Marry* by Darlene Love and The Blossoms on *Theme Time*.

Laura Nyro: Bob Dylan reportedly startled a young Laura Nyro when he approached her at a party and declared *"I love your chords!"* [279]

Donna Summer: Both Dylan and Summer have been linked to the Vineyard Fellowship. Summer could be seen in the audience at the 1980 Grammy Awards during Dylan's performance of *Gotta Serve Somebody*.

Joe Tex (born Joseph Arrington, Jr.): In *Chronicles: Volume One*, Dylan wrote about watching Tex on Johnny Carson's *Tonight Show*, commenting that Carson didn't interview him, and how he related to Tex by not being part of the mainstream either. Dylan introduced the late Joe Tex's *I Believe I'm Gonna Make It* on *Theme Time*, saying he took his last name from the state of his birth. Tex was a country music fan, according to Dylan, and mixed it with the stories heard from preachers he knew from his youth, creating a unique form of country soul. Dylan said Tex would make himself hoarse before each performance. He also said his pallbearers were Ben E. King, Don Covey, Wilson Pickett, and Percy Mayfield.

Tom Waits: Bob Dylan named Waits as one of his *"secret heroes."* [280] Not only did Waits appear numerous times on *Theme Time*, he was also one of the most-played artists on the show. Last fall, Dylan jokingly introduced Tom Waits as a special guest at two shows, only to have Stu Kimball sing truncated versions of two Waits songs.

Chuck Willis: While growing up in Minnesota, Dylan said he used to listen to Willis on the Little Rock radio station KTHS. On *Theme Time*, Dylan said he was playing Willis' *Hang Up My Rock and Roll Shoes* because they liked to play records by musicians who wore turbans when they performed. The Band also covered that song on their live album, *Rock of Ages*.

---

[279] http://lauranyro.bobfinnan.com, *Laura Nyro Tribute Page*, Retrieved 11/27/2016

[280] http://www.tomwaits.com/press/read/9/alice_biography/ *TomWaits Press: Alice Biography*, Retrieved 11/27/2016

Promoter Bill Graham

January 8, 2011

Wolodia Grajonca was born January 8, 1931. As Bill Graham, he was known as a rock concert promoter, and was involved in everything from the Fillmore Auditoriums to the Last Waltz and Live Aid.

Bob Dylan and Graham worked together various times in the 1970s and 1980s. However, the first documented interaction between the two was at an earlier press conference televised on public television.

On December 3, 1965, Bob Dylan gave a press conference at WQED studios in San Francisco. Among those in attendance were critics Ralph Gleason, Phil Elwood, Robert Shelton, and Jonathan Cott; concert producer Mary Ann Pollar; photographer Jim Marshall; poets Michael McClure, Lawrence Ferlinghetti, and Allen Ginsberg; members of comedy troupe The Committee; and a young promoter named Bill Graham. [281]

According to his autobiography, *Bill Graham Presents*, Graham snuck in through a side door, and started placing handbills for a concert on every seat. Danny Weiner, who worked for Dylan, asked what he was up to. Graham stopped while Weiner spoke to Dylan, and, luckily for Bill, Dylan said it was OK. Graham then asked Dylan to hold up a large placard advertising the concert during the press conference.

At the conference, Graham was able to say to Dylan, *"Going back to what you said a minute ago, about not really being concerned, not really knowing, why you are in the midst of this popularity. That's in direct opposition to what most people who reach this popularity say, and I ..."*

Dylan interrupted and, unlike some of the other questions, took this one seriously, answering that *"A lot of people start out to try to be stars, I would imagine. This had nothing to do with it when I started. . . "*

Graham continued, stating he agreed with Dylan's right not to care, then said that people might be disappointed if they knew Dylan didn't feel the same way about his fans as they do about him, and that was the reason for Dylan's popularity.

"No," Dylan answered for humorous effect. *"I don't want to disappoint anybody. Tell me what I should say!"*

This prompted someone (Gleason?) to direct Dylan's attention to the placard for the concert Graham was promoting. The show took place at San Francisco's Fillmore Auditorium one week after the press conference, and was to feature Jefferson Airplane and the Great Society (with Grace Slick), among others, to benefit the S.F. Mime Troupe. After reading the information for the press, Dylan said, *"I would like to go if I could, but unfortunately I won't be here, I don't think."* The press conference was released on DVD under the title, *Dylan Speaks: The Legendary 1965 Press Conference in San Francisco.*

When Dylan went on the road with The Band in 1974, Bill Graham organized the entire 40-date national tour. It was the first of its kind, where one organization arranged the bookings for an entire tour. Graham would be working for Dylan, so that Dylan would get more money. Graham would also rent the plane and take care of just about everything else.

For the tour, Graham arranged for other people to take care of the day-to-day responsibilities, and to respect Dylan's privacy. This worked just a little too well. Just a few dates into the tour, Dylan knocked on Graham's hotel door at midnight and, according to the promoter's autobiography, Bob asked, *"Bill, why isn't anybody talking to me?"*

---

[281] http://kripes.proboards.com/thread/1, *Bob Dylan's 1965 San Francisco Press Conference*, Retrieved 11/27/2016

On the final date on the tour, Dylan brought out Graham and said, *"We're gonna do one more, but before we do, we need to bring out the man ... he brings us to you, Mr. Bill Graham - You know him!"* Graham was brought on stage, then soaked with soda. After the tour, Graham told *Rolling Stone*, *"It'll be hard going out on another tour. I can tell you 9000 stories how great it was."* [282]

Graham worked on-and-off with Dylan over the next decade or so, with too many shows to list here. Some examples:

When Graham organized the S.N.A.C.K. benefit in 1975, Dylan was a surprise guest, performing with Neil Young and members of The Stray Gators and The Band.

In 1976, for The Last Waltz, Dylan was being his usual, idiosyncratic self. Warner Brothers was doing the film because Dylan was in it. It's been well-documented that, at intermission, Dylan changed his mind and refused to be filmed. It was decided that Graham would speak with Dylan, and, after much drama, it was agreed that only Dylan's last two songs could be filmed.

Graham would later promote Dylan's 1984 European tour. For the Slane Castle concert, Graham spoke to Bono, Van Morrison, and Dylan individually, and said to each performer that the others would like to play with Dylan, which led to a once-in-a-lifetime live collaboration.

The American portion of Live Aid was organized by Graham. Again, according to his autobiography, Graham was asking many acts to shorten their sets. Dylan, however, refused. Originally, Dylan was to close the show, not Lionel Richie, who led an all-star version of *We Are The World*.

"I minded the song," Graham said. *"Certain songs are like postage stamps . . . Everybody could have sung* (Blowin' In The Wind). *I felt that using* We Are the World *was a retread."*

Bill Graham died in a helicopter crash on October 25, 1991.

At the memorial concert, Neil Young, backed by The Grateful Dead, played Dylan's *Forever Young*.

---

[282] *Knockin' on Dylan's Door - On The Road in '74*, Pocket Books, New York, 1974

The Bob Dylan - Dolly Parton 'feud'

January 19, 2011

Dolly Rebecca Parton, one of the 'Queens' of Country Music, was born on January 19, 1946.

In 1986, Parton was inducted into the Nashville Songwriters Hall Of Fame. Bob Dylan followed in 2002.

Dylan and Parton have occasionally worked with the same musicians and singers, including Emmylou Harris, Fred Carter Jr., Pete Drake, Shelly Kurland, David Lindley, and Steve Cropper.

In 1997, Parton covered Bob Dylan's *Knockin' On Heaven's Door* with Ladysmith Black Mambazo on their album, *Heavenly*.

Eight years later, Dolly released *Those Were The Days*, an album of cover versions from the 1960s and 70s. The concept was to sing with the artists or writers who originally recorded the songs. While Parton was able to recruit Mary Hopkin, Yusuf Islam (Cat Stevens), Roger McGuinn, Kris Kristofferson, Judy Collins, Tommy James, and others for the project, two artists did not participate - Joni Mitchell, due to illness, and Bob Dylan.

On October 17, 2005, Parton appeared on Comedy Central's *The Daily Show*. Host Jon Stewart asked if she was turned down by anyone. *"Yeah, Bob Dylan,"* Parton replied. *"Actually, to be fair to him, he wrote the song, that's all he needed to do, but I didn't actually speak to him personally . . . I got the message back that he didn't want to do it, so I got Nickel Creek ... to sing on it, so, in a way, it worked out better ... I was going to do a whole album of his* (songs) *and I was going to call it 'Dolly Does Dylan.' Now I'm having second thoughts. "*

In 1973, Parton's had a #1 hit with her signature song, *Jolene*, which has been covered in concert by The White Stripes in recent years. When Dylan released his 2009 album, *Together Through Life*, it included an original song with the same title. Was this Dylan's way of commenting of the 2005 "feud"? In March, 2009, in his interview with Bill Flanagan [283], Dylan said his song was about *"a different lady." Jolene* is, by far, the most-played song Dylan has performed live from *Together Through Life*.

---

[283] http://www.huffingtonpost.com/2009/04/19/bob-dylan-interview-revea_n_188782.html, *Bob Dylan Sounds Off On The Origin Of His New Record, Parlor Music, Dr. Dre, And Who His Songs Are About*, Retrieved 11/27/2016. (Originally posted on bobdylan.com. Dead link.)

Singer-songwriter Joe South dead at 72; guitarist on Dylan's 'Blonde On Blonde'

September 5, 2012

Singer, songwriter, and musician Joseph Alfred Souter died earlier today. He was 72.

In the late 1960s and early 1970s, as Joe South, he had a string of hit singles, including *Don't It Make You Wanna Go Home*, *Games People Play*, and *Walk A Mile In My Shoes*. South was also a well-known session musician, playing on the hits Aretha Franklin's *Chain of Fools* (including the distinctive opening tremolo riff), Tommy Roe's *Sheila*, and Bob Dylan's *Blonde On Blonde* album.

Dylan played some of South's records on his *Theme Time Radio Hour* program, including *Walk a Mile in My Shoes* (*Shoes* episode) and *Rose Garden* (*Spring Cleaning*). When introducing the latter, he talked about South's own hits like *Games People Play*, and the ones he wrote for others, including Deep Purple's *Hush*, Elvis Presley's *Walk a Mile in My Shoes*, and Billy Joe Royal's number one hit, *Down in the Boondocks*. Dylan then praised his guitar playing, citing his overdubbed contribution to Simon & Garfunkel's first hit, *The Sound of Silence*. He also mentioned South's 1979 Nashville Songwriters Hall of Fame induction.

His songs were also covered by Gene Vincent, Kula Shakar, the Osmonds, Lynn Anderson, Bryan Ferry, and others.

Blonde on Blonde Sessions:

According to Michael Krogsgaard, [284] "Joseph Souter" participated in the November 30, 1965, New York session from 2:30 to 7:30, while "Joseph A. Souter Jr." was in Nashville starting on Valentine's Day the following year, playing guitar and bass. South, with fellow Nashville musicians Jerry Kennedy, Hargus "Pig" Robbins, and Henry Strzelecki, was the choice of producer Bob Johnston. [285] (Trivia: Kris Kristofferson was the janitor.)

In 1969, *Rolling Stone* publisher Jann Wenner asked Dylan about playing with South in Nashville during the *Blonde on Blonde* sessions. [286] Dylan, in a mellow country mood, said South was quiet, but liked him, and enjoyed his guitar playing and his records. When asked if South did any of the solos on *Blonde on Blonde*, Dylan claimed he couldn't remember any, but believed he played a Chet Atkins model Gretch guitar. When pressed, Dylan said he might have played on *Absolutely Sweet Marie* or *Just Like a Woman*, adding, *"He played so pretty."*

Al Kooper, in the liner notes to *Bootleg Series Vol. 7*, wrote, *"Just a few credits to pass out that have been hidden over the years. Joe South is playing the soul guitar on* Stuck Inside ... *He is also playing the great bass line on* Visions of Johanna.*"*

When Dylan played his longest show ever, on January 12, 1990, at Toad's Place in New Haven, he opened with a one-off cover of *Walk A Mile In My Shoes*.

---

[284] http://www.punkhart.com/dylan/sessions-1.html, *Bob Dylan: The Recording Sessions, Part One*, Michael Krogsgaard. Retrieved 11/27/2016

[285] http://www.oxfordamerican.org/magazine/item/186-mystic-nights, *The Making of Blonde on Blonde in Nashville*, Retrieved 11/27/2016

[286] http://www.jannswenner.com/Archives/Bob_Dylan.aspx, *The Rolling Stone Interview: Bob Dylan*, Jann S. Wenner - RS47: November 29, 1969. Retrieved 11/27/2016

Johnny Cash bassist Marshall Grant, dead at 83, played with Bob Dylan

August 7, 2011

Marshall Grant, the bassist of Johnny Cash's original backing duo, the Tennessee Two, has died at the age of 83. Grant also served as road manager for Cash and his touring show company.

Rosanne Cash, Johnny's daughter, tweeted:

Marshall Grant, original of Johnny Cash & The Tennessee Two, died lst nt. Grateful I was w/ him last 2 days. Boom Chicka Boom, old friend.

So grateful I was w/ Marshall Grant last 2 days of his life. He was my 'back-up dad'. Lot of bass players owe him a debt.

He was meant to be on Jonesboro show Thurs; came to rehearsal. Played his bass on stage 1 last time, with so many friends.

Marshall used to say 'if you want the REAL story, ask ME!'. Truth.

Grant recorded with Cash from 1954 until 1980, which means he probably played bass on Cash's covers of Dylan's *Blowin' In The Wind, Don't Think Twice, It's All Right, Mama You Been On My Mind, One Too Many Mornings, Wanted Man, Country Pie,* and *It Ain't Me Babe,* according to *Dylan Cover.*

It was originally reported that Grant played with Bob Dylan, Johnny Cash, Carl Perkins, W.S. Holland, and Bob Wooten, in 1969: [287]

18 February 1969

5th Nashville Skyline session, produced by Bob Johnston.

1-2. *One Too Many Mornings*

3-4. *Mountain Dew* (Bascom Lamar Lunsford/Scott Wiseman)

5-8. *I Still Miss Someone* (Johnny Cash/Roy Cash Jr.)

9. *Careless Love* (trad.)

10-12. *Matchbox* (Carl Perkins)

13-14. *That's All Right Mama* (Arthur Crudup)

15. *Mystery Train* (Sam Phillips - Herman Parker)

16-17. *Big River* (Johnny Cash)

18-20. *Girl From The North Country*

21-22. *I Walk The Line* (Johnny Cash)

23. *How High The Water (Six Feet High and Rising)*

24. *You Are My Sunshine* (Jimmie Davis/Charles Mitchell)

25-27. *Ring Of Fire* (June Carter/Merle Kilgore)

28. *Wanted Man*

29-33. *Guess Things Happen That Way* (Jack Clement)

34-35. *Amen*

36. *Just A Closer Walk With Thee* (trad.)

---

[287] http://www.bjorner.com/still.htm, *Still on the Road*, Retrieved 11/27/2016

37-38. *Blue Yodel # 1* (Jimmie Rodgers)

Bob Dylan (vocal, guitar & harmonica), Johnny Cash (shared vocal), Carl Perkins (guitar), Marshall Grant (bass), W.S. Holland (drums), and Bob Wooten (guitar).

The current listing for *Still On The Road*, however, has been updated to say:

Bob Dylan (vocal, guitar & harmonica), Johnny Cash (shared vocal). No further information on musicians available but most probably: Bob Wilson (piano), Charlie Daniels (guitar), Charlie McCoy (bass), Norman Blake (guitar), Hargus "Pig" Robinson (piano), Peter Drake (steel guitar), Kenneth Buttrey (drums).

If you listen to the recordings, however, Cash clearly introduces Perkins on guitar - more than once - so I'd say the line-up was most likely Grant, Perkins, Holland, and Wooten.

Some sources placed Grant at the February 17 session as well. If this is true, it was at the latter part of the session on the tracks with Johnny Cash - *One Too Many Mornings*, *I Still Miss Someone*, and *Don't Think Twice, It's All Right*.

In his memoir, *I Was There When It Happened: My Life With Johnny Cash*, Grant wrote:

Today, as I look back at what we did, I realize that it really didn't matter whether John had written a particular song - or whether it was Bob Dylan, Peter LaFarge, Shel Silverstein, or Harlan Howard - he made it his own. Very few artists had the talent John did, or could sing with the same kind of feeling.

Robert Johnson

May 8, 2011

Today, May 8, is the 100th anniversary of the birth of Robert Johnson, "King Of The Delta Blues." Despite recording only a handful of songs in 1936 and 37, Johnson's legend probably looms more now than ever. Eric Clapton has covered just about all of his songs, while everyone from the Rolling Stones and Hot Tuna to Lucinda Williams and the White Stripes have paid tribute either on stage or in the studio.

While not as obvious an influence as Woody Guthrie, Hank Williams, or even Jerry Garcia, the ghost of blues legend Robert Johnson can be seen throughout the work of Bob Dylan.

Listening to the new and improved release, *The Centennial Collection*, one hears some lines that Dylan may have either directly or indirectly borrowed from Johnson: "*She's a brown skin woman . . . last fair deal gone down . . . killing me by degrees . . . little queen of spades . . . love's in vain . . .*"

In 1995, Dylan mentioned [288] that "*Robert Johnson only made one record. His body of work was just one record. Yet there's no praise or esteem high enough for the body of work he represents. He's influenced hundreds of artists. There are people who put out 40 or 50 records and don't do what he did . . .* "

It's unclear if Dylan was being serious or even correctly quoted when he added, "*He made a record called* King of the Delta Blues Singers. *In '61 or '62. He was brilliant.*"

That LP was released in 1961, compiled by John Hammond himself. He gave a "thick acetate" to Dylan the day he signed with Columbia Records, according to a passage in *Chronicles: Volume One*.

Johnson, of course, had died years earlier, on August 16, 1938. (Elvis Presley died 39 years later on the same day.) A second volume followed in 1970, and a massively successful box set was released in 1990. Dylan soon incorporated some of Johnson's material into his early set lists, including *Ramblin' On My Mind* and *Kindhearted Woman Blues*. He also covered *Milk Cow's Calf's Blues* for an early *Freewheelin'* session.

Dylan referred to Johnson repeatedly in *Chronicles: Volume One*. Not only does he spend a few pages writing about his excitement at discovering Johnson's music, he later goes into detail about seeing footage of Johnson, writing it "*couldn't be anyone else.*" Dylan described the man's hands, his clothes, and he appeared to be the opposite of someone who made a deal with the devil. Unfortunately, according to subsequent research, [289] it could not have been footage of Johnson (assuming this is the same thing Dylan viewed), as the movie seen playing in the theater was not released in Johnson's lifetime; evidence the man in the film could not have been Johnson.

When Dylan recorded his solo acoustic album *World Gone Wrong* in May, 1993, one of the out-takes was a cover of Johnson's *32-20 Blues*. It was finally released on the 2008 set, *Tell Tale Signs: The Bootleg Series Vol. 8.*

In 1999, Dylan joined Eric Clapton at A Benefit Concert For The Crossroads Centre In Antigua. They ended their six song closing set with a joint cover of Johnson's *Crossroads*.

When he was awarded a Grammy in 1998 for "Album Of The Year," Dylan recalled seeing Buddy Holly in concert, then quoted Johnson from his song, *Stop Breaking Down*:

"In the words of, you know, the immortal Robert Johnson, "the stuff we got'll bust your brains out," and we tried to get that across."

---

[288] http://articles.sun-sentinel.com/1995-09-28/lifestyle/9509270260_1_songs-sunrise-musical-theatre-tour, *A Midnight Chat With Dylan*, Retrieved 11/27/2016

[289] https://www.youtube.com/watch?v=ZSV69BO2Uak *Alleged Video Footage Of Robert Johnson*, Retrieved 11/27/2016

Kinky Friedman: 'Bob Dylan wanted to write an album's worth of songs with me'

August 15, 2015

On Thursday night, the B.B. King Blues Club & Grill in New York City hosted a Lone Star Cafe reunion. According to the venue's website, [290] *"The Lone Star Cafe, the brainchild of Mort Cooperman, was THE joint in New York City for Texas country, rhythm and blues, boogie woogie, rock-a-billy and zydeco music (and almost everything in between) .... The Lone Star was unofficial home of the New York Rangers, the New York Yankees, the Blues Brothers, Larry King, Ann Richards, Levon Helm, Doug Sahm, and Willie Nelson. Even the Hells Angels hung out regularly, always on their best behavior, having been admonished by Willie that he would never play for them, if they caused any trouble at the club... Doc Pomus had a regular seat in the third row of tables, and he never ever missed a good rhythm and blues act. A single seat will be held open at the party for Doc and all the others who won't be there with us (here's to you, Levon and Rick)."*

Bob Dylan twice appeared at the venue, in 1983 at a Rick Danko/Levon Helm gig, and again in 1988 at one of Levon's shows.

Before the festivities began, many of the musicians playing that evening headed to the local SiriusXM studios to promote the concert on the *Freewheelin'* program, which can be found on the *Road Dog* channel (146). Among the performers who converged on the station were artists associated with Bob Dylan in one way or another:

- Larry Campbell (Dylan's former guitarist)

- Kinky Friedman (Rolling Thunder Revue alumni, L'Chaim - To Life, Telethon '91)

- Tony Garnier (Dylan's bassist)

- Michael Simmons (*MOJO* Magazine, liner notes for Dylan's *Another Self Portrait*)

- Larry "Ratso" Sloman (Author, *On the Road with Bob Dylan*)

Also along for the ride was former Mountain drummer, Corky Laing.

The lineup for the evening also included Austin Music Hall Of Famers Greezy Wheels, Robert Gordon, Commander Cody, Teresa Williams, Dave Keyes, Aztec Two-Step, Carolyn Wonderland, Popa Chubby, George "Frogman" Worthmore, Hank B., Chuck McDermott, Rob Stoner, emcees Jessie Scott and Buddy Fox, and others.

You could tell by listening that there was a very loose atmosphere in the SiriusXM studios, with people talking over one another in a feeling of anarchic bonhomie. The subjects ranged from Campbell's new album and his work with the late, great, Levon Helm, to the old days of the Lone Star itself. In the second segment, author, singer-songwriter, and self-proclaimed "Texas Jewboy" Kinky Friedman, known for such songs as *They Ain't Makin' Jews Like Jesus Anymore* and *Get Your Biscuits in the Oven and Your Buns in the Bed*, was the focus, and he shared a few anecdotes about his experiences with Dylan.

Here are the highlights:

Friedman said he spent six weeks on the island of Yelapa, Mexico, with Dylan and Dennis Hopper in 1976. Dylan wanted to write an album with Friedman at the time, harassing him to do so. Friedman said that since they'd just finished the second leg of the Rolling Thunder Revue tour, he wanted to take it easy. Kinky kept putting it off, and it never happened. That would be unlike Dylan, who Friedman said would have been more *"practical,"* squeezing out a few albums with the bigger

---

[290] http://www.bbkingblues.com/bio.php?id=5585, *A Lone Star Cafe Reunion party! Hosted By Austin Music Hall Of Famers Greezy Wheels*, Retrieved 11/27/2016

name. Friedman said this was a pattern in his career, as he also blew chances to work with Paul Simon and Shel Silverstein.

Cleve, an employee of Friedman's, talked Kinky into auctioning off Dylan's Rolling Thunder coat, presumably a gift from Dylan himself. It was a Nudie original, *"with Jesus' head and palm trees"* on it, according to Kinky. It was successfully sold, and the winner was Tel Aviv's Hard Rock Cafe. When he told the former owner of the jacket he had sold it for $7,500, Dylan replied, *"Bad move,"* meaning, it would be *"worth a fortune"* if he'd kept it.

Friedman's next story was about Dylan playing his guitar on the beach, almost alone, when suddenly he drew a crowd. Dylan then put the guitar away, saying *"he really liked it when he played for people just having their dinner ... and he can't do that anymore."*

Friedman had one more story, which Sloman said Friedman *"appropriated from him."* Friedman went on to tell a tale about when they were flying on Southwest Airlines, *"which has no first class, so we're with regular people."* The woman who wound up sitting next to Dylan, in her excitement, kept saying, *"I can't believe it, I'm sitting next to Bob Dylan!"*

So Dylan said, *"Pinch yourself."*

Bob Dylan and B.B. King - Singers, songwriters, guitarists, and satellite DJs

September 15, 2011

Birthday boy B.B. King was born Riley B. King in Mississippi, on September 16, 1925. He was raised by his grandmother, sang in the local church's gospel choir, and owned his first guitar by the time he was 12-years-old.

In 1943, King left home to work as a tractor driver and as a musician. Three years later, King followed his cousin, blues legend Bukka White (author of *Fixin' To Die, Shake 'Em On Down*, and *Po' Boy*) to Memphis. King soon left and went back to Mississippi to practice, then headed out for West Memphis, Arkansas, in 1948.

Here, King began to make a name for himself, both in clubs and on radio. Eventually he worked as a disc jockey and singer at R&B radio station WDIA. Here King became known as "Beale Street Blues Boy," which was eventually shortened to B.B. He went on to become one of the most popular and influential blues guitarists of all time.

In 1981, Bob Dylan wrote a song with bassist Tim Drummond called *Fur Slippers*. According to *Searching For A Gem*: [291]

"(Dylan) recorded during Shot Of Love *sessions at United Western Studios, Los Angeles, CA, 02 Apr 1981, short-listed for* The Bootleg Series Vols. 1-3. *Covered by B. B. King on the soundtrack of the 1999 CBS TV mini-series* Shake Rattle And Roll *(Uni/MCA records)."*

Like Bob Dylan, King became a satellite radio DJ. The SiriusXM Bluesville channel was renamed *B.B. King's Bluesville* in 2008.

B.B. King and Bob Dylan were photographed at the Adelaide Entertainment Centre in Adelaide Australia, on April 19, 2011.

On *Theme Time Radio Hour*, Dylan played some of B.B. King's records, including *Bad Luck Soul* and *Walking Dr. Bill*. Referring to the latter, Dylan talked about titles that made no sense, thinking he didn't know who "Dr. Bill" could be, until he heard the lyrics and discovered King, a wreck since his woman left him, was a *"walking doctor bill."*

Bob Dylan and B.B. King shared the same stage at the February 24, 1990, Roy Orbison tribute. Like Orbison, some of King's early sides were produced by Sam Phillips.

During the finale, everyone gathered on stage for a version of *Only The Lonely*, including:

Cindy Bullens, Gary Busey, Bob Dylan, Joe Ely, Chris Frantz, John Fogerty, Larry Gatlin, Emmylou Harris, Jerry Harrison, Levon Helm, John Hiatt, John Lee Hooker, Chris Isaak, Booker T, B.B. King, Al Kooper, Michael McDonald, Slim Jim Phantom, Iggy Pop, Bonnie Raitt, Lee Rocker, Brian Setzer, Ricky Skaggs, Harry Dean Stanton, Syd Straw, Don Was, David Was, Tina Weymouth, Dwight Yoakam and others, including The Byrds: Roger McGuinn, David Crosby, and Chris Hillman, with John Jorgenson and Steve Duncan. [292]

---

[291] http://www.searchingforagem.com/Starlight/BobUnrelF.htm, *"Starlight In The East" - Directory of Bob Dylan's Unreleased Songs: F*, Compiled by Alan Fraser. Retrieved 11/27/2016

[292] http://www.bjorner.com/still.htm, *Still on the Road*, Retrieved 11/27/2016

Billy Preston covering Bob Dylan in 1965, plus *Blood On The Tracks* controversy

William Everett "Billy" Preston was born on September 2, 1946. He started as a child prodigy, and performed with Mahalia Jackson, James Cleveland, and Andrae Crouch by the time he was 10. Soon, he was making appearances with Little Richard, Sam Cooke, and Ray Charles. In the mid-1960s, he was a regular on the mid-1960s ABC-TV musical variety series *Shindig!* In the 1970s, Preston had hits with *Outa-Space, Will It Go Round in Circles, Nothing From Nothing, Space Race*, and with Syreeta Wright, *With You I'm Born Again*. He also wrote *You Are So Beautiful*, a major hit for Joe Cocker.

In January, 1969, George Harrison recruited Preston for the Beatles's *Get Back/Let It Be* sessions to ease tensions within the band: [293]

Billy was in London playing organ for Ray Charles. George Harrison caught Ray's show at the Royal Festival Hall and spotted someone he recognized in the band. George said in *The Beatles Anthology* book: *"I thought, 'That guy looks familiar,' but he seemed bigger than I remembered... I thought, 'It's Billy!' Since we had last seen him in Hamburg in 1962, when he was just a little lad, he had grown to be six foot tall."* [294]

Preston was rewarded with a credit on the *Get Back/Don't Let Me Down* single, and was suddenly in demand, playing sessions for various solo Beatles, the Rolling Stones, and many others.

The Beatles then signed Preston to their Apple Records label, where he covered Dylan's *She Belongs To Me* for the album *That's The Way God Planned It*. Later, while on A&M, he recorded a version of *It's Alright, Ma (I'm Only Bleeding)* on his 1973 album, *Everybody Likes Some Kind of Music*. Preston also covered *Maggie's Farm* back in 1965 on *Shindig!*

Preston and Dylan both played at The Concert For Bangla Desh, but did not appear on stage at the same time.

Preston later toured with Ringo Starr in 1989, along with Levon Helm, Rick Danko, and others. He also toured with The Band in the early 1990s, but reportedly couldn't accept an invitation to permanently become a member due to legal problems.

If you believe postings on the internet, Billy Preston played bass on Dylan's album, *Blood On The Tracks*. It's even been hinted at on his official Apple Records page. [295]

However, there is no evidence he ever played on sessions for Dylan's 1975 masterpiece (especially the bass), or any other Dylan recording. It appears someone confused Preston with Minneapolis musician Billy Peterson, and the error has been copied ever since. [296]

Here's Preston on (not) playing with Dylan: [297]

(Preston muses when asked about the making of Dylan's 1975 milestone, *Blood on the Tracks*.) *No, Mr. Preston, I was asking about the making of Blood on the Tracks.*

"What? Is that Michael's record?" he asks. (Michael who?) (Note: Preston was possibly referring to Michael Jackson's *Blood On The Dance Floor* 1997 remix album.)

---

[293] http://www.applerecords.com/#!/albums/Album_ThatsTheWayGodPlannedIt, *That's the Way God Planned It*, Retrieved 11/27/2016

[294] *The Beatles Anthology*, The Beatles, Chronicle Books, San Francisco. 2000

[295] http://www.applerecords.com/#!/albums/album_thatsthewaygodplannedit, *That's the Way God Planned It*, Retrieved 11/27/2016

[296] http://www.bjorner.com/DSN02710%201974%20Blood%20On%20The%20Tracks %20recording%20sessions.htm, *Still on the Road*, Retrieved 11/27/2016

[297] http://www.metrotimes.com/detroit/prestons-follies/Content?oid=2176514, *Preston's Follies*, Retrieved 11/27/2016

"No, that's a record by Bob Dylan."

"I don't know, I forget a lot of sessions from way back then."

Preston's phone kept ringing. Clapton called. Dylan called. Or did he?

Bonnie Raitt covers two Bob Dylan songs on her first album in seven years

January 3, 2012

Bonnie Raitt has interpreted two songs from Bob Dylan's *Time Out Of Mind* on her upcoming release, *Slipstream*.

The Dylan compositions Raitt covered were *Million Miles* and *Standing In The Doorway*, both first released in 1997. Interestingly, Adele had some recent success with Raitt's *I Can't Make You Love Me*, and another *Time Out Of Mind* track, *Make You Feel My Love*.

Raitt previously covered a Dylan rarity, *Let's Keep It Between Us*, on 1982's *Green Light*, and the classic *It's All Over Now, Baby Blue* for the soundtrack of the 2000 movie, *Steal This Movie*. Raitt also contributed to Tom Corwin and Tim Hockenberry's *Mostly Dylan* project.

Dylan and Raitt once shared the stage at the 1990 Roy Orbison tribute at the Los Angeles Universal Amphitheater, and both appeared on the Artists United Against Apartheid *Sun City* single. However, she reportedly declined an invitation to 1992's 30th Anniversary Concert Celebration (a.k.a. "Bob-Fest") when she learned that none of the proceeds would go to charity.

Dylan mentioned Bonnie and her father, actor John Raitt, on the *Fathers* episode of *Theme Time Radio Hour*. According to CBS/Associated Press, [298] Bonnie's parents, her brother, and her best friend, all died since the release of her last studio album seven years ago. Similarly, *Time Out Of Mind* was Dylan's first album of original compositions in seven years.

Slipstream is expected to be released April 10 on her new label, Redwing. Musicians on the album include Joe Henry, Bill Frisell, Paul Brady, Maia Sharp, Al Anderson (NRBQ), and members of Raitt's touring band.

---

[298] http://www.cbsnews.com/news/bonnie-raitt-to-release-first-album-in-seven-years/ *Bonnie Raitt to release first album in seven years*, Retrieved 11/27/2016

Time Out Of Mind guitarist Duke Robillard to join Bob Dylan's touring band

December 23, 2012

It appears blues guitarist Duke Robillard will be joining Bob Dylan's touring band next year.

The following was posted yesterday to the Byron Bay Bluesfest forum (with typos fixed): [299]

Duke Robillard was to be toured by an Australian Blues promoter who had sold a date on the tour to Bluesfest.

It has transpired that he was unable to get the number of shows needed to proceed with the tour, and then advised us, and Duke's agent, he was canceling.

Bluesfest then attempted to resurrect the tour, but found it impossible when Duke Robillard subsequently advised he needed to cut the tour short due to his being appointed by Bob Dylan as his new guitar player - and needing to get back to the US by April 1 for rehearsals, and only being available for a much shorter run of dates, which did not make coming to Australia at this time viable...

Sincerely,

Peter Noble Bluesfest Director

Robillard, a co-founding member of Roomful Of Blues, was brought in by Dylan to play on his 1997 album *Time Out Of Mind.* According to Olof Bjorner, [300] Robillard appeared on the following songs from those sessions: *Million Miles, Tryin' To Get To Heaven, Can't Wait, Mississippi, Red River Shore,* and *Marchin' To The City.*

Here is a quote from engineer Mark Howard about the sessions, courtesy *Uncut* magazine: [301]

"(Co-producer Daniel Lanois) had put together a band, and then Dylan had put out the call for these guys like Jim Dickinson, Augie Meyers, Duke Robillard, Cindy Cashdollar. Dylan brought in all these Nashville people, and I think that made Dan a little mental having all these Nashville strummers strumming, it was a bit too much. As I'm sure Jim Dickinson has said, there were a lot of ingredients in there that you don't actually hear on the record, because things were filtered down so we could take a cleaner path on some of them."

As of now, dates posted on the Duke Robillard Band's tour page still list shows past April 1.

This development has not been confirmed by Dylan's management. It is unclear who, if anyone, Robillard will be replacing in Dylan's touring band.

Of course Robillard's career expands much wider than his time short time with Dylan. After his stint with Roomful Of Blues, he played with The Fabulous Thunderbirds for a few years before forming his own band. He has played with everyone from Pinetop Perkins and Jimmy Witherspoon to Jay Geils and Tom Waits. He has been nominated for many awards, including Grammys for Best Contemporary Blues Album (2007) and Best Traditional Blues Album (2010).

Report: Duke Robillard confirms rumors, and Bob Dylan to tour Europe in the fall

March 4, 2013

It appears the rumors are true. As reported here late last year, Duke Robillard will join Bob Dylan's touring band next month.

Robillard is currently on tour in Europe, and played a gig in Landshut, Germany, last night. Afterwards, he spoke to fans. This is the exclusive report, from Dorothee Kern:

---

[299] http://forum.bluesfest.com.au/Default.aspx?g=topics&f=5 Dead Link.

[300] http://www.bjorner.com/still.htm, *Still on the Road,* Retrieved 11/27/2016

[301] http://www.uncut.co.uk/features/bob-dylan-tell-tale-signs-special-mark-howard-37964, *Bob Dylan: Tell Tale Signs Special,* Retrieved 11/27/2016

"Last night, the Duke Robillard Band played at Jimmy's Cafe, and it was fantastic! After the show, I met him and all of his band, and they signed his new CD, Independently Blue, *which is scheduled for release in April.*

"I got a chance to ask him about his touring with Bob Dylan in April and, big news, at least for me ... He confirmed the rumors! I also asked him whether Bob will come to Europe and he answered, 'Yes, in the fall.'

"He was busy signing his CD's, so I didn't dare question him more. He added, 'Well, see you then!' I don't know when and where he will tour with Bob, but this was exciting news anyway!"

According to his official website, Robillard is currently on tour with his band until the end of the month, and again in May. Nothing is scheduled for April, when Dylan is on the road. There are currently 12 concerts listed on Dylan's official site.

Besides playing on *Time Out Of Mind*, Robillard has covered Dylan's *Love Sick*, *Pledging My Time*, *Down Along The Cove*, and *Everything is Broken*, according to the *Dylan Cover* website.

Robillard's Facebook posts

June 30, 2013

There has been some drama in the Dylan camp. New guitarist Duke Robillard's Facebook page has some intriguing posts: [302]

Early this morning: For sale Bob Dylan CD and record collection for sale slightly used. Later this morning: I will be selling a lot of guitars and amps soon. I'll keep you posted ...

What does it all mean? Stay tuned for *As The Record Spins*. I hope it's some sort of "in" joke.

Robillard leaves

July 7, 2013

According to posts on his Facebook page at about 7 p.m. ET, Duke Robillard confirmed that he is no longer touring with Dylan:

I will make one small non-cryptic post hear (sic) *to clear up any confusion or misinterpretation. I left the Bob Dylan tour of my own accord. All I can say is it wasn't for musical reasons and please don't ask any more. I enjoyed my brief stay there and had a lot of fun with the band playing Bob's music. I have great respect for him as an artist. I will miss everyone in the organization as they are all wonderful people. I wish them continued success and I will miss them all. Case closed!*

Earlier messages included this one from Robillard: *How can you NOT love BD? Guess I'll be keeping CDs! LOL*

---

[302] https://www.facebook.com/duke.robillard.1?fref=ts, *Duke Robillard's Facebook page*, Retrieved 11/27/2016

Etta James dead at 73 - Bob Dylan joined her on stage at the Marriott in 1986

January 20, 2012

Etta James, the R&B legend, has died after a long illness. She was 73.

About a year ago, it was first reported that James was undergoing treatment for leukemia, and had been diagnosed with dementia.

Etta James was born Jamesetta Hawkins on January 25, 1938. She was discovered by Johnny Otis, who died earlier in the week.

James has been inducted into the Rock and Roll Hall of Fame, the Blues Hall of Fame, and received a Grammy Lifetime Achievement Award. [303] [304] Two of her recordings - *At Last* and *Wallflower (Roll With Me, Henry)* – were entered into the Grammy Hall of Fame. [305]

There are a handful of connections between James and Bob Dylan.

Bob Dylan dropped in on a late 1970's Etta James session in Los Angeles to speak with producer Jerry Wexler, where he previewed some new songs:

" ... He just happened to drop by one Tuesday evening to tell me he was a fan and play Wexler some of his new ideas... That record, Slow Train Coming, *featured* Gotta Serve Somebody, *my favorite Dylan tune, which, years later I wanted Wexler to produce for me, only to have Jerry refuse 'cause the song was too religious!* [306]

James eventually recorded the song as the opening track on her 2000 album, *Matriarch Of The Blues*. She also covered *Blowin' In The Wind* in 1983, and again in 2002.

From the same book:

"In the early eighties ... I'd be at the Vis at the edge of the Fillmore, an all-the-way black club, where one night they said Bob Dylan was pulling up in a limo. 'Cool,' I said. 'I like Bob, but you better put his name at the door 'cause black folks don't know who Bob Dylan is.'" [307]

On July 8 and 9, 1986, Bob Dylan, while on his True Confessions tour with Tom Petty, The Heartbreakers, and The Queens Of Rhythm, played at the brand new Great Woods amphitheater in Mansfield, Massachusetts, now known as the Xfinity Center.

In the early hours of the 10th, Bob Dylan joined Etta James and Johnny Otis' son, Shuggie, on stage at the Providence Marriott Hotel. You can almost hear Dylan smile as he kept repeating the same suggestive verse of *"I'm A King Bee"* (the one about *"making honey"*). Here's the information: [308]

Marriott Hotel,

Providence, Rhode Island 10 July 1986

1. *You Win Again* (Hank Williams)

2. *I'm A King Bee* (James Moore)

3. *Let The Good Times Roll* (Leonard Lee)

---

[303] http://www.aceshowbiz.com/celebrity/etta_james/awards.html, *Etta James Awards*, Retrieved 1/25/2017

[304] https://www.grammy.org/recording-academy/awards/lifetime-awards, *Lifetime Achievement Awards*, Retrieved 1/25/2017

[305] https://www.grammy.com/blogs/etta-james-dies, *Etta James Dies*, Retrieved 1/25/2017

[306] *Rage To Survive: The Etta James Story*, David Ritz, Etta James. Da Capo Press, New York, 1995

[307] *Rage To Survive: The Etta James Story*, David Ritz, Etta James. Da Capo Press, New York, 1995

[308] http://www.bjorner.com/still.htm, *Still on the Road*, Retrieved 11/27/2016

4. *Earth Angel* (Dootsie Williams/Curtis Williams)

5. *Goodnight, Sweetheart, Goodnight* (James "Pookie" Hudson)

Bob Dylan (guitar), Etta James (shared vocal), Shuggie Otis (guitar), Jack McDuff (organ), Richard Reid (bass), Paul Humphrey (drums).

1- 4 Bob Dylan (solo vocal)

Bob Dylan played a handful of Etta's recordings on his *Theme Time Radio Hour* radio program, including *842-3089 (Call My Name)*, *Only Time Will Tell*, and *Stop The Wedding*.

Talking about James in 2006, on the *Telephone* episode of *Theme Time*, Dylan said that she was still *"strong,"* and thought he should congratulate her on receiving a star on the Hollywood Walk of Fame. He also mentioned Otis was the one who discovered her.

On the *Time* episode, Dylan played her recording of *Only Time Will Tell*, and said there was a rumor she was the daughter of the legendary billiards player, Minnesota Fats, adding he didn't ever hear *his* version of the story.

Dylan's current drummer George Recile, and former background singer, actress Katey Sagal, each collaborated with James.

Here is a sample of posts on Twitter about James' death:

@r0bbier0berts0n: (Robbie Robertson): RIP Etta.

@sandibachom: (Sandi Bachom): RIP Etta, simply the best blues singer of all time IMHO!

@Spotify: RIP Etta James. Truly one of the most amazing voices of all time.

@rosannecash: The great Etta James

@alecbaldwin: Etta James. Put down your magazine, kindle, e- mail, catalog or telephone. Turn off the TV and spend some time with this great artist.

@Raekwon: RIP to the lovely etta james

@joejonas: R.I.P. Etta James :(

@SteveWinwood: Etta James… You'll be missed.

@thewarrenhaynes: RIP Etta James - @thewarrenhaynes band performing I'd Rather Go Blind on 5/14/11 in Philly - bit.ly/AuP9V6

@BBKingBluesClub: Etta James in her last BB Kings appearance in 09' fb.me/LqXC3fY4

@hughhefner: Sorry to learn of Etta James passing. RIP.

@YO_RANDYJACKSON (American Idol): Sadly today the world lost one of the greatest ever, Etta James.

@brianrayguitar (Brian Ray, Paul McCartney's guitarist who also played with James): Thank you for you kind words on this sad day RIP Etta James "Take It To The Limit" & "Can't Turn You Loose" [with me at 26] ... I am thinking of Etta's kids, Sametto (my Godson), Donto this evening. And Johnny Otis who discovered her. LOVE and RIP, you 2.

Interview with Canned Heat's Harvey Mandel, Bob Dylan's Grammy guitarist

February 17, 2011

When Bob Dylan played at The Grammys on Sunday night, bandmates Sku Kimball, Donnie Herron, and Tony Garnier joined the Avett Brothers and Mumford & Sons to perform a raucous version of *Maggie's Farm*.

Missing were George Recile and Charlie Sexton, but someone else was brought in - Harvey "The Snake" Mandel.

Mandel has been playing almost as long as Dylan, starting off with Charlie Musselwhite in 1966, later hooking up with Canned Heat (*Let's Work Together*), John Mayall, Barry Goldberg, and the Rolling Stones (*Black and Blue*), among others.

"Yeah, I got a call Saturday morning (the day before the Grammys), *flew into L.A. that day,"* Mandel told me over the phone. *"It was literally that morning that I got contacted. It was very exciting, much better than watching it on TV."*

The way Mandel heard it, albeit secondhand, *"for some reason, Bob said, 'We need one more guy.'"* Mandel's name came up, and Dylan's *"people"* tried to get in touch with "The Snake."

"That's as far as I know. They contacted one of my collaborators from my website. I was in Colorado and they didn't know how to get in touch with me. They left a message and I followed up. Bob Dylan's people wanted me to know that he wanted me to play on Maggie's Farm *at the Grammys. Next thing I knew, I was flying to L.A., and everything started to happen."*

This was the first time Dylan and Mandel collaborated. *"We travel in the same circles, but never played together before. Barry Goldberg and I do shows, and he played with Dylan. I play with Canned Heat, and they knew Dylan, I'm sure. John Mayall, The Rolling Stones. We'd met before, he knew who I was. We never played together before. I'm surprised, but that's how it works out sometimes."*

Once Mandel flew into L.A., it was time to get down to business. *"There wasn't really a rehearsal, really just a run-through. What you saw on TV was the same as the run-through, except there were producers and people twisting knobs. All we did was play. It was over in two minutes, no going over anything."*

From the beginning, Mandel knew he would be playing *Maggie's Farm*, which is comprised of only three chords.

"I already knew it was a simple song. When I got there I asked if it was in the key of G like on the record, but either Stu or Tony said, 'No, it's in E.'"

While he didn't get to speak with Dylan after the performance, Bob let Mandel know he was pleased. *"While we were putting our equipment away, he definitely waved, and gave me the 'good look.' By the time I got everything packed, I think he took off. But he gave me the vibe that he was happy. It was exactly what he asked for."*

Mandel got to watch the delayed telecast back at his hotel room. *"It was exciting. I got about a million phone calls and more people emailed me - a crazy amount - than over anything I've done in years."*

"I didn't even have to be there, but it was an honor to play the Grammys, and I always wanted to play with Bob. I hope that it leads to more real playing, not just part of some 30 man entourage."

Mandel appeared on The Rolling Stones' album, *Black and Blue*, playing lead guitar on *Hot Stuff* and *Memory Motel*, but didn't get a chance to say hello to Mick Jagger while at the Grammys.

"Unfortunately not. It's weird in the Staples Center, it's even bigger than it looks. There are hundreds of dressing rooms, and everybody is surrounded by security. You only see people if you happen to bump into them. Bob's was a secret dressing room behind all the others. You had to be escorted in."

The entire experience reminded Mandel of when he was invited to play with the Stones in 1975. *"I was at home. Mick Jagger called me at midnight. At first I thought someone was goofing on me, but after a while I could tell it was really him. He said, 'I'd like you to fly to Germany tomorrow.' The next day, I'm on my way to Germany."*

"It was the same with Bob. At first I thought I was being goofed on again, but then I did some investigating, and forged ahead immediately."

So, the big question is - are you the new guitarist in Bob Dylan's band, or was this just a one-off gig?

"At the moment, it's just a one-off. I have plans to tour with Canned Heat again starting in June. We only play in the warm weather. We don't like the cold."

Interview: D.A. Pennebaker reflects on Dylan in *Dont Look Back* and *Eat the Document.*

November 26, 2015

It's time for Bob Dylan fans to take a break from listening to *The Cutting Edge 1965-1966*, and head for the couch in front of that big, flat screen TV. *Dont Look Back* is back, and it's better and more expanded than ever.

Pennebaker's 1967 documentary of Bob Dylan's 1965 acoustic tour of Britain is considered a classic for its groundbreaking cinéma vérité style, as well as encapsulating a pivotal moment in the history of popular music. The film was included in the Library of Congress' National Film Registry in 1998, and is often near - or at - the top of any "Best Music Documentary" or "Greatest Rock Film" polls.

Pennebaker, still going strong at 90, has been involved in filmmaking for more than 60 years, and his movies have covered a wide variety of topics. *Dont Look Back* was not the first music-based documentary directed by Pennebaker, nor would it be the last. However, this film in particular stands out for a variety of reasons, most notably the intimate, hand-held grainy camerawork used in a portrait of the artist as a young man, a musician attempting to avoid allowing fame to swallow him up as his blazes his own path, oblivious to whomever else gets burned.

Dont Look Back now joins other Pennebaker films as part of the Criterion Collection, a company that prides itself on catering to the cinematic connoisseur. I spoke with "Penny" on the eve of its re-release. He was expansive, giving in-depth and detailed answers to whatever question he was asked. He was also self-deprecating, giving most of the credit to his subjects, and his cohorts. However, none of this would have happened without the skills and talents of one Mr. D.A. Pennebaker.

Movie making has evolved quite a bit in the six-plus decades since you've been involved in the process. What are your thoughts on all of these changes?

The whole thing is just incredibly astonishing! I heard the new film, Tangerine, *was filmed entirely on iPhones. No cameras were involved! This is what I always thought would happen ... When we started (Dont Look Back), we had to make a camera, because there were no cameras that you could carry around that would be safe, that you could shoot dialogue with ... It's kind of wondrous. In 20 years - well I'm sure I won't be around - people will be using equipment we now don't even know could exist.*

How was the original process of making the film different from the new Criterion version?

We shot on negative. We pretty much handed it over (to Criterion). In the beginning, when we were shooting it, we had a lab in England that we liked ... They made everything look OK. The secret was not having a good knowledge of exposure, but of having a very good lab.

Dont Look Back was available in limited release for a short while in 1967 and 1968, then was out of circulation for about 15 years...

It came and went. To some degree because of some problems (manager) Albert Grossman and Dylan were having with each other. Dylan, who was my partner in the film, was trying to figure out what to do with the film. I didn't know, I wasn't a distributor. To get it into a movie house was complicated ... The films were distributed by a distributing annex that was really a marketing operation out of Hollywood ... So when I show up with a ratty looking film ... the guy in the theater can't believe it. He has no way conceiving (of showing this to a mainstream audience.) If it hadn't been for a porn film operator, who saw it and eagerly grabbed it ... because, he said it looked like a porn film, but wasn't ... a 16mm print ran (in a San Francisco theater) for almost a year, and it managed to generate enough money for us to make a 35mm blow up and open it in New York.

When I first saw Dont Look Back, it was unlike anything I'd ever seen, even though it was already 15 years old...

It was rather ratty looking, don't you think?

Being a fan, it was like watching a Bob Dylan bootleg on the big screen. I thought it was cool, and a bit disturbing, to see such an unflattering portrait of someone I admired. However, with the DVD commentary, more research, and more life experience, a more sympathetic aspect did emerge.

I was reminded of this English writer who collected all the letters to and from (Lord) Byron ... He went to Italy with (Percy) Shelley ... All the English sort-of intellectuals came down to hang out with him ... Byron wasn't even 30. He was a young scamp! I kept thinking, if I had been there and been able to have a camera and just watch, the way I could do with Dylan, people would be watching that film for hundreds of years afterwards, because Byron was so interesting. It wasn't my camerawork that would be fascinating, but they were interested in: 'What is this guy like? ... How could he command such a huge hunk of history at the age of 28, having written a few poems?' That's kind of what I felt I had here, that I made it for the future ... It has to be the subject who makes it work.

A few years back, there was another documentary you made, from the outtakes, titled *65 Revisited*, and now there's even more footage in the Criterion version, titled *Snapshots From the Tour*.

I felt I had been target shooting (for Dont Look Back), and I'd been a little off of the target. Then I went back and shot it again, and got closer. The assumption was that I fucked up the first time (laughs), and got it straightened out for the second!

When I got there, I was under the impression that Albert wanted a musical film to promote Dylan's concerts, or records, or whatever he was doing, and this would be kind of a music film. So I brought along Bob Van Dyke, he was our sound guy ... Any music we did, he was in charge. He recorded every concert from beginning to end. But after less than a week, going around with Bob, I began to get a sense the film I wanted to make was not a musical film, but about this guy who might be a poet, and he, himself, was trying to figure out if he was a poet. The way he used language was just amazing sometimes. I kept filming dialogue with just people on the street. So I was making a film about Dylan as a persona, rather than Dylan as the organ grinder.

What we did was to put together a film (65 Revisited) where he sings complete songs, and when I saw it, I thought, 'Oh my god. I did make a mistake (the first time)!' The poetry is really in the songs, not in the conversations. People who saw the early film and said, 'Dylan is kind of shit,' with the new one they said, 'God, he's just lovely.'

I expect everything I shot to be put out on some sort of format eventually. Whether we put that out in a film format as we know it, or in some format that hasn't been discovered yet, I don't know.

The opening sequence of Dylan holding cue cards while *Subterranean Homesick Blues* is playing has been copied and parodied many times...

It was a good idea, and it was a very "home movie" idea. It was Dylan's idea. In a bar, he asked me, and I said I thought it was terrific. We took along hundreds of shirt cardboards on the trip, and we sat down with Donovan and Joan (Baez), and just did different signs. I did some too, but I can't remember which ones I did.

Things must have been a bit different on the 1966 tour, where the rare documentary *Eat the Document* was filmed...

It was a different kind of film. He said, "You've got your film, and now you're gonna film, and I'm gonna direct." But the problem was neither of us had the least idea of how to direct it. We kept stumbling around, and we kept shooting things, but it had to be put together. Editing was very important in this type of film. It has to be theatrical, it can't be explorative ... It was Dylan's film, and I didn't want to grab it away from him, or struggle with him. That was the deal we made. It was a handshake deal. And he didn't know what to do with it. It didn't go anywhere, until (Martin) Scorsese got hold of it and put it together (for No Direction Home). Eventually, (I think) it will all appear, and some of it is extraordinary.

You were on stage with the whole band there ...

You'd normally film it from a distance ... I didn't want to do that. I wanted to be on stage with them, because he was having a great time and jumping around out on that stage...

I made a (special) lens that was extremely wide angle, and it flared at the edge, which I thought was kind of beautiful. I just got up on stage, and he didn't know I was gonna do it. So when he came out on stage, there I was, and he really cracked up. And we filmed the whole show, with me between everybody, filming!

Well, it's been a real pleasure speaking with you again, and thank you for your time.

I really appreciated anyone who is interested not just in the film, but in Dylan, and why he survives after 50 years.

The impact of Andy Griffith on Bob Dylan

July 3, 2012

Andrew Samuel "Andy" Griffith, actor, singer, director, producer, and writer, died earlier today. He was 86.

Griffith was probably best known for his starring roles in the television shows *The Andy Griffith Show* (featuring Don Knotts and a very young Ron Howard) and *Matlock*. Although he eventually became a Grammy Award-winning gospel singer, it was an early movie role that reportedly made a big impact on a young Bobby Zimmerman.

Almost ten years ago, Sean Wilentz, currently George Henry Davis 1886 Professor of American History at Princeton University, posted an article on Bob Dylan's official website, where he is the historian in residence. In an article titled *The Roving Gambler at Scenic Newport*, he wrote about the significance of Dylan returning to the Newport Folk Festival in 2002, and performing the song, *Roving Gambler*. [309] Wilentz wrote about the effect the 1957 film, *A Face in the Crowd*, directed by Elia Kazan, had on a young Bobby Zimmerman. Griffith starred as the singing Lonesome Rhodes, a former convicted hobo, who became *"a nationwide T.V. celebrity and reactionary demagogue -- a forerunner of Rush Limbaugh and Bob Roberts. Bob Dylan saw* A Face In The Crowd, *and, reportedly, was more shaken by it than by any film he'd seen since* Rebel Without a Cause. *At a crucial moment in the film, Griffith's character realizes he's going to make a fortune and starts singing an exuberant and menacing version of* The Roving Gambler."

Wilentz went on to connect the song with *Highway 61 Revisited*, among other things: *"Now the rovin' gambler he was very bored."*

At the end of an outtake [310] version of *I Shall Be Free* from the *Freewheelin'* sessions (December 6, 1962, Mx. CO 77023-5), [311] after Dylan sings about making love to Liz Taylor and catching hell from Richard Burton, you can hear him say as the song fades out, *"Get tested by Elia Kazan,"* as in "Screentest," presumably.

Like Dylan, Griffith received the Presidential Medal of Freedom. His was awarded in 2005.

---

[309] http://web.archive.org/web/20041209094434/http://bobdylan.com/etc/wilentz_newport.html, *The Roving Gambler at Scenic Newport*, Sean Wilentz, Retrieved 11/27/2106

[310] http://www.bjorner.com/DSN00150%201962.htm#DSN00320, *Still on the Road*, Retrieved 11/27/2016

[311] *I Shall Be Free, 50th Anniversary Collection - 1962* (Limited release in Europe only), Bob Dylan, 2012.

Eddie and Carrie Fisher

September 24, 2010

Pop singer Eddie Fisher died of complications from hip surgery on September 22 at the age of 82.

While Bob Dylan had little connection to Fisher, it has been reported that they shared some of the same Nashville musicians on their recordings.

Both Dylan and Fisher were spotted at Temple Israel of Hollywood. [312] Eddie Fisher once sang Kol Nidre from the choir loft on the High Holidays, while Marlon Brando and Dylan attended a Passover Seder at the Temple in 1975, where Bob allegedly sang, *Blowin' In The Wind.*

Carrie Fisher, of *Star Wars* fame, is the daughter of Eddie Fisher and Debbie Reynolds. She has a couple of interesting Dylan stories to tell, [313] saying she once mocked Dylan at a cocktail party for wearing sunglasses and a parka, saying, *"Thank God you wore that, Bob, because sometimes late at night here the sun gets really, really bright, then it snows."*

Sometime after Fisher got out of rehab in the 1980s, Dylan, through someone at his office, called and asked for Fisher's number. She said she felt like saying, *"No, you keep that stalker away from me. I don't want any more Sixties icons fucking up my life!"* but thought the better of it, and she picked up the phone. Apparently, a perfume company wanted Dylan to endorse a fragrance named after his song, *Just Like a Woman.* [314] Dylan disapproved of the name, so he asked Fisher, for reasons only he would know, for some some suggestions. She came up with *"Ambivalence – for the scent of confusion,"* *"Arbitrary – for the man who doesn't give a shit how he smells,"* and *"Empathy – feel like them, smell like this."* She apparently thought Dylan was hitting on her, but George Harrison explained that Dylan gets easily distracted and bored on the road: *"Bob had phoned George the week before to see if he wanted to open the Traveling Wilburys Hotel."* [315]

Carrie Fisher was once married to singer-songwriter Paul Simon, making him Eddie Fisher's son-in-law. Simon, of course, has known Dylan for many years.

---

[312] http://www.tioh.org/WELCOME/history/, Dead Link. See http://www.iamnotastalker.com/2012/11/15/temple-israel-of-hollywood-from-will-grace, *Temple Israel of Hollywood from "Will & Grace"*, Retrieved 11/27/2016

[313] http://www.avclub.com/article/carrie-fishers-wishful-drinking-23641, *Carrie Fisher's Wishful Drinking,* Retrieved 11/27/2016

[314] *Wishful Drinking,* Carrie Fisher, Simon & Schuster, New York, 2009

[315] *Opinion: "Wishful Drinking",* Maureen Callahan New York Post, 11/30/2008

Elizabeth Taylor

March 23, 2011

It is being reported that Hollywood icon Elizabeth Taylor has died. Dame Elizabeth Rosemond Taylor, DBE, was 79.

Taylor was born on February 28, 1932. Pop singer Eddie Fisher, who died September 22, was involved in a scandal when he left his first wife, Debbie Reynolds, for Taylor, in 1959. Fisher and Taylor divorced on March 6, 1964, and she married Richard Burton for the first time nine days later. Liz and Dick met on the set of the film, *Cleopatra*, in early 1962. [316] By December of that year, Bob Dylan was already singing, *"I make love to Elizabeth Taylor . . . Catch hell from Richard Burton!"* in his recording of *I Shall be Free*.

Fast forward to March 31, 1986. When Dylan was presented with a Founder's Award from ASCAP at Chasen's in Beverly Hills, he was photographed sitting with Taylor. According to Howard Sounes in his book *Down The Highway*, Taylor was *"giddy"* over Dylan when he played at the Martin Luther King, Jr. tribute earlier in the year. They were both on stage for the finale, a version of Stevie Wonder's *Happy Birthday*.

In the book *Nothing to Turn Off: The Films and Video of Bob Dylan*, a connection was made between Dylan and Taylor in the video for *Emotionally Yours*, from 1985's *Empire Burlesque*, a song some think was written for her. [317] (The video opens with a photograph of Taylor.)

According to producers Eddie Arno and Markus Innocenti, who had previously worked with Dylan's friend, Dave Stewart with his band The Eurythmics, *"During the filming of Emotionally Yours, when it was after six o'clock in the afternoon, Dylan suddenly started to have ideas of his own. He noticed that Monica Getchell, who was playing the 'discarded girlfriend,' had a similar bone structure to the young Elizabeth Taylor."* Dylan then requested a wig for Getchell to get her to look like Taylor. He was pleased with the results, and revealed that he had been thinking of Taylor when he composed the song. *"When Dylan saw his concept going from initial idea to film action in a matter of hours, he was thrilled by it."* [318]

It's also been reported Michael Jackson and Dylan performed together at Elizabeth Taylor's 55th birthday party in February, 1987. Dylan was in California around that time, making a surprise appearance at the Palomino club with Taj Mahal, George Harrison, and John Fogerty, and recording with Warren Zevon.

---

[316] http://elizabethtaylorthelegend.com/Elizabeth%20Taylor%20-%20Cleopatra%20Timeline.html, *The Cleopatra Timeline*, Retrieved 11/27/2016

[317] http://www.expectingrain.com/discussions/viewtopic.php?f=-6&t=41326, *Expecting Rain Discussions: Track Talk 56: Emotionally Yours Via the book Nothing to Turn Off*, p162

[318] *Nothing to Turn Off: The Films and Videos of Bob Dylan*, Vince Farinaccio, Vincent Farinaccio (Standard Copyright License), 2008

Jeff Bridges talks about acting and jamming with Bob Dylan

August 11, 2014

Actor/musician Jeff Bridges was interviewed by Howard Stern on the latter's SiriusXM satellite radio show this morning. Bridges and the radio host talked for almost 90 minutes, ostensibly to promote Bridges' new movie, *The Giver*. The subjects ranged from acting in the shadow of Bridges' father, Lloyd, to Jeff's kids, from acting in *The Big Lebowski* to his appearance in Bob Dylan's 2003 film, *Masked & Anonymous*. In each case, the Dude abided.

About one hour into the interview, Stern asked, out of the blue, if Bridges, who played the part of "Tom Friend" in *Masked & Anonymous*, had got a chance to "jam" with Dylan. Bridges said it was a "high point" in his life, then imitated a knock on his trailer door, followed by Dylan asking if he wanted to "jam." Bridges said he felt like he was "in another zone."

Bridges went on to talk about the movie, how it was shot in a couple of weeks, and how Dylan wrote the screenplay with Seinfeld co-creator, Larry Charles. Charles was "a very cool and open cat" who was directing his first movie. Charles asked Bridges to jam and improvise with Dylan, which he did for "half a day." Bridges said Dylan was "just incredible," trying to get to the "reality of the scene."

When Stern asked what they would play, Bridges mentioned Dylan's cover of *You Belong to Me*, from the film, *Natural Born Killers*. He also praised Dylan's guitar-playing skills, calling him "an incredible … masterful guitarist."

In typical Stern fashion, he said he would have defecated if he was in that position. Bridges joked that he may have "had a bowel movement, man!"

When asked, Bridges said he considered Dylan a friend, although he doesn't really ever see him anymore.

Later, Stern joked that Dylan heard his playing once, and asked him to stop.

Sally Kirkland on her 'favorite person' Bob Dylan: "God bless him"

May 18, 2011

"I'm staying with Aunt Sally, but you know, she's not really my aunt / Some of these memories you can learn to live with and some of them you can't" [319]

Actress Sally Kirkland has been a star of stage and screen since the early 1960s. For the film *Anna*, she was nominated for the best actress Oscar award and won the Golden Globe, Independent Spirit Award, and L.A. Film Critics EDtv Award. Her credits also include *The Sting*, *The Way We Were*, *Revenge*, *JFK*, *Cold Feet* (with Tom Waits), *Best Of The Best*, *The Haunted - A True Story*, *EDtv*, *Bruce Almighty*, and over 150 others.

She also appeared in Neil Young's *Human Highway*, and the video for Bob Dylan's *Unbelievable*. Kirkland has known Dylan for decades, and reportedly writes poems to him. [320]

On her new Facebook "Official Fan Page" [321] you can view a picture of the night Kirkland introduced Dylan to Robert De Niro. Photographer Brad Elterman commented on photographing Dylan and Robert DeNiro the evening they were introduced by Kirkland in Los Angeles, August 18, 1976:

"Bob Dylan made a big deal about me taking his photo with a young actor named Robert De Niro. He wanted the photo in the worst way! Bobby sent Sally Kirkland (the blonde in this photo) to go downstairs at The Roxy and drag up an amazed De Niro. I just happened to be the lucky kid hanging around with the camera back then in 1976. The other chick in the photo is singer Lainie Kazan and we were all backstage after Ronee Blakley's performance. If only these kind of cosmic evenings happened today! … Since I did not have a clue who De Niro was, I thought that he was just some guy getting in the way of my Dylan photo." [322]

In a 1994 issue of *Femme Fatales* magazine, Kirkland talked about Dylan, saying that in order to prepare herself to act in the role of a rock star, [323] *"I followed my lifelong friend, Bob Dylan, through six cities of a concert tour. I tried to incorporate him into my role as Starr. I met him in the early '60s when he was playing with Joan Baez."* Kirkland lived on Christopher Street in Greenwich Village from 1961 to 1966. Kirkland went on to reveal how important he's been to her, calling Dylan a *"mentor, brother, father, lover. In almost every emotional scene I've done over the years, I've listened to his music. You'll always see me with a Walkman on right before the scene, and the music just gets me."*

Kirkland went on to say she *"fantasized about living happily ever after with … Bob Dylan. Maybe when I'm in my nineties, he will agree to settle down. I am utterly convinced that we have known each other in at least five previous lifetimes."*

In a *Bob Dylan Examiner* article from last year, Kirkland commented on her cameo in Dylan's *Unbelievable* video, where she played the motel receptionist:

"Paris Barclay was a terrific director. I was thrilled to be in it. Always been a fan of Molly Ringwald's… and I LOVE ALL THINGS BOB. What a blast."

When I mentioned I was writing this article, Kirkland emailed me, saying, *"He's my favorite person in my life, along with my spiritual teacher … God bless him."*

---

[319] *Sugar Baby, Time Out of Mind*, Bob Dylan, 1997

[320] http://www.broadwaytovegas.com/February27,2000.html, *Lusting After Bob Dylan* (Scroll Down), Retrieved 11/27/2016

[321] https://www.facebook.com/Sally-Kirkland-Official-Fan-Page-177689438946542, *Sally Kirkland* (Official Fan Page), Retrieved 11/27/2016

[322] http://marthajefferson.tumblr.com/post/34295972416/bradelterman-bob-dylan-made-a-big-deal-about-me, *Would You Shut Up About Lando*, Retrieved 11/27/2016

[323] *In Bed with Sally Kirkland*, Gary Garfinkel, Femme Fatales, Summer 1994 (Vol. 3 #1).

Tony Curtis

September 30, 2010

Actor Tony Curtis, born Bernard Schwartz in 1925, the star of *Some Like It Hot* and father of actress Jamie Lee Curtis, died on September 29.

In *Chronicles: Volume One*: Bob Dylan mentioned that Curtis told him *"fame is an occupation in itself,"* and that helped liberate him from the pressures of celebrity.

Tony Curtis played Ira Hayes in the movie, *The Outsider*. Hayes was the Native American and American Marine who was one of the six men immortalized in the iconic photograph of the flag raising on Iwo Jima during World War II. Bob Dylan's 1970 version of Peter LaFarge's *The Ballad of Ira Hayes* appeared on the 1973 album, *Dylan*.

In Dylan's 1978 movie *Renaldo & Clara*:

Bob Neuwirth, in a mask, is on stage in a small club reading a poem written by a badly disabled black guy named Tony Curtis who sits watching. At the end of the poem Tony Curtis asks for money (asking for money for poems or songs will be a recurring motif in the film.) [324]

Trivia: Life-size cutouts of both Dylan and Curtis grace the cover of the Beatles' album, *Sgt. Pepper's Lonely Hearts Club Band*.

---

[324] http://www.litkicks.com/Films/RenaldoAndClara.html, *Renaldo and Clara: a synopsis*, Retrieved 11/27/2016

A look back - Bob Dylan's appearances on David Letterman's talk shows

April 20, 2014

David Michael Letterman has been a fixture on American late night television since 1982, and recently announced he would retire in 2015. Below, we take a look back at Bob Dylan's appearances on Letterman's talk shows, collecting, updating, and expanding articles I wrote a few years back.

Dylan performed on Letterman's show three times - *NBC's Late Night with David Letterman* on March 22, 1984, a 10th anniversary special on January 18, 1992, and *CBS's Late Show with David Letterman* on November 18, 1993. Dylan also made a cameo appearance on October 20, 1994, while rehearsing for a gig at Roseland.

For his Letterman debut, Dylan was backed by J.J. Holliday (a.k.a. Justin Poskin and Justin Jesting) on guitar, Tony Marsico on bass, and Charlie Quintana (a.k.a. Chalo Quintana) on drums. Marsico and Quintana were in the band The Plugz, which later morphed into The Cruzados. In late 1983 and early 1984, Dylan reportedly rehearsed with Marsico, future Cruzado Steve Hufsteter, and, at later sessions, Holliday, among others. Quintana was recruited by Dylan about a week before the Letterman appearance. Future Dylan guitarist Charlie Sexton also briefly participated around this time.

According to Olof Bjorner, [325] the quartet practiced at Dylan's Malibu home on March 21, 1984, although Clinton Heylin [326] stated that the rehearsals occurred in New York, which would make more sense. Maybe Dylan rehearsed in Malibu on an earlier date? Quintana was quoted as saying that the quartet loosely rehearsed dozens of songs the band didn't know, and did not work out any endings. Attempted songs included Hank Williams' *Lost On The River*, *We Three (My Echo, My Shadow And Me)*, a hit for Frank Sinatra and the Tommy Dorsey Orchestra, *Jokerman*, *Don't Start Me Talkin'* by Sonny Boy Williamson II, *Saved*, and a couple of unidentified songs. Other possible titles rehearsed include *My Guy*, *Just One Look*, *Who Loves You More*, *Lonely Dreamer*, *Back in My Arms Again*, *Johnny Too Bad*, *A Woman Will Give You The Blues*, *Shake*, *Baby I Do*, and *Mary Lou*. Backup vocal duties were probably handled by Clydie King.

The following day, Dylan and his backing band arrived at NBC Studios, in Rockefeller Center, New York City. The afternoon rehearsal was videotaped. The songs performed were:

- *I Once Knew a Man*

- *Jokerman*

- *License To Kill*

- *Treat Her Right* (by Roy Head)

- *My Guy* (by Smokey Robinson)

Late Night with David Letterman had only been on the air a couple of years when Dylan was booked as a musical guest in 1984, so it was quite a coup to get him to appear. The show aired following *The Tonight Show with Johnny Carson*, in the early hours of March 23, but the actual show was taped around dinner time on March 22. The other guest that evening was the flamboyant pianist Liberace, there for a cooking demonstration.

Letterman and his sidekick and bandleader Paul Shaffer were almost giddy with excitement. Shaffer in particular was hysterical in his faux showbiz mode, exclaiming, *"What a night! Liberace cooking? In my*

---

[325] http://www.bjorner.com/still.htm, *Still on the Road*, Retrieved 11/27/2016

[326] *A Life in Stolen Moments - Bob Dylan Day-By-Day 1941-1995*, Clinton Heylin, Schemer Books, New York, 1996.

book, that cat always cooks. And Dylan—I'm shocked. I was listening to him in rehearsal . . . (pause) . . . Did you know he went electric?" Shaffer also mentioned he had secretly been playing along with the band during rehearsals. Letterman chided him not to screw things up. Soon after this appearance, Shaffer and members of his band would accompany just about every act that appeared.

Shaffer wrote about Dylan's appearance in his memoir, *We'll Be Here for the Rest of Our Lives.* [327] After the show, Shaffer went to see Dylan, who was unresponsive at first. From the book:

"When you sang Roy Head's Treat Her Right *in rehearsal today, Bob, it sounded just great. I wish you'd record it."*

Finally Bob looked me in the eyes. I'd obviously made a connection.

"Paul, do you think you could introduce me to Larry 'Bud' Melman?" he asked, *referring to the lovable nerd who was a running character on our show.*

I thought Dylan was kidding. But he wasn't.

This television appearance is often cited as one of Dylan's best. It certainly was one of his most exciting. The report before the show was that Dylan would perform two, or possibly three, songs, depending on how things went. He started with a blistering, animated version of *Don't Start Me Talkin'.* Afterward, Letterman gingerly said, *"Bob Dylan .... Very impressive ... Mr. Dylan and the band ... you will be back ... perhaps two more songs?"* Dylan paused a moment, nodded, and said, *"Okay."* Letterman joked, *"I'm almost sure it's gonna happen."* Dylan returned to sing *Licence to Kill*, and then *Jokerman.* You can tell Letterman was apprehensive, but by the end it was obvious Dylan was pleased, even if he picked the wrong harmonica for *Jokerman.* Letterman asked if Dylan would appear every Thursday, to which Dylan kiddingly agreed.

Soon after the appearance, I bumped into Eddie Gorodetsky in a Greenwich Village record store called It's Only Rock and Roll. I knew of him from his days as a DJ in Boston. He had been a writer for *Saturday Night Live*, and was working for Letterman at the time. I asked him what Dylan was like. *"He's a very private man,"* was his reply.

Gorodetsky was soon in Dylan's inner circle. He wrote the liner notes for the 1991 Rhino compilation, *I Shall Be Unreleased: The Songs Of Bob Dylan.* Dylan was responsible for releasing one of Gorodetsky's legendary Christmas CDs in the early 1990s. Dylan made a cameo appearance on the sitcom *Dharma & Greg* in 1999, when Gorodetsky was a writer for the show. Gorodetsky then appeared with Dylan in the *"Love & Theft"* [328] TV commercial and the movie *Masked & Anonymous.* Gorodetsky was also thanked in the credits for *No Direction Home.* Gorodetsky not only produced *Theme Time Radio Hour with Your Host Bob Dylan*, appearing (allegedly) on-air as "Pierre Mancini," but is often cited to have had at least as much input into the series as Dylan, if not more.

The next time Bob Dylan appeared on television with David Letterman, it was prime time. The occasion was a 10th-anniversary special edition of *Late Night*, broadcast February 6, 1992, on NBC.

The show was taped a few weeks earlier on Saturday, January 18, at New York's Radio City Music Hall. Dylan appeared with an eclectic, all-star ensemble. Here's the line-up: Chrissie Hynde (guitar), Steve Vai (guitar), Carole King (keyboards), Jim Keltner (drums), Edgar Winter (saxophone), Jim Horn (baritone saxophone), Rosanne Cash, Nanci Griffith, Emmylou Harris, Michelle Shocked, Mavis Staples (backup vocals), Doc Severinson from *The Tonight Show* (trumpet) and Maceo Parker, Fred Wesley and Pee Wee Ellis from James Brown's horn section, plus "The World's Most Dangerous Band" from Letterman's show - Shaffer (keyboards), Sid McGinnis (guitar), Will Lee (bass), and Anton Fig (drums).

---

[327] *We'll Be Here for the Rest of Our Lives*, Paul Shaffer with David Ritz, Doubleday, New York, 2009

[328] *"Love & Theft"* in quotes (Official title)

Shaffer also wrote about this Dylan appearance in his memoir. [329] According to the book, Letterman first suggested Dylan sing *Stuck Inside Of Mobile With The Memphis Blues Again*. Shaffer wanted *One Of Us Must Know*. However, it was obvious they needed a more famous song. They wanted Dylan to perform *Like A Rolling Stone*.

It was Shaffer's job to speak with Bob. *"Dylan loves me,"* Shaffer wrote. After tracking him down, Dylan acted lukewarm to Shaffer's request for *Rolling Stone*. *"That's a little obvious,"* he said. *"There's gotta be something else ... It's a big catalog, Paul."* After some convincing, Dylan invited Shaffer to a rehearsal in New York, and tried a version of Dylan's greatest hit, with Shaffer's piano playing augmenting Dylan's regular band. *"It was on,"* Shaffer wrote.

When Dylan arrived for the rehearsal on the Friday before the taping, he was not happy. He would not sing with the all-star band, and barely strummed his guitar: *"I don't need this band to play my music. Me, I got four pieces. That's all I need. All this other stuff don't make no sense."* Jeff Kramer, Dylan's manager at the time, assured Shaffer that all was OK, and to just continue. The band went through the song a third time, but Dylan still wouldn't sing. Then Dylan left early to observe the Sabbath.

Shaffer then stood where Dylan was, to hear what Dylan was hearing. It turns out that Dylan's monitor had no sound. Shaffer did his best to improve it.

When he arrived for the dress rehearsal, Shaffer said Dylan gave about 30 percent. By show time, he estimated that Dylan gave about 70 percent. After the taping, Shaffer asked Dylan how it went:

"Lemme be honest with you, Paul. When I'm in the hotel room at night, I flip on the show only to catch a glimpse of Larry 'Bud' (Melman). *I've never really keyed in on you. But tonight, man, I saw that you know what you're doing. If I had realized this could have been something, I would have given more."*

Noel Redding, bassist for The Jimi Hendrix Experience, was in the audience. On January 29, 11 days after the taping, he appeared on Howard Stern's radio show, and talked about Dylan's appearance. Redding talked about Dylan sitting at his table, and inviting him to a session. Stern was skeptical about Dylan following through.

After a brief interruption, Redding continued, saying at the afterparty, while sitting with Anton Fig (who played on a couple of Dylan albums) and his wife, Dylan (*"he's like a hero to me"*) joined them at the table. Redding got an autograph for his mother, and again mentioned that Dylan asked him to a session. When Stern co-host Robin Quivers asked if he got a phone number, Redding said he had *"a couple."*

(Side Note: Dylan recorded *Hey Joe*, a song The Jimi Hendrix Experience covered as their debut single, and *Dignity* in a New York studio around this time, according to Bjorner. [330] Could one of the "unidentified musicians" Dylan used be Noel Redding? Maybe Dylan warmed up with *Hey Joe*, then tried *Dignity*, an unreleased song at the time, a leftover from his 1989 album, *Oh Mercy*. Since these recordings are not in circulation, one can only speculate. Noel Redding died on May 11, 2003.)

Dylan performed on CBS's *Late Show with David Letterman* on November 18, 1993. Dylan had just played his legendary Supper Club shows on November 16 and 17. It may have been Dylan's first time in the venue, now known as The Ed Sullivan Theater, since May 12, 1963, when Bob got word that he would not be allowed to perform his song, *Talkin' John Birch Paranoid Blues*, on Sullivan's Sunday night variety show. For this Letterman episode, Dylan performed an acoustic, full-band version of *Forever Young*.

For his most recent *Late Show* appearance, Dylan was featured as part of a comedy skit. On October 20, 1994, after a commercial break, Letterman noticed Shaffer was not in the television studio. Dave

---

[329] *We'll Be Here for the Rest of Our Lives*, Paul Shaffer with David Ritz, Doubleday, New York, 2009

[330] http://www.bjorner.com/DSN12845%20-%201992%20Early%20Sessions.htm#DSN12845, *Still on the Road*, Retrieved 11/27/2016

rushed out the door, only to find Shaffer jamming with Dylan and his band across the street at Roseland, during a soundcheck. At first, it was unclear who the musicians were, until Letterman stopped by to apologize to Dylan on the way out. At the Roseland concert that night, Bruce Springsteen and Neil Young joined Dylan for the encore.

Will Dylan make one more appearance before Letterman retires? Well, we can always hope.

Addendum, 2016: Dylan appeared on the penultimate broadcast of *The Last Show with David Letterman*.

Dick Clark

April 14, 2011

When Dylan appeared at The Band's 1976 Last Waltz farewell concert, he played the following set:

Winterland, San Francisco, California Thanksgiving, 25 November 1976

1. *Baby Let Me Follow You Down*

2. *Hazel*

3. *I Don't Believe You*

4. *Forever Young*

5. *Baby Let Me Follow You Down* (Reprise)

6. *I Shall Be Released*

For the first five songs, Dylan was backed by the Band. The last song featured some of the other musicians who had performed earlier in the evening, with the addition of a Beatle (Ringo Starr) and a Rolling Stone (Ron Wood).

Dylan sang and played guitar. He did not play harmonica.

Or did he?

According to an article in *The New York Times*, dated October 25, 2006, [331] Dick Clark (of *American Bandstand* fame) was putting some rock and roll memorabilia up for auction, including *"the harmonica that Bob Dylan played in 'The Last Waltz.'"* It was estimated to sell for somewhere between $20,000 to $40,000, according to the report.

I emailed *The Times*, casting my doubt that Dylan played harmonica at The Last Waltz. On November 2, 2006, I received a reply which included the following quote from the office of Mr. Clark, "informing" me that some of Martin Scorsese's footage was not used in the film, but was eventually released:

When performing Hazel, *Dylan typically played a harmonica, such as on the* Planet Waves *album ... Members of the film crew who often worked with Dick Clark's staff vividly recall Bob carrying a harmonica on the set. Following The Last Waltz, the harmonica entered the Clifford Glass Collection where it was recorded as having originated from the set of the film. In 1992, Dick Clark acquired the instrument from that Collection. Dick placed the harmonica on public view at that time, indicating that the harmonica was from that filming. It has remained publicly displayed until it recently was removed from inclusion in the coming auction.*

I sent an email back, stating that there was audio, video, and written documentation of the event, and there was not one shred of evidence that Dylan played a harmonica, or even wore a harmonica rack, at the concert. He may have "carried" it, but he certainly didn't play it. I even sent a video link for an outtake version, in black and white, of the performance in question.

Later that night, I received another reply: *"Thanks, whoever you are. We'll look into it."* I never heard another word.

In another report, CBS' *The Early Show* [332] reported that Dylan's Last Waltz harmonica was autographed:

---

[331] *Dick Clark Puts Some Rock 'n' Roll History Up for Auction*, James Barron, New York Times, 10/25/2006

[332] http://www.cbsnews.com/news/memories-on-the-auction-block/, *Memories On The Auction Block*, Retrieved 11/27/2016

Bob Dylan Autographed Harmonica from "The Last Waltz." This harmonica was used by Dylan during the Band's farewell gig in San Francisco on Thanksgiving 1976. This Hohner harmonica, autographed in black ink by Dylan, is mounted in a framed display accompanied by a black-and-white image of Dylan with harmonica and guitar.

An *AP* version of the claim was repeated in *USA Today,* [333] *The Los Angeles Times,* [334] and *MSNBC,* [335] among others. Cinema Blend went so far as to say *"the harmonica Bob Dylan played in Scorsese's documentary* The Last Waltz.*"*

The harmonica and listing, with a photograph, at Live Auctioneers: [336]

Lot 785: Bob Dylan Autographed Harmonica: This Hohner harmonica, autographed in black ink by Bob Dylan, c. 1976. The instrument is mounted in a framed display accompanied by a black and white image from another occasion of Dylan with harmonica and guitar. Framed display: 20 1/2 x 26; Photo: 14 x 10

The web page listed the estimated price as only $2,500 - $5,000, not the $20,000 - $40,000 originally listed in *The New York Times*. Notice there's no mention of The Last Waltz in the description. On December 6, 2006, the harmonica reportedly sold for $15,000, according to the Live Auctioneers site. Much of the money raised reportedly went to various charities.

Notes on *Hazel*: Dylan sang *Hazel* for the first time on stage that night. Although he played it at a soundcheck in 1978, Dylan did not perform it on stage until 1994 for the *MTV Unplugged* sessions. In 2004-5, Dylan finally brought the song out and played it in public six times. [337]

UPDATE: From Dick Clark Memorabilia Auction - Dec 5, 2006: *"I just was lucky enough to 'bump' into the memorabilia auction for much of Dick Clark's Stuff. Timothy said that Bob Dylan came in early in the morning with Yoko Ono. He wants to buy back the harmonica that he gave to Dick Clark years ago."*

Thanks to Enrique D. for the inspiration.

---

[333] http://usatoday30.usatoday.com/life/people/2006-10-25-clark-auction_x.htm, *Dick Clark plans auction of memorabilia*, Retrieved 11/27/2016

[334] http://articles.latimes.com/2006/nov/06/entertainment/et-auction6, *Dick Clark's curios to rock auction block*, Retrieved 11/27/2016

[335] http://www.today.com/id/15413773/ns/today-entertainment/#.WBEgVVf0ejs, *Dick Clark to auction 'Bandstand' microphone - Famed host to sell other pieces of musical memorabilia in December*, Retrieved 11/27/2016

[336] https://new.liveauctioneers.com/item/2735826 785, *Bob Dylan Autographed Harmonica - Sold For $15,000*, Retrieved 11/27/2016

[337] http://www.bjorner.com/still.htm, *Still on the Road*, Retrieved 11/27/2016

Bob Dylan, avowed Shemp fan, allows one of his songs in new Three Stooges' film

April 10, 2012

Bob Dylan has allowed one of his songs to be used in the new Farrelly Brothers film, *The Three Stooges*, because he is apparently a fan of the vaudeville and comedy legends.

According to an article posted on *USA Today*'s website, [338] Dylan is *"a 70-year-old Stooge-aholic,"* and that's one of the reasons he allowed his song *Just Like Tom Thumb's Blues* to be included on the movie's soundtrack. Filmmaker Peter Farrelly was quoted as saying, *"We love Bob Dylan ... We contacted his people to use one of his songs and turns out he is a big Stooges fan."*

Dylan mentioned on his *Theme Time Radio Hour* program that Moe was *"arguably the smartest"* Stooge. However, he considered himself a Shemp fan. Of course, he may have been joking. Nyuk, nyuk. Unfortunately for the 70-year-old Stooge-aholic, the new movie is not a Shemp one (real name Samuel Horwitz). It features actors playing Larry (real name Louis Feinberg), Curly (Jerome Lester Horwitz) and Moe (Moses Harry Horwitz).

While researching this article, I came across this totally unrelated quote that I thought would be of interest to Dylan fans. It was written by Toronto Maple Leafs Blogger Howard Berger, about the time he sat next to Dylan on a plane: [339] *"Notoriously shy; a fedora pulled slightly downward to cover his face, I nudged him with my right elbow and nervously asked: "Are you who I think you are?" He looked at me; smiled, and said, "Yup." I told him, "Okay, it'll be our secret." We did chat a bit during the four-hour flight. I wondered how a person so bashful and introverted could comfortably perform in front of thousands of people: "Just natural," he shrugged. "I don't even think about it."*

---

[338] http://usatoday30.usatoday.com/life/movies/news/story/2012-04-11/three-stooges-returns-to-roots-say-farrelly-brothers/54158058/1, *Farrellys' 'Three Stooges' film gets back to trio's roots*, Retrieved 11/27/2016

[339] http://www.hockeybuzz.com/blog/Howard-Berger/44-Leafs-Notes-and-Opinions/3/43475, *44 Leafs Notes and Opinions*, Retrieved 11/27/2016

Lenny Bruce

October 11, 2010

. . . Lenny Bruce was really, along with Bob Dylan and Miles Davis and a handful of others (maybe Joseph Heller, Terry Southern and Allen Ginsberg in another way) the leader of the first wave of the American social and cultural revolution which is gradually changing the structure of our society and may effectively revise it, if the forces of reaction which are automatically brought into play by such a drive, do not declare military law and suppress it. Liner notes by Ralph J. Gleason, *Lenny Bruce - The Berkeley Concert*, Bizarre/Reprise Records, 1969. [340]

Leonard Alfred Schneider was born on October 13, 1925, and died on August 3, 1966.

Bob Dylan and Lenny Bruce were both performers in Greenwich Village during the early 1960s. They've often been mentioned in the same breath, whether it was in a *Village Voice* article, [341] in a Paul Simon song, [342] or on a Frank Zappa album cover. [343] Cut-out figures of both Dylan and Bruce appear on the cover of The Beatles' 1967 album, *Sgt. Pepper's Lonely Hearts Club Band*.

Bruce was arrested numerous times for obscenity as well as possession of narcotics. On April 3, 1964, before going on stage at the Cafe Au Go Go, he was arrested on obscenity charges. [344]

Bruce's New York arrest [345] inspired a protest from many of the city's artists, authors, and actors. The formation of an "Emergency Committee against the Harassment of Lenny Bruce" was formed, as proclaimed by Allen Ginsberg. A petition protesting the treatment and prosecution of Bruce, dated June 13, 1964, was signed by more than 80 people. [346] Among the signatories were entertainers Woody Allen, Theodore Bikel, Richard Burton, Godfrey Cambridge, Bob Dylan, Herb Gardner, Ben Gazzara, Dick Gregory, Tommy Leonetti, Paul Newman, Elizabeth Taylor, Rip Tom, and Rudy Vallee; novelists and playwrights Nelson Algren, James Baldwin, Saul Bellow, Kay Boyle, Jack Gelber, Joseph Heller, Lillian Helman, James Jones, Norman Mailer, Arthur Miller, Henry Miller, John Rechy, Jack Richardson, Susan Sontag, Terry Southern, William Styron, John Updike, Gore Vidal, Arnold Weinstein; artists Jules Feiffer, Walt Kelly and Ben Shabo; and poets Gregory Corso, Lawrence Ferlinghetti, Allen Ginsberg, Leroi Jones, Peter Orlovsky, Louis Untermeyer, in addition to theologians, critics, editors and publishers.

On November 4, Bruce was found guilty.

Dylan mentioned Bruce in his book *Chronicles: Volume One*, while describing a night at the Cafe Wha? evening shows, which included Joan Rivers, Richard Pryor, Allen, and Bruce. While recalling a conversation with U2's Bono, he mentioned that names like Idi Amin, Lenny Bruce, and Soutine the painter had a certain "feel."

---

[340] http://globalia.net/donlope/fz/related/Berkeley_Concert.html, *The Liner Notes*, Retrieved 11/27/2016

[341] *Dylan in October*, Jack Newfield, The Village Voice, 10/7/1965 (Vol. X, No. 51)

[342] *A Simple Desultory Philippic (or How I Was Robert McNamara'd into Submission)*, *Parsley, Sage, Rosemary and Thyme*, Simon and Garfunkel, 1966.

[343] http://aln2.albumlinernotes.com/Freak_Out_.html, *The Mothers of Invention Freak Out! Original 1966 double album liner notes*, Retrieved 11/27/2016

[344] http://law2.umkc.edu/faculty/projects/ftrials/bruce/brucechrono.html, *The Trials of Lenny Bruce: A Chronology*, Retrieved 11/27/2016

[345] http://law2.umkc.edu/faculty/projects/ftrials/bruce/bruceaccount.html, *The Trials of Lenny Bruce*, Doug Linder (2003), Retrieved 11/27/2016

[346] http://law2.umkc.edu/faculty/projects/ftrials/bruce/brucepetition.html, *Petition Protesting the Arrest of Lenny Bruce*, June 13, 1964, Retrieved 11/27/2016

Bob Dylan supposedly wrote *Lenny Bruce* the night before he recorded the song at an April 29, 1981, session. [347] Later the year, while he was in London, WNEW-FM DJ Dave Herman asked him about the song, but he said he didn't know why he wrote this particular song, many years after Bruce's death. *"I wrote that song in five minutes!"* Dylan said. *"I found it was a little strange after he died, that people made such a hero out of him. When he was alive he couldn't even get a break."*

The lyrics for the song, along with a picture of a 45 release, were included on page 68 of the 2004 Shout Factory box set release, *Lenny Bruce - Let The Buyer Beware.*

In Closing:

"Bruce stands up against all limitations on the flesh and spirit, and someday they are going to crush him for it." – The *New York Post* [348]

"Lenny Bruce died from an overdose of police" – Phil Spector. [349]

On December 23, 2003, Governor Pataki pardoned Bruce. It was the first posthumous pardon granted in New York State's history. [350]

---

[347] http://www.bjorner.com/DSN06131%20-%201981%20Shot%20Of%20Love%20Sessions.htm#DSN06141, *Still on the Road,* Retrieved 11/27/2016

[348] https://shadowproof.com/2011/08/27/saturday-trolls-bruce-lennon-nilsson-spector/, *Saturday Trolls: Bruce, Lennon, Nilsson, Spector,* Retrieved 11/27/2016

[349] https://shadowproof.com/2011/08/27/saturday-trolls-bruce-lennon-nilsson-spector/, *Saturday Trolls: Bruce, Lennon, Nilsson, Spector,* Retrieved 11/27/2016

[350] http://www.cbsnews.com/news/lenny-bruce-pardoned/, *Lenny Bruce Pardoned,* Retrieved 11/27/2016

Michigan Representative Thaddeus McCotter abruptly resigns, quotes Bob Dylan

July 6, 2012

Republican Representative Thaddeus C. McCotter of Michigan has abruptly resigned, and in his restless farewell, quoted Bob Dylan.

His resignation letter, which was posted in its entirety on his Facebook page, [351] was described in the press as *"bizarre, rambling and error-riddled,"* [352] McCotter quoted a line from the closing song on Dylan's 1965 album, *Bringing It All Back Home.*

Here is an excerpt:

Today I have resigned from the office of United States Representative for Michigan's 11th Congressional District … The recent event's totality of calumnies, indignities and deceits have weighed most heavily upon my family. Thus, acutely aware one cannot rebuild their hearth of home amongst the ruins of their U.S. House office, for the sake of my loved ones I must 'strike another match, go start anew' by embracing the promotion back from public servant to sovereign citizen.

The quote *"Strike another match, go start anew"* comes from the Dylan song, *It's All Over Now, Baby Blue.* The Michigan Representative has been under fire lately. His recent election campaign collected what turned out to be a slew of fraudulent signatures. Only 244 out of 2,000 signatures were deemed to be valid, which led the Michigan Attorney General's office to investigate the election fraud accusation. [353]

After his unsuccessful presidential bid last year, McCotter also tried his hand at writing a "lowbrow" television pilot. [354]

---

[351] https://www.facebook.com/notes/representative-thaddeus-mccotter/mccotter-strike-another-match-go-start-anew/10151111945933132, *McCotter: "Strike Another Match, Go Start Anew"*, Retrieved 11/27/2016

[352] http://thehill.com/homenews/house/236517-rep-mccotter-resigns-after-nightmarish-month-and-a-half, *GOP Rep. McCotter resigns after 'nightmarish' month and a half*, Retrieved 11/27/2016

[353] http://www.washingtontimes.com/news/2012/aug/9/mccotter-staffers-charged-michigan-election-fraud, *McCotter staffers charged in Michigan election fraud*, Retrieved 11/27/2016

[354] http://usatoday30.usatoday.com/news/washington/story/2012-07-14/antics-prompt-resignations-from-congress/56205160/1, *Public shows little tolerance for lawmakers' bad behavior*, Retrieved 11/27/2016

'Hibbing's' Bob Dylan uncomfortably accepts honor from 'fan' President Obama

May 29, 2012

Bob Dylan fidgeted in the East Room of the White House this afternoon, but eventually walked over and accepted his Medal of Freedom award from President Barack Obama.

After the ceremony, Dylan's official Twitter page tweeted, *"President Obama awarded Bob with the Medal of Freedom at the White House today, the nation's highest honor,"* with a link to a photograph, [355] *"It's the highest civilian honor, awarded for contributions to the national interest, to world peace, or to other significant endeavors."* The entire ceremony has been archived at C-SPAN.org. [356]

Dylan was the twelfth, and final, recipient at the 40-minute ceremony. One of the honorees, Shimon Peres, was not present and will receive his honor next month.

The festivities began about 15 minutes late, just after 3:40 p.m. ET. The ceremony was webcast at c-span.org and whitehouse.gov/live, and broadcast on C-SPAN with a 15-second delay. The recipients were announced and filed in first, although the microphones did not start working until after the President began his speech. Dylan sat in the front row on the far right, often out of the range of the television cameras.

At 3:43, Dylan could be seen through an open door as Tennessee basketball coach Pat Summitt entered the room. Dylan followed soon after, wearing shades and stroking his chin, as someone called out, "Bobby!" The honorees all stood in front of their seats, posing for photographs. Dylan, of course, was fidgety, not used to standing still, or on ceremony.

After about a minute, President Obama entered amid the usual fanfare. Immediately beforehand, the camera swept from left to right, but Dylan could barely be seen through the crowd. Dylan clapped along with his peers as Obama entered, nodding his head, and seemingly making some humorous, but not disrespectful, facial expressions.

The President began by saying, *"Welcome to the White House... I have to say just looking around the room ... this is a packed house, which is a testament to how cool this group is. Everybody wanted to check 'em out!"*

The President went on the say that it was *"the highest civilian honor this country can bestow, which is ironic because no one set out to win it. No one ever picks up a guitar, or fights a disease, or starts a movement, thinking, 'You know what? If I keep this up, in 2012, I could get a medal in the White House from a guy named Barack Obama.'"*

Obama indirectly referenced Dylan while honoring John Doar, Assistant Attorney General in charge of the Civil Rights Division of the Department of Justice, who convinced protesters leaving the 1963 funeral of Medgar Evers to go home and, in turn, avoid a riot. Dylan, of course, wrote about Evers in his composition, *Only A Pawn In Their Game*.

Next, Obama spoke specifically about Dylan.

"Bob Dylan started out singing other people's songs, but as he says, there came a point where I had to write what I wanted to say, because what I wanted to say, nobody else was writing. Born in Hibbing (sic)*, Minnesota, a town he says, where 'you couldn't be a rebel, it was too cold!'"*

As the President and the crowd laughed, there was a cut to a shot of Obama and Dylan, with the musician remaining expressionless, tapping the front of his seat, marching to his own drummer. Of

---

[355] https://twitter.com/bobdylan/status/207598758555435008/photo/1, *President Obama awarded Bob with the Medal of Freedom at the White House today, the nation's highest honor,* Retrieved 11/27/2016

[356] https://www.c-span.org/video/?306291-2/medal-freedom-ceremony, Medal of Freedom Ceremony. Retrieved 11/27/2016

course, Robert Zimmerman was born in Duluth, not Hibbing, but maybe Dylan was indeed born in northern Minnesota?

Obama continued, *"Bob moved to New York at age 19. By the time he was 23, Bob's voice, with its weight, its unique gravelly power, was redefining not just what music sounded like, but the message it carried, and how it made people feel. Today, everybody from Bruce Springsteen to U2 owes Bob a debt of gratitude. There is not a bigger giant in the history of American music. All these years later, he's still chasing that sound, and searching for a little bit of truth, and I have to say, I am a really big fan."* It was a touching, and sincere, moment.

While praising Dolores Huerta, co-founder of the National Farmworkers Association, there was another shot that showed Dylan, still tapping away, the only honoree not looking at the President. Again, not disrespectful, but either uncomfortable, or in another world, or both. During Summitt's turn, Dylan could be seen looking to his left, then straight ahead.

As the President awarded the first 11 honorees, Dylan was craning his neck to view some of the presentations, with his right hand steadied by his left. Often he did not appear to clap, and sometimes fiddled with the locks of hair hanging down the back of his neck. He would also sometimes shift his feet, or lick his lips.

At 4:16 p.m., it was Dylan's turn. When his name was announced, Dylan did not immediately stand up, and had to be prompted by the President who said, *"C'mon, Bob!"* It was humorous, and I would say it was one of those Chaplinesque moments for which Dylan is known. Dylan got up and walked behind the podium, then past Obama to the front, as a clearly amused President watched from behind. Dylan fidgeted in place, wearing a bow tie and some award-like ribbons hanging from the front of his black jacket, as a voice off-stage said:

A modern day troubadour, Bob Dylan established himself as one of the most influential musicians of the 20th century. The rich poetry of his lyrics opened up new possibilities for popular song and inspired generations. His melodies have brought ancient traditions into the modern age. More than 50 years after his career began, Bob Dylan remains an eminent voice in our national conversation and around the world.

The President then presented Dylan with the medal, and tied the ribbon behind his neck. Nothing much appeared to have been said between the two, unlike some of the other honorees, although they shook hands, and Obama touched Dylan's right arm before leaving the stage. Once seated, Summitt patted Dylan's right leg.

After a standing ovation for the medal winners, the President announced that the honorees were invited to a private reception, for which Dylan may or may not have stayed. It would be interesting if he and astronaut John Glenn would have discussed the song *License To Kill*, with the lyrics, *"... man has invented his doom, first step was touching the moon."*

The ceremony ended at 4:19. Was Dylan really that uncomfortable, or was he just putting everyone on? Maybe it was a commentary on awards in general? Who knows? That's why we love Bob ... He always keeps us guessing.

Congratulations, Mr. Dylan. We're proud of you today, as we are all other days.

President John F. Kennedy

November 20, 2013

John F. Kennedy was inaugurated as the 35th President of the United States, in Washington, D.C. on January 20, 1961, during a snowstorm. Bob Dylan arrived in a snowbound New York four days later.

Kennedy appeared in Dylan's early songs both by name and by association. The president's name was used for humorous effect, in a fictionalized account, in 1963's *I Shall Be Free*. In the song, the President phoned him for hints to help *"the country grow."* Dylan's advice? *"Brigitte Bardot, Anita Ekberg, Sophia Loren ..."* [357]

Since many of Dylan's compositions during this period were of the topical variety, Kennedy's name can be attached to songs addressing the battle for civil rights, especially *Oxford Town* and *Only A Pawn In Their Game*. Dylan also appeared at the "March On Washington" at the Lincoln Memorial on August 28, 1963. The march was originally opposed by Kennedy, but he eventually lent his support.

Dylan wrote his anthem, *The Times, They Are A-Changin'*, in the fall of 1963, and recorded it on October 23 and 24 as the title song of his next album, which was released the following January. President John F. Kennedy was assassinated in Dallas, Texas, on November 22, 1963. Dylan and his girlfriend, Suze Rotolo, spent the weekend watching television coverage of the aftermath. Dylan appeared in concert at an upstate New York theater on the 23rd. He told biographer Anthony Scaduto [358] that he felt compelled to sing it, even if it evoked a hostile response. Although the audience applauded, Dylan told Scaduto nothing made any sense in the aftermath. [359]

On December 13, less than one month after the assassination, with the country still in mourning, Dylan was presented with the Emergency Civil Liberties Committee's Tom Paine Award. His remarks, which referenced Kennedy's accused assassin, were controversial, and not well received:

"... I got to admit that the man who shot President Kennedy, Lee Oswald, I don't know exactly where —what he thought he was doing, but I got to admit honestly that I too - I saw some of myself in him. I don't think it would have gone - I don't think it could go that far. But I got to stand up and say I saw things that he felt, in me - not to go that far and shoot. (Boos and hisses) *You can boo but booing's got nothing to do with it. It's a - I just a - I've got to tell you, man, it's Bill of Rights is free speech and I just want to admit that I accept this Tom Paine Award on behalf of James Forman of the Students Non-Violent Coordinating Committee and on behalf of the people who went to Cuba.* (Boos and Applause)*"* [360]

It's been widely interpreted that Dylan's speech was his attempt to avoid being anybody's puppet, and he began to move away from overt political statements in his songs. Tom Paine was later referenced in the 1967 song, *As I Went Out One Morning*.

Another song Dylan had been singing, *He Was A Friend Of Mine*, was rewritten and recorded by The Byrds as a tribute to Kennedy. *Chimes of Freedom* had been interpreted as a song inspired by Kennedy, but Dylan has denied this.

---

[357] *I Shall Be Free, The Freewheelin' Bob Dylan*, Bob Dylan, 1963. (Copyright © 1963, 1967 by Warner Bros. Inc.; renewed 1991, 1995 by Special Rider Music)

[358] *Bob Dylan: An Intimate Biography*, Anthony Scaduto, W.H. Allen, London/New York, 1972.

[359] https://www.rockhall.com/songs-shaped-rock-and-roll-times-they-are-changin, *Songs That Shaped Rock and Roll: "The Times They Are A-Changin"*, Retrieved 11/27/2016

[360] Dylan's comments to the Emergency Civil Liberties Committee were supplied to the author in a transcript the committee prepared, from its executive director, Edith Tiger. Per *No Direction Home: The Life And Music Of Bob Dylan*, Robert Sheldon (Revised and Updated Edition: Edited by Elizabeth Thomson and Patrick Humphries), Backbeat Books, Milwaukee, WI, 2011.

According to Scaduto's book, [361] Dylan went on a road trip in 1964, and stopped at the site of the assassination. Dylan wanted to check out Dealey Plaza, but the people they asked would not admit to knowing where Kennedy had been shot. *"The seventh man they asked, answered, 'You mean where they shot that bastard Kennedy?' Dylan didn't answer, and the Texan gave them directions. For about a half hour they wandered around the murder scene, Dylan grim and silent, and then back in the car and on their way, and all of them shouting out the windows, condemning all Texans as assassins."*

After the first few "electric" concerts of 1965, keyboardist Al Kooper wanted out, fearing a visit to Dallas on an upcoming tour. As he recalled in his book, *Backstage Passes & Backstabbing Bastards*, *"I mean, look what they just done to J.F.K. down there ... So what was going to happen to Bob Dylan? ... I wasn't sure I wanted to find out."* [362]

Bob Dylan married his first wife, Sara, on November 22, 1965.

In 1966, Dylan told biographer Robert Shelton, that the world goes on, no matter what happens, citing Kennedy's assassination.

The spirit of Kennedy hovered over Dylan throughout the 1980s. He played Dick Holler's song *Abraham, Martin, and John* 23 times in concert in 1980 and 1981.

In 1983, Dylan recorded *Blind Willie McTell* for his *Infidels* album, but it remained unreleased until 1991's *The Bootleg Series Volume 1-3*. It included a reference to East Texas, and fallen martyrs.

In 1985, Bob Dylan headlined Live Aid, which took place at Philadelphia's John F. Kennedy Stadium. The following year, Dylan appeared with Stevie Wonder and Peter, Paul & Mary at the John F. Kennedy Performing Arts Center Opera House to celebrate the first Rev. Martin Luther King, Jr., holiday. Dylan returned to Kennedy Stadium in 1987, backed by The Grateful Dead.

On the first leg of his tour with Paul Simon in 1999, both artists shared the stage at the end of the first set of whoever opened the show. One song they performed together was the Dylan-inspired *The Sound(s) of Silence*, whose lyrics were written by Simon in the aftermath of that fateful day in Dallas.

In 2008, Dylan referenced President and Mrs. Kennedy multiple times during a special two-hour *President's Day* episode of his *Theme Time Radio Hour* program. Dylan played a clip of Jackie Kennedy's televised tour of the White House, contrasted the radio and television interpretations of the Richard Nixon-John Kennedy debates, and played Frank Sinatra's rewritten, pro-Kennedy version of *High Hopes*, before describing the fallout between the two.

In December, 1997, Dylan, along with actor Charlton Heston, actress Lauren Bacall, opera singer Jessye Norman, and dancer Edward Villella (who danced for President and Mrs. Kennedy), was honored at the Kennedy Center. At the ceremony, President Clinton said:

"His voice and lyrics haven't always been easy on the ear, but throughout his career Bob Dylan has never aimed to please. He's disturbed the peace and discomfited the powerful. President Kennedy could easily have been talking about Bob Dylan when he said that, "If sometimes our great artists have been most critical of our society, it is because their concern for justice makes them aware that our nation falls short of its highest potential."" [363]

Addendum 2016: When it was announced Bob Dylan had won the Nobel Prize in Literature, President Bill Clinton tweeted: *Congrats @bobdylan on a well-deserved Nobel for wise, powerful lyrics that touched minds & hearts. And TY for this amazing orig. sculpture!*

[361] *Bob Dylan: An Intimate Biography*, Anthony Scaduto, W.H. Allen, London/New York, 1972.

[362] *Backstage Passes & Backstabbing Bastards*, Al Kooper, Billboard Books, New York. 1998

[363] http://www.presidency.ucsb.edu/ws/?pid=53674, William J. Clinton, XLII President of the United States: 1993-2001, *Remarks at the Kennedy Center Honors Reception*, December 7, 1997. Retrieved 11/27/2016

Michael Gray on writing, talking, and meeting Bob Dylan

November, 2010

In 1981, while traveling in England, I came across a book called *Song and Dance Man*. I was intrigued by the premise, and the pictures, and soon bought and devoured the book. The observations and opinions about Bob Dylan I found inside opened not only my mind about Dylan's work, but about "art" in general. Since I was away from home, and most of my Dylan collection was inaccessible at the time, the book made me long for my vinyl so I could rediscover his music armed with an updated, educated view. When I returned home, I found a new appreciation for LPs such as *Street Legal* and *Self Portrait*, as well as a greater understanding of where his greatest works came from.

The book was written by British music journalist Michael Gray. Over the years, he wrote (or co-authored) the books *Mother! Is The Story Of Frank Zappa*, *The Elvis Atlas: A Journey Through Elvis Presley's America*, and *All Across The Telegraph: A Bob Dylan Handbook*. His 2008 book, *Hand Me My Travelin' Shoes: In Search Of Blind Willie McTell*, was awarded the Certificate of Merit at the 2010 ARSC (Association for Recorded Sound Collection) Awards for Excellence in Historical Recorded Sound Research.

Over the years, Gray's knowledge of Dylan's work has led to some interesting side projects, including writing the liner notes for *The Songs Of Bob Dylan* (Start Records), a collection of various artists covering Dylan compositions.

"That was nothing special," Gray said. *"I just happened to know the guy in charge. I was asked to write the notes and suggest tracks, Iain McLay had to sort out the licenses. We got most of what we wanted. I like that it was the first time Elvis Presley was included in a multi-artist compilation. You'd never see him on any hits-of-the-50s-type records. The price was that we also had to include Bobby Bare's terrible version of* Don't Think Twice. *I was thankful there were songs most fans didn't know about, like Gary U.S. Bonds' version of* From A Buick 6, *and Jason & The Scorchers'* Absolutely Sweet Marie. *It was an interesting selection . . . I wouldn't have thought to include Tina Turner's* Tonight I'll Be Staying Here With You."

Gray currently lives with his wife, food writer Sarah Beattie, at their home in the southwest of France, where together they host "Bob Dylan Weekends." He recently called me from home to discuss the "Weekends," his early days as a music fan and journalist, and all things "Bob."

Today, there are countless numbers of fans who take Bob Dylan very seriously, and are studying his every move. That was not always the case. In the mid-1960s, the mainstream press did not cover rock acts that came to their towns, or treat them with any respect or credibility. Sure, there was occasional praise (or bafflement, or scorn) for The Beatles, but otherwise daily newspapers would not lower themselves to acknowledge the frivolous passing fad of pimply adolescent "pop" music.

Things started to change with the advent of the underground rock press, in such upstart magazines as *Crawdaddy* ("the first magazine to take rock and roll seriously," they claimed) and *Rolling Stone*. Musicians like John Lennon, Pete Townshend, Bob Dylan, and others were seen as "Artists," with thoughts and art worth serious examination - just as one would study any "serious" novelist or composer.

In the early 1970s, Michael Gray was a teacher, freelance music journalist, and Bob Dylan fan. In late 1972 in the U.K., and the following year in the "States," Gray published *Song and Dance Man*, a scholarly study of the work of Bob Dylan, the first book of its kind. As he told me, *"I created quite a niche for myself."*

With the acclaim of *Song and Dance Man*, Gray was able to quit his day job, and devote himself to writing full-time. He has updated the book twice, in 1981 and 1999. It is an essential book for any serious music fan. He also wrote and compiled *The Bob Dylan Encyclopedia* (2006).

As a child, Gray rummaged through his parent's record collection. *"Shellac 78 r.p.m. records,"* Gray recalled. *"I found some weird things I really liked . . . Spike Jones and His City Slickers,* Chloe *. . . Jo Stafford,* Buttons and Bows *. . . Tennessee Ernie Ford,* 16 Tons *. . . That was when I was young . . . 6, 7, 8."*

The first rock music that resonated with Gray was Tommy Steele singing *Hound Dog* on the British television show *6.5 Special*, when Gray was about ten-years-old. *"I was blown away, although I would not have used that expression at the time. I liked him for a couple of years until he started recording the music rock and roll was supposed to abolish. I asked my grandmother to buy (the Steele single), but there wasn't one. There was one by Elvis Presley on 78. So Elvis became my idol and remained so, despite making very disappointing movies, until I got to university in 1964. Then I met someone who told me about an artist who was on a very different level. . . I was very shocked by the very notion of that."*

"This turned out to be Bob Dylan, of course."

Back in the 1960s, the world was a much different place. Before the Internet, music fans were left to solve the mysteries found inside far-out rock albums on their own. To get information about this music, there were basically two resources: Underground (or pirate) radio, and the burgeoning rock press.

Gray started out as a freelance writer. *"I didn't give up my day job until I got an American deal for the publication of the first* Song and Dance Man. *I was teaching languages. My first piece was in* Melody Maker. *Broadstreet newspapers didn't lower themselves to write about pop music - you could only write for* Melody Maker, The Guardian *or* The New York Times, *they didn't write about Bob Dylan. In 1968, Greil Marcus was writing about the underground. 'Grown-ups' were not."*

When *Song and Dance Man* was published, it was the first book devoted to the serious study of one artist. *"It was the first time that a mainstream book like this was published on both sides of the Atlantic,"* Gray told me, almost with a sense of wonder. *"It was not a leaflet. It discussed Dylan in the same breath as William Blake and T.S. Eliot, outside of the hippie underground. I didn't even know it was going to be the first book. I work slowly, and had no idea if anyone else was doing the same thing. It was surprising that it had not been done before.*

"The feedback was very mixed, but there were a lot of people who were struck by it. It was overshadowed at the time, because (Anthony) Scaduto's (Dylan biography) came out first. More people wanted to read about Dylan's life than a lit-crit study of his work."

While the book was influential, and groundbreaking in many aspects, it was not a huge seller. *"At the time, Dylan was unfashionable. He was already passé. 1973 was really the last year of the 1960s. Music was not yet swamped by the gigantism of the record industry."*

Song and Dance Man was updated twice. *"The third edition was definitely the best. The great pleasure was that I was able to write at enormous length (the book is over 900 pages). They let me have footnotes on the same page, which I think was crucial. That was great for me, it enabled me to do a running commentary. The other thing the length enabled me to do was make the occasional joke. Humor is a virtue."*

Even though the book ends with the release of 1997's *Time Out Of Mind*, Gray has no plans to update the book a fourth time around. *"I still enjoy writing essays and writing my blog, but there are a million people writing about Dylan, and there are other books I'd like to write.* Song and Dance Man *III was 530,000 words,* The Bob Dylan Encyclopedia *was 750,000. If I haven't said all I've got to say already, I never will."*

For Gray, the Encyclopedia was an enjoyable endeavor, but involved an enormous amount of time on interviews and research. *"The Bob Dylan Encyclopedia was very hard work. The Internet was up and running by then so that sped things up. I enjoyed writing about people this time, instead of songs. It was nice to have an email dialogue with everyone from Bruce Langhorne to Rob Stoner to Freddy Koella. Winston Watson was also very helpful and cooperative. I like the book. It was satisfying for myself to learn about people that I already knew about. I don't know how I did it so fast! I was tired a year after I wrote it."*

Gray received his first feedback from the Dylan camp after he finished writing the first edition of *Song and Dance Man*. *"I had to submit the manuscript - this was before (manager) Jeff Rosen - to the New York office to show that (the book) was an honorable project. I needed permission for over 100 songs, and they let me quote them very cheaply, so that was being near to a 'thumbs up.' Each time, I've always been given permission to quote the lyrics cheaply. With A.J. Weberman, the so-called concordance quote was (allegedly) something like $200 a line."*

This led to an actual invitation to meet Bob Dylan when the "Song and Dance Man'" himself toured England later in the decade. *"The closest I ever got to Dylan was about twelve inches, backstage at Earl's Court in 1978. He got the London CBS Records press officer to ask me if I'd like to say 'Hello'"* Not too surprisingly, Gray agreed.

"By 1978, Dylan did not like critics. He wasn't going to say anything nice about the book, so the press officer said that Dylan liked a piece I wrote in Melody Maker *about the 1978 tour. That was his way of not saying anything nice about the book.*

"We talked. It wasn't so bad. I had my son with me, who was a child at the time. He was nice to my son, therefore it was fine. I didn't really expect anything more, really. It was a little weird that he was someone who means so much to you, and you mean nothing to him."

Nora Ephron, dead at 71 - Interviewed Bob Dylan, broke news of his first marriage

June 26, 2012

Writer and filmmaker Nora Ephron died in New York City earlier today. She was 71. Ephron is probably best known for her Academy Award-nominated screenplays - *Silkwood*, *When Harry Met Sally...* and *Sleepless in Seattle*.

Ephron was born five days before Robert Zimmerman. In 1965, she interviewed Bob Dylan, and the following year broke the news in the United States that he had secretly wed.

Dylan was reportedly interviewed by Ephron and Susan Edmiston in late summer, 1965, at the office of his manager Albert Grossman, [364] soon after Dylan played an electric set at Forest Hills. Asked if folk-rock was indeed a mix of intelligent lyrics and a backbeat, Dylan replied, *"Yes. It's very complicated to play with electricity. You play with other people. You're dealing with other people. Most people don't like to work with other people, it's more difficult. It takes a lot. Most people who don't like rock and roll can't relate to other people."*

Asked if he was a poet, Dylan answered, *"No. We have our ideas about poets. The word doesn't mean any more than the word 'house.' There are people who write poems and people who write poems. Other people write poems. Everybody who writes poems do you call them a poet? ... Some people work in gas stations and they're poets. I don't call myself a poet because I don't like the word. I'm a trapeze artist."* [365]

It also featured other famous quotes, including *"Chaos is a friend of mine. It's like I accept him, does he accept me"* and *"Queen Jane is a man."*

Dylan married his first wife Sara on November 22, 1965, in a private civil ceremony. According to Robert Shelton in his book *No Direction Home*, the ceremony was a well-kept secret until the British music paper *Melody Maker* reported the news at the end of the year. In the U.S., Ephron broke the story in the February 9, 1966, issue of *The New York Post*, with the headline, *"HUSH! BOB DYLAN IS WED."*

---

[364] http://www.interferenza.com/bcs/interw/65-aug.htm *Bob Dylan Interview*, Nora Ephron & Susan Edmiston, Retrieved 11/27/2016

[365] http://www.interferenza.com/bcs/interw/65-aug.htm, *Bob Dylan Interview*, Nora Ephron & Susan Edmiston, Retrieved 11/27/2016

Bob Dylan's connection to Norman Raeben, and *Fiddler on the Roof* author Joseph Stein

October 25, 2010

Joseph Stein, best known for writing the books for such musicals as *Zorba* and *Fiddler On The Roof*, has died at the age of 98.

Fiddler On The Roof was based on *Tevye and his Daughters* (or *Tevye the Milkman*) and other tales by Solomon Naumovich Rabinovich, written under the pen name of "Sholem Aleichem." The original Broadway production surpassed 3000 performances, a record that stood for almost a decade.

The youngest of Rabinovich's six children was Norman Raeben, the American painter who influenced Bob Dylan in the mid-1960s.

In The Mysterious Norman Raeben, Bert Cartwright wrote about the painter's history and influence on Dylan, especially on his albums *Blood On The Track* and *Street Legal*, and the movie *Renaldo & Clara*.

Dylan's interest in Raeben began sometime in 1974, when several friends of Sara came to visit. They were discussing common words, like truth and beauty. When Dylan asked where they learned the definitions of these words, they told him about Raeben. When Dylan returned to New York in the spring of 1974, he decided to pop in and visit Raeben. The artist asked Dylan if he wanted to paint, and he said, *"Well, I hadn't gone up there to paint, I'd just gone up there to see what was going on. I wound up staying there for maybe two months. This guy was amazing…"* [366] When Dylan looked back upon what happened during those two months, he came to believe that he was so transformed as to become a stranger to his wife. *"It changed me. I went home after that and my wife never did understand me ever since that day. That's when our marriage started breaking up. She never knew what I was talking about, what I was thinking about. And I couldn't possibly explain it."* [367]

---

[366] http://www.willamette.edu/~rloftus/ChangingTimes/BOTNormRaeben.htm, *The Mysterious Norman Raeben*, Bert Cartwright, Retrieved 11/27/2016

[367] http://www.willamette.edu/~rloftus/ChangingTimes/BOTNormRaeben.htm, *The Mysterious Norman Raeben*, Bert Cartwright, Retrieved 11/27/2016

Liz Thomson on restoring Robert Shelton's Dylan bio, *No Direction Home*

June 14-15, 2011

To celebrate, or exploit, Bob Dylan's 70th birthday, many books were republished, expanded, and updated last month. Dylan even sarcastically commented about the flood of literature that was about to engulf the publishing world in his essay, *"To my fans and followers,"* [368] which was published on his website on May 13, suggesting anyone could write a book about him. (Ahem.)

One book, however, was a long time coming, and it was a labor of love.

In 1986, Robert Shelton finished his biography of Bob Dylan, *No Direction Home.* The version published was not what Shelton had in mind, but compromises had to be made for his book to see the light of day. Shelton actually hung out with Dylan during his most explosive creative period: from 1961 - when Shelton wrote a rave review of the unknown singer in *The New York Times* - through 1966, when Dylan withdrew from public view after a motorcycle mishap. The book was written with Dylan's encouragement and cooperation, and the two remained friends until Shelton's death in late 1995.

Liz Thomson recently took on the task of restoring Shelton's vision - with help from Patrick Humphries on the notes and chronology - and an updated version of *No Direction Home - The Life and Music of Bob Dylan* was published last month. I recently spoke with Thomson on the phone while she was in New York. Thomson has been a journalist, author, and broadcaster for over 25 years, and was a friend of the author.

Thomson herself became a Dylan fan at a fairly young age, she told me. *"I'm 53, and I wasn't quite the generation to be a Dylan fan ... I was a weird kid. In 1969, I got into Joan Baez, then Judy Collins. It was the gateway to the 1960s social-political climate, and I was obsessed. How I got into Dylan when all my friends were into Donny Osmond, I don't know. I was into* (Dylan's 1970 album) New Morning. *My generation got into Dylan a bit later on. I was early, he wasn't in fashion. I loved his other albums, but I didn't understand, for instance, what* Desolation Row *was about. It didn't fit into my 13-year-old frame of reference. But I was hooked."*

Thomson met Shelton in 1979, at the "Dylan Revisited '79" conference, and eventually became friends. *"I'd gone and seen Dylan the previous year, and it was an exciting experience. In the last hours of the conference, Shelton and I were introduced. After speaking for a short while, he asked, purely platonically, if we could meet in London."*

Shelton had put a lot of time, sweat, and money into his research in this pre-internet era. He hadn't heard back from the intended American publisher, Doubleday, and was concerned about what was happening with his project.

"He was still worrying about the book. He'd sent it off six months previously, and Doubleday was taking too long. It was a serious book, with lots of insight into the New York folk scene. Originally, Shelton wanted it to be published in two volumes - one through 1966, and a second one through the late 70s. The publishers didn't want that. This was after Albert Goldman's book on John Lennon."

Thomson said Shelton was offered more money to add more salacious material. *"Robert was not going to sell out his friend like that,"* she said.

According to Thomson, there was a *"horrible battle,"* and the book was eventually resold to the New English Library in the U.K., who then sold it to William Morrow and Company in the United States. *"They were more sympathetic,"* Thomson said. *"However, as time went on, they had to take out more from the 60s, in order to update the book."* Shelton referred to the published version as *"abridged over troubled waters."*

---

[368] http://bobdylan.com/news/my-fans-and-followers/, *To my fans and followers*, Retrieved 1/25/2017

"I knew Shelton 15 years. For 15 years, he was my mentor. If I hadn't met him, I might have ended up as something different, probably a teacher. (Shelton) wasn't an easy man, but he was a good man and had good ears. He was the father of popular music journalism, at a time when it wasn't taken seriously. Others have denigrated his work, while those that have done less have claimed more. Shelton never claimed he had discovered Dylan. He always said 'He discovered himself,' but Shelton did much of the groundwork. Part of my goal was that he should have his moment in the spotlight."

In 1980, Shelton gave Thomson a copy of the *No Direction Home* manuscript to read and critique, and the two remained friends. The original 365,000-word manuscript was edited down to 260,000 for the original edition.

"We decided the best way to create the new edition was to work with a scan of the published text and my old carbon of the original manuscript, amalgamating the two - sometimes big chunks, sometimes a sentence or a paragraph, sometimes just a few words. I still have the back ache and eye strain to prove it. My overarching aim was to have the original text reinstated, never to bring it up to date. It's basically Dylan in the 60s - the formative years of artists are always more interesting, I feel. The idea was to publish what Shelton first aimed to publish in 1978-79. Dylan's 70th birthday loomed, it seemed like a good opportunity."

"The book (No Direction Home) *was not an authorized collaboration, but he was able to interview Baez, Dylan's parents, members of the inner circle. From 1961 to 1966, Shelton and Dylan were buddies who lived a few hundred yards from each other* (in Greenwich Village). *They'd go out drinking and dining, bringing their girlfriends - for Dylan it was Suze* (Rotolo) *and Baez."*

"Shelton's 1961 review put Dylan on the map, and they became friends. It was a journalist/artist relationship (between Shelton and Dylan), *but they were able to separate that. They became friends. What struck me was how unsophisticated it was in those days, living in ratty apartments in the Village. It was a naive time, without a music business as such. It was just a scene they were a part of. There was a trusting of the press. Now a journalist would sell the story to the National Inquirer."*

The centerpiece of the book is a long, intense interview that took place on a plane flight during Dylan's 1966 tour. Large chunks were removed from the original book, and have been restored in the new revised edition.

"In an effort to make it shorter (in the 1986 edition), *there were parts taken out. The edits meant a loss to the stream-of-consciousness of the interview. The interview was man-to-man, friend-to-friend. You get a real sense of a closeness to Dylan. The new, complete version gives you more of a sense of Dylan in 1966. It now, I hope, gives a much better sense of how Dylan actually sounded, of the rhythm and patterns of his speech, which had been lost in the conflation of the original text."*

What did Thomson have to say about the so-called "revelation" that Dylan "took heroin" and was "suicidal"?

"I don't know . . . 45 years on, what a revelation - Dylan took drugs! I haven't sorted it all out. Was he putting us on? He sounds very strung out. It's hard to say if he was using the harder stuff. The specific passages about heroin may not be in the book, but, as Shelton always said, 'Everything's there if you break the code.' There's quite a lot about his 'death obsession' from Dylan himself in that chapter and, elsewhere, from Suze.

"What was interesting was the tsunami of articles over two-and-a-half minutes of tape (originally linked to a BBC article). *We - all of us - don't get to hear Dylan chatting very often. This was like eavesdropping on two old friends, it's of prime interest. He's Dylan! Here's Dylan talking about his life. I would suspect there's truth in this. It shows the extraordinary pressure he was under. There was no protective system, he was out there, exposed. (Manager Albert) Grossman overworked him, he was tired beyond exhaustion and trying to cope."*

Thomson then addressed the accusation that Shelton was "defending" Dylan, saying that *"everything is in there, except he wouldn't write about* (Dylan's) *wife and children."*

When putting the new version of *No Direction Home* together, Thomson's goal may have been to restore Shelton's original vision, but she still had to make revisions.

"I think I made the right decision that it should end in 1978. From Gerde's to the 1978 world tour, that makes sense for the book. Looking back at the manuscripts - I can't even read some of my original 1980 notes anymore - but even then, I had some tentative suggestions to make and some of them still made sense. I moved sections around - some of the flashbacks and fast forwards made it unnecessarily complicated - so it would appeal to those that are not mega-fans, trimmed some parts, restored 20,000 words."

Thomson said she felt sad that Shelton is not around to see Dylan's resurgence in recent years. *"They remained in touch,"* Thomson said. Shelton moved to Europe, Dylan moved to Woodstock. They met a few times, including 1969 at the Isle of Wight and the triumphant return to London in 1978. Indeed, the book ends with the two men having dinner after the last of the Earls Court concerts.

"In 1986, during the filming of the film Hearts of Fire, *Dylan summoned Shelton to his trailer. It was Dylan's way of saying he was OK with the book.*

"I wish Shelton could have lived to see the revival of Dylan's career. He would have been thrilled, but not surprised."

Sean Wilentz on his book, *Bob Dylan in America*

December 18, 2011

Sean Wilentz is not only one of the nation's most prominent historians, but a huge admirer of Bob Dylan. He grew up in New York City, and his family owned the 8th Street Bookshop in Greenwich Village. In fact, Allen Ginsberg first met Bob Dylan in his uncle's apartment above the shop.

Since 1979, Wilentz has taught at Princeton, where he is currently George Henry Davis 1886 Professor of American History. Wilentz has also gone on to write the Grammy-nominated liner notes for *The Bootleg Series, Volume 6, Bob Dylan Live, 1964: Concert at Philharmonic Hall*. Since 2001, he has served as historian-in-residence at Dylan's official website. For more on Wilentz' many accomplishments, please visit his website. [369]

Last year, Doubleday published his book, *Bob Dylan In America*, a *New York Times* bestseller. It has recently been published in paperback by Anchor Books, a division of Random House.

Can you tell our readers about your first exposure to Bob Dylan?

I dimly recall hearing about him first in 1963. Not long after that, a friend turned up in my Sunday School with a copy of Freewheelin'. *(It was quite a Sunday School.) I first laid eyes on him in 1964, at Philharmonic Hall.*

What inspired your unique perspective of Bob Dylan in your book?

If there's anything unique about my perspective, it comes from being a young fan — not-quite and then barely in his teens — who grew up inside the Greenwich Village milieu where Dylan first made his name as a performer and writer. I think one's early surroundings, the feel of them, sink into the marrow, and that feeling surely went into the book.

Your book received widespread praise. Were there any unexpected comments or reactions from anyone since *Bob Dylan In America* was published?

I was gratified that, among the reviewers, musicians like Philip King, the Irish songwriter and filmmaker, thought so highly of the book. In general, musicians have been particularly friendly and have seemed to connect with what I was trying to say. I'm a historian by trade, so I was a little worried that the book wouldn't do justice to the musical fundamentals in Dylan's work. It's been a pleasant surprise.

When I heard you speak in Cambridge, Massachusetts, in October, many long-time Dylan followers attended, including those that saw Dylan at Newport in the 1960s. I was surprised that despite their love for Dylan's music, these fans appeared to be unaware of Dylan's recent post on his website refuting his alleged "censorship" in China, or knew little other than superficial accusations of plagiarism for his recent paintings. What is your take on this?

It seems to confirm that, once they are created, modern-day pseudo-scandals are very hard to dispel. Then they harden into conventional knowledge, even in circles that ought to know better. Most people, and maybe even most Democrats, still take it for granted that Al Gore really did claim he invented the Internet! This kind of misinforming by the press has been going on a long time. I've seen it transformed into pseudo-history. I do think it's worsened, though, over the past twenty years or so. The plagiarism charges are especially silly. If Dylan is a plagiarist, so was Cezanne.

There were two particularly interesting observations you made in your lecture. One was about the 2003 film, *Masked and Anonymous*, the other was Dylan's version of *Lone Pilgrim* (from *World Gone Wrong*). Could you please elaborate?

Thanks for saying so. In 2003, Masked and Anonymous *got creamed by the movie critics, who greatly preferred* My Big Fat Greek Wedding. *They dismissed* Masked and Anonymous *as an incoherent vanity vehicle made by a rich rock star, with help from the guy who wrote* Seinfeld *(Larry Charles). I think the film deserves more serious attention as a layered, glancing quasi-allegory -- with the emphasis on the "quasi." The book describes it as "a*

---

[369] http://www.seanwilentz.com/about/ *About SW*, Retrieved 11/27/2016

manic film about the death throes of one America and a chilling portent of a new one." Maybe, someday, everybody will take another look.

World Gone Wrong *is the album on which I think Dylan finally recaptured his muse after his struggles of the mid-to-late 1980s.* Lone Pilgrim, *the final track, is an old Sacred Harp hymn. Dylan says he took his version from Doc Watson's. But Dylan inhabits it in his own powerful way. In the book, I call it "a reprieve, a coming to rest, a ghost note of a different order [that] is also a benediction." Dylan's performance brings me solace.*

You have written the liner notes for the upcoming benefit album, *Chimes of Freedom: The Songs of Bob Dylan Honoring 50 Years of Amnesty International.* **How did that come about? It's an impressive collection. Were there any unexpected favorites?**

The album has been in the works a while. I got involved when my friend Julie Yannatta, who produced the project, asked me to write the notes. It is impressive, so much so that it's taken four CD's to include everything worth including. The roster is so diverse, in every way, that there is something (or there are some things) for Dylan fans of all ages and inclinations. I'm especially taken with the Carolina Chocolate Drops' rendition of Political World. *It may just be generational, but I also liked Patti Smith's* Drifter's Escape *and Mark Knopfler's* Restless Farewell. *The ticking "false clock" on the latter brings back what you said earlier, Harold, about the China fracas. That track also brings to my mind the late Liam Clancy, on whose rendering of* The Parting Glass *Dylan based the song's melody. If this be plagiarism, make the most of it.*

Remerro Trotsky Williams, and the mural on the cover of *Oh Mercy*

August 15, 2011

One of Bob Dylan's most acclaimed albums, 1989's *Oh Mercy*, is being reissued on vinyl tomorrow, August 16.

Interestingly, it is being released not on Sony or Sundazed, but by 4 Men with Beards, a San Francisco-based label that specializes only in vinyl reissues. While there is no confirmation on the official Runt website, [370] Amazon lists the release date as tomorrow.

The cover artwork was chosen by Dylan as he passed a mural that caught his eye while biking to the studio (probably for mixing sessions in New York). The piece was called *Dancing Couple*, and it was signed "Trotsky."

Remerro Trotsky Williams already had a connection with Dylan. Trotsky grew up in Washington, D.C., and attended the 1963 March on Washington for Jobs and Freedom. The march is best known for Dr. Martin Luther King's "I Have A Dream" speech, but Dylan performed at the event as well. The event changed Trotsky's outlook:

"I learned that differences in acceptance could be attributable to color ... and my journey for balance and harmony [in my life] *began."* [371]

The artist's life changed again when Dylan wanted artwork by Trotsky for an album cover. According to a 1989 article in *People* magazine, [372] Dylan had agents sent to locate the mysterious artist who painted a mural on the wall of the side of a Chinese restaurant at 9th & 53rd in Manhattan's Hell's Kitchen district. Dylan wanted to use the image for the cover of his next album, *Oh Mercy*, and Columbia representatives went looking for this elusive artist, along with a check for $5,000. Trotsky was finally located a few weeks later:

"There I was in early July, returning from landlord-tenant court, completely exhausted, and the phone rings," says Trotsky, 36, who owed back rent on his ramshackle $369-a-month studio near his mural. "I answered with a whine." And utter disbelief when told of Dylan's intent. "I said, 'You're full of it,' " he recalls... [373]

Trotsky was also quoted in *New York Magazine* as saying, *"I was just about to give up and move to Atlanta or Istanbul, and I get this phone call: 'CBS (who owned Columbia Records pre-Sony) calling - we want to use one of your paintings for the Bob Dylan LP,' and I say, 'You're kidding; this is some cruel joke; go away, but give me your number, and I'll call you back.' I called back and it ended up being the real thing."* [374]

In the aftermath, Trotsky's career took off, and he even met Dylan at one of his concerts. *"He told me my painting blew him away,"* says the artist. *"He was also concerned that I liked the title of the album to go with my artwork. That was very nice."* [375] Trotsky elaborated for *New York Magazine*, saying Dylan asked him

---

[370] http://www.runtshop.com, 09/26/11: *Bob Dylan's hard-to-find 1989 classic back in print on LP, The first Dylan album produced by Daniel Lanois*, Retrieved 11/27/2006

[371] http://www.thebody.com/content/art46257.html, *Visual AIDS - A Gallery of Art by HIV-Positive African Americans: Remerro Trotsky Williams. Home: New York, N.Y. Age: 53. Diagnosed: 1990*, Retrieved 11/27/2016

[372] http://people.com/archive/trotsky-whose-lively-street-art-became-an-off-the-wall-album-cover-for-bob-dylan-vol-32-no-17/, *Archive: Trotsky, Whose Lively Street Art Became An Off-the-Wall Album Cover for Bob Dylan*, Retrieved 11/27/2016

[373] http://people.com/archive/trotsky-whose-lively-street-art-became-an-off-the-wall-album-cover-for-bob-dylan-vol-32-no-17/, Archive: Trotsky, Whose Lively Street Art Became An Off-the-Wall Album Cover for Bob Dylan. Retrieved 11/27/2016

[374] *Off The Record: Positively 53rd Street*, Lauren Spencer, New York Magazine, 9/25/1989

[375] http://people.com/archive/trotsky-whose-lively-street-art-became-an-off-the-wall-album-cover-for-bob-dylan-vol-32-no-17/, Archive: Trotsky, Whose Lively Street Art Became An Off-the-Wall Album Cover for Bob Dylan. Retrieved 11/27/2016

for advice when they finally met. *"He said, CBS was scared the title… Oh Mercy sounded religious. I said Oh Mercy had guts and feeling, and it matched the art."* [376]

On the album's credits, Street Art is credited to "Trotsky."

[376] *Off The Record: Positively 53rd Street*, Lauren Spencer, New York Magazine, 9/25/1989

Bob Dylan in 1975 - The 'Night of the Hurricane,' the tale of the tape

December 13, 2011

In December, 1975, the Rolling Thunder Revue played a benefit concert, "The Night of the Hurricane," at New York's Madison Square Garden. I attended, and recorded most of the show. If you are a serious Bob Dylan collector, you probably have a copy of it.

In the autumn of 1975, I was glued to New York's legendary underground radio station, WNEW-FM, even more than usual, since it was the only way to find out what was happening with Bob Dylan's mysterious, hit-and-run Rolling Thunder Revue tour. I wanted to attend at least one of the shows, but figured any concert would be over before I even knew about it. If I did get the information in time, would I even be able to attend? I wasn't even old enough to drive at night.

After seeing an advertisement on November 30 for the December 8 show in the *Sunday New York Times*, my parents let me skip school the next day to go to the Garden box office to get a pair of tickets for the concert. I took the Long Island Rail Road to Pennsylvania Station, where the Garden is located, and arrived 15 minutes before the advertised on sale time.

However, with fans lining up overnight, tickets had gone on sale about eight hours early. I walked up to the ticket window and was just glad to be able to purchase last row, left of stage, tickets. One week later, less than two years after I saw Dylan and The Band at the Nassau Coliseum, I was seeing Dylan again.

At my previous Dylan concert, one of my friends snuck in a portable, fairly large, Panasonic cassette player to record the show. Even though our seats were in the back, and my friend skipped most of The Band's performances to save on batteries, we had the show captured for all eternity, just like real bootleggers.

It was probably only a few weeks before my friend let me borrow the tape, although it felt like an eternity at the time. I took two cassette players and placed them side-by-side, without the aid of any RCA cables. I played the recording in one, and recorded the show with the other. Primitive. Analogue. Golden.

I was obsessed with the scratchy sounding tape and listened to it constantly. That summer, I got my own cassette recorder, this one a compact, handheld model. My next three concerts, all in 1974, were Crosby, Stills, Nash & Young, Rick Wakeman, and George Harrison, and I recorded them all.

In those days, going to a concert was still a big deal. In 1975, I didn't go to any shows until December's "The Night Of The Hurricane." Since I couldn't find any friends to take to the show (most parents thought it was too dangerous), I went with my sister. I was armed with my trusty Panasonic and three Maxell LN-90 cassettes. I thought it important to record all the acts for posterity, not just Dylan and the other big names. Who knows, maybe this T-Bone Burnett guy would amount to something?

I heard the Rolling Thunder Revue played for about three hours, and this special event was rumored to be even longer. This was a mixed blessing, as I had to catch the 12:30 a.m. train home whether the concert was over or not.

The tape started with me talking to my sister about the vendors loudly selling popcorn and soda during the Wakeman show. I was incensed that they were oblivious to the music, as if a rock concert was the same experience as a basketball game.

Over the next four hours or so, I dutifully recorded every act: Bob Neuwirth, Burnett, Rob Stoner, Mick Ronson, actress Ronee Blakley, Joni Mitchell, Muhammed Ali, "Hurricane" Carter (via the telephone), Ramblin' Jack Elliott. Then Dylan, with special guest Robbie Robertson on one song, followed by an intermission. Part two featured Dylan with Joan Baez, then Baez solo, Coretta Scott King, Roberta Flack, Roger McGuinn, then Dylan's closing set.

After Dylan sang *Hurricane* (*"This is what this concert, or this show, is all about, and this person, he's a beautiful man, and beauty should never be imprisoned"*), we had to go. I kept the tape rolling until my sister and I sat down on the train, with the strains of Dylan's new song, *One More Cup Of Coffee*, fading as we walked out of the Garden and into Penn Station.

Fast forward to the early days of 1999. I was finally online, and one of the first things I did was find Dylan fan sites. An important aspect of the Internet for a Dylan fan like me was finding like-minded souls who shared my passion, and who appeared to be willing to trade all this great unreleased music. However, there was a code - the tapes were not to be sold, which was fine by me. All you had to do was find some generous person who wanted to trade.

At first, that was the difficult part. Most of the serious Dylan collectors already had the good stuff. What would they want with my measly collection?

There was a list of "traders" on Bob Links, [377] but only one person would trade with me, an Englishman named Peter Baker. He was very generous, patient, and informed. Baker was interested in owning everything, including the audio from a VHS rough-cut of Dylan's movie *Hearts of Fire* a friend had given me. However, I could not convince him, or anybody else, that my 1975 recording was something a Dylan collector would want to add to his collection.

One day I saw a posting by Les Kokay on an old Dylan fan site. He wrote he was chronicling the Rolling Thunder Revue tour, and while Dylan's performances were often captured on tape, he was having trouble getting detailed information on the other acts. I had been discouraged by the previous lack of enthusiasm for my "Night Of The Hurricane" recording, but decided to offer it anyway.

I could not have predicted the response from offering the recording this time. There were multiple requests for tape copies from all across the globe. Not only had Kokay expressed interest, but so had Baker, plus others with whom I had no previous contact.

Multiple trades were arranged. I used a pseudonym (Dave Peters) and a P.O. Box to disguise my identity for a variety of reasons, including hiding my activities from my co-workers. I copied the shows with my dual tape deck, editing out the very beginning, when I was talking with my sister, and anything after the song *Hurricane*, when I pouted all the way to the train.

Packages started arriving in my P.O. Box. I received unreleased Dylan recordings on cool-looking Japanese Maxell cassettes from someone I eventually friended on Facebook, and met at a Boston Paul McCartney concert in 2013. Kokay sent me a collection of shows I attended, to make up for the postage I would have to pay to send my tapes to his home in New Zealand. After spending some time with the tapes I had sent, Baker even asked if I could lend him the originals so he could make superior copies. However, I would not even consider parting with them.

I remember my recording creating quite a buzz for a short time. Then life went on.

Eventually, Kokay completed *Songs of the Underground - Rolling Thunder Revue (a collector's guide to the Rolling Thunder Revue 1975-76)*, and it was posted online. [378] Here's what Kokay had to say about my recording:

"There is a (VG+) tape of almost all the full show ... This is a super tape and show. One of the best. Essential listening."

About six years ago (I think), someone posted recordings of The Night Of The Hurricane in two parts to a music sharing site - one with Dylan's performances, another with the other acts.

---

[377] http://www.boblinks.com/trade.html#trade, *Trader Lists*, Retrieved 11/27/2016

[378] http://www.bjorner.com/RTR%20Tour%20Guide%20Letter.pdf, *Songs of the Underground - A collection guide to the Rolling Thunder Revue 1975-1976*, Retrieved 11/27/2016

In the description section, there was information citing "Dan (sic) Peters" as the source for the second, non-Dylan segment. A friend of mine downloaded both parts and made a copy for me, not realizing that I was Dan, I mean Dave, Peters. It was amusing to see my 1975 recording made available for everybody to enjoy 30 years later.

Of course, now anyone can listen to the entire concert, because it's currently streaming over at *Wolfgang's Vault*. It doesn't have the extra flavor of Madison Square Garden vendors selling Coca Cola, but it's not a bad way to spend a few hours.

Fee, fi, fo, fum: The Bob Dylan - Muhammad Ali connection

January 16, 2012

Boxing legend Muhammad Ali was born Cassius Marcellus Clay, Jr., on January 17, 1942.

There are a few obvious connections between Ali and Bob Dylan, and others more obscure. For your entertainment, here's a match-up of the two icons.

Dylan and Ali both:

- changed their names.

- changed their religious affiliations.

- wrote poetry.

- loved boxing (Dylan has been known to practice the sport to keep in shape, and has been seen in the audience at matches).

- sang and recorded for Columbia Records.

- appeared at 1975's "Night Of The Hurricane" benefit concert at Madison Square Garden.

Dylan has performed numerous songs about the sport of boxing. He wrote the "topical" songs *Who Killed Davey Moore?* and *Hurricane,* and covered Warren Zevon's *Boom Boom Mancini* and Paul Simon's *The Boxer.*

Dylan sang about Clay in his 1964 song, *I Shall Be Free, No. 10,* writing in (and mocking?) the style of the boxer's famous poetic pronouncements, boasting he would *"clean (Clay) right out of his spleen."* [379]

When I went to see Dylan and The Band at Nassau Coliseum on January 29, 1974, the news of the day - besides Dylan's area concerts - was Ali defeating Smokin' Joe Frazier at Madison Square Garden the previous evening, the second of their three famous bouts.

Less than two years later, on December 8, 1975, it was my turn to see Ali - and Dylan - at Madison Square Garden. I was fortunate to witness (with binoculars) Ali speak at The Rolling Thunder Revue's "Night Of The Hurricane" concert to benefit imprisoned boxer Rubin "Hurricane" Carter.

He appeared after Joni Mitchell's set, introduced by WNJR's Bill Franklin:

"There are three types of great in the world. There's the great, the near-great, and the ingrate. Tonight I have 'The Greatest!' ... "

Ali received a hero's welcome. It started off well, joking that he expected cheers because he was *"The Greatest,"* and thanked the *"rock and roll"* crowd that *"had the connection and the complexion to get the protection."* Later, Ali interviewed Carter from prison on the phone. After a while, Ali started to lose the crowd when he brought out a "Mr. Sapier." When Ali introduced Tennessee attorney and entrepreneur John Jay Hooker as the *"next president of the United States,"* Ali was booed off the stage.

Later, Dylan joked from the stage, *"We're gonna do this song now for Mr. Albert Grossman. Hello Albert! Who won't be the next president, don't even want to be president!"*

Dylan and Ali were photographed backstage. Apparently the two got along, and Dylan did not *"knock him clean right out of his spleen."*

---

[379] http://bobdylan.com/songs/i-shall-be-free-no-10/ *I Shall Be Free No. 10, Another Side of Bob Dylan,* Bob Dylan, 1964, (Copyright © 1971 by Special Rider Music; renewed 1999 by Special Rider Music)

Beastie Boy Adam 'MCA' Yauch, dead at 47, and his connection to Bob Dylan

May 4, 2012

Founding member of the Beastie Boys, Adam Andrew Nathaniel Yauch, also known as "MCA," "Bloach," and "Nathanial Hörnblowér," died earlier today after a long battle with cancer. He was 47.

Dylan and the Beasties appeared to be mutual admirers. Early in their career, the Beasties mentioned they wanted to help Dylan out by getting him to wear a pair of Groucho Marx glasses, complete with fake nose and mustache. While this never occurred, Dylan has been referenced directly on at least four Beastie Boys tracks: *3-Minute Rule, Finger Lickin' Good, Don't Play No Game That I Can't Win*, and one unknown unreleased song. Here is the rundown:

3-Minute Rule, from the album *Paul's Boutique*, featured the following lyric: *"A lot of parents like to think I'm a villain, I'm just chillin' like Bob Dylan."*

Bob Dylan's original 1965 studio recording of *Just Like Tom Thumb's Blues* was sampled on the track *Finger Lickin' Good*, from the album *Check Your Head*. In the June 1992 issue of *Boston Rock*, Beastie Boy Michael "Mike D" Diamond revealed the cost of sampling Dylan: *"Seven hundred bucks, but he asked for two thousand dollars. I thought it was kind of fly that he asked for $2000.00, and I bartered Bob Dylan down. That's my proudest sampling deal."* [380]

When the album *Check Your Head* was re-released in 2009, the bonus disc featured a commentary track informing listeners that Dylan would appear on the upcoming Beastie Boys album, *Hot Sauce Committee, Pt. 1*. It turned out that it was actually scheduled to be included on *Hot Sauce Committee, Pt. 2*, and it was not a "collaboration," but a sample of Dylan talking about the Beasties on the *New York* episode of *Theme Time Radio Hour*. Host Bob Dylan played the Beasties' track *No Sleep 'Til Brooklyn*, from their debut, *Licensed To Ill*, on the show. In his introduction, he praised the trio's longevity, crediting their tough New York upbringing.

In a June 2009 interview in *Drowned In Sound*, [381] the Beasties discussed Dylan's role on the Hot Sauce Committee:

Ad-Rock: Bob Dylan is guesting on ... Pt 2. He talks about us. More of a spoken word thing...

MCA: We sampled his ass.

Mike D: He has a radio show on satellite and he was speaking about Beastie Boys...

Ad-Rock: He played one of our songs and was talking about us; he's a big fan ... Bob Dylan is one of the greatest songwriters of all time.

Hot Sauce Committee, Pt. 1 was originally scheduled to be released in September, 2009, while *Pt. 2* would follow later. The whole project was delayed, however, when Yauch announced, in July 2009, that he had cancer. Soon after, Yauch said he was *"hopeful"* after his surgery, which successfully removed a cancerous tumor from his left salivary gland. The albums and all tours were postponed.

Last year, the Beasties released an album called *Hot Sauce Committee Pt. 2*, which was expected to include the *Theme Time* sample. Instead, *Pt. 2* was a slightly altered version of the original *Pt. 1*. However, the Beasties do quote Dylan's *Subterranean Homesick Blues* in the song *Don't Play No Game That I Can't Win*. The original version of *Hot Sauce Committee Pt. 2* remains unreleased.

Bucky Baxter, who played over 700 shows with Dylan in the 1990s, also had a Beastie Boys connection. Baxter played on *Country Mike's Theme* and *Railroad Blues*, from 1999's Beastie Boys

---

[380] http://jaaam.com/post/41256648/seven-hundred-bucks-but-he-asked-for-two-thousand, From *Boston Rock*, 6/1992.

[381] http://drownedinsound.com/in_depth/4137232, *Interview - Boys Will Be Boys: Beastie Boys Talk Hot Sauce Committee Pt. 1*, Retrieved 11/27/2016

Anthology: *Sounds of Science*. The tracks originally appeared on a rare album called *Country Mike's Greatest Hits*. According to *Beastiemania*, [382] Baxter probably played pedal steel on every track of that album, plus fiddle on *Country Christmas*.

The first Beasties track that ever caught my attention was *Cookie Puss*, which became an instant classic at Boston's college radio stations. As the major label buyer at a New England music store chain, I watched their full-length debut, *Licenced To Ill*, become a best-seller in the Boston area, then spread out into the suburbs. *Licenced* sold unusually well in all three formats - LP, CD, and cassette. However, we eventually had to hide the cassettes behind the counter to avoid an unprecedented amount of shoplifting.

The Village Voice reviewed *Licenced* under the heading, *"Three Jerks Make A Masterpiece."* A rewritten version of the Beatles' *I'm Down* was initially planned for inclusion but could not overcome publishing/licensing issues.

Before experiencing the band in concert, I saw future Beastie Adam "Ad-Rock" Horovitz, son of the playwright Israel Horovitz, play with the Young and the Useless as a support act for Public Image Ltd., and can still remember smelling the shaving cream on their freshly shaved heads. A few years later, I saw the Beastie Boys at the Worcester Centrum with Public Enemy and Murphy's Law. The Beasties were as much fun in concert as they were on their album, even taking time to mock local big name acts like Boston and J. Geils, before mentioning the hardcore band SSD.

The Beasties have had their ups and downs, but eventually became elder statesmen in the world of hip-hop, and were inducted into the Rock and Roll Hall Of Fame on April 14. Yauch was too sick to attend the ceremony, but fellow Beasties Mike D and Ad-Rock accepted and read a speech that Yauch had written.

The ceremony was broadcast on HBO with the ending of the program altered due to the day's sad news:

An HBO spokesperson tells Billboard.com that the show's ending has been changed to include a photo of the rapper and musician - who passed away on Friday at the age of 47, following a nearly three-year battle with cancer - with text that reads "In Memory of Adam Yauch." The two-and-a-half-hour show had already been altered to include Levon Helm and Dick Clark during the In Memoriam section, even though both died during the week following the event.

For now, I have the yellow vinyl version of *Hello Nasty* on my turntable. Rest in peace, MCA.

---

[382] http://www.beastiemania.com/whois/baxter_bucky/, *Bucky Baxter*, Retrieved 1/25/2017

David Plentus, webmaster of Bob Dylan Cover site, dead at 55

January 31, 2011

David Plentus, webmaster of the *Dylan Cover* site, has apparently died in a fire, according to *Ojornal*. [383] Plentus lived in East Taunton, Massachusetts, with his older brother, John, who was away on vacation at the time.

Alan Fraser, webmaster of the Dylan rarities site, *Searching For A Gem*, sent me a link to the article, and confirmed that it was the same David Plentus that ran the *Dylan Cover* website. Fraser wrote, *"I found his site a valuable resource and he was a frequent contributor to my site. He'll be greatly missed and I hope the* Dylan Covers *site can be continued."*

Fraser's sentiment was echoed on his website: [384]

31 Jan 2010: I'm very sad to have heard from Bill Hester and Arie de Reus of the death of David Plentus, who died in a fire at his home in East Taunton, MA, on 19 Jan 2011. Dave was the webmaster of the Dylan Covers *site, which has proved a valuable resource for* Searching For A Gem.

Among the comments on the *DylanCovers.com* Facebook page: [385]

Friday: Has anybody heard from Dave in the last two weeks?

No. I have been wondering that myself! I hope he is ok and just taking a well-deserved vacation. I have never met him in person but consider him a friend and kindred spirit.

Me too, he's one of the kindest persons I know. What worries me is that he doesn't answer since more than a week. He's normally very quick in answering, and normally he would have left a "I'll be back soon" message ... I hope he's not seriously in trouble.

Today: It is with great sadness that I post this information - that David Plentus passed away two weeks ago - a tragic victim in a house fire at his home in Massachusetts. May Dave rest in peace.

. . . a huge loss to the Dylan community, our thoughts and love to his family. I will miss this guy immensely. His contribution to the Dylan community was immense, and he was one of the most friendly and responsible people I have known. My thoughts and love to him and his brother.

I'm sorry to read this...

RIP David. I just read on a link from Expecting Rain that David Plentus, the creator of DylanCover died in a fire on January 19th . . . DylanCover and all the associated links and blog has been a great source for over 10 years. He will be missed.

The last Facebook post by Plentus was on January 13.

I recently started incorporating links to Plentus' extensively researched and documented website into my *Bob Dylan Examiner* articles. On October 10, I contacted Plentus to inform him that a new Dave Stewart song co-written by Bob Dylan was being released. I also mentioned that I linked to the *Dylan Cover* website in a Solomon Burke article. The next day, Plentus replied that he had seen the link to the Stewart article on *Expecting Rain*, and had subscribed to my *Examiner* feed.

The fruits of Plentus' labor can been seen at *DylanCover.com*, which contains over 30,000 Dylan covers, now hosted by Karl Erik Andersen at *ExpectingRain.com*.

Plentus was obviously a diligent and hardworking Bob Dylan fan, and had many friends and admirers.

---

[383] http://my.ojornal.com/sports-news/east-taunton-fire-victim-identity-confirmed Dead Link.

[384] http://www.searchingforagem.com, *Searching For a Gem*, Retrieved 11/27/2016

[385] https://www.facebook.com/pages/DylanCovercom/107718325947876 Dead Link.

Don DeVito, Columbia Records A&R executive and Bob Dylan's producer, has died

November 26, 2011

Columbia Records A&R executive and record producer Don DeVito has died, according to a tweet by Peter Fletcher, President Of Plan R Marketing, and "favored" by Sony's Greg Linn: *"My Hero, Don Devito. A great record man RIP #columbiarecords".*

DeVito is most known to Bob Dylan fans for his production of the 1976 album, *Desire*. He also co-produced the live albums *Hard Rain* and *At Budokan*, was "Captain In Charge" (and behind the remix of the 1999 reissue) on the 1978 album *Street-Legal*, and produced the "concert audio" for The 30th Anniversary Concert Celebration. He also worked on various compilations and archival projects, and was thanked on the album, *Dylan & The Dead*. DeVito has even been described as Dylan's publicist.

Emmylou Harris has credited DeVito for enlisting her on the *Desire* sessions. DeVito was a friend of Mary Martin, who among other things, suggested Bob Dylan check out The Hawks (later The Band):

"There was a fellow at Columbia that was a fan, who was like an executive producer, and I think Dylan told him 'I need a girl singer.' Don DeVito was his name and I got a call that Dylan wants you to sing, but that wasn't true because he just wanted a girl singer." [386]

In addition to his work with Dylan, DeVito produced, executive produced, or remixed recordings by Aerosmith, Carole King, Goo Goo Dolls, Tony Bennett, The Byrds, Ron Wood, Mott The Hoople, and many others. He has also worked with Bruce Springsteen, James Taylor, and Pink Floyd.

---

[386] http://www.gibson.com/News-Lifestyle/Features/en-us/emmylou-harris-0709.aspx, *The Gibson Interview — Emmylou Harris. The music legend discusses her signature guitar, her activism and her collaborations with Bob Dylan and Gram Parson*, Retrieved 11/27/2016

Don Kirshner accepted 'Rocky' award on behalf of Bob Dylan

January 18, 2011

Don Kirshner, known as "The Man With the Golden Ear," is dead at the age of 76.

Kirshner had a long and varied career, beginning in the 1950s as a co-owner of Aldon Music Publishing (Carole King, Gerry Goffin, Neil Sedaka). He went on to promote the careers of other acts (Neil Diamond, Bobby Darin), and run his own record labels (The Archies, Kansas). Kirshner is probably best known for producing early records by The Monkees, and hosting his own musical variety program, *Don Kirshner's Rock Concert*.

In the mid-1970s, [387] Kirshner tried to go up against the Grammy Awards with his own "Rock Music Award Show." The goal was to reward critically-acclaimed artists that Kirshner felt were routinely snubbed by the mainstream Grammys. However, the show has largely been lost to history. It appears to have been panned by critics, [388] and ran for only three years. At the time of writing, I can not find an official listing, but there is evidence that "Rocky" awards were presented to Linda Ronstadt, Dan Fogelberg, The Eagles, Bad Company, Stevie Wonder, Randy Newman, and Bob Dylan.

Dylan's 1975 release, *Blood On The Tracks*, was awarded a "Rocky" for "Album Of The Year." When the award was announced, Dylan was not present, so Kirshner revealed that Dylan suggested Don himself accept the award on Bob's behalf.

---

[387] http://vintagetourjackets.blogspot.com/2010/11/don-kirshners-rocky-awards-1977.html, *Don Kirshner's Rocky Awards 1977*.

[388] http://www.superseventies.com/sdmc_81_Sep_76.html, *Seventies Daily Music Chronicle*, September 1976, (Saturday, September 18)

Stax bassist Donald 'Duck' Dunn dead at 70, his connections to Bob Dylan

May 14, 2012

Donald "Duck" Dunn, legendary bassist for Stax Records, Booker T. & the M.G.'s, The Blues Brothers, and countless sessions, died yesterday in his sleep while on tour in Tokyo. He was 70-years-old.

His many accomplishments can be found elsewhere. For the purpose of this article, however, I will focus on his connections to Bob Dylan.

Dunn twice played with Dylan. The first time was 31 years ago tomorrow, when Dunn was the bassist at the final recordings for Dylan's *Shot Of Love* album. The information from the session follows, courtesy of Olof Bjorner's *Still On The Road*: [389]

Clover Recorders

Los Angeles, California

15 May 1981

Shot Of Love recording session # 16. Produced by Chuck Plotkin and Bob Dylan.

1. *Minute By Minute* (Sam & Dave)

2. *Heart Of Mine*

3. *Instrumental*

4. *Instrumental*

5-7. *Heart Of Mine*

8. *Glory Of Love*

9-11. *Heart Of Mine*

12-14. *Watered-Down Love*

15. *In A Battle*

16-21. *Watered-Down Love*

22. *Mystery Train* (Sam Phillips - Herman Parker)

Dylan (vocal & guitar), Fred Tackett (guitar), Danny Kortchmar (guitar), Willie Smith (keyboards), Donald Dunn (bass), Ringo Starr (drums), Jim Keltner (drums), Carolyn Dennis & Madelyn Quebec (backing vocals). The site also states the track was *"overdubbed 15 and 16 June 1981 with Jim Keltner on drums and Tim Drummond on bass."*

The song *Heart Of Mine* (#11) was included on *Shot Of Love* and released as a single. The liner notes on the inner sleeve of the original album lists Bob Dylan (vocals and guitar), Clydie King ("2nd vocal"), Jim Keltner and Chuck Plotkin (drums), Donald "Duck" Dunn (bass), Wm. "Smithy" Smith (organ), Ron Wood (guitar), and Ringo Starr (tom tom).

Dunn later appeared with Booker T. & the M.G.'s as the house band for the Bob Dylan 30th Anniversary Concert Celebration at New York's Madison Square Garden on October 16, 1992. For the finale, G.E. Smith, Al Kooper, Stan Lynch, Jim Keltner, and the M.G.'s (Booker T. Jones, Steve Cropper, Dunn, and Anton Fig) backed Dylan, Neil Young, Eric Clapton, Tom Petty, Roger McGuinn, and George Harrison on *My Back Pages*, and then Dylan and the entire crew on *Knockin' On Heaven's Door*. Footage of rehearsals was added to the 2014 expanded Blu-ray/DVD version.

---

[389] http://www.bjorner.com/still.htm, *Still on the Road*, Retrieved 11/27/2016

Solomon Burke, dead at 70, covered Bob Dylan's *Stepchild*

October 10, 2010

According to various sources, soul legend Solomon Burke died today in the Netherlands. He was 70-years-old.

Burke was inducted into the Rock and Roll Hall of Fame in 2001.

Bob Dylan played some of Burke's songs on *Theme Time Radio Hour*, including *Home In Your Heart* and *Cry To Me*. The latter was a hit twice - in the 1960s and again when it was featured on the soundtrack of the 1980's film, *Dirty Dancing*. In Dylan's introduction to Burke's *Cry To Me* on his *Theme Time Radio Hour "Tears"* program, he mentioned all of his kids (21), grandkids (64), and great-grandkids (8), which explained why he was crying.

Burke recorded Dylan's rare song *Stepchild* in 2002. According to *Searching For A Gem*, [390] via Tim Dunn and his book *The Bob Dylan Copyright Files 1962-2007*): [391]

Copyrighted from a live performance at Oakland, CA, 13 Nov 1978, and performed several times in late 1978 - no studio version is listed by Krogsgaard. Also known as AM I NOT YOUR STEPCHILD? And YOU TREAT ME LIKE A STEPCHILD. Covered by Solomon Burke on his album Don't Give Up On Me *(Fat Possum Records, July 2002, . . . this version has amended lyrics mentioning Bob). Helena Springs has implied in an interview that she co-wrote this song, but the copyright records do not list her involvement.*

He also recorded Dylan's *Maggie's Farm* in 1965, *The Mighty Quinn* (1970, unreleased until 2000 CD *Proud Mary: The Bell Sessions*), and *What Good Am I?* on his 2005 album, *Make Do With What You Got*.

---

[390] http://www.searchingforagem.com/Starlight/BobUnrelS.htm, *"Starlight In The East" - Directory of Bob Dylan's Unreleased Songs: S*, Compiled by Alan Fraser, Retrieved 11/27/2016

[391] *The Bob Dylan Copyright files 1962-2007*, Tim Dunn, AuthorHouse, Bloomington, IN, 2008

Interview with 12-year-old who got Bob Dylan's autograph at The Ryman

August 14, 2011

When Bob Dylan played The Ryman Auditorium on August 1, he did the unthinkable - he autographed the harmonica of a 12-year-old boy standing in the front row.

The boy in question was Dylan Thomas May, named not after the Welsh poet, but two members of the Traveling Wilburys.

His mother, Kerry, had always wanted to take her son to see Bob Dylan when he was old enough, but did not hear about the concert at The Ryman until it had already sold out.

After many negotiations, dramas, and financial transactions, Kerry was able to obtain front row seats for the show.

Before leaving for the concert, young Dylan picked out one of his harmonicas to bring to the show - a 1937 Hohner. It had belonged to his grandfather, who had died three years before. Despite the odds, he hoped to get it autographed by Bob Dylan.

While biding their time between picking up the tickets and the start of the show, the family waited in the alley to the left of The Ryman, hoping to see a glimpse of Dylan entering the venue. While that didn't happen, the lucky young Dylan was able to get guitarist Charlie Sexton and bassist Tony Garnier to autograph his T-shirt.

All night, things kept going Dylan's way, as one of Leon Russell's guitarists (either Chris Simmons or Beau Charron) threw the boy his guitar pick, and drummer Brandon Holder walked over and handed him his pre-signed drumstick.

During the encore, after *Blowin' In The Wind*, young Dylan waved the harmonica and a Sharpie, yelling, *"Bob, please!"* As the band was leaving, the elder Dylan walked toward the microphone, paused, then went up to the boy, took the Sharpie and harmonica and, without saying a word or making eye-contact, signed the instrument.

I spoke to May on the phone a few days after the show. He was a very nice, polite, and articulate young man, and appeared to be wise beyond his years. Here's what he had to say:

So, you've had a very exciting week!

Yup.

How did you get into Bob Dylan?

Well, I've listened to his music as long as I can remember, so I automatically liked it.

Any favorites?

Yeah, Forever Young, Tangled Up In Blue.

Have you ever been to a rock concert before?

This was my first.

Did you sense Bob Dylan was looking at you during the show?

Oh yeah - The whole time! My mom told me that everyone wants to think (the performer) is looking at you, but he was staring straight at me the whole time. When he was in front of me, he would be singing, he'd pause, look around, then when he stopped, he'd look at me again.

Where do you keep the harmonica?

Well, we're hoping to get a glass case to put it in, and a picture of him signing it. It's in my room. I look at it a lot.

Did your mom make you go to sleep after the show, or did you stay up late?

Well, we got home, we were tired but still very excited. My mom and I stayed up and talked about the show and getting the autograph until it was almost daylight and we couldn't figure out whether the harmonica case should be opened or closed. We were afraid it would rub the autograph off if we closed it. We closed it and kept checking it!

Are you a celebrity in school? Do the other kids even know who Bob Dylan is?

Just me ... I don't even think they know his name, so I didn't even go there. My teachers know who he is. They think it is great! Some of them knew it before I told them. The story spread fast!

How do you listen to music, and who do you like?

On my computer, CDs. I've liked classical music ever since I first heard it in (the school) band, Bob Dylan, Johnny Cash, Elvis. I was even Johnny Cash for Halloween last year. I don't like new music.

You must have heard of Bob Dylan's Buddy Holly quote by now. (See Buddy Holly chapter.) Do you know who he was?

Yeah, we had just watched (the movie) La Bamba *a few months ago.* (The story of Ritchie Valens, who went down in the same plane that killed Holly and "The Big Bopper.")

I watched a video of you playing *Nearer My God To Thee* on piano and harmonica. What instruments do you play?

I play French horn, piano, trumpet, and harmonica. I tried harmonica before, but not seriously. After the concert, I was gonna record myself on the piano only, to put it on YouTube. I just started to play it on the harmonica while my mom went out shopping, and it sounded really good. So I wanted to play both, but I only have two hands! So we went to Sam Ash and got one of the harmonica holders you put around your neck. I made up the harmonica part to that song in an hour! Actually, you can see the (signed) *harmonica in the* Nearer My God To Thee *video, on top of the piano.*

In the video of your Tchaikovsky French horn recital, I noticed you'd only been playing for a few months by that time. How much do you practice? Does it seem like fun, or is it hard work?

Well, I go in early every day to school. On a normal day, I usually practice 45 minutes to an hour before school, and I usually stay after about one-and-a-half, two hours. Then I practice when I get home. I often practice seven hours a day - I think it's fun!

So what would you like to be when you grow up?

As of right now, I'd like to play for a classical music orchestra.

Was there anything about the show that you wish had happened?

The only other thing I have to say - the only thing a little bit disappointing was that I'd like to have a conversation with (Bob Dylan) *about music. But I'd heard that he doesn't really do that.*

Close encounters of the Dylan kind

Anneke Derksen is a self-employed professional writer, editor and proofreader working on a freelance basis for Reed Elsevier. She also is a Gestalt Therapist, but closed her practice when she moved from Holland to Belgium. Anneke currently lives in Antwerp, Belgium. She met her husband, Hans Derksen, while waiting in line for a Bob Dylan concert, and they married on the fifth day of May in 1999. They are both devoted collectors and maintain the website *Another Site of Bob Dylan*.

Derksen met Dylan on more than one occasion. Here's her story of one encounter in Dunkirk, France, in 1992, courtesy of the author.

On June 30, 1992 my sister and I drove from Holland to Dunkirk, France, to attend a Bob Dylan concert there that night. While waiting for the doors of the venue, the Kursaal, to open we decided to take a walk down the boulevard when someone suddenly grabbed me from behind by the shoulders and hissed in my ear that I "get rid of that guy." I turned my head and looked straight into the eyes of an angry Bob Dylan.

A young Belgian man was following Bob, taking pictures as he walked down the Dunkirk streets. Bob must have thought the man was with us.

I told Bob that I didn't know the man and while we were speaking, the man took yet another picture. I kindly asked the man to stop and without a word he disappeared.

Bob apologized for bothering me and asked me to have a drink with him.

We walked a few minutes to the café Espadrilles followed by my sister who asked Bob for his autograph, which he hesitantly gave, though he seemed a bit miffed by the request.

While in the café, Bob was looking around a bit nervously, because the place was filled with fans from England, France and Belgium, waiting for the concert, but they did behave very well and didn't bother us in any way although they kept staring at us with open mouths.

Bob and I chatted for about 15 to 20 minutes over a cup of coffee about what happened in Dunkirk during WWII, we talked about Holland and the tulips and we had a more serious talk about the differences between being Jewish in the US and being Jewish in Europe (the past is close behind) and he couldn't take his eyes off the Chai pendant, mounted in a horseshoe, around my neck. I also drew a map on a napkin to show him in which part of France he was and where I lived. He made an effort to put his signature on the napkin but to my bewilderment the pen didn't co-operate. I suggested to get my sister's pen who was sitting at another table but he waved it away saying "Why, it's not that important."

I even got the nerve to ask him to do a better job that evening than he had in Utrecht a year before when he appeared to be drunk on stage. He laughed out loud, telling me he remembered.

As I realized that he wasn't walking the streets of Dunkirk solely to hang out with me I stood up from the table and I said goodbye. He stood, looked me straight in the eyes, and said, "You know, I really like you." Then he kissed both my hands and bid me farewell and disappeared through a side door in the back of the café.

After Bob left, all hell broke loose in the café. The fans who have been sitting there watching us chatting surrounded me and started to ask all kinds of questions like what brand of cigarettes did he smoke, did he have milk and/or sugar in his coffee, what were you talking about etc. etc. When my sister and I arrived at the Kursaal we were welcomed with a big round of applause. The story already had run ahead of us and had reached the people who were waiting in front of the doors.

I must admit that it took me several weeks to get over it. I was so overwhelmed when I realized what happened that I don't remember anything of the concert that evening. (The Girl On The Greenbriar Shore, on Tell Tale Signs, was taken from this show - HL.) In fact, I don't even remember how I got home driving my car from France to Holland that night.

Even after all these years, with a picture of the encounter prominently hanging on my wall, I still cannot believe that this really happened, especially because I know that Mr. Dylan is a very private man.

Derksen briefly met Dylan more recently in October, 2011. Here's her story:

Better than alchemy. I did it again.

Coincidentally meeting Bob Dylan three times in twenty years in Europe is just unbelievable. Maybe "coincidence" is not the right term. This time, it had more to do with strategy.

On the evening of October 18, in the lobby of an Antwerp hotel, I met Bob Dylan for a third time. Claude Boni, the French artist who makes Bob Dylan collages, drawings and paintings, stayed with us so we could all attend the Antwerp show together. Claude arrived earlier in the day, and in the evening we decided to go into town, just the two of us.

On the "Groenplaats," a square in the heart of the city with a big statue of Rubens in the center, some student event was in progress. I think they were being "hazed." While we were observing the activities, we noticed two men standing next to us. One was a big guy and the other one was smaller, and dressed up like a hobo. I immediately saw that the big guy was Baron, his bodyguard, and deduced that "the hobo" had to be Bob Dylan!

I took a quick look and yes, it was unmistakably Bob's profile. Because nothing special was happening except these students making noise, both men stopped watching and left. I told Claude that we had just stood next to Bob Dylan, but she didn't believe me. As we looked at them walking away, I noticed that they were heading for the side entrance of the hotel. To see them again, my strategy was to enter through the front, walk through the restaurant and into the lobby, so that we had to cross paths.

And so it went.

Claude still didn't believe me. She was hesitant and didn't follow close enough to be with me when I "coincidentally" bumped into Bob and Baron. I put on my highly "surprised" face, and walked right up to Bob, saying, "Hey, Mister Dylan ... Great to see you again, and now in my hometown. It's been a long time since I saw you." He looked surprised, put out his hand to shake mine and mumbled something like "Hey, hello there." I told him of our "coffee" in Dunkirk and he said, "Yes, I think I remember." Of course he probably didn't, but it was very polite of him to act as if he did. He leaned his head in so that his face was close to mine, and there was something like a kiss in the air or a rub on my cheek. Then I said, "It was nice meeting you again. I will leave you now. Have a good night."

The entire exchange lasted only 10 seconds or something. All the while that Baron character was looking at me as if he wanted to kill. Maybe he was angry at himself because he failed to protect Bob from a harmless fan. There was nobody there who took any notice of the hobo with his guard, and I'm sure that nobody knew who he was. Even Claude didn't believe that it was Bob until I was speaking with him and she could see his face.

After this "coincidental" encounter, they walked toward the hotel rooms. I was very happy that I again managed to talk with Bob, but was now in need of a cigarette, so we decided to go for a smoke. On our way out, we saw the band members having supper in the restaurant. Once outside, we saw Dylan manager Jeff Kramer already smoking a cigarette. That was a great opportunity to start a conversation about the "non-smoking mafia" in the U.S. and Europe. We had a lot of fun, and after we were done with our cigarettes, we all went back in and had a good time with Stu, Charlie, and Tony from Dylan's band, along with Kramer and a very nice woman (identity unknown).

As all my friends know, I'm no longer that eager to go to see Bob in concert, but I have to admit that the Antwerp show was 100% better than the last one I saw in Amsterdam two years ago. I thought the band was fresh, strong and enthusiastic. My thoughts on Dylan's voice and his stupid organ, however, are not quite as positive. I know a lot of fans disagree, but in my opinion his voice is worn out, broken. It sounds like he's doing some kind of alternative rap.

And to come back to Baron. During the final song of the Antwerp show, a big guy jumped on stage and Baron captured him and dragged him away, like he was a feather. This Baron guy must be very strong, like a Kung Fu fighter.

Bucks Burnett on his Eight Track Museum, meeting Dylan, buying his harmonica, and managing Tiny Tim

Bucks Burnett is opening The Eight Track Museum in Texas, [392] which will include a display of the harmonica Bob Dylan threw to a young woman in the audience in 1978.

Here's the press release:

The Eight Track Museum of Dallas, Texas has acquired Bob Dylan's stage harmonica, used at his Ft. Worth performance on Nov. 24, 1978, during his Street Legal tour.

"I was sitting second-row center, and saw Bob throw the harmonica to a girl I knew in the front row, Linda Williams, during Blowin' In The Wind," *explains Bucks. "It was quite a moment. All of us gasped."*

Linda Williams gave the harmonica to her date, Dallas music writer Tim Schuller, who kept the harmonica for 32 years. Burnett and Schuller met in 1977 when they both worked at Peaches Records in Dallas.

Says Burnett, "I've wanted this harmonica ever since that night when Bob threw it to Linda. I'm grateful to Tim for selling it to The Eight Track Museum, and looking forward to giving it a home where people can see it."

I contacted Burnett, and asked him a few questions about the museum, the harmonica, meeting Dylan, and managing Tiny Tim. Here are his responses:

Who is Bucks Burnett?

I am a 51-year-old Dallasite. I write and record music (guitar, lyrics, vocals), produce albums, including Tiny Tim's last album Girl (1996), *and am also a writer and graphic artist. My new band Rachel Bazooka just released a debut album on 3 formats.*

Tell me about the Eight Track Museum.

The Eight Track Museum, which was featured on the front page of The Wall Street Journal *in March,* [393] *fulfills two dreams; sharing my love of all music formats with the world, and getting my 8-tracks out of the garage. It will be in Deep Ellum, the area of Dallas where Robert Johnson recorded some of his music. Street address not confirmed - a space has been chosen, I expect to sign a lease in about a month - just don't want to reveal the exact location before the lease is signed. (There are) 3,000 8-tracks plus assorted other formats/objects, including a dental mold of Tiny Tim's teeth.*

Dylan 8-tracks pre '75 are fairly hard to locate, even on Ebay. But I collect all formats, and recently obtained a sealed first run stereo LP of Blonde On Blonde *with a sticker that reads "Bob Dylan's Amazing New Album" ... I have several complete 8-track collections of many artists, but not Bob. Dylan collectors should note that CBS used red plastic on their 8-track cartridges through 1975 before switching to gray, so a* Blood On The Tracks *8-track was on red plastic only briefly. I also have some Dylan 4-track tapes made with green plastic - much harder to find than the 8's.*

Oh, and through a friend, I got Milton Glaser to sign the greatest hits poster to me a year ago!

I also have a lot of white label promo LPs, but do not consider my collection significant - yet. Too overwhelming a concept!

What's the story behind acquiring Bob Dylan's harmonica?

I first saw Dylan live on Nov. 24, 1978 in Ft. Worth. I went with a bunch of coworkers from Peaches Records. Since our store sold concert tickets, we were not above grabbing all the best seats for ourselves. So we were all in the center of the first few rows. In the front row were the beautiful Linda Williams and a Dallas writer Tim Schuller. During Blowing In The Wind, *Bob smiled at Linda and gracefully leaned over and dropped the harmonica to her.*

---

[392] Closed, for now.

[393] http://www.wsj.com/articles/SB10001424052748704754604575095310056590490, *Play It Again: Promoter Has One-Track Mind About Eight Tracks. Tiny Tim's Former Manager Hopes to Open Museum for Obsolete Music Format,* Retrieved 11/27/2016

She kindly gave it to Tim for taking her to the gig, and Tim kept it in a drawer for 32 years. Every 2 or 3 years, I would ask Tim if he would sell the harmonica. Last week, I finally convinced Tim to sell it to me, for display in The Eight Track Museum. There is a white piece of tape on it with the letter C to indicate the key - have not authenticated the handwriting yet - may just be a stagehand's writing. Might be Bob's. The harmonica has not been played since.

I found a setlist online which shows that he did play the song, about a week ago - don't have the link, but Google his name, date 11-24-78, Ft. Worth, and you can probably find it, along with a photo of him playing harmonica at that same gig. He played the harmonica part, threw it down gently to Linda right away (she was a stunning girl - like Patti Smith cast as Cleopatra), and finished the song, so it was during, not after, the song. We are all sure he threw it deliberately to her, as opposed to just tossing it in the crowd.

While there is the possibility of error regarding the song, I'm pretty sure it was Blowin' In The Wind.

How did you meet Bob Dylan?

It was January 26, 1976, I believe - I was trying to meet Joni Mitchell at her sound check in Dallas at 4 p.m. (the day following the Rolling Thunder Revue's "Night Of The Hurricane 2" at Houston's Astrodome). Sadly I did not see the "Night Of The Hurricane" show - I was in high school, I think it was on a weeknight. I was 17.

A limo pulled up, and out stepped Kinky Friedman and Bob Dylan. I said, "Hey Bob," expecting him to ignore me. He literally spun around on the heel of his boots and said, "What's up?" I offered to give him some money for Hurricane Carter (Bob had just held the all-star benefit in Houston the night before). He casually explained that he was not allowed to accept any money, that it would look bad. I asked where I could mail it and he rattled off the address, and asked "Got it?" I repeated it back to him and he grinned real big. They got back in the limo and then Bob got back out and came back over to me and said, "Hey man - anything else?" I said "Are you playing with Joni tonight?" He said, "I don't think so - we just played last night - just gonna watch the show. Anything else?" "No," I said, "just have a great time in Dallas." He smiled and said "Okay!" and got back in the limo. He looked like he had just stepped off the Desire *cover - same clothes, scarf, hat. Was it luck or was it fate? A simple twist.*

At Joni's show at the Dallas Convention Center, she pointed Dylan out as "a famous friend of mine," to much applause, but he did not play.

I met her after the show and asked to for an autograph and she said "What should I write?" I said, "Anything." So she wrote "Anything, Joni Mitchell." A banner day!

(Side note: Dylan showed up at Joni's show in Austin on the 28th. He duetted on *Both Sides Now*, and performed a solo version of *Girl From The North Country*.)

What about your other interests?

Too many things interest me. Led Zeppelin, Tiny Tim, meeting my heroes, Kubrick... obsessed with everything but cooking, war and sports. I managed Tiny for 14 years until his death, producing records, booking his Texas gigs, running his fan club, etc. By the way, I gave Dylan's manager Jeff Kramer in 2007 a copy of the Tiny CD Girl *for Bob, which he later confirmed he passed to Bob. Then Bob mentioned* Brave Combo *and Tiny's music when promoting his Christmas album.*

What was it like producing Tiny Tim's album, *Girl*?

It was a labor of love - we really tried to help Tiny make a more legit record, having no idea it would be his last. It took 7 years to complete due to complications.

This dental mold of Tiny's teeth was made a few months before he died in 1996, for planned dental surgery. His widow, Sue Khaury, gave it to a fan, who eventually put it on Ebay. It was purchased for me as a gift to the Museum, by my friend Randy Reeves, who paid the "buy it now" price of $1500. And yes, I am going to take a picture of the harmonica holding the teeth at some point, thus symbolizing the unity of Bob and Tiny.

Eyewitness account of Bob Dylan's exclusive Legion D'Honneur ceremony

November, 2013

Last week, Bob Dylan was in Paris to receive an award, d'officier de L'Ordre de la Légion d'honneur. Danielle Labadie, professeur d'Anglais at Education Nationale France, posted on Facebook she was one of the lucky few to attend the ceremony. I contacted her, and she sent this exclusive report.

During the fall, 2013, segment of his "Never Ending Tour," Bob Dylan was scheduled to perform shows at the Grand Rex in Paris on the 12th, 13th, and 14th of November. While in the area, he was presented la Legion D'Honneur, the highest decoration in France, at the Culture Ministry, 3 rue de Valois, Paris, 1er, by French Minister Aurelie Filippetti, on the 13th at 2 p.m.

I was there at this special and historic ceremony, and so happy to have this privilege. I had previously written a long letter to our minister, explaining my work as an English teacher in a Parisian high school, where I introduced Bob Dylan's songs, music, and poetry to my students, who usually responded with great interest, care, and attention. I followed up and continued to make a case to show my deep commitment. After many calls, emails, and discussions, I was eventually, and unexpectedly, invited to attend this momentous ceremony. I am at a loss of words to express how happy and enthusiastic I was! It would be quite a week, as I also bought front row tickets to all three Paris shows.

I arrived at the Culture Ministry just before 2 p.m. There were not many in attendance, maybe about 50 people, I would say. I felt honored and privileged to be among the happy few. The ceremony took place on the first floor, in the huge, 18th century styled Salon de Reception. It was requested we wait a few minutes before entering this beautiful and historic place, as Mr. Dylan had only just arrived.

As we entered, I had no idea what to expect. I was surprised to discover there were no seats at all, that everybody had to stand, including Mr. Dylan and the minister. So we all stood behind a rope barrier that separated us from the small stage where Bob Dylan and Aurelie Filippetti would appear.

After waiting a few moments, there was an announcement, and Mr. Dylan and our minister entered through a door at the back of the room. While Ms Filippetti gave her speech in French, an interpreter, standing behind Mr. Dylan, apparently whispered the translation into his ear.

Ms Filippetti's speech referenced Mr. Dylan's unique career and personality, as well as his artwork, and special sense of humanity and commitment. She then pinned the medal on Mr. Dylan's jacket, and congratulated him.

An official picture was taken, along with a few others, by the official photographer, the only one allowed at the ceremony. Indeed, I had heard Mr. Dylan requested that he be excused from interacting with the press at all.

Before his quick exit, Mr. Dylan, who looked somewhat uncomfortable and rather shy, said a few words as the minister turned the microphone toward him: "Thank you, I am both humble and proud." There was a pause of a second or two, with everybody listening intently, waiting for the rest of his speech, so Mr. Dylan added, "That's all." Everybody applauded, then Mr. Dylan disappeared quickly, exiting through the same door through which he entered.

There was a cocktail reception after the ceremony, but unfortunately Mr. Dylan had already left. I was very happy and moved to attend this fantastic event, but I had just one regret. I hoped to give Mr. Dylan a book, along with a little note I had written for him. That was impossible, even though he was just two meters in front of me.

First-hand report on Bob Dylan's *Mood Swings* exhibit preview

November 15, 2013

This morning, John A. Baldwin wrote in his *Desolation Row Information Service* bulletin he attended a preview of Bob Dylan's newest art exhibit, *Mood Swings*, at the Halcyon Gallery website. He has kindly permitted me to reprint a slightly edited version of his review here:

Thursday, November 14, was the press day for the exhibition at the Halcyon plus for a small group of individuals who were given private guided tours of about an hour's duration. For some reason, I was one of the lucky ones to have a private tour in the morning. The entire gallery was buzzing with camera crews from all over Europe and reporters in interview with gallery management. Other than that general organized chaos, what struck me immediately on walking through the door was the enormity and beauty of the exhibition. I'd gone along expecting to be disappointed but I was awestruck ... to the extent that when my appointed salesman came over, I couldn't speak for a short while because I was simply lost for words.

The gates, of which there are eight, some single, some double, form the centerpiece of the exhibition, but there are also four tables and a number of metal wall ornaments. All were based on the same theme - carefully chosen, reworked and positioned scrap metal that tells a story - in true "Dylan sense," any story you want it to be. Look at the detail and you cannot but be impressed with the little added extras: The birds here, the guitar there, the musical notes, the skate, the mincer, the spurs, cog wheels, pistons, etc., all lovingly turned into works of art. There was nothing in the metalwork section that I didn't like; there was nothing that I did not want to take home with me, if only I could afford it.

Move downstairs to see the gangster car doors, each with a poster detailing the life and times of a particular hoodlum such as Pretty Boy Floyd or Machine Gun Kelly and each has been riddled with bullet holes in the metalwork and glass by Mr. D. in person, and touched up with paint or artificial rust to give it a particular feel ... inspired.

In the same room you'll find the Revisionist paintings, but they are mainly different from the ones exhibited in NYC and, in my opinion, more amusing, more pithy and more of a piss-take on modern society. One is particularly rude, involving an almost naked lady with legs wide open; this is meant to be an attack on the mad state of the art market (but I'll spoil your fun if I tell you how).

Go up to the top floor and see some original Drawn Blanks *and the new* Train Tracks *range – Spare Tracks – which are a disappointment. There are only three on display out of the 320-odd available. They are all orange and all have added original artwork by Dylan, with some clouds and extra details on the track sidings, etc. They are all very slightly different and, because Mr. D. has spent a few minutes adding some extra detail to make it almost a one-off, you pay £25,000.*

Turn your back on them and look to the other side of the room – or perhaps you notice it as soon as you walk in – there is the biggest Train Tracks *you've ever seen, the biggest Bob has ever done, some 12 foot by 8 foot (or at least that's what it seemed to be to me), landscape rather than portrait, far more colour, far more detail, far more vibrant, far more expensive. Look out for the glass around the stairwells on which they've etched copies of Bob's paintings ... very effective.*

There is a catalogue of the metalwork aspect of the exhibition that is available at the desk. I think it was £40 or £45 but I'm pleased to say that I got mine for free. Also, look out for the special limited edition giant, luxury, Drawn Blank *catalogue. They weren't available for sale on the day but I've ordered my copy.*

I honestly cannot believe that you won't enjoy this exhibition thoroughly. Oh, and people were buying and quite a few pieces were sold that very morning. I was standing in front of my favourite piece (cost £145,000) and someone walked over and said, "Sorry, you can't have it. I've just bought it." He came all the way over from the Carolinas for it and told me that the gallery manager had informed him that one of our royal princes (he couldn't remember who) had ordered a gate on commission from Bob as a present for her Maj or, more likely, Prince Charles, and that Bob was supposed to be popping along to Buck House whilst he's in London. [394]

---

[394] Courtesy John A. Baldwin, Personal Correspondence, 11/24/2016

Confirmed: Bob Dylan played Rutgers University on February 10, 1965

February 9, 2013

It had bothered Michael Perlin for years.

Perlin attended Rutgers University in New Brunswick, New Jersey, class of '66. While there, he remembered seeing Bob Dylan give a concert in the school's gymnasium. However, in all the literature and web pages devoted to the famously documented singer-songwriter, there was no evidence this show had ever taken place.

The only clue was to be found on page 24 of the 1999 book, *Early Dylan* (Bulfinch Press). There's a photograph taken by Daniel Kramer of Johnny Cash backstage with Dylan at a *"concert in New Brunswick, New Jersey, in February."*

Perlin had previously seen Dylan perform numerous times: at Gerde's Folk City in May, 1963 (*"The night before my Political Science 102 exam"*), where Dylan thanked him for the quarter he dropped into the folk singer's hat; [395] the historic March On Washington later that year in August; and the legendary Halloween concert of 1964, officially released on CD in 2004. (He also has a memory of seeing Dylan perform at a Johnson-for-President rally in Madison Square Garden around that time, although he has not found any corroborating evidence so far.)

The Rutgers show itself, however, had remained a mystery. In those days, it was unusual for a rock, pop, or folk music concert to receive much attention from the mainstream press. It would be a year or two before the burgeoning underground scene began reporting such events with the reverence we take for granted today.

"This has been on my mind for a long, long time," Perlin told me. *"I became editor of the* Rutgers Daily Targum *in February 1965, and recalled it was right around the time of the show. I was sure that I had written a review, but there was no record of it."* He continued, *"In 2005, I wrote a letter to the* Rutgers Alumni Monthly *asking whether others had recollections. In response, I received many letters ... but still, no documentary evidence. I put the idea aside, figuring I would come back to it one day in the future. Soon after that, I received a copy of a review that had appeared in the* Douglass Caellian, *but it was so lacking of detail, that I felt I needed more before I could 'go public.'"*

"At some point over the next couple of years, I contacted the then-editors of the Rutgers paper, *but was told, if I recall correctly, that no issues could be found discussing the concert. Paper archives back then, of course, were not perfect. In 2010, there was a reunion of editors of the* Targum *and the* Douglass Caellian *(at that time, Rutgers was all-male, and Douglass all-female, and there were two separate newspapers published) spanning a seven year period. At that point, I mentioned this quest to someone, and one of the attendees recalled the* Caellian *review. But again, that review was so empty that I decided to wait until I had more.*

"In November, 2010, in line for a Bob Dylan concert at Terminal 5 in New York, I struck up a conversation with the woman behind me, who was also at the Rutgers concert. Coincidentally, her home town, Middletown, New Jersey, was the same as my friend Hank Wallace, who also attended the show with me. That again reminded me to try to do something.

"A couple of months ago, I received an email from a historian at Rutgers who was writing a book about Rutgers and student activism in the 1960s, and was trying to track down something entirely different in Targum *that I had written at about the same time. When he and I started corresponding, I asked about the concert. The historian, Paul Clemens,* [396] *then sent me what I sent you* [copies of old newspaper clippings]. *The timeline is this: The concert was February 10. I coincidently became editor-in-chief on the 12th. I know copies of the February 13 issue of* Targum *exists. But there is no record of any surviving issues from February 11 or 12 anywhere. The review was in one of those, I am sure."*

---

[395] *Another Side of Bob Dylan*, Nick Paumgarten, The New Yorker, 11/18/2002

[396] http://fas-history.rutgers.edu/clemens, *Paul G.E. Clemens*, Retrieved 11/27/2016

After years of inquiries, Perlin has finally been able to secure documentation of Dylan's Wednesday, February 10, 1965, 8 p.m. concert at Rutgers University, 48 years ago tomorrow, through articles in the *Rutgers Daily Targum*, as well as the *Douglass Caellian*, preserved on microfilm.

The *Targum* and *Caellian* articles are all brief. On January 14, the same day as Dylan was in New York City recording songs for his upcoming album, *Bringing It All Back Home*, there was a front page *Targum* piece titled, *"Anti- establishment Bob Dylan Professes 'Concern for People'."* The accompanying photograph, an already outdated Guthrie-esque pose, also described Dylan with the equally antiquated title, *"... protestee extraordinaire."* On February 4, there was another article headlined, *"Dylan Concert to Aid SISCAP."* (SISCAP is an acronym for "Students in Support of Community Actions Projects.") Two days before the performance, there was an ad with ticket prices listed as $4, $3, and $2, and another short article promoting the show.

On the Friday after the concert, there was a short, three-paragraph review in the *Caellian* by Ruth Winfield, describing the first half as *"satisfactory"* except for those in the balcony, *"where Dylan dialect comes out garbled."* She much preferred the shorter second half, where Dylan was *"a stronger, more confident performer."* Remember, this was a solo acoustic show, five-and-a-half months before Dylan "went electric" at the 1965 Newport Folk Festival.

After obtaining copies of these reports, Perlin wracked his brain trying to remember any details not included in the articles.

"I am trying to think about the set list at Rutgers, and working really hard in my mind," Perlin told me. *"So far, this is all I have come up with. I wouldn't bet the ranch, but am I fairly sure he performed* With God on Our Side, All I Really Want To Do, Mr. Tambourine Man, *and* Seven Curses.

"I remembered Seven Curses *because I adored the early Judy Collins albums, especially the first three, and of course,* Seven Curses *was similar to* Anathea *that was on one of those LPs. It may have been the last time he ever performed it."*

To try and find out more details, Perlin asked other Rutgers alumni what they remembered. One wrote:

"While I was only a first-semester sophomore pledge at Delta Phi, I remember that some Delts drove to Greenwich Village and picked up Dylan at Gerde's Folk City. After the concert, at the chapter house located at 17 Union Street, Dylan asked someone for their army jacket. We paid him $75 and returned him to Manhattan."

Another replied:

"For what it is worth, my memory of the Dylan concert at Rutgers has to do with his harmonica. If I remember it correctly, Dylan's harmonica 'malfunctioned' part way through the concert. He must have said something, for I remember someone in the front row or near the front handing him a replacement, and the show went on."

There were also these memories shared regarding the Rutgers swimming team. One friend wrote:

"We had a hilarious experience with one of Bob Dylan's cadre. He was dressed in full uniform. Heavy hiking boots, grubby jeans, wide leather belt with a Bowie knife lashed to his hip. This individual walked into the pool and told us we were disturbing Bob during his practice session. He asked us to stop and our coach George Hurych ... said, 'No way,' because we were practicing for a major championship. He, Bob's lackey, became very pissed and stomped out of the pool area. He made one big mistake, however. He went through the door to the locker rooms down below the pool. Perhaps you might recall that there was a four-inch deep disinfectant pool just inside that door. He got both feet into the pool and then there was dead silence. About 10 seconds later he came storming out from his disinfectant bath and proceeded to go out the correct door. We all laughed ..."

Perlin's friend, Hank Wallace, [397] had this to add:

[397] http://wsln.com, *Hank Wallace, J.D.: Write & Speak Like the News*, Retrieved 11/27/2016

"All I remember is hearing occasional splashes while Dylan sang, splashes I later learned were from Rutgers swim team members diving into the pool behind the stage's back wall. I only wish I could approximate the number of splashes I heard, or remember a (specific) reaction by Dylan or anyone else."

Perlin said, *"Hank, like me, recalls a joke Dylan made when the sounds of the divers in the pool behind the stage almost drowned out his singing."*

Someone else indicated Dylan may have appeared at an earlier Joan Baez SISCAP benefit concert on July 29, also at the Rutgers gymnasium (mentioned in one of the *Targum* articles), just days after the 1964 Newport Folk Festival.

Perlin is a professor at New York Law School, and continues to use Dylan lyrics in the titles of many of his articles, including, for example, *What's Good Is Bad, What's Bad Is Good, You'll Find Out When You Reach the Top, You're on the Bottom: Are the Americans with Disabilities Act (and Olmstead v. L.C.) Anything More than 'Idiot Wind'?* (*University of Michigan Journal of Law Reform*, Fall 2001-Winter 2002). [398]

---

[398] https://papers.ssrn.com/sol3/papers.cfm?abstract_id=335500, *What's Good is Bad, What's Bad is Good, You'll Find Out When You Reach the Top, You're on the Bottom: Are the Americans with Disabilities Act (and Olmstead v. L.C.) Anything More Than 'Idiot Wind'*, Retrieved 11/27/2016

Filmmaker Sandi Bachom on Dylan's 1966 warm-up show at Riverside College

January 12, 2011

Bob Dylan played a warm-up gig in 1966 at Riverside College that does not appear to be documented in any book or on any website, according to filmmaker and "New Media Maven" Sandi Bachom. [399]

In a recent telephone interview, Bachom told me she attended an open rehearsal concert by Bob Dylan and the Hawks, then attended the after-party, where Donovan was one of the guests.

I was contacted by Bachom after a friend sent her a link to my *Examiner* story about Dylan's appearance at the 1963 March On Washington. She informed me that her "old man," the late Stuart Scharf, played guitar with Dylan, Len Chandler, and Joan Baez on Chandler's song, *Hold On (Keep Your Eyes On The Prize)*.

I thanked her for the information, and asked if she had any other Dylan-related stories. Bachom informed me that she not only attended a 1973 mixing session, with Dylan in the room, for *Knockin' On Heaven's Door*, but had seen an electric mid-1960s show, probably with her friend, a young Jackson Browne.

Bachom is the daughter of two Walt Disney Animation Studio artists, film editor Jack Bachom and airbrush artist Dorothy Higgins, who worked together on such classic "Golden Age" films as *Bambi*, *Fantasia*, and *Pinocchio*. Sandi grew up in Hollywood, California, where she was a folksinger and a surfer. In 1965, Sandi moved to Boston for a while, went back to California, then joined Scharf in New York City in 1967, where she lives to this day.

Bachom went on to become an award-winning producer of television commercials, and has created hundreds of films she calls "Schlockumentaries." She has also written three books, and created an online tribute to Manny's World after the legendary music store closed (which features an autographed photo of Dylan).

Once we got onto the subject of the mid-1960s concert, we spent the next couple of hours trying to figure out when she saw this rare, electric Dylan show.

Although she had been a fan since his early folkie days, Bachom was surprised to discover that Dylan was initially "electric" only from July 25, 1965, (Newport) to July 29, 1966 (motorcycle accident). *"I didn't realize how rare that was,"* she said, referring to seeing a concert during this one-year time frame.

Bachom remembered that she saw the electric Dylan show *"at Riverside College, in Orange County. That's* The Barricades Of Heaven *Jackson* (Browne) *sang about."*

So when, exactly, did this concert take place?

We both went into detective mode. While I was rummaging through my Dylan books, I directed her to Olof Bjorner's *Still On The Road* [400] site, to show her where Dylan played during this time period. *"I'm amazed such a site even exists!"* she said. On the "1965 Concerts, Interviews & Recording Sessions" page, it listed a one-off gig at the Hollywood Bowl on September 3, then a return to California at the end of the year.

"When did (The Beatles album) Rubber Soul *come out?"* Bachom asked, trying to figure out when she was in Boston. When I told her it was early December, 1965, she said, *"I associate my time there with* Rubber Soul . . . *It was new at the time. I know I was there for the great blackout of* (November) *1965."*

---

[399] http://sandibachom.com, *Sandi Bachom: New Media Maven*, Retrieved 11/27/2016

[400] http://www.bjorner.com/still.htm, *Still on the Road*, Retrieved 11/27/2016

So the Riverside College date could not have happened in late 1965. *"How old were we in 1965?"* Sandi asked herself out loud. Then she laughed, *"In '65 . . . he was 17"*, quoting the famous Jackson Browne line.

"I'm pretty sure our friend Jackson was with us but I'm not sure... Hey, it was the 60s after all! Jackson and I were friends in California, so we probably went to the show. He was so influenced by Dylan. He idolized him. I have a picture he signed some place, he wrote on the back, 'Sandi babe . . . motor highways . . . something . . . ' . . . very Dylanesque. He signed it 'Jack.' We called him 'Jackie' in those days."

I pointed out to Sandi that, according to Clinton Heylin in *A Life In Stolen Moments*, Dylan was on the West Coast in March and April of 1966, although no California shows were listed during this time.

Information about the show was still a puzzle. Sandi asked various friends to help her figure out when she saw this "mystery" concert. She finally heard, via email, from her friend Richard Alderson, who professionally taped Dylan's shows around this time:

"This was a warm up for the '66 world tour. Why it doesn't exist on any site is weird, except that I think it was not really a booked concert, just sort of a rehearsal with an audience. I missed it because I was in NYC building the sound system for the tour - the next stop was Honolulu, Hawaii. The Hawaiian and the Australian parts of this tour are sketchily documented and I did not tape them as I did the European ones."

Dylan and The Hawks played the Honolulu International Center Arena on April 9, 1966. It has been documented that Dylan rehearsed with The Hawks and new drummer Mickey Jones, in Los Angeles, on March 30. So the concert probably took place during the first week of April.

As for the show itself, Bachom recalled, *"We were total Dylan freaks. We were folkies, and just starting to get into the protest thing. I just remember it was a huge theater. It was fancy.*

"So we went to this concert and the first half was Mr. Tambourine Man *and all that... and then he came out with* THE BAND... *It was like the scene from* (the Mel Brooks movie) The Producers, *the audience's jaws dropped. I remember that pretty well. They played* Like A Rolling Stone. . ."

I pressed her to see if she could remember what other songs he did. She thought Dylan sang an acoustic *Masters Of War*, but he had dropped this from his set list during this period, although that doesn't mean he didn't dust if off for this performance. I mentioned *Gates Of Eden*, and she remembered that, then I said *She Belongs To Me*, and she started singing, *"She's an artist, she don't look back,"* then said, *"Yeah, he did that too."*

"You're scraping the plaque off my memory," she laughed at one point. *"I was an eyewitness to history!"*

There was a party after the concert which Bachom attended. *"It was a big deal. Donovan was there, and Dylan. They spent a lot of time in another room, probably getting high and playing guitars."*

Looking back, Sandi is amazed by the attention Dylan still receives from his fans.

"When I told Paul Colby (owner and manager of legendary Greenwich Village club, the Bitter End) *that I was being interviewed about Dylan, we both talked about how dumbfounded we were. Paul asked, 'What is it about Dylan'?"*

"To me, it appears to have the sort of reverence usually reserved for dead people, like Elvis or John Lennon."

In closing, Sandi said she'd *"love to urge people to join and share their memories of seeing Dylan or other artists in the village. I started this thing on Facebook, and the 65 comments so far are amazing!"*

The day Victor Maymudes brought over an early Bob Dylan acetate

November 18, 2011

Carol Stief is a grandmother currently living in Copenhagen. She moved there 46 years ago after her divorce from her husband, August Maymudes, brother of Victor. In the 1960s, Carol and Augie lived in Los Angeles, and encountered Bob Dylan on a few occasions. This is her story:

I was married to Victor Maymudes' brother Augie. Sometime in early 1962, Victor called to ask if he could come over with something he wanted to play for us. We said, "Sure, come on over!"

At the time, Victor was Bob Dylan's closest friend, confidant, protector and troubleshooter. They met in New York and went to Los Angeles and hanged together all of the following years. Victor lived with Lenny Bruce for a period above the Whisky-A-Go-Go on Sunset Strip. He knew everybody. I met Bruce and Bo Diddley through Victor.

Those were the days.

Anyway, Victor came in, and in his hands he had a record with no label on it, just some scribbling. I had never seen an LP without a label before. He said that he had just gotten it, and it was the first one off the press. It was practically still warm. Victor said he wanted us to hear it and tell him what we thought of it.

He put it on the record player and we listened. At the time I was into regular pop and had never heard anything like this.

I asked Victor who it was, and he said that it was his friend Bob. I had heard Victor mention his friend "Bob" who played chess a lot with my father-in-law, but I had never met the guy.

Anyway, when the record was finished, Victor looked at us with great expectation and asked us what we thought of it. Augie said nothing. I told him flat out that I hated to disappoint him but this Bob guy whoever he was, was never going to make it with a voice like that!!!

I don't remember what he said, but Victor stormed out the door and slammed it shut behind him. He forgave me later, of course, but teased me about it a long time after his friend Bob became famous, as Bob Dylan!

Anyway my ex-husband Augie and I were among the very first to ever have heard Bob Dylan's debut album. It's a good thing Victor didn't listen to a dumb 20-year-old Sinatra fan! It actually took a while for me to see the light. But I finally did.

Augie and I were also at the Newport Folk Festival in 1963. After the concert, Victor took us to a small house on the festival grounds and Dylan and Joan Baez were already in the bedroom, sitting on the bed and jamming together. It was very intimate and felt really cool to be a part of.

While Augie and I were living in Los Angeles, Victor invited his brother and me to a Dylan concert at the Santa Monica Civic Auditorium on March 27, 1965. The experience was nearly traumatic. After the concert, Dylan offered to drive us home. We said, "Fine, thanks a lot!" We got into the car and proceeded to drive out of the backstage entrance. My husband and the driver in the front seat, and me sandwiched between Dylan and Victor in the back seat. When we drove out, there was a giant crowd waiting for the car to pull out. As the driver inched slowly forward, the crowd began to rock the car. In the beginning it was just a bit, but then it moved more and more violently. I honestly thought that the car would land on its side. But it didn't. Bob was totally cool about it. He smoked his cigarette and waved his hand and said not to worry, that it was all OK!!!

These events have been a part of my past for such a long time that I take them for granted. I have never thought that anyone might find them interesting. After all, I can't say that I was a part of Dylan's inner circle. Victor was, but I wasn't. I was just lucky enough to have a brother-in-law who was Dylan's closest friend and confidant.

Bob Dylan, Patti Smith, and the Nobel Prize

No wonder he didn't show.

The announcement alone of the choice of Bob Dylan for the 2016 Nobel Prize in Literature caused unnecessary controversy. Reminiscent of the famous 1966 world tour – his public aural assault on the unsuspecting, or disbelieving, public, playing electric rock and roll with a beat combo – the very idea of a singer-songwriter receiving such a prestigious honor divided the world. For some, this was an insult ... an outrage! Who was this beatnik interloper infiltrating the serious world of genuine auteurs? Surely there must be many more deserving candidates who have suffered for their art, and continue to toil in obscurity? Someone who could use the publicity, the money! Not someone who has already greatly profited from the unsightly world of the commercial pap? Hasn't Mr. Dylan already received enough accolades?

The other side argued, why *wouldn't* Dylan deserve the prize? In the past 50 years or so, who has done more with the power, and the artistry, of the written word? And, by extension, who has done more to lead people to the works of other authors based on his influences and references, both obvious and obscure? Then, of course, there's the debate over whether songs can be literature at all, which was affirmed at the ceremony in the presentation speech by Professor Horace Engdahl, Member of the Swedish Academy, Member of the Nobel Committee for Literature:

In itself, it ought not to be a sensation that a singer/songwriter now stands recipient of the literary Nobel Prize. In a distant past, all poetry was sung or tunefully recited, poets were rhapsodes, bards, troubadours; 'lyrics' comes from 'lyre'. But what Bob Dylan did was not to return to the Greeks or the Provençals. Instead, he dedicated himself body and soul to 20th-century American popular music, the kind played on radio stations and gramophone records for ordinary people, white and black: protest songs, country, blues, early rock, gospel, mainstream music. [401]

The prize was acknowledged on Dylan's official website, briefly, and on Twitter, both of which I'm sure receive little input from him.

From Dylan himself, we heard ... nothing.

Cue the "experts."

It's no secret newspapers are suffering financially these days, and have been ever since Craig's List inadvertently siphoned off their Want-Ad revenues. Now it's all about the clicks. Online newspaper sites collect profits based on the traffic they generate to their content, and by the comments posted beneath. It doesn't matter if the comments are good or bad, or if the content is sincere or manipulative. With so many alternatives to get information, newspapers and other news outlets are prostituting themselves, left and right, in order to generate revenue.

So when it comes to the Nobel Prize, once again, like a rock and roll Moses, a Dylan-based news story parted the journalistic seas. It was an outrage to some, or at least baffling. Why did Dylan not immediately respond; clearly a snub. Such an insult! On the other hand, what could be more Dylanesque? How cool not even to acknowledge one of the most prestigious awards anyone could ever hope to receive. Dylan never played "the game," it was argued, so why start now?

Apparently, according to one source, Dylan, with his son Jakob, met with his manager in New York to discuss how to accept this honor soon after receiving the news while on tour. Then the word came from on high, or at least from Edna Gundersen's late October interview in *The Telegraph* [402]

---

[401] *The Nobel Prize in Literature 2016, Bob Dylan, Award Ceremony Speech*, December 10, 2016, https://www.nobelprize.org/nobel_prizes/literature/laureates/2016/presentation-speech.html, Retrieved 1/8/2017

[402] http://www.telegraph.co.uk/men/the-filter/world-exclusive-bob-dylan---ill-be-at-the-nobel-prize-ceremony-i/, *World exclusive: Bob Dylan - I'll be at the Nobel Prize ceremony... if I can*, The Daily Telegraph, Retrieved 12/28/2016

(U.K.) that Dylan, apparently, was pleased, and would attend "if it's at all possible." See? There's nothing to see here. Move on.

As it transpired, though, Dylan would not attend, but singer-songwriter-poet-author Patti Smith would sing one of his songs in his stead, and an unnamed person, who we later found out to be the U.S. Ambassador to Sweden, would read a speech written by the recipient in honor of the occasion. Again, there was outrage. False, attention-grabbing outrage, but outrage nonetheless. What an insult. Blah, blah, blah. Click, click, click.

Dylan often, but not always, takes December off. According to the most reliable rumors, this is the time he spends with family, and this year there was some added intrigue – he was rumored to be in the planning stages of recording with Daniel Lanois, producer of the highly acclaimed Dylan albums *Oh Mercy* and *Time Out of Mind*. (Dylan reportedly recorded 30 more standards not that long ago as well. Will they be shelved?) Dylan enjoys his privacy, so we rarely know anything until it is announced, or leaked.

The recipient of the Nobel Prize in Literature has six months to claim his award. In order to do this, Dylan has decided to tie in the ceremony with a European tour. As it stands now, his first six dates of 2017 are in Scandinavia, starting with two nights at the Stockholm Waterfront on April 1 and 2. What will Dylan do when he accepts the Prize? Well, if history has taught us anything, Dylan will try to keep this a secret, but it may somehow be (strategically?) leaked beforehand. Dylan is at his best when he's in control, in focus. After all, no one does Dylan like Dylan. When too many cooks start messing with Dylan's recipe, he often withdraws, or acts passive-aggressively. From the Tom Paine Award of 1963 to his Live-Aid closing set in 1985, from his 1998 appearance at the Grammys to his 2012 Presidential Medal of Freedom Award, Dylan has to deal with expectations, executives, and the omnipresent "experts," which can interfere with whatever artistic vision he has. He can be eloquent and engaging, as he was during his 2015 MusiCares speech, or uncomfortable, as he appeared to be when he received his Grammy Lifetime Achievement Award way back in 1991.

At this stage of the game, he can do what he wants. At *every* stage of the game, it was "Critics be damned!" Each of his marriages has been conducted in secret. He tries, as much as a person of his fame can, to live a normal life. He also tries to live the life of an artist, always on call to his muse. In this age of celebrity worship, where people hunger for attention on social media, and become famous through reality TV, Dylan does not participate. He is not part of the Kardashian/Simon Cowell nightmare-overload-bombardment culture carnival which we all suffer through, no matter how hard we try to avoid it. Dylan keeps it real, on the DL, living by an antiquated code of dignity, standing on a soapbox to anyone within the sound of his voice, analyzing on the present, couched in poetry and metaphor, with a moral compass deeply rooted in his American and Jewish upbringing.

Patti Smith makes a spectacle of herself

Patti Smith was the ideal choice to perform at the Nobel Prize ceremony in Dylan's place. I remember reading Smith's 1974 review of *Planet Waves* in *Creem* magazine, and, growing up on Long Island, was hyper-aware of the ascension of both her and her fellow New Jerseyite, Bruce Springsteen. It was clear both of their 1975 albums, *Horses* and *Born to Run*, respectively, would battle *Blood on the Tracks* (and *The Basement Tapes*) for album of the year, at least among the elite New-York-WNEW-FM music cognizanti. Smith so impressed and endeared herself to Dylan when they met that year, he asked her to join his upcoming Rolling Thunder Revue tour, but she declined in order to follow her own path. 20 years later, after the death of her husband, the MC5's Fred "Sonic" Smith, Dylan took her with him on a mini-East Coast tour.

Everyone, including Smith herself, has written and/or commented about her performance. Of course much of the media, again in order to generate traffic and needlessly mock an artist, focused on Smith's forgetfulness of the lyrics instead of her performance, which was, to these ears and eyes, one of the most powerful I've ever experienced.

The song choice, *A Hard Rain's A-Gonna Fall*, was perfect for a number of reasons. First of all, it was one of Dylan's early major works. It not only upped the ante after such signature songs as

Blowin' in the Wind, it took songwriting to a whole other level. Verse after verse, image after image, a dizzying protest storm, kind of like an early viral folk tweet. It was based on *Lord Randall*, the traditional British ballad, which would be evidence enough that Dylan was worthy of an invitation into this exclusive Nobel Prize club. The myth, perpetuated by Dylan, was that the song was written in response to the Cuban Missile Crisis, even though he'd already debuted it in concert a month earlier. It's not unlike Dylan's *"Love & Theft,"* forever associated with the day of its release, September 11, 2001, which sounded as though it had been written in response to that tragic episode.

The composition broke ground for songwriters. It not only set the stage for lengthy songs in pop music, but the poetic imagery hinted at a new type of expression, one that would become a major ingredient in psychedelia, set to emerge and explode a couple of years later.

It's a song Dylan has come back to time and time again, often under heavy circumstances. When he made his rare early-1970s appearances at The Concert(s) For Bangla Desh, he began each set with a honey-voiced *Hard Rain*; for 1975's Rolling Thunder Revue, he recast the song as an almost Bo-Diddley-meets-The-Yardbirds type glam-rocker (courtesy of David Bowie's guitarist, Mick Ronson); and in 1994, when the public perception of his performances was somewhat in decline, Dylan gave an impassioned reading backed by an orchestra, which help redefine his public image.

Although a complex song, *Hard Rain* has been covered with great success in various guises by a variety of artists. From the early folkie versions by Pete Seeger and Joan Baez, to Leon Russell's swampy take, to Bryan Ferry's devilish retransformation, the song has continued to expand and grow.

As great as those versions are, Smith's may have topped them all. If you've been following her career, or read her recent books – *Just Kids* and *M Train* – you get a sense of where her place is in rock music history, and her respect for those who came before. She's a true artist, who almost stumbled into the CBGB's spotlight, to become the first true poetic songwriting female artist. Smith does have her detractors, and has been dismissed as arty and derivative and pretentious, but these criticisms, without the misogynistic undertones, could also be hurled at Dylan. Dylan gets her, and that should be enough for anyone.

Smith's performance last December 10 was reverent. Spiritual, even. A monochromatic figure, in white blouse, black jacket, and long, flowing gray hair, the so-called "punk priestess" captured on Robert Mapplethorpe's iconic black and white *Horses* cover, 40-plus years down the road. You could feel the weight on her shoulders. Her nasal vocals echoing Dylan's, her twang when singing the title line reached back to Dylan's first idol Hank Williams. Smith wasn't just singing the song, not just reciting it. She was inside it, inhabiting the poetry, engulfed in the imagery.

Smith's eyes appeared to be almost closed. She was not wearing her glasses. It's unclear whether the lyrics were in front of her, but in any case, she was singing the song from memory, from the heart. Like Dylan, she was a conduit, a vessel. There was a controlled intensity.

And then … she faltered.

At about two minutes in, Smith stumbled over a lyric. Unable to get back on track, she looked up at the conductor, humbly asked to start that section again, then admitted to the assembled multitude that she was nervous, charming the crowd in the process. The acoustic guitarist began again, and Smith rose to the challenge. Her voice was shaky, echoing the emotions in the song. The intensity increased, as a flute, the weeping sounds of the pedal steel guitar, and other instruments of the orchestra, added extra tension. Her hand over her heart, she stumbled again, but it didn't stop her. When she got to the part about the young girl and the rainbow, Smith suddenly strengthened, and there was no turning back. Unconscious hand gestures added to the performance, arms swinging by her side as if walking, hands outstretched to emphasize her quest for answers, expanded when the enigmatic answers were given; fists punching the air during the climax.

It should be noted that in addition to the respect she has for Dylan, and literary figures in general, the dignitaries to whom she was performing could only have added to the burden she had placed upon herself. People were wiping away tears. She connected.

The song ended with a defiant Patti. She grappled with the phrase about knowing her song well, realizing the irony, and emerged victorious. After the song ended, to rapturous applause, Smith hid behind her gray locks, maybe embarrassed, maybe disappointed.

While the imperfections of her performance could be interpreted negatively, Smith turned them into strengths. The song, and the performance, spoke for itself. It didn't need dancers or lasers, flashing lights or giant screens. There was a direct connection between Smith's soul and yours. It was a human moment.

Smith's decision not to wear glasses reminded me of when I first saw Dylan in concert. It was January 29, 1974, with The Band, at the Nassau Coliseum on Long Island. I sat with friends who knew much more about Dylan than I did, way back in the loge section at the opposite side of the arena. In fact, I felt unworthy of even being there. Danny, my oldest friend, and the one who turned me on to Dylan, brought a Panasonic tape recorder and a pair of binoculars with him. Dylan did not use big screens to amplify his image, since there were no big screens at concerts in those days. He still doesn't. There was nothing between you and his music. I did look occasionally through the binoculars to get a closer look, but I did not want any artificial barriers. I wanted a direct connection.

When he accepted his Grammy Award for Album of the Year in 1998, Dylan mentioned that he felt the presence of Buddy Holly while recording *Time Out of Mind*. He recalled being in the audience, just a few feet away from Holly when he performed at the Duluth National Guard Armory, and said he looked directly at the teenaged Robert Zimmerman. Again, a direct connection. Nothing between the music and your soul. These days, we don't go to see musicians when we go to big concerts. We go to watch giant televisions. Smith could have used a big teleprompter, or she could have worn her glasses, but she defiantly decided not to. It was the poet connecting to the poetry directly.

The Nobel Prize ceremony took place in early December, 2016, during a time of particular global unrest. The threat of a "hard rain" is as great now as in any period of my lifetime. One of the strengths of Dylan's greatest works is its timelessness. His music lives on, and, against all odds, so does he. Following his journey for more than four decades has had such an impact on my life, not just for the content of this book, and the friends I have made, but on the way I think, and the way I view the world. And for that direct connection I made with Dylan back in 1974, I will always be indebted.

CPSIA information can be obtained
at www.ICGtesting.com
Printed in the USA
BVOW07s2313230217
477023BV00010B/87/P